BOOTH
A JOURNAL

EDITOR: Robert Stapleton

ASSOCIATE EDITOR: Bryan Furuness

POETRY EDITORS: Krista Ramsay, Kelly Thomas

PROSE EDITORS: Corey Michael Dalton, Carol Divish

ART DIRECTION: Nogginwerks

COPY EDITOR: Ashley Petry

READERS: Jenna Caschera, Emma Faesi, Melissa Friedman, Erin Hall, Jim Hanna, Rebecca Huehls, Wendy Jones, Heather Kauffman, Sarah Knoth, Susan Lerner, Doug Manuel, David Marsh, Mallory Matyk, Deanna Morris, Jennifer Moss, Colin Murray, Craig Parker, Ashley Petry, Terri Procopio, Zach Roth, Shannon Siegel, Chris Speckman, Maggie Wheeler.

CHAPTER ONE

Calamity's Child by Kevin Ducey 06

The Un-Game by Kathleen Founds 26

STORIES

Monitors by Ryan Boudinot 38

Run Time by Jesse Goolsby 47

Gravity by Sherrie Flick 50

Sorrel by Sherrie Flick 52

The Mathematics of Waiting by Kirsty Logan 55

What They Did with the Body by Mike Meginnis 60

Playing House by Sarah Scoles 76

NONFICTION

Migration by Kelsea Habecker 92

Three Cardboard Gods by Josh Wilker 96

ART

Photography by Dale Bernstein 104

POETRY

Sam and Lulu at the Very End of the World by Aubrey Ryan 114

Furrow and Plow by Aubrey Ryan 115

Stable by Mark Petrie 116

Orgasm by David LaBounty 118

My First Love Asks Me to Stop Writing About Him by Elizabeth Wade 120

Goldfinches by Tasha Cotter 121

The Mailman by Dana Kroos 122

Cleveland, Ohio, 1964 by Tara Mae Mulroy 124

INTERVIEWS

The Philosophy of Space, An Interview with Jonathan Lethem 128

The Van Halen Brown Sound, An Interview with George Saunders 142

COMICS AND MISCELLANY

Tokyo by Nick St. John 164

Nine Possible Observations to Consider by Michael Bazzett 168

Vampire Story by Zeynep Alpaslan and Nick St John 170

CONTRIBUTORS

....174

NO. B 134

★ ★ ★ ★ ★ ★ ★ ★ ★
CALAMITY'S CHILD
BY KEVIN DUCEY
★ ★ ★ ★ ★ ★ ★ ★ ★

NO. A 917

★ ★ ★ ★ ★ ★ ★
THE UN-GAME
★ ★ ★ ★ ★ ★ ★ ★
BY KATHLEEN FOUNDS

CHAPTER ONE

CALAMITY'S CHILD

By Kevin Ducey

✴ ✴ ✴

The story has been told many times with variations. Sometimes the daughter is a stepchild. Sometimes the girl is a boy. Coursey claims Calamity gave birth to a son in Sydney. Senn reports the incident as follows:

'Deadwood citizens confirm the story of her arrival in Deadwood accompanied by her husband and a bright young girl about ten years old ...'

— J. Leonard Jennewein, *Calamity Jane of the Western Trails*

Letters to Edison [excerpt]

8 June 1903

Electric, Montana

Dear Mr. Edison,

...I didn't hear the train come in. There was no horse riding up either, though I didn't, generally speaking, have a lot of time to sit around waiting for the train like some people might. Carl decided somewhere along the line I needed more stuff to do to keep me out of his hair. He has been a dentist as well as a saloon owner and has taken it into his head that I should grow up to be the dentist for our town. Carl tells me that what this town needs is a young dentist. Since there aren't any dentistry schools anywhere in this part of the world is how come I find myself most afternoons down on my knees on the bar floor filling in the tiny cracks in the planking with a spackling compound that Carl says acts most like a dentist's oxyphosphate of copper cement as any sealant he can find. The floor of Carl's bar is about halfway sealed in enameling like a giant tooth at this point when I look up from the floor (not because I heard the sound of a particular train or horse, but mainly I reckon because all the low murmuring of cards and drinking stopped all of a sudden) and I look up into the bright sunlight coming in through the saloon doors and a shadow falls on me where I was kneeling there with putty knife in hand.

Now Carl generally likes to keep the room dark on account of the heat and he always says people spend too much of their time out in the sun. He says that and then he's just as liable to launch into some homesick story about Quebec as not, and the way the sun spoke to him one morning with a French accent, the same day his stake in the Black Hills finally yielded up its mineral wealth and gave him the idea to open a bar called 'Chez Carl' in Montana along the Milwaukee Road. Even though he swears he never talks to the sun or moon anymore, his face went pale as a full moon of whey cheese when the sun, je suis désollée, was eclipsed by the figure of a stranger standing in the open saloon doors. With the sun settled on the stranger's left shoulder it was hard to see who it was, but I knew it wasn't one of our townies. I've seen most of 'em from the knees down for years and the newcomer's boots were worn so bad you could see the traces of glue and tar signifying several lifetimes of comfortable re-shoeing. The stranger's jeans were chapped and filthy dark brown, the color of our street, but it was clear the raggedy ends carried the stink of horse manure from the Bitterroot to the Mogollones. The stranger's hips were wide and belted with a simple leather belt. Slung low on one leg nestled a holster with an old revolving pistol even I could tell was old and a coughing puppy, like Carl would say: "That horse is a coughing puppy," or, "that fire ain't gonna catch, it's a coughing puppy." The stranger wore a dark shirt of unknown color. Traces of fringe still trailed from the sleeves. Saddlebags and a poncho rested across a shoulder. One heavy step, then two, into the room and I saw the stranger's hand, gnarled and rough like old burlap. The head came slowly into the darkness showing me the ugliest face I've ever had the pleasure to appreciate, Mr. Edison. Cruelly scarred by the pox, the skin hung from the skull. The long hair, pulled back from the craggy, flying dutchman forehead, was brown, and streaked with white. The lips twisted in a half smile, half sneer and the eyes were deep socketed with a hunger I've only seen in the eyes of Indians out along the road if Carl doesn't shoot 'em first. The eyes of the traveler fixed on Carl's ashen face and I don't ever know how I would react if I had someone look at me with eyes like that. Staring and angry and hopeful and other things I couldn't name all in that look. As if the face held a secret on the rest of us, it came steadily into the room and stopped across from Carl.

"Jane?" Carl said.

The stranger swung her saddlebags onto the bar and stood straighter. The ceiling came swooping down on her as she drew herself up another five feet into the air and ducked as the rafters went past. Or so it looked to me from where I was still down on my knees. I was watching her, but I kept glancing over at Carl. Something in his eyes had gone shiny and he says again:

"Jane Canary?"

Almost like it's a question that he knew the answer to, but didn't want to hear it spoken out loud where his ears would have to listen to it; like it was a question he didn't ever expect to hear spoken where the world would grab ahold of it. But if the newcomer heard anything in Carl's voice she didn't pay it any mind. She took off her old hat and threw it on top of her saddlebags.

"Hello, Carl. How about a drink?"

"By God, it's been a long time, Jane," Carl says.

"Not so long, Carl. I had a bottle coming outa Billings."

Before Carl could answer she turned quick-like to me, because I moved, or something that caused her to look at me like I was some kind of ghost sneaking up on her with a club of bad memories. She looked scared of me almost and I stood up slowly, thinking maybe she was afraid of short people. She narrowed her eyes at me and took a step or two closer.

"Sweet Jesus, boy," she says to me, "what're you doing crawling around Carl's floor?"

Carl spoke up and explained about the lack of dental schools and the spackling compound oxyphosphate of copper and this Jane character looked from Carl to me and then at the carefully enameled half of the barroom floor that I'd spent my last several months making shiny and smooth and then she did it all again; she looked from Carl to me to the floor all over again like she hadn't heard right.

"I'll have that drink now," she whispered. And Carl went about setting up the glasses, one for himself and one for her. Although he usually only drank beer, this time he poured a whiskey for himself as well as a tall glass for her.

"Thank you, Carl," she said and I got up my nerve and cleared my throat. I could tell by the way Carl was leaning over the bar that he was settling in to chew her ear off. I said:

"Ma'am? Excuse me, but ma'am, I'm not a boy. I'm a girl." But I didn't say it loud enough and they went on talking, so I said it again louder and this time Jane and Carl stopped and looked at me like they'd forgotten I was alive. Some of the regulars in the bar who'd been watching this all go on started to laugh and I felt the heat in my face.

She looked down at me and then around at the room where the other folks were laughing and they shut up and she looked back at me. "Course you are, I see that now. My eyes is just getting used to the light. Why ain't you wearing a dress, girl? Shoot, you gave me a fright a moment ago you look so much like someone I used to know. What's your name, child?"

"Jane," Carl said, "I figured you'd know my kid Andy—I mean, Andrea."

I put out my hand to shake hers—like I shook the cowboys' hands. They were always shaking hands with me and each other. She turned to me and took my hand in both of hers. Then before I could grab it back, she bent from the waist over my hand and pressed her lips to the skin. Her lips felt light and dry, like a grasshopper or butterfly lighting on my skin. Nobody had ever kissed my hand before. I'd read about gentlemen kissing hands attached to the arms of French ladies, but I wasn't a French lady and I didn't know what I was supposed to do next and while all this was going on she straightened up, looking me in the eye all the while, and said: "I'm so happy to meet you, Andrea."

By way of reply I ran out of there as fast as I could.

Forgive me for writing so much, Mr. Edison. Carl told me I was only supposed to write and say thank you for the photo of yourself that you were kind enough to send us. If you don't mind my saying so, sir, I must say you look tired out. Doubtless you are still working night and day on your new problems.

I will send Carl's diagrams for a new light bulb when I find the old receipt that has his design sketched out on the back. I also wanted to tell you that I have taken your advice and have given away my Buntline novels.

June 1903
Electric, Montana

I usually relied on my dog, Bain, for advice but since he'd taken himself for a walk the day before and hadn't come home yesterday, or yet today, I ended up at Kuzma's Mercantile. Greta Kuzma ran Kuzma's Electrical Emporium & Mercantile in partnership with her husband, Marcus. The place was always dusty, decrepit, and overstocked, so you entered it holding your life egg-like in your hands because of all the large sacks of things that might fall on a child's body and crush the life from you as you lay under a mountain of dry goods and mercantile. Like what happened to that Swede boy who slammed the door too sudden once and the big parrot there in the rafters screamed and the fresh load of pintos carefully stacked bean by bean (in one of Marcus's famous full-scale displays of the architecture of his beloved Bohemia) came avalanching down on that boy like it was God's avenging anger for that noisy character's plundering Viking heritage.

Even if the threat of a wall of beans doesn't frighten you, it's better for you if you step quietly when entering because Greta and her friend Mrs. Gorvitch would usually be back there somewhere in the hazy shadows amidst the wagon wheels and canned goods from Illinois, sipping their laudanum-laced tea, and loud noises might startle them too quick from conversation. It was that or somebody would be getting the electroflux treatment in Mrs. Kuzma's chair and she liked it quiet. I always found it went easier if I showed up at Greta's elbow as if I'd always been there. Usually the conversation then came around to what I wanted when they noticed me standing there quiet as a door.

I arrived as quietly as possible, my hand still burning with the application of a stranger's lips, and I must have been agitating the spot because Greta and Mrs. Gorvitch looked up from their talk as I came in and Greta asked me what in God's good name was wrong with my hand and I said, 'nothing.' And so they went back to their talk. They were sitting across from each other, Greta still had her blouse loosened from her electroflux session. I wanted to tell them what had happened but they shushed me and I held my tongue and listened as Mrs. Gorvitch finished the story she was telling. Mrs. Gorvitch had very pale skin. The blue veins of her forehead could be traced along her skull, disappearing under her high starched collar and then rediscovered crawling out from under the long, lace sleeves of her blouse. Up to that day she was the oldest-looking person I knew. She offered me a piece of the tea cake they had been eating and I accepted before I realized Greta was glaring 'no' at me. Then I didn't know if I should eat it or not as Mrs. Gorvitch stuck a piece on a plate and put it in front of me.

There was a long silence while I looked at my cake, watched Greta out of the corner of my eye and acknowledged Mrs. Gorvitch's smiles at me with smiles of my own. Greta's old parrot tottered back and forth on the beam above our heads squawking something that sounded like 'strudel.'

Mrs. Gorvitch went back to the telling of her story about the distant cousin she'd hoped to marry back in Hungary, but he fell from a horse and down a deep well where he died calling out for his mother and breaking Mrs. Gorvitch's heart. We hung our heads as we always did at that point in the story because it was so sad. After we sighed, Greta roused herself to ask what it was that called me away from my dental work on the floor of Chez Carl. I didn't answer directly, because I knew they weren't really interested in the work I still had to do, but they were asking out of not politeness really, but out of their sense of what one did. So I told them about my progress on the barroom floor in such a way that it might seem as if I believed in their interest and that I felt a sense of gratification that they should take an interest. Finally, because I felt the need to pee, I asked them directly if they knew a lady named Jane Canary.

Greta's face colored bright red when the name dropped from my mouth. Mrs. Gorvitch leaned across the tea table toward her friend.

"What's wrong, Greta?"

Greta picked up an illustrated magazine and began fanning herself, but she stopped and looked at me. "First," she said, "that woman is not a lady."

"No, ma'am. 'Course not."

"Second, and I've told you this before, and you ought to know by now, that people don't show up without a reason. There's a plan to everything. Nothing's ever 'accidental' in this electrical world. People come and they pass on for a reason. Everything –"

"Yes, ma'am. Everything flows and seeks valence."

"That's right," she said and then thought for a moment, biting her lower lip. She said to Mrs. Gorvitch: "Marcus probably brought her in. He's always up to something." Then back to me she said: "And third, I would appreciate a glass of water. Why don't you quit squirming around in your chair like that and go get me some?"

I ran out to the outhouse and forgot about the water for Greta. Instead, I went out to the fields. I ran so far I forgot who I was for a minute and I stood in the field with all the grasses waving their arms and fuzzy heads in the wind. The breeze patterned the fields as if it was God's hand, smoothing down the velvet cloth of the earth so it was showing all one color, and then shoving it back the other way, making patterns of the wide fields for the hell of it. Out on the edge of my sight, I saw the heat dancing on the horizon. The edge of the world waved with all the heat that was busy sucking the sweat out of my forehead. I'd forgotten my hat. I squinted my eyes up and thought I could see arms waving out there: Somebody waving at me in every direction I looked.

When my mother was still walking about the earth, she would have had me in the electric chair at least once a week to make sure my valence didn't get unbalanced. Some days I felt anymore like those grasses in the field—pushed this way and that, repelled by one body's electrical charge, only to be attracted by another's. If you've never done it, I recommend an afternoon in the chair as it is a wonderfully spiritual exercise to have all your electrical energies spinning in harmony with the world. Sometimes as I sat in the chair, feeling the thrum of the machine rising through my body, I could feel a rise in the pulse of energy as though it were the swelling of tomatoes in our power plant heaving a gentle sigh of exhaustion and green desire. I wondered what a tomato might desire and when I asked my mother that she didn't say anything for a while, and then I remembered her laugh, clear as the heat out there on the horizon. I wondered if it was because I was in the chair getting electrocuted that she laughed like that. Maybe she was thinking the tomatoes were doing the talking—just as she used to say the liquor did most of the talking in our bar. She then told me that those fluctuations I felt were the "sweeping wings of the solar wind." Maybe that's a desire that the tomatoes are aware of. It sounded like something a tomato would like.

Letters to Edison [excerpt]

June 1903

Electric, Montana

Dear Mr. Edison,

I will finish this letter soon and mail it off with our parts order and please expedite the return so Carl will get his parts. I have to finish telling about what happened that day Jane showed up and I have some questions that I'm sure you can answer for me. On that particular day, I ended up walking out to the fields thinking about how I missed my dog, Bain. (Bainbridge happens to be the name of Carl's dental college in Ohio.) Whenever Carl shows me how to coil the imaginary gold leaf prior to insertion in the oral cavity he says, "this is how we did it in Bainbridge."

The day Marcus brought Bain into Chez Carl the critter came over to me a curious (not a coughing) puppy—wondering what it was I was up to on the floor. I didn't notice it right away, 'cause sometimes my eyes might not be seeing right and Carl was yelling something that day about how rough my denture work was and Bainbridge, Bainbridge, Bainbridge, when I felt something wet and cold poke me in the cheek and it was this big, ugly dog sniffing me. Bain was a sly dog from the first. He knew most of my secrets eventually. Bain was part dog, part moose, brown body with a black face and the softest ears that made the telling of secrets easier. I told him everything, which makes his return even more urgent. I need to get him back before the whole world knows everything. Now that he's disappeared, Mr. Edison, I lay awake at night, listening to the coyotes repeating a story I'd told Bain and nobody else. Like I said, he is a sly dog.

Mr. Edison, in your article in Columbia you say it is the entities that rule our lives. I have been considering your statement and was wondering about the nature of the entities. I had to ask Mr. Kuzma what an entity is. I have been thinking about the story you tell about that time when you cut off the skin on your thumb and then the skin came back. Is it true that the fingerprints were the same as before? Didn't you have a scar? If there's something inside us telling our fingertips how to grow, where does that something go when we die? Maybe, after leaving the body, the entity moves like a butterfly landing on a flower. How do the entities know where to land? Once a person knows the character of an entity is that knowledge an invention or a discovery? I reckon you'd find that an invention. If an entity landed like a butterfly on you while you were out in the wind hanging laundry on the line, what would it feel like? Is it like a kiss on the hand? Or is it like an itch that makes you crazy?

✳   ✳   ✳

That night, Carl butchered the fatted calf for his visitor. He built a fire in the pit and had the dead animal turning on a spit. It looked like it was going to be a late night. I didn't know where Carl had gone, but when I got back from Kuzma's he'd set out a table and chair in the shade in the backyard and Jane was sitting there with a glass of beer at her elbow. She was getting up to turn the cow over when I came up to the house. When she saw me, she straightened up and shouted, "Hey you. Andy. Have you seen my revolver? It's missing." She turned her hip to me to show the empty holster. "You didn't take it, did you?" I shook my head and tried to walk past her into the house.

"I'd understand it, if you had taken it: every girl wants her own gun. And it ain't just for self-protection." I pretended she wasn't there and kept walking.

Carl was inside and he told me to make up some cornbread for dinner. Carl went outside and came back a few minutes later leading that Jane person into the kitchen. They didn't pause, but went down the hall to Carl's dental office.

Carl keeps his office in a room off the bar. He has a fancy chair with a headrest that doubles as a vice. It has handles and spring-loaded levers all around the bottom of the seat and you can just about launch a person to Kansas if you get the settings right and press them all at once. I know because I've tried a couple of times, but haven't got the combination right. Carl started locking up his office after I strapped one of the Sweeney boys in there and left him overnight. Carl's also got a small chaise lounge that patients recover on and a woodstove that he uses for melting paraffin and making coffee. He's got a couple of magazines on the coffee table. The subscriptions ran out years ago, but Carl says that nobody reads in a dentist's office anyhow, they're too scared. He keeps illustrated magazines of the Spanish War. Some of the drawings are especially gruesome—this is to Carl's liking, since he looks at them over and over again. I tried to throw them out, but he stopped me. "Pictures like these, Andy, help to set the mood." He also has several copies of the American Magazine and Columbia—especially those issues that have your articles in them, Mr. Edison.

He also has a small, windowless workshop, a large closet, really, where he makes his dentures and keeps his safe. He's covered the walls with pasted calendar pages and prints. He's stuck them up with dental plaster; the dust is all over everything in the room. He lights the workshop only by the bunsen burner that also keeps his coffee warm and heats up metals for his fillings. My father's blasphemous proud of his dental work and the research he has conducted to further the cause of dentistry here on the frontier. I don't know if it's true, but he says the best thing he's ever done for dentistry is his procedure for breaking and re-setting jaws to cure overbite. He says one day he'll write a scientific article on the "talum usum aere figere dente" (application of brass knuckles in certain operations), but he says he's still in the research stages. I will let you know when his article is ready for publication. Carl's denture work is more popular. He specializes in making sets of dentures that look just as nasty and discolored as the patient's original teeth.

Coffee-colored, tobacco-stained, and gap-toothed, my father's denture work is the wonder of Montana.

Carl and his patient were still in his office when I put the cornbread on the stove, so I went out to turn the cow.

✻   ✻   ✻

When the locals began showing up, Carl dished out the cow with beans, sauerkraut and cornbread. He doesn't usually put on a feed like this and when word spread, people came in who normally wouldn't and grabbed a plate. They set up along the bar and at all the tables around the room and I heard a lot more talking and laughing than I usually heard in my father's bar.

By the time I finished washing up the supper dishes it was already past midnight. I like to sit in the dark far corner of the saloon. Carl stores some barrels in that corner and a couple of them stand between me and the bar, so if I'm quiet Carl doesn't notice and he forgets to chase me off to bed. But the night this Jane showed up I didn't really have to worry about being quiet, it was so loud with people carrying on. A new piano player had come in on the same train as Jane, but he hardly had a chance to play; people wanted to listen to Jane's stories about her travels.

I watched Carl working the bar, laughing at these stories this hand-kisser was telling. I've never seen him laugh like that, Mr. Edison. I guess usually when Carl laughs everybody gets sort of quiet. The stories didn't seem that funny to me. I worry for Carl's immortal soul sometimes from all the cussing he does, but he's a saint compared to Jane standing at the bar with a tumbler of whiskey in her big hand.

The men seemed to have forgotten all their arguing and card playing and picking on each other and they lined the bar calling out questions and peculiar notions that came into their heads. They asked Jane again and again about Hickok and how did he manage to get himself killed when he was so fast with a gun? She laughed and remembered out loud how some of them bad hombres used to shoot like regular coughing goddamn puppies. And they laughed kind of nervous-like 'cause they all knew she meant Carl (that was his patented phrase and nobody ever said 'coughing puppy' around him, except me maybe when I was in my room and the house was quiet and I knew that he couldn't hear me. Then, sometimes, I whispered 'coughing puppy' or even 'coughing palomino' because I knew it was a magic phrase and maybe I'd get some of Carl's power if I could master it). But Jane, she just threw it out there as though she had all Carl's words down and the cowboys were scared because nobody ever kidded Carl, but I saw Carl throw his head back and laugh. He slapped the bar with his hand and the barrels along the back wall jumped with his pounding.

Back of the bar's a painting of a naked lady. It's been there since Carl bought the place. He's whitewashed the walls and hung his framed magazine pictures up there (one of them is of you, Mr. Edison) where the mural of a naked woman used to be (the cowboys called her Rosie). The whitewash has started to fade and the out-line of Rosie re-appears under the white paint. She's reclining on a big red couch. I think it's supposed to be a couch covered in drapery, but it looks like that rocky patch over in Eberson's field. Her thighs are big and she's crossing her knees and she has her hair piled up on the top of her head. Her face is turned to the side and maybe it's because it's been painted over, but it looks like Rosie's two eyes are on one side of her nose. They're beautiful brown eyes with long lashes. I don't get to see her face very often because Carl has hung a portrait-photograph of you-know-who looking thoughtful where Rosie's head used to be and Carl has a landscape of the Wizard's Lair over her bosom (she has a large bosom, Mr. Edison) and we forget about Rosie mostly, except when a newcomer like Jane shows up and starts asking about her. This happened now and the cowboys gathered around, marveling at Rosie's wonderful persistence.

Marcus came in the door then carrying his old accordion and Jane insisted he play them funny goddamn Bohemian songs he used to play in the old days. Marcus obliged, playing songs I'd never heard him do before. They did sound happier

than what he usually played. But despite the whooping, hollering, and foot stomp-
ing that Marcus put on, nobody laughed. Carl got quiet and several of the older
cowboys, big, leather-faced men, put their heads down on the bar like they didn't
want the others to see their faces in the yellow glow of Chez Carl's big electric light.
Marcus sang:

> O, the grass grows high
> where the cows go by
> away on the long yerba night.
> Will you sing for me
> my Molly McGee
> on the trail
> by the sad Rio Grande?
>
> O the proud Brahmin bulls
> of the Kansas cow towns
> carry ticks by the score, or more (or more).
> Will you sing for me
> of the rough chapparal
> on the road
> by the sad Rio Grande?
>
> From the Yellow Slave Lake
> to the Brown Musselshell
> the cows wander 'way from me.
>
> Will you light up that smoke
> my Molly McGee
> on the trail
> of the sad Rio Grande?

At the end of the night when I was starting to nod, I woke up as the usual
crowd of them with any money left set off for the whorehouse down the street. They

talked Jane into going along and she went saying something about being interested only if they had some pretty ones.

Carl went about locking up, dragging the passed-out drunks outside where he left them on the front porch. The night was warm and wasn't going to hurt any of them, so Carl could just leave 'em there: a big mess of men on the boardwalk.

I crept down the hall past my bedroom to the room that Jane had taken. The door was open, so I went in. Hanging on the wall was the coughing pistol she'd accused me of stealing. On the floor, by the side of the bed, she had a small traveling box, and thrown across the chair by my old dresser were her saddlebags.

Through the window I saw the full moon rise on the horizon and from a long ways off I thought I heard the train whistle calling. It was probably only Carl though, scraping the chairs in the bar along the half-enameled floor. In a minute or two he'd be ready to head across the street and turn off the Yellowstone Power Company for the night. I slipped out the door and ran back to my room.

It is now very late and I have to be up early. I'll close here, Carl will wonder why it took so long to send out our order for parts.

Good night, Mr. Edison,

your friend,

Andrea

P.S. Carl says we're still waiting for the repair parts we need for the commutator I wrote to you about in April.

P.P.S. After I finished writing I heard Jane come in the back door and walk down the hall, but instead of passing on to her room two doors down she opened my door, walked in and sat on the foot of my bed. She took off her hat and scratched her head for several minutes, muttering to herself. I didn't know if she was talking to me or not. I'd left my French lesson on the bed and she picked it up and looked at it, turning the pages over, wondering. I shifted in my bed and she looked up surprised and said: "What are you doing in here?"

"This is my room."

"Oh."

"Yours is down the hall."

She indicated my book and said: "Say, it looks like you like to read. I've got a book you can read. I wrote a book. It's my oughttabiography, full of things I ought'ta done."

She pulled a folded pamphlet from her back pocket and handed it to me. The cover had a picture of Jane dressed in buckskin, holding a little squirrel gun.

"I usually sell them for two bits," she said, "but you can have that one there, gratis."

I took the pamphlet and studied it for a few moments. "It says here you were a scout for General Custer and you rode for the Pony Express," I said.

"Would you read that part to me?" she asked. "I like that part about the stage robberies and I never get to hear it anymore."

"Can't you read it?"

"No. I can't read."

"But you said you wrote it," I said.

"I *did* write it. I learned the writing business all right, but I never had any patience for reading. Writing seems reasonable, because you know what you're putting down there on paper, but when you pick up something to read, god knows what you're getting into."

I sat up and read aloud the story of the death of Bill Hickok in Deadwood. She grasped my hand as I read and wept until my bedclothes were damp.

"Darling, that is such a sad story," she said.

"Yes'm, it is. I heard Carl say that you had a daughter."

"A sweet little girl. That's in there too."

"Was Hickok her dad?"

"Why, yes. Wild Bill *was* the father of my little girl. She can read and write letters and shoot from a galloping pony and drink tea with her goddam little finger stuck out if she needs to."

"What's your daughter's name?" I asked her.

"I call her Janey, but her name is really Elizabeth."

"She must be a young woman by now. Is she married? Where does she live?"

"She isn't that old. She's still my darling little girl."

"But Bill Hickok died twenty-five years ago, Miss Jane."

"I know that. Don't you think I know that? Don't you think I think about that every day? My little daughter was born in the petrified forest and everything moves slower in the petrified lands. Plants, minerals, children. You might think you're living life at railway speed in the petrified places, but you're not: you're still a young kid in spite of yourself. In fact, I've spent a lot of time petrified myself—that's how I've managed to keep my looks, honey. You've seen how all the boys are still crazy about me. But I had to give my little girl up you see, even though she was petrified."

"Petrified? You mean, like a stone?"

"Well, she wasn't *quite* like a stone. She just didn't move very fast. She was slow to grow. I think she spent extra time in every year. But I've not seen her now since I gave her up to adoption."

"Even though she was petrified?"

"I think that being petrified made the girl even more attractive to folks. Except you know you gotta feed kids and watch out for them, and a petrified child is harder to watch out for cause they're such slow growers."

"I've heard about petrified forests, but I never heard about petrified people—"

Jane said: "I think it has to do with all those underground minerals and things. The Indians believe these places to be holy and they avoid 'em because none of 'em want petrified children running around—an Indian child's gotta be on her feet and helping out from a young age. It's the way of the Cheyenne you know to avoid petrification."

"Where is she now?"

"I don't know, child. I stay away from her. She has a fine respectable life. She don't need no disreputable old woman getting in the way."

"How do you know? Do you ever write to her?"

"No writing," Jane said.

"I could write a letter for you."

"You could?" She thought about it for a moment, moving her lips, and she looked off somewhere to my left. "No. We better not," she said and then she stopped and looked at me out of the corner of her eye. "You want to know about her?"

I nodded.

"Wait."

She went down the hall, a little steadier than when she came in. After a few minutes she returned with her traveling box. She set it down on the floor. I sat up and looked over the side of my bed as she sat on the edge and opened the lid of the box. She rummaged around inside, taking out some old clothes, a dress, rubber boots, a few extra shirts.

"Miss Jane, I'd wash those for you, if you like."

She grunted something in response, lost in her search. She pulled out parts to a broken shotgun wrapped in oilskins. When she set it on the floor, shotgun pellets rolled under the bed. She had a bundle of her pamphlets tied up in twine. She reached deeper into her trunk, pulling out more hardware: bits of coffee mills, cigar tins, empty medicine bottles.

"Here it is," she said. She uncovered a small rag, a gunny sack with the faded lettering 'bea...' The sack had a couple of holes knocked out on the top and sides.

"What is it?" I asked as she put it into my hands.

"That's my darling's christening gown," she said.

"Mmm."

"Here." She took it back from me and ran her hand under the unravelling fabric. Her gnarled fingers caught and twisted in the moth-eaten holes of the gown.

"Dammit," she said as a fingernail tore the cloth.

"But do you see?" she asked. "Do you see?" And she moved her hand gently inside the gown. Her eyes searched out my own and I nodded.

"I did all the lace work myself," she said.

"It's lovely, Miss Jane. It looks like a butterfly. Yes, like a butterfly caught in a net."

She stopped the motion of her hand when I said that and we watched the dirt brown of her wrist and the dark-veined back of her hand through the gray burlap gown. And it did look a little something like a butterfly—or maybe a prairie dog—caught in a net.

"It took me weeks of work," she said. "I used a 20 gauge loaded with birdshot. For the really fine Armenian lace here," and she showed me the shotgun-laced hem, "I soaked the cartridges in pigfat so's the pellets stuck together and they made this nice bricbrac. Oh, remember how her tiny body filled out this old gown?"

She fixed me with her eyes, and I nodded 'yes' or maybe I meant 'uh huh.' "Why did it take weeks if you used a shotgun?"

She looked at me to see if I was pulling her leg—pretending not to know about the uses of firearms in lacemaking. "Oh honey, when you make a lace like this you don't shoot directly at the fabric. Like all the important things in life, girl, you aim *in*-directly. That's how it's done. Why, a straight-ahead shotgun blast would tear big ol' holes in this little dress. And the sooner you learn that, the better the whole deal will go."

She folded it up reverently before stuffing it back into the bottom of her traveling box. This done, she replaced her hat on her head and left, taking her box with her.

THE UN-GAME

By Kathleen Founds

✳   ✳   ✳

Dear Ms. Freedman,

We kept asking Mrs. Calderon why you abandoned us after break. She said you had "health issues." Adam Sandoval says he knocked you up, but don't worry, barely anyone believes him, especially the part about it being the medical miracle of Siamese twins. I kept bugging Calderon until she ripped a kid's drawing off the bulletin board and scribbled your address. Ms. Laura Jane Freedman, Bridges, 400 Pecan Blvd., Austin, TX. At first I was like, ah, shit, Ms. Freedman's a druggie! Because a cousin of mine went to a rehab called Bridges. On the home page, though, it says, "Guests unwind in the whirlpool, contemplating the exquisite beauty of arid plains." Which sounds like a super-deluxe get-away spa. Then I used my critical-reading skills, like we practiced with the toothpaste ads. I realized: you are in the looney bin.

I feel bad, Ms. Freedman. Plenty of teachers have thrown a terrarium out a window and shouted, "You're driving me crazy!" But you're the first who actually followed through. You were so nice to us, too. You gave us extra credit for wearing costumes on Halloween, and you brought in all that cardboard on Bastille Day so we could make funny hats. I don't know if you remember, but I made mine look like a pope's hat. I wore it after school to confirmation class, and even Sister Gloria tried it on.

The substitute we got for the last few months of school is not so nice. El Corporal. He is really into discipline. The first time Adam Sandoval sassed him, El Corporal screamed, "Drop and give me fifty!" We watched while Adam tried. He barely made twenty. We felt bad for him, Ms. Freedman. We pretty much shut up and did our work after that.

While school is not so great, I got promoted at The Rising Dove. Kind of. I am "temporary activities coordinator," while the real activities coordinator gets a gastric bypass. Instead of wiping butts, I wheel the fogies into a room with moldy encyclopedias and tall windows to read "Dear Abby" and the horoscopes. Last week I taught poetry. "The haiku is an ancient artform," I read from an internet printout. "It contains three lines, in a syllable pattern of 5-7-5:

An old silent pond

A frog jumps into the pond

Splash! Silence again."

The old people sat there. Carl started eating a crayon. Finally Joan—who is in the rest home at fifty for getting fat and depressed and not taking her meds—scrawled out some lines.

"Joan," I said. "Want to share?"

She scraped back her chair and read:

"A swarthy old pirate, McPhee,

chased after them lasses with glee.

'til his wife seized an axe,

Made one hearty whack,

and tossed his old jewels out to sea."

I did the only thing I could do, Ms. Freedman.

I led them in a round of applause.

After ten minutes of poetry failure, the walking fogies up and left, and the cripples asked to be wheeled back to their rooms. I looked at the blank papers and broken crayons. So much for my plan of including old people poetry in El Giraffe, the Joseph P. Anderson High School Lit Mag. I thought it could add variety. Being the student advisor, Ms. Freedman, you know we get mostly suicide poems. I thought old people might write on different themes, such as tarnished lockets with pictures of dead babies, or gout. I am hoping to God El Corporal does not replace you as Giraffe advisor. I have such weak-ass arms, Ms. Freedman, I can only do like two push-ups, so he'll probably fire me as editor and choose someone in JROTC, like Julie Chang.

Anyways, I have still been writing poetry a lot, even though you're not here. I included a poem I just finished. It is called Eclipse. I thought maybe if you felt like it you could read it.

Your friend,

Janice

Dear Janice,

Thank you for sending me your poem, Eclipse. I was impressed. Your journaling exercises were always strong, but this poem demonstrates a clarity and awareness that is new and exciting. I especially liked the lines, "Does the darkness hide/ the verses written in your eyes/ the spots upon your soul?" And I was impressed with the narrative turn at the end of the poem. "I walked with you for a while/ But soon I found that I / prefer to walk in the light." And nice use of enjambment! You do remember the term? Come to think of it, I'm not sure we made it to enjambment. I think our last literary term was simile. There were no similes in your poem.

You will have to forgive me, Janice. My memory is a bit shaky these days. It's not professional of me to go into this, I know, but I feel I owe you an explanation. In short: there are some pills I take to balance my brain chemistry. In November, I flushed them down the toilet. I had an initial rush of energy—I imagine you recall the lit-term Jeopardy board coated with industrial-grade glitter glue (I've been told El Corporal burned it in the gravel pit). Soon, though, I felt a strong need to curl in the fetal position in a dark, enclosed space. Towards the end, I hallucinated that a great bird appeared at my window and wrapped me in its downy wings.

My brother tracked me down to Phoenix, Arizona, where I'd been sitting on a park bench, feeding hamburgers to birds. He brought me back to Austin and checked me into Bridges. The doctors have gotten my medication straightened out, but I still wake up each morning feeling exsanguinated (look it up).

I want you to know, Janice, that though I had a hard time managing the class-room as a whole, I do care deeply for each of you. It means a great deal that you've taken the time to write. Your nursing home story made me smile. To the orderlies at Bridges, I must seem like one of your intractable charges—I refused to attend clay modeling class three times this week. Do keep sending me poetry. I have a lot of time on my hands, here, and I'd rather spend it reading your work than filling out my mood chart.

Fondly,

Ms. F

Dear Ms. Freedman,

I'm glad they got you on the right pills. I looked up exsanguinated and it means, "drained of blood and life." I feel that way a lot of times when I get home from work. Maybe I need some mental meds and a week at Bridges, ha ha.

In order to waste time at the rest home on Thursday, I inventoried the sup-ply closet. As I counted crates of tangled string and stacks of brittle magazines, I realized: the "supplies" are just things geezers leave behind when they die. Then I saw the "Un-Game," battered in the corner. I thought: damn, a real supply. An activity for tomorrow!

Me and the Un-Game, we go way back. I first played it at Amelia Basil's house. Amelia's parents believed in exact fairness. They liked the Un-Game, because no one wins. You just take turns pulling question cards like "Who do you trust?" and "What is your favorite: triangle or dodecahedron?" While I played the game on Amelia's rug, shoveling Cheez-its in my face, I learned that Mrs. Basil's happiest mo-ment was eating jumbo shrimp dipped in cocktail sauce a week before her wedding.

This seemed sad to me.

Today I wheeled old folks onto the sun porch to play the Un-Game. Aurora leaned down to pick up the lid of the game-box. Her eyes wobbled. She put the box on top of her head.

"It's to shade myself," she said.

"Do you want me to get you a hat from your room?"

She held it there, arm shaking. "I have no hat."

"Okay," I said, feeling bad she had Parkinson's, plus also a box on her head. "You can go first." I flipped through the deck, discarding downers (Share a big letdown in your life. What do you think it's like after you die?).

"Okay, Aurora. I found a question for you!"

It was hard to watch Aurora's emaciated body tremble. It was like watching a grandma be crucified.

"What is your most sentimental possession?"

"My Bible."

"A classic! What's your favorite story?"

"The cripple at the well."

"I like it when Jesus overturns the tables in the temple and drives out money-changers with a whip of braided cords."

I turned to Helen, whose body swelled out of her wheelchair like a rising mound of dough. "Helen. 'What advice would you give a young man about to get married'?"

"Buy her . . . flowers," Helen croaked, trying to adjust her thick, terminator-style shades.

"That's sweet. Did your husband buy you flowers?"

"My lover . . . did."

I imagined a lover climbing Helen's mountain of flesh, planting a flag in her perm. "Good for you, Helen. Way to live fully." I turned to Nancy, a frail woman with puffy orange hair. "What are you most proud of?"

Nancy brushed an imaginary crumb from her arm.

"Like, what have you done in your life that you feel good about?"

She rubbed her eyes.

"Nancy. C'mon. Participate."

"I'm not proud of anything," she sobbed. Tears streamed down her face.

So much for the Un-Game.

Before I worked here, I thought living a long time would automatically make you kindly and wise. Not so much. The old people cheat at bingo and throw hissy fits about toast. Anyways, I'm going to see if I can steal some beer from my aunt, and get wasted, and forget about my day. Don't tell.

Your friend,

Janice

P.S. This is a kind of weird poem I wrote on my break today. It is called, *Nicoli, Who Was Thrown To the Wolves Behind the Sleigh, 1845.*

Dear Janice,

I suppose I don't have to tell you that your prefrontal cortex is not fully formed until the age of twenty five. Abusing alcohol in the teen years may cause your brain to re-circuit, wiring you for dependence on alcohol or other substances.

But I understand why you'd want to drink. Sometimes the mind whirs and pinwheels, rising and contracting on roller coaster stairs, and you need a little something to blur the flashing lights to shade forests of tree green.

At least postpone your drinking until you make it to college. Please. Alcohol could be your camel's straw—the weight that tips you into the world of perpetual rest-home employment. Try that for purgatory.

Sorry I'm jangly. They've augmented meds, seeking that which won't exsanguinate. This new cocktail (of drugs) makes me feel I've swallowed batteries. Energizing yet artificial. I do not recommend.

Naptime!

Ms. F

Dear Janice,

I haven't heard from you in a while, and I worry my last letter offended you. If so: apologies. It's hard for me to tell, sometimes, when I should staple back my tongue. Your choices are your own. God knows my adolescence wasn't the picture of propriety. (And look how well I turned out. Ha!)

As for your poem. What a strange, lovely opening. "You used to pet the/ soft fur that grew on the tips/ of my ears. Pleasure in the seat of my belly/ as you held me, mother." I wonder if you might consider adding one more verse. As it is, it's a bit difficult to tell exactly what happens after the mother wanders into the snow. Overall though, fine work.

Best,

Ms. F

Dear Ms. Freedman,

Sorry I didn't write. It's just I found out the Smucker's plant is closing down. My dad is being transferred to Piggot, Kentucky, which just happens to be where his jam factory girlfriend (Glenda) was transferred six months ago. According to the brochures, Piggot is famous for hand-carved canoes and Kentucky's only life-size wax museum. I HATE WAX FIGURES! I screamed, throwing a light fixture at my dad. THEY ALWAYS COME TO LIFE AND TRY TO KILL YOU! According to him, that's not the point. According to him, he can't get another job here, unless he works the fields, and his back can't take that. The worst part is, he wants me to stay here, and live with my fat aunt. He says it's because I'm already in school here, but I know it's because Glenda doesn't want me living with them. So now I get to share a room with my cousin Macy, who is always saying things like, "Planning on grow-ing boobs this year, Janice?" Plus, she is pregnant, so I am also going to be sharing my room with a screaming baby. God. I hate my life. Maybe I could come be your roommate at Bridges. Ha. Ha ha ha ha. Seriously, though, I'd rather live pretty much anywhere than with my aunt.

Cross My Heart & Hope to Die,

Janice

Dear Friend of <u>Laura Freedman</u>,

This letter is to inform you that, due to the complexity of this therapeutic juncture, *Bridges Psychiatric Wellness Solutions*^{TM} has deemed it best to isolate our client from outside stimuli. All mail for Laura Freedman will be returned to sender until further notice. Thank you for your concern.

Spirit Engaged,

Andrew Schaffer, Outreach Coordinator

From: janthepiratespy@hotmail.com

To: lfreedman@anderson.edu

Subject: ?!?

Dear Ms. Freedman,

I am e-mailing you because maybe you will get a chance to sneak away from a nurse and look at your e-mail. They are not giving you my letters because you are apparently on lockdown. God, what did you do, assault an orderly? Jesus. I looked at the Bridges website again and I have to say the place creeps me out. First of all, who signs anything "Spirit Engaged"? Second, the section on electro-shock therapy says "To ameliorate the stress of temporary memory loss, Bridges staff eliminates potentially stressful stimuli." Which I am thinking means you are getting electro-shock therapy. God. I didn't think they even did that anymore. Does your hair stick out crazy all over the place? I hope you're okay. I really hope you're okay.

Your Friend,

Janice

From: janthepiratespy@hotmail.com

To: lfreedman@anderson.edu

Subject: RE: ?!?

Dear Ms. Freedman,

I guess they are not letting you check your e-mail. Who knows, maybe they don't even have computers there. Maybe it's "excessive stimuli." Ha ha. Well guess who is teaching our English class this year? El Corporal. Yes. Mrs. Hinojosa liked the way he licked us into shape, so she hired him full-time. We are learning lots of literature under this totalitarian regime, if learning lots of literature means filling out worksheets while El Corporal paces the room, bristling. I have to admit, though, it's kind of cool to see him shut down the cocky kids like Juan and Adam. Even Juan looked nervous when El Corporal made him stay during lunch hour for a "conversation." I was lounging on the grass, drawing a yeti on my jeans, when Juan stumbled out of the classroom. He looked like he'd been through a wind tunnel.

"Did he get you with the bullwhip, Juan?"

"He made me clean out the hamster cages."

"What does that have to do with you throwing a stapler at Timon?"

"He accused me of 'inciting irresponsible reproductive activity among rodents.'"

"You put Kojax in Tulip's cage?"

"I wouldn't have done it if I knew that bitch would eat her babies."

"Dude, you deserved what you got."

Juan looked me over. "Janice. Way to get boobs this summer."

I flipped him the bird. I was about to let that punctuate our conversation, but then I thought, hey. You know what would serve my dad right? If he heard I was hanging around with losers, such as Juan, who has been in my class since kinder. Back then he had a head like a T-Rex, and he brought his toys crashing down on my head without reason. My dad hated him.

"What are you doing right now?"

"Ditching PE and taking you to the lake?"

"The last time I hung out with you, Juan, you cut the hair off all my troll dolls."

"Aw, Janice, come on. You're too old to play with dolls, anyway."

So I went to the lake with Juan. On the way we stopped and got slurpees and when we got to the lake we poured rum in them and they were cold and good as we sat on the hood of his car. When you get to know Juan, it's surprising. Beneath the cocky asshole exterior, there is a sticky marshmallow interior. We reminisced about old times, like when Adam Sandoval choked on a golf ball in second grade and the janitor saved him. Juan told me that his dad had always wanted him to be a doctor. He worked double shifts at the Discount Mattress Outlet to save for Juan's college, until the night he had a heart attack while stacking kings. They found him the next morning, hands over his heart. Dead.

"You should be a doctor, though, J. You were always smart and stuff. You could be one of those pretty doctors like on TV."

"Not if I keep failing."

"You do good in school."

"Um, El Corporal's PE class?"

"Smart people suck at sports. It's like, one of those inverse scenarios."

"Wow. It's like you were almost paying attention in math."

"You probably just suck at push-ups because you have brains in your arms instead of muscles." Juan drew a diagram in the mud with a stick. "Actually, your boobs are probably all filled with brains, too," he said, adding two wiggly lumps to his diagram.

"If I have brains in my arms, how am I about to punch in your face?"

"You're the doctor." Juan flicked the stick into the lake. "Don't ask me."

Don't worry, Ms. Freedman. I'm not stupid enough to get knocked up like Christina Sackburn-Reyes. I just want to hang out with dino-head enough to freak out my dad.

Xo

Janice

MONITORS

By Ryan Boudinot

✳ ✳ ✳

I.

A room lit by a bank of monitors. Two technicians, Ross and Andy, watch the progress of the subjects. If the subjects perform outside the performance parameters, there are a number of contingency strategies in the Standard Operating Procedures (SOP) manual to which Ross and Andy must refer.

Ross and Andy are males between the ages of 25 and 40. Both wear the codified uniforms of their positions as technicians. They intently watch the subjects who are themselves performing monitoring activities, observing the activities of certain sub-subjects. It is difficult for Ross and Andy to make out the activities of these sub-subjects, as Ross and Andy do not have direct access to what their own subjects are watching on their (the subjects') monitors. Not that Ross and Andy haven't tried. They have squinted and pressed their noses against their monitors trying to make out what the sub-subjects are doing on the monitors their subjects are viewing.

Occasionally one of the subjects violates their Personal Performance Parameters and Ross and Andy must refer to the SOPs for the appropriate contingency strategy. These contingencies consist solely of referring to the appropriate escalation pathway and submitting an alert, after which corrective action is taken. When corrective action is taken, the monitor displaying the subject in question goes blank, or is supposed to. Ross and Andy have postulated that their equipment needs replacing because occasionally the monitor view has been left on while a particular corrective action is taking place. Corrective actions can be as simple as a Corrective Referee visiting the subject and talking to them a short while, or perhaps giving them some medicine. Twice Ross and Andy have witnessed a Corrective Referee discipline a subject with violence. They have never seen outright termination, but they have seen restored monitor views showing just an empty, disheveled room, and in one case a custodian cleaning a bloody hand print off a wall.

Ross thinks these sightings are accidental, but Andy has a theory that they have been purposely shown the outcome of their taking the appropriate contingency strategy with regard to their subjects performing outside their Personal Performance Parameters. Andy is of the opinion that being able to infer the nature of a more intense kind of corrective action has made them—Ross and Andy—better performers.

Ross finds this hard to believe, and notes that they aren't even being observed.

Andy challenges Ross on this point. How does Ross know they are not being observed?

Ross notes that they certainly have never had a visit from a Corrective Referee, which would prove that they were being monitored.

Exactly, Andy says, because they have never deviated from their Personal Performance Parameters. So the only way to determine whether they are being observed is to violate them.

Ross thinks this is a ridiculous plan and refuses to go along with it. Andy says that Ross secretly believes he is being observed and is afraid of corrective action, that he has spent countless hours in this room soldering in his mind a connection between deviating from the Parameters and receiving correction. But if they are not being observed, as Ross claims, they have nothing to fear.

So Andy reaches out and turns off a monitor. They have watched their subjects perform this very action, for which they received stern words from Corrective Referees. Ross asks Andy to turn the monitor back on. An argument ensues, and perhaps driven by boredom, Ross struggles with Andy physically and strikes him with his fist, then turns the monitor back on. Andy slowly rises from the floor, wiping blood off his lip, and makes a pointed comment about how Ross would make a great Corrective Referee.

A few minutes pass wordlessly as they observe the subjects on their monitors. Then there is a knock on the door and both technicians jump, startled. They typically—actually never—get visitors. Andy opens the door and the Corrective Referee appears, seemingly proving Andy's theory. He wears the suit and the tidy hair of all Corrective Referees, and his tie is decorated with little cartoon characters. There are only two chairs in the place, so Andy yields his and leans against the table their monitors sit on. It is meant to be a casual posture, but his arms are crossed and it is clear he is having troubling thoughts.

Say, the Corrective Referee says, I know things can get a little uncomfortable here with the close quarters and all. You fellows have a real tough job, and hey, it's only human that from time to time nerves get frayed. I'm here to help. So say, tell you what, I've got a couple cards with entertainment codes I'd like to give you. Here, take them, use them in your rooms tonight. You know, relax. I understand there's a great batch of new releases. And if you need anything else, feel free to contact me per the appropriate contingencies. Buck up. You guys are doing a fabulous job.

The Corrective Referee leaves and seems to take with him whatever animosity Ross and Andy shared in that brief, explosive moment. It goes without saying that they are indeed being observed, though via what means it's hard to surmise. They survey the walls and ceiling, trying not to be conspicuous, knowing they are being observed in the act of trying to determine how they're being observed. Ultimately, the technology is too sophisticated for them to detect. What would come of finding the miniature cameras anyway? If they were to locate them and obscure them they would certainly be violating their own Personal Performance Parameters.

The end of their shift finally comes and both technicians retreat to their private rooms, eat, and enter their respective entertainment codes. Andy settles on an entertainment in which the righteous prevail and the wicked are vanquished swiftly and without prejudice. Ross watches an entertainment about a big dog and how it disrupts one family's routines with hilarious results.

Both technicians return to their work space the next day with their coffees and pastries and proceed to monitor their subjects. Ross, feeling horrible about the previous day's outburst, apologizes to Andy. Andy mumbles something noncommittal in response, and for the better part of the day, they don't speak to each other.

A little after lunch, Ross spots a violation on monitor four. One of the subjects is violently smashing his own monitors with the base of his swivel chair.

Ross says, I believe that's a section seven violation right there. He taps the screen with a pen. Andy sits doing nothing but watching the monitor, so Ross takes it upon himself to report the incident. A few minutes later the monitor goes into stand-by mode. The Corrective Referee has no doubt paid his visit to their subject.

This is bullshit, Andy says. You and I are both one centimeter from doing exactly what that subject just did.

You're talking crazy, Ross says.

I'm crazy? You're the one who brained me yesterday, don't you remember?

Yeah, I remember. And for the second time today, I apologize. Whatever mood you're in doesn't justify neglecting your monitoring responsibilities.

Bullshit, Andy says again. He pauses a moment before an expression of surprise passes over him, as if something he once knew but had forgotten had been revealed anew. He stands, walks from the room, and doesn't return the rest of his shift.

Ross smolders throughout the rest of the day. Not only does he have to monitor twice as many monitors as he usually does, he suspects that his inability to keep Andy focused on his tasks will reflect poorly on his own performance. He performs as best he can, and that night in bed falls into a forest of nightmares.

The following morning Andy is already in his seat when Ross arrives. He doesn't look good. He appears fatigued and there's a bandage over one of his eyebrows. He hasn't touched his coffee or pastry. His eyes move from one monitor to the next, but Ross can't tell if he's actually processing what he's seeing. The only way to find out is to wait until one of the subjects on Andy's monitors violates a Performance Parameter. Ross again performs double monitoring duty, just in case. Mid-morning he notices one of Andy's subjects slumped in a sleeping position in his chair. Apparently Andy doesn't notice, so Ross scoots his chair over and submits the alert using Andy's keyboard. As the subject on the monitor is being visited by a Corrective Referee bearing a pot of black coffee, the door to Ross and Andy's workspace opens and their own Corrective Referee appears, his shirt sleeves rolled up and his tie loosened.

Hi Ross, the Corrective Referee says, turning a spare chair around so he can sit on it backwards. I appreciate the effort you're putting into helping Andy out, I really do. It's commendable.

Ross says, He'll snap out of this funk, I know he will. He's a good guy.

For your sake I certainly hope so. You can't expect yourself to maintain your own Performance Parameters if you're doing two monitors' jobs.

He'll get better. I promise.

I know he will, the Corrective Referee says, nodding at one of the monitors. I wouldn't want what happened to that guy to happen to our Andy.

Ross glances at the monitor to see that the subject who fell asleep is clutching his eyes, twisting his body around on the floor in a pool of steaming coffee.

The next morning Andy is already at his station when Ross arrives, busily typing commands into his keyboard. Andy greets Ross warmly and offers him his pastry. Ross feels relieved, happy that his faith in his colleague was correct. They spend the morning talking about entertainments as they perform the functions of their jobs, just like years ago when they began monitoring together.

Some time after lunch Andy swivels around in his chair excitedly and asks Ross to look at something on one of his monitors. They peer closely at two subjects, except the view has been magnified significantly and they can make out what is on the subjects' monitors.

I finally figured out the secret zoom command, Andy says, see? Just a few keystrokes and I can zoom in even closer.

Ross says nothing, riveted by the image he sees on one of the subject's monitors. He raises his left arm to test his hypotheses and realizes that it's true. He and Andy are the subjects of these subjects' monitors.

When the Corrective Referee arrives with his assistants in their rubber aprons and gloves, Ross does not struggle, but Andy does. The referee uses the eye core.

II.

They made me watch the procedure. The eye core looked like something you might use to drive nails into a wall, a vibrating, battered machine with a pistol grip and hoses running to a portable tank/battery pack. Our Corrective Referee and his assistants held Andy to the chair and placed the eye piece over Andy's face. It didn't take longer than thirty seconds. Once Andy's eyes were removed, they inserted two white ceramic plug-like objects, from the bases of which trailed two cables. Our Corrective Referee plugged these cables into two ports beneath one of Andy's monitors.

How's it looking? our Corrective Referee said, Is the signal coming through? Andy nodded.

All good then, our Corrective Referee said as the assistants wiped up some blood with pre-moistened absorbent wipes.

When they left, I leaned over and whispered, Andy? Are you okay?

Andy nodded.

Andy, I'm so sorry, I said, and started to cry. I took hold of his closest hand. It felt cold and drained of blood, probably from the medications they inserted during the procedure.

Can you see anything? I said.

Yes, Andy said, I can see what's on the monitors. It's like looking down a tunnel at the image. The resolution is better.

In my peripheral vision I spotted a violation and quickly submitted the appropriate alert. Andy groped for his keyboard to log some violations of his own. They were coming in waves—subjects falling asleep, defacing their monitors, breaking furniture. Thanks to my quick work, the misbehaving subjects were instantly visited by their Corrective Referees, who delivered the variety of punishments they deserved. By the end of my shift I started hoping something I could barely admit to myself, that the subjects would violate their Performance Parameters. I considered the possibility of the subjects wising up and behaving within their Performance Parameters, and the prospect oddly disappointed me. The broken fingers and black eyes that resulted from their disobedience were my reward for a job performed well.

At the end of our shift our Corrective Referee visited to unplug Andy from his monitors and escort him to his quarters. He gave us both unlimited entertainment cards. That night I watched three. One was about a kid who learns how to be cool when a more popular kid shows him how to dress. Another was a historical entertainment about Vikings. The third was a pornographic entertainment that I'm too ashamed to describe.

The next day Andy arrived before me. He was in a talkative mood.

I can plug these suckers into my ports at home and see the entertainments with crystal clarity, Andy said. Cool, yeah? The Corrective Ref says pretty soon I'll be allowed to hook these things into a video camera so I won't be restricted to just seeing whatever monitor I'm plugged in to.

Do they hurt? I said.

They're a little sore, yeah, Andy said, but that's supposed to wear off in a couple days.

I slowly became accustomed to Andy's new way of monitoring. The more content he seemed with his new apparatus, the more bored I became. My subjects entered a long streak of faithfully performing within their Parameters. I waited with itchy fingers for them to slip up, make some fatal error that brought upon them the wrath of a Corrective Referee, but for the most part their transgressions were minor. I daydreamt about a subject smashing a monitor with a chair or getting up and walking out an hour before his shift ended. Then I considered an awful thought, some dark and buoyant fantasy that kept bobbing to the surface regardless of how I tried to push it down. I wanted to submit an alert on someone who was completely innocent, who had not deviated from their Performance Parameters. With Andy locked into his own personal monitor view, I knew I could probably get away with it. Nobody would see me, not even the hidden others who observed me from miniscule cameras hidden somewhere in the acoustic tile overhead. Whoever was watching me would not be able to discern whether my subjects had in fact deviated from their performance parameters. There was a half hour left on my shift. I could simply shelve the idea, go home, eat pizza, and watch some entertainments. Instead I chose my subject randomly and submitted an alert for vandalism.

A couple minutes passed and I stared at the back of my subject's head. Before him a screen of fuzzed out, inhuman pixels behaved. The Corrective Referee entered and I considered submitting an alert correction, but knew that alert corrections reflected poorly on one's own performance. The Corrective Referee selected an instrument from his belt and went to work. I could not bear to watch. I had to watch. When the occasion of correction passed, my subject crawled back to his chair and pushed it toward the camera, then climbed onto it so that his face took up nearly the entire monitor. How he knew where to find the camera I had no idea, but his knowing where it was located seemed to me an admission of his guilt. Then he opened his mouth to show me the bleeding pits where his bottom teeth had been.

At home I vomited for an hour then sat down in my favorite chair to watch an entertainment about a beloved teacher whose unorthodox teaching methods simply aren't understood by the school administration.

The following day I numbly went about my work. I considered submitting a vacation request. My mind wandered to entertainments I had seen, people's faces I had passed in the hallway. Andy hummed and tapped the wrist protector of his keyboard with a pencil in time to a song. Then right before noon all the monitors went blank. Hardware failure. I banged on my monitor with the ball of my hand, but all they displayed was static.

What's going on? Andy said.

Dang monitors blew, I said.

I can see mine just fine, Andy said, What are you seeing?

Nothing, I said.

Must be a connection between the servers to the monitors, Andy said. Hey, it looks like my subjects are having the same problem. I guess this is system-wide.

Can you pull up a Performance Parameter menu? I said.

Yeah, Andy said, hold on a second. I've never had to access this one before. Okay, here. It says that... This can't be correct. "In case of monitor failure please continue following performance parameters and submit alerts on all violations."

But we can't even see our subjects! I said.

It's happening to everyone, Andy said. Oh, Jesus.

I started toward the door. The Corrective Referee and his two assistants met me. On the Corrective Referee's face was an expression of deep, compassionate sadness as he sighed and asked for his tools.

RUN TIME

By Jesse Goolsby

✳   ✳   ✳

1. I've heard stories that once you get to heaven you sit in front of everyone you know and they replay your life so everyone can see. It's movie hour. I imagine all those folding chairs, the murmurs of anticipation, the projector warming for the arrival.

2. During high school my girlfriend and I would select which movies to watch by their run times: the longer the better. We'd curl up under a blanket—even in the summer—and play with one another's bodies. Once, in late August, we thumbed through titles, checking the backs, when I spotted *The Sound of Music.* I flipped the movie over and like a gift from on high I read 174 minutes. I felt like shouting thanks to the heavens. We turned off the lights, took up our position on the couch, and nestled under the blanket. Before Julie Andrews could finish *the hills are alive with the sound of music* my singing mother walked in and sat a foot away from our heads. She stayed until the end credits.

3. My parents didn't allow rated R movies in our home. But every so often, out of the blue, one would sneak in. I remember *Braveheart* getting a pass. *Schindler's List* got a pass. I was fifteen then. I remember the little girl in a red coat running through the Jewish ghetto, the naked, starving people, the part where Schindler tells the bad concentration camp commander that real power is pardoning, not executing the Jews. My head spun. In the end, my mother was angry about the sex scene in the beginning. *It showed her breasts,* she said. *Completely unnecessary.*

4. One afternoon, a high-school friend brought over *Faces of Death.* Some cows had their heads chopped off. There were a couple of executions by electric chair, firing squad scenarios, and a few hangings. In one scene, a tight-rope walker:

He stood in beautiful balance between two tall buildings; a crowd gathered below, shouting and pointing. The walker gripped a long balancing pole, but soon it fell away, and for a few seconds the man teetered between safety and horror: he went on his toes, angled his hips; he thrust his arms to one side, then another. I wondered if he'd prepared for the moment. Surely tight rope walkers consider their fall; they imagine where and how, the few seconds of gravity. And suddenly, the man slipped, but snagged the rope under his armpits. He dangled, his legs kicking, but there was nowhere to go but down. His body slid another couple feet and he hung by his hands. The scene took far too long. *Let go,* I said. But he wouldn't. He hung on to the rope, and for awhile, it seemed as though the movie paused: just the still frame of the man, hanging, the V shape of the tight rope, and the crowd, eyes above, silent and waiting.

5. While my mother was dying in the San Francisco hospital, I wasn't thinking of her. Occasionally, I would, but not for the right reasons. When I was seventeen I asked to miss school to go see her. It was mid-week and I told Dad that I couldn't take it anymore—I missed my mom—and had to make the four-hour trip south. He said *yes, of course you can go,* looking proud and tired through his red eyes, and I ran back to my room and picked up the phone and called Jill, my on and off again girlfriend who lived on the way to the hospital. We were currently off, but she said I could stop by, so the next morning, a sunny Wednesday, I stopped in Davis.

I know my mother was lonely and scared. I know she was bored. I know the beeps and shining floors drove her mad. But I was in Davis. I went to a movie—*The Horse Whisperer*—hoping the darkness would guide Jill's hand to my thigh, her blonde head to my shoulder. The long movie was overproduced and sappy, and Jill never touched me, not even when I overtook the armrest between us and bent close, smelling her jasmine perfume. Still, on the ride to her apartment, I hoped for the best. Dusk was fading out, and the sky turned purple.

At her apartment she let me kiss her. I started leaning on her, but she held me up, said, *I want to know you mean it.* Her eyes shook. I told her, *of course I mean it,* but it was a lie. She let me kiss her again. Then, she backed away. *Your mother,* she said.

6. I made a movie once, a documentary. I filmed quite a bit over my four

years in university. I interviewed my friends, took the camera on spring break, and to other events. When I edited the film one of my friends helped. We wanted to make sure it was authentic, so we left most of the stuff in.

In one scene, my friend moons the camera, says, *full moon out tonight, fuckers.*

In another, a Mexican prostitute bares her chest and sings in Spanish.

In one, I'm naked and drunk. I recite Dylan Thomas's "Do Not Go Gentle into That Good Night" in a downpour in Montana. I get most of the words right, and perform a twirl for the camera.

I showed the film to my family. I don't know what I was thinking. Near the end I realized I'd brought an R-rated film home.

7. The other day *The Horse Whisperer* was on television. It's been fifteen years since the night in Davis with Jill. I recall driving the rest of the way to my dying mother later that evening. I drove through Vacaville, Vallejo, and Oakland. I drove the Bay Bridge over the dark water. I passed the tall buildings of downtown San Francisco, so close they seemed to touch. I parked at Kezar Stadium and walked up the hill to the university hospital. When I walked in my mother had just shit herself, and the staff was changing her diaper. They finished, but the smell lingered. A nurse brought me a cot. There wasn't a whole lot to say. My mother was dying and I was confused and tired. I asked her if she wanted me to read to her, but she said no. We lay there for awhile, not saying anything. They brought her red Jello and she ate it half heartedly. Her face was bloated from the anti-rejection drugs, and she struggled to open her mouth. She groaned. We walked a lap of the floor. I pushed her IV machine and she stared at the gleaming tiles as her organs toiled. I hated myself, but my mind swung to Jill—how she hadn't moved toward me, her smell, her dry lips.

Later, with the lights out, my mother turned on the television. She asked me what I wanted to watch, but I didn't care. She said we could watch a movie, my choice. I didn't object. We scrolled through the titles on the menu screen a couple times, but there was nothing worth our time.

GRAVITY

by Sherrie Flick

✻   ✻   ✻

"If he was a pet, we'd put him to sleep." That's what my sister says. If she was in a story, she would be an unlikeable character. She says this about our father, who's in the hospital with all kinds of problems. Liver, kidneys, heart, you name it. Beeps and burps and monitors screeching.

My sister tries her best. She does. But it's hard to have empathy for her most days. And it isn't the typical story. Our father wasn't, isn't, a monster. He drank too much, sure. But he was kind to us, spoiled us most days. My sister, she won't have any of it. Needs to feel abused and neglected and put out over everything, including the type of pizza I've brought to her house. The red wine, when she wanted white.

"I'm just saying," she says. "If my cat had the problems dad has? The vet would say: 'I'm sorry Kathy. We have to put her down.'" I stare at her, pizza midway to my mouth, suddenly unhungry.

"Kathy," I say. "Our dad is not a cat. He can drive and use his thumbs. He paid for your college education. Fluffy over there bats around that little mouse toy on a good day. On a bad day she pukes up hairballs on your carpet."

"Sure, yes. But that isn't what I'm talking about," Kathy says. "I'm just articulating the reality of the situation."

My dad played badminton with us in the summers. Built us a tree house. Sure, he couldn't handle girl adolescence; that's when my mom stepped in and fucked things up a bit, sure. But, you know, he tried. He tried until he couldn't try any more and an ambulance came and brought him to St. Mary's. And now he's a beeping mess of wires, and my sister refuses to visit him, like she's proving a point.

"All I'm saying," I say, "is you're going to hate yourself if he dies and you don't visit. Could you just visit. You know, for like 5 seconds? You'd visit Fluffy if you had to put her down, right?" I've succumbed to the pet metaphor against all better judgment.

"The cat's name isn't Fluffy. Do you honestly think I'd name an animal some-thing like that? It's Gertrude. You know that. Gertie. Get it right," she says, avoiding the question.

Now I feel that old need to drink a lot of wine. It's coming on strong, an itch in my neck, down deep where you can't scratch. Glasses of wine. Goblets of wine. Wine enough to shut my sister up. My mom won't talk to my sister because my sister won't visit dad so the last few days have been me ping-ponging between everyone, acting like a social worker or a flight attendant, depending on where I am.

I pour another glass of Syrah. A big, fat glass.

My sister rummages through her fridge for a beer. "From what you're telling me, he isn't going to know if I visit or not," she says and pulls out a cantaloupe, a green pepper. Starts slicing them both.

"Are you going to eat those together? What's happened to you?" I say. I don't understand anyone anymore. I move away for a few years and everyone changes. My mother does yoga. Kathy eats weird food. My dad decomposes. My old boyfriend is fit and wealthy. I have stayed exactly, exactly the same except for the overwhelming realization that I love my dad. I have always loved him. And right now my sister is breaking my heart. He is also breaking my heart, because—honestly—he's the only one who could set everyone straight.

He'd say: "Kath—put that food back in the fridge. Sit down and talk with your sister you never see." He'd say: "Drink the red wine, it won't kill you, Joyce." He'd say: "Mommy, you look ridiculous in those yoga pants, but hey grab your little mat and do what you can." He'd say: "Joyce, get me a beer. Let's talk about Johnny. Sure, he looks good and rich, but he never once remembered your birthday. You remember crying on the back porch about that? You remember how he once took you to Taco John's to make up?" He'd say: "Me? Don't worry about me. I've got everything under control."

SORREL

by Sherrie Flick

✻   ✻   ✻

The rain streaked the windows of the little yellow house and made a stitching noise against the glass, sealing up the world. Yellow rubber boots. Mud and puddles. Car tires rubbed down the street, tiny waterfalls spraying at their heels. The gray sky pushed down, making the world contract, come inside, where Elizabeth's oatmeal pan had boiled dry.

How had that happened, she wondered. Time wasn't right anymore. And in her confusion, her constant confusion of late, she'd lost her reading glasses. She stood in her housecoat—a frilly, pink shell—with her ostrich legs, her puffy slippers. Elizabeth held a wooden spoon in her hand. But why? She was lost in this aquarium, would be lost now for a long time, she knew. She thought to pick up the phone. The hard black plastic in her hand gave her confidence. Elizabeth gripped it and for a moment a slippery fish of memory drew some numbers on a screen in her head. She dialed.

When the voice said hello, Elizabeth said, Hello. Who is this? And of course, yes, it was her daughter, wasn't it? A daughter who would come right over, now, yes? But this daughter didn't live nearby, had moved away years ago she reminded her mother right then. And then this daughter asked, "Where's dad, mom? Isn't he there to help you?"

Of course, how could she have forgotten. There was Stanley on the stairs, hair sticking up, so gray. When did it get so gray? And stumbling now and looking alarmed and grabbing the phone from her hand and talking, talking, talking into it. Charming, really. He'd always been that way, hadn't he? Or no. Stanley had been dull at times and then gained a kind of charm later in life.

He set down the black plastic thing, looked at Elizabeth in a way she believed was love. She said, Are you concerned?

And he looked out the window at the drizzle, looked at Elizabeth. He said, Elizabeth, what did you try to cook this morning? I thought we'd agreed we'd only cook together, remember?

Elizabeth looked at the spoon in her hand, a big wooden spoon, too big to eat from. It was most certainly used for stirring things. She hid it behind her back. She said, The rain?

Stanley hugged her then, and in hugging her gently took the spoon away. Elizabeth felt her body flatten against his, naked under her housecoat. She so badly wanted so many things she could no longer name. This, for instance. What was it?

Stanley set her down in a chair, smoothed his hair, pulled his own robe a little tighter over his pajamas. Did he clean this kitchen, she wanted to know? It was really very nicely done.

He told her that no, Sammi came in twice a week now, but yes, Sammi did a great job, didn't she? It made them both more comfortable, didn't it? A clean house. Stanley made her toast, spreading the butter and jam carefully with his thick fingers. He didn't have much practice at this kind of thing, she could tell.

And she ate, and the rain continued to move throughout the town. A slow sweep of it, dense and unforgiving. The silence in the kitchen seemed natural. Perhaps they'd sat in silence this way many times? She wanted to know, did he want to read the newspaper? Hadn't he always done that? But now he said, no, he wanted to be with her instead. And that seemed sweet. He held her hand.

I used to make you marvelous meals, she said, guessing.

Yes, he said.

And I was beautiful, she said.

Yes, he said. And you're still beautiful. It's just that we're getting so much older now, you see?

She said, We were lovers and happy. We had a good, simple life, didn't we?

And now Stanley was tearing up a little, but he said, yes, we did, we had a good life. We had children and several pets—although some of the pets and some of the children were impossible at times. Yes, we had a good life that was complicated by some mistakes but might be called simple and happy.

Elizabeth smiled. Yes, I remember, she said.

Stanley said, I'm sorry, Elizabeth. You know that, right? I'm sorry for what I put you through. I was a fool for a while, and then a jackass. But you see now, now I'm taking care of you? I can love you like I've always wanted to.

Yes, of course, she said. Sorry. It's such a nice word, isn't it? She thought about sorrow and sorry and sorrel, which she used to grow, that she remembered clearly. The spring rains, the green leaves, the tiny plants reaching up to the sun.

She didn't remember the bad times. She believed that no one did, anymore. The world had changed and now everyone was happy.

THE MATHEMATICS OF WAITING

By Kirsty Logan

✻   ✻   ✻

1. Landscape

At five to nine we take the metal grilles off the window-frames. When we lift, our arm muscles tense to the size of garlic cloves. We already have crumbs in our hair. Clouds reflect on the spilled liquid on the table. A baby throws chewed raisins on the floor. Children thumb grease onto the cake cabinet. The music changes; the CD skips; it's changed back. The roots of our hair grow in the same color as coffee grounds.

2. Commerce

I waitress to buy the time I need to write. One day of waitressing is equal to two days of writing, because I share rent with my girlfriend and quit smoking and mostly eat rice and vegetables.

Waitressing saves money because I walk to work (+£2.50 on bus fare), get my lunch for free (+£5 on food), get as much coffee as I need to stay awake (+£4 on double macchiatos), and get paid in cash (+£200 p/a tax).

Waitressing turns every purchase into a trade-off: is this thing worth the hours of my life I wasted making lattes? A dress (−5 hours), a DVD (−2 hours), going out with my girlfriend for dinner and drinks and a film (−8 hours). I don't buy much because not much is worth those hours of work. Not much is worth wasting my life.

3. The Mathematics of Tips

being aloof ≠ more tips

being slutty ≠ more tips

being friendly ≠ more tips

wearing blue = more tips

rainy days = more tips

Marvin Gaye on the stereo = more tips

more tips = fewer hours spent waitressing = more hours spent writing = a better writer

hypothesis based on transitive relation: wearing blue = a better writer

4. Monologue

A skinny cappuccino doesn't negate the fat in a cheesecake. I can tell she's been crying. Every day he orders a black coffee, adds three sugars, and then doesn't drink it. I hate when people stub out cigarettes in their cups. Chin up, back straight. Keep your tattoos covered. I hope he doesn't try to bring that dog inside. Put this check on make this coffee put through this bill *yes sir what can I get you* refill the salt shakers get fresh butter *I'll be right with you madam* go downstairs for more pudding plates get ice-cream while you're there sorry about that, sir, *I'll get you another* smile smile I know you're tired I know you ache but it's midnight and it's almost over so just—

5. British Weather

Some days I am snowblown and shivering, steaming milk even when there are no new checks on so I can wrap my hands around the jug to un-numb my fingertips. Every new customer heralds me with a faceful of frigid air. The windows don't steam up until lunchtime; it takes all morning for the room to be heated by the bodies. My shoulders ache from being constantly hunched and my toes sting from cold. I worry that I will get fewer tips because people will order less: the jumpers make me bulky and no one wants to order cake from a fat waitress.

Other days I am sunbleached and flapping, sweat in the small of my back. I wear a vest even though it shows all my tattoos and I have to hear the question 'what is that on your wrist?' and I have said 'it's a book' so many times that I can't even smile when I say it anymore. My feet slide in my pumps and when we bring ice up from the machine it melts within minutes. I pass plates with my elbows pressed to my sides in case I smell of sweat; waitresses must always be clean and fresh, to match the food we are serving.

6. Dialogue

Things I want to talk to the other waitresses about:

Sex politics

Sentence structure

Feminism

Whether it's better to work on short stories and build a name or just try to write an amazing novel and hope it gets picked up by a big publisher

Suicide Girls

Vincent Van Gogh

Metaphors

Things the other waitresses want to talk to me about:

Screen-printing

The morality of Catholicism

Teaching methods

How to get an Arts grant to design fabric

Greek islands

Open-source software

Spanish politics

Things we actually end up talking about:

Eyebrow-waxing

Mortgage rates

Nail polish colors

T in the Park

Calories

Floor tiles

Indie bands

7. The Mechanics of Writing

Every story I've ever written began on a check pad. I write each story over three evening shifts, lurking behind the coffee machine, serving up G&Ts and meringues with strawberries. Sometimes my imagination will not rise above my burned fingertips and I write about pissed-off girls with shitty jobs, girls who paste on smiles, girls who never get to make their own mess because they're too busy cleaning up after other people. But if the checks are spaced out enough, I can forget where I am and go somewhere else. I can write about sea monsters and Ancient Roman goddesses and groupies and Japan and fucking behind all-night garages. When I have to lift my pen and measure out two small red wines, three large white wines, a jug of tap water, I'm still halfway across the world or under the sea or two thousand years in the past. Once I'm elsewhere, it's hard to drag myself back.

At the weekend I tape all the check pad sheets together and type them up on my laptop. The taped sheets arch over the kitchen table where I work and when I get up to make tea I tear the tissuey paper with the chair legs. It takes a long time for my imagination to rise up beyond my fingertips again.

8. More Mathematics

The credit card machine is slow to spit out receipts. It dials through the phone line and if someone is on the phone then it won't connect, just stutters out millimeters of receipt paper while I stand there and smile at the customers. Even when it does work it is the slowest credit card machine I have ever used: one minute to dial, one minute to check, one minute to print the confirmation.

I add up the hours I have spent standing awkwardly by a napkin-strewn table, staring down at the tiny green screen.

Three minutes each time + ten times a shift + three shifts a week + two years = 156 hours / 6.5 days / just under a week.

I could write seven short stories in a week. I have lost seven short stories waiting for the credit card machine.

The next time I am staring down at that little green screen, I resolve to write a paragraph in my head.

9. Observations On My Way To Work

#1. Seventeen slices of white bread, spread across the top of a bin in an arc, frost making its surface glitter brighter than my Christmas decorations. I consider bringing them home, taking my third-hand angels off the tree, and bejeweling my home with these glittering shards; then I remember they will soon melt, leaving me with a damp carpet and a tree covered in old bread.

#2. A girl with white shoes and shiny hair hunching in a doorway as her boyfriend screams down at her *why couldn't you just leave it alone?*

#3. My girlfriend's ex-girlfriend buying broccoli at the greengrocer; she has puffy eyes and wears black skinny jeans that are two sizes too small. Her cheeks are so round and pink that she looks like she's holding her breath.

#4. A winter sunrise that staggers me so much that I forget how to walk; I stumble off the pavement, my shoes too big and my brain too small because I can't take it all in. The sky is the color of bluebells, of marigolds, of ice-capped hills, of the insides of fruit, of pigs' tails, of hunger and solitude, of joy burning through me from my scalp to my heels. It makes me ten minutes late for work—my boss docks 50p off my tips and I stare at the check pad for the whole shift without writing a single word.

WHAT THEY DID WITH THE BODY

By Mike Meginnis

✳   ✳   ✳

Once the community had agreed that Mr. Reed would have to die, including Mrs. Reed and the sheriff and all the sheriff's deputies, everything was simple and easy, and the murder came quite naturally. John Taylor was chosen for the job, on account of his relative neutrality concerning Mr. Reed—they did not want this to be a hateful act, unduly painful or otherwise immoderate—and his ownership, legal but generally frowned upon in their town, of a handgun. The gun was a .357 caliber Smith & Wesson Model 60, which some believe to be the most widely-owned handgun in America, though 9mm models have become more popular in recent years.

Because of what Mr. Reed had done, it was easy to point the gun at him, and it was simple to pull the trigger. Mr. Reed was shot three times. Once in the right shoulder, once in his gut, and once in his heart.

The entrance wounds were small, and though they bled profusely this was not a cause for concern, because Don Knight owned a carpet warehouse, and his sons would replace the carpet the next day. Mr. Reed had been watching television when the murder took place. They also disposed of his easy chair, and this was simple, as well.

When Mrs. Reed came home with her children, she told them the stains on the floor and the chair were from ketchup. "You know your father, how he puts ketchup on everything," she said, "and what a messy eater he is." This was, of course, a slander; for all that had been wrong with the living Mr. Reed, he ate neatly, and was scrupulous in using his napkin. His son and daughter were young, and believed what they were told.

When he died, Mr. Reed changed the channel, which he had just begun to do before the door opened and John Taylor shot him three times. Because he was alone before they killed him, no one knew what he had been watching before. In any case he died watching a slug crawl into a conch shell. The music in that moment was soothing—breathy woodwinds and cool, synthetic burbles—which the community agreed was a good thing for Mr. Reed, who in any case shouldn't be blamed for shortcomings that may well have been God's handiwork.

Mr. Reed's body became hard and cruel in death. His toes curled up in his shoes. His prick became stiff, and his guts clenched as if to strangle some live game trapped inside them. His hands squeezed themselves into tight balls of muscle. His right hand broke the television remote. When the children asked where their father was three days later, Mrs. Reed explained that he had disappeared, and that he'd taken the remote with him, which answered their next question.

There was a brief moment where Mr. Reed was still conscious, watching the slug crawl into the conch shell, feeling all the blood fall out. He did not look at John Taylor, possibly out of contempt, possibly because he could not turn his head. "So it's true," he said. "Everyone wanted me dead, and always has for as long as I've been here."

John Taylor had been struck by the same feeling often. He said, "I'm sorry, Hal. There was a vote."

It had been easy to agree that Mr. Reed would have to die, for reasons no one in the town felt bore repeating. The name of their community was Floyd, and Floyd prized discretion, so there was little recounting of Hal Reed's crimes, or those of anyone else. It was better to kill him than to talk of what he'd done. On this point even the minister agreed.

Floyd had also come to quick agreement about how the cover-up would be done. Of course they would not discuss the killing any more than they would what precipitated it, except in closed meetings at the town hall, and they would file a missing persons report, and should anyone come asking after him—which was unlikely—they would only say Hal Reed was gone, and perhaps insinuate something about a long-distance girlfriend in one of the western interior states. One of those Internet sex perverts, no doubt.

The trouble came when it was time to dispose of the body.

Hal Reed was laid out on the desk that served as a podium in the city hall, eyes weighted shut with old pennies, fists still clenched (and the left embedded with shards of the controller's plastic), packed in ice, from which thick vapors rose.

There was a crematorium in a neighboring city, but this would not be sufficiently discreet. (Surely those places made you identify the deceased.) There were several citizens of Floyd who thought it best to boil the flesh away and bury the bones. Doris Crabtree said they should attempt a cremation themselves and scatter the ashes.

Paula Sharp, a farmer, observed that her pigs would eat nearly anything.

Steve Price had been researching dangerous chemicals in which the body could be dissolved, leaving only a fine white powder like baking soda.

Warren Reed, Hal's estranged older brother and a former student of anthropology, had been studying the Voodoo practices of apocryphal African cults. The growth of this interest was somehow connected to the growth of a lump behind his testicles, about which he had told no one. He suggested that they eat the body to absorb its strength, and also out of respect for the deceased.

Fat Steve, twenty-six, had lived alone in his mother's house ever since she died from sudden cardiac arrest. The volunteer firefighters of Floyd had been called after the ambulance came, and they had knocked down three-foot sections of wall with sledgehammers in order to extract her body while the paramedics smoked out back. Fat Steve shouted over the rising discord, "Having deprived this man of his life, we could at least give him a proper burial!"

For the first time in several decades, the neighbors fought with each other loudly, and in public. Owen Peachtree struck Mr. Cobb, who was kind enough to ignore it. Meanwhile flies were settling on Hal Reed's body, and his widow had begun to cry.

Mayor Osborne called the meeting to order by striking the desk where Mr. Reed lay with his coffee cup, which said, "NUMBER ONE MOM." He proposed another vote like that which had started them down this path in the first place. Every method was put to the vote, and each member voted for his or her own method, so that no real majority could form.

"I've got a solution that should work for all of us," said Ross Reed, Hal's son by his first marriage, who was seventeen, paid $75 a month to live in his girlfriend's family's basement, and wore a leather jacket to obscure his growing paunch, even when it was too warm. "Since none of us can agree on what should be done with his body, we should carve him into pieces—one for each. And each can dispose of our share as we please."

The town handyman had foreseen his tools might be needed and brought them from his rusted Ford.

Mr. Reed was divvied up among Floyd. They did their best to keep their portions equal, measuring each helping by his left middle finger, with the exception of indivisible units like the eyes, and heart, which proved too hard for cutting. His brother Warren was given four inches of large intestine. Fat Steve got the penis. Ross Reed took an eye.

The widow Reed was given the heart because it was known to be hers.

Sally, Warren's wife, offered to prepare him a bowl of menudo and cook the intestine inside it, to disguise his brother's flesh. "I'm going to put my toe in the mulch," she said, "so at least a part of Hal can become one again with nature." She did not believe in Voodoo, but in gardening. There were soiled rubber work gloves scattered all over their home, and she liked to pour her homemade ice tea from a watering can with a sunflower painted on the side. Warren didn't mind picking leaves from her hair because she looked sweet in overalls.

Warren said, "The body should be devoured raw. Fire cooks away the spirit. It leaves with the steam." The intestine was sitting on a plate in front of him, which was smeared with some watery blood. He tried to imagine how it would feel in his mouth. Probably, he thought, like biting your own cheek – except that he would need to push through.

And it was going to be cold. He adjusted his bifocals. The world shifted around his eyes.

"You're having second thoughts," said Sally.

"Do you remember when I first brought you home?"

"He couldn't take his eyes off me."

"Later he said I should be grateful you were willing to go with a guy like me."

"Is that why you voted against your brother?"

"Not at all," said Warren. "It was only something I remembered about him just now."

Their daughter came in through the front door and left her muddied shoes on the tile floor of the entry way. She hung her dripping yellow coat on the rack. "It's raining," she said.

Fat Steve cradled Mr. Reed's penis in his hands. He was standing in front of his full length mirror, mentally comparing the severed prick with his own. He had to push his gut up and out of the way to do this, which inflamed his stretch marks. They were like cross-hatching, and made his belly seem full and round and three-dimensional. His torso looked like the breasts he drew on super women, in other words.

When they cut the penis from Mr. Reed's body, it was still hard. Most of the blood poured out after, though, like wine from a skin, and when it was done all that was left was some red-brown tissue with pale, hairy softness wrapped around it. Hal was not circumcised. The skin puckered around the tip of his penis head, pink and faintly purple. Another man had the balls.

Fat Steve's penis was nearly as long as Mr. Reed's, but they hadn't been so careful to cut it at the root. There was more of it, he knew, in Mrs. Koch's share. Fat Steve had been circumcised. Some women like that better, while some do not. They never tell you which in advance, any more than they will really tell you what the biggest one they ever had was.

In a few days he would bury the penis in a shoe box. He would not mark the grave or say a sermon, because they could not risk a gravestone. Anyway, he didn't know any prayers meant strictly for the penis.

It was hard to suppress his erection. There was a girl coming. As far as he could tell it would be a date. He set the penis on his bed, on a paper plate, so it could not ooze onto his blankets. It reminded him of making Play-Doh snakes in preschool, of rubbing the purple clay between his hands until it was long and fragile.

He dressed in brown slacks, a white collared shirt, and an argyle vest. It was his own home; he wore sandals with velcro straps over fun Mario socks. The table was draped with a maroon cloth and piled with various candles. There were Michigan craft beers sweating in an ice bucket. Someone knocked on his door.

He ran to the door because it was raining. "Come in," he said. There were two girls on the other side. His date, Joanna Dillard, and a fat girl named Pamela. Their faces looked molten and waxy with all the water beading on them. They were framed by the heavy black chemical smoke of the latex factory. "Come in."

"Pamela's depressed," said Joanna. "She feels bad for Mr. Reed. I told her she could come along. I hope that's alright."

Pamela nodded. This submerged her walnut-shaped chin, and made her neck divide into several dozen folds, which did not improve her appearance. There was a faint pink ring around her mouth—perhaps misapplied lipstick.

"Sure," said Fat Steve. He wasn't really shocked to discover this was not, had perhaps never been, a date.

"That's a lot of candles," said Pamela.

"I didn't know how to choose. There's all sorts of scents and colors. Banana and strawberry, lavender and vanilla, things like that." Fat Steve pulled a third chair up to the table and cleared a space of several candles so that she could eat. "Do you like beer?" he asked them.

Joanna said she did, though not for the taste. Pamela only sniffed and nodded again.

Fat Steve twisted open three beers and set them on the table. "I made us breakfast for dinner, because that's my favorite dinner. Come into the kitchen and you can serve yourselves."

There were eggs with cheese and sausage in them. There were fat sausages that burped hot air and brown grease when stabbed with a fork. There were buttermilk biscuits and honey and jam. When Pamela came to the hash browns she burped once, immediately swallowed, and flew to the washroom.

Joanna followed Pamela. Fat Steve followed Joanna.

They found Pamela kneeling at the toilet, clutching her arms around herself, shivering. A bloody spit string hung from her lip. The toilet was full of red water, which had also splashed on the tile floor and the outside of the bowl.

Joanna knelt to rub her friend's back. "It's going to be okay," she said. "There, there."

Pamela lunged forward and sprayed blood from her mouth. It hit the seat, which was up, and ran down the back of the toilet. It poured from her mouth and down her chin.

"What's wrong?" asked Joanna. "Are you okay?

Whenever Pamela seemed ready to answer, another stream of gore came rushing out. Gore and other things: granola bar, fruit candy, Cheeto dust, cashew crumbs, carrot chunks, soda pop, Redvines, Nutter Butter sandwich cookies.

The citizens of Floyd disposed of the body in their own ways and in their own time. People did not ask each other what they had done with their shares, though sometimes the information was volunteered, or so public as to be inescapable. Joanna Dillard stomped her quarter of his right lung on the pavement of the outdoor basketball court in front of several other teens, including her sister. She stomped and stomped until the lung was pulped, and then she stomped until it was only a gray stain on the cement. Some felt that this was too far, while others did not. This was the virtue of each person acting on his or her conscience—they could all judge for themselves where the line of decency fell.

Joanna came home to a message from Fat Steve. She thought he should have used her cell phone's voicemail—it would have been more discreet. He said he enjoyed their evening together. He hoped Paula wasn't worrying about what she did in his bathroom. He had cleaned it all up and everything was fine now. He hoped they would be able to get together again some time soon. He wanted to hear all about her university applications.

Joanna poured herself a tall glass of milk. Her parents wouldn't be home from work for several hours, which meant her sister was downstairs with Ross Reed. There was $75 in dog-eared cash on the kitchen counter, left by Ross for her father to discover. She pocketed the money. This was the third time she stole his rent. As far as she could tell, no one really cared, which was typical of her family. Probably her sister was sucking Ross Reed off right now. Or maybe—and this was worse, way worse—Ross was eating Joanna's sister out, working his tongue and lips on her like she was made of cotton candy, which was just about how her pubes looked ever since she gave up shaving (against Joanna's advice).

Joanna wondered when Floyd would meet again. At the meeting where it was decided that Mr. Reed would have to die, he hadn't been invited. He stayed home to watch television. Of course Mr. Reed must have known there was a meeting coming, and no one had asked him not to come. He stayed home anyway. It was possible he didn't know what Floyd would say, or how they would come to vote on his life. She thought it was more likely that he had some idea about all this—his last words to John Taylor seemed to suggest as much—and had concluded there was nothing to say in his defense. Joanna knew what that was like. She had felt, for as long as she could remember, very much the same.

Joanna decided she wanted to tell her sister all about her day. She went downstairs and into the basement without giving any warning beyond the sounds of her bare feet on the wood steps. Ross Reed and Joanna's sister, Diana, were watching television by the time she could see them, which was all they ever did when Joanna was around. Ross was rolling his father's eye around in his hand. The colored ring around its pupil was blue like a beer can. Earlier that day, he had stripped the nerves with his pocket knife, leaving only the glassy sphere, and the grime that accrued on its surface.

Ross balanced his father's eye on the tip of his nose. It quivered, rolled up the bridge of his nose, then slipped back down. He was continuously surprised by the weight of it.

Diana had a fistful of Mr. Reed's nerves. These had been pulled out of his body like the long white worms that threaded through the bloated bellies of starved African boys. Diana couldn't decide what to do with hers until Ross knew what to do with his. In the meantime, she worked it between her fingers, imagining static electricity from the nerves explained the tingle in her skin. They felt like coarse hair.

Ross said, "Joanna."

"Ross," she said.

Ross was trying to think of a way to ask her how it felt to stomp his father's lung into a fine paste. There was no polite way of asking. He rolled the eyeball over his knuckles like he was doing a coin trick.

Diana said, "You should knock before you come down here." And then, "What do you think I should do with my share?"

"You could see if they'll burn."

"That's a good idea. You don't want to leave anything identifiable."

Ross Reed offered his lighter. It had a polished chrome case, into which he had carved the sign for anarchy. Diana spread the nerves out on the coffee table, on a mirror they kept there, which they liked to say was for cocaine, though it was really for fixing her makeup after they smeared it. She flicked the lighter open and held the flame to Mr. Reed's nerves. The flame licked her fingernail several times before the nerves took. They were like kindling, and the fire spread quickly throughout them. There was a sizzling sound, and sparks popped from the nerves, which glowed from their insides.

"Pamela would hate this," said Joanna. "She won't say what she did with hers."

"What did she get?" said Ross, who dropped the eye in his pocket.

"It was his liver," said Joanna. "Not the whole thing, I mean, but a big piece."

"Well she'd better get rid of it," said Diana.

Ross Reed said, "My dad was a fucker. He liked to wrestle. He would get angry or horny or something, or he would say I was making a fool of myself, and then we had to fight about it. When I was a little kid I thought it was funny. His secret weapon was tickling me. All he had to do was tickle me and I would fall over, and then he could work my back over with his elbows. He called that Chinese Massage. Sometimes he would sit on me and fart. He thought he was so funny. I guess I encouraged him. I did laugh."

Diana warmed her hands over the burning nerves. Joanna sat down between them on the couch and pretended not to notice the way her thighs touched theirs, or the warmth that rolled through them. She was conscious of not having shaved anywhere for seven days.

She checked their faces to see if they felt what she did. There was nothing.

"It got more serious as I got older," said Ross. "One time I punched him in the cheek. The next time he gave me a black eye. His knee got put in my stomach.

I dug my nails in his thigh. He pulled my hair. I actually broke one of his ribs after that. He told the doctor we were playing football. I felt awful, even though really it was his fault. My step mom made us stop after that."

"That's fucked up," said Joanna. Her sister was sweeping the ashes off of the mirror and into his garbage pail, which was overloaded with soda cans, strawberry Gogurt tubes, Snickers wrappers, fun-sized M&M pouches, and pieces of broken glass from a lamp he'd thrown the night before against the wall. The broom that stood in the corner still glittered in its bristles with grains from the shatter.

"You should bury that too," said Diana. "Do what you will with the eye, and then bury that memory. Say it into a hole and close the hole up."

"Do you think people like me?" asked Ross. Diana and Joanna pretended not to hear.

They watched television for several hours, saying very little, ignoring the smells their bodies made, until the girls' father was due home, and then they went upstairs to pretend to do their homework. Through their windows they could see the latex factory, and its many various smokestacks, and the heavy black plumes like long apostrophes that it poured into the air, and the smoke shadows on the dead land that surrounded the factory. The pink teddy bear she liked to squeeze between her thighs was sitting on her bed like it was waiting for her. She knocked it to the floor with the back of her hand, and took the other, wholesome bear (the mint green one, which she only held like a baby) to her desk.

There was a folded piece of yellow notebook paper hidden in a seventh-grade social studies book beneath several others on Diana's desk. She excavated the paper and unfolded it, smoothing the creases. There were several names written on the paper in a very small hand. It was a list of people Diana thought should die. She had written Ross' name at the bottom to see how it felt, and then erased it, but the pencil's impression remained.

Beneath that shadow of a name she wrote her own.

The next day Ross Reed took the eye to a concrete bridge that stood over the highway that split Floyd in half. The bridge was covered with graffiti and fliers for basement bands. He waited until a sixteen-wheeler came. He dropped the eye so it hit the windshield, which made the truck swerve. All the way to the gas station he thought about what it would be like to see an eye burst on your windshield. Maybe like the sky was looking back.

At the gas station Ross bought a pack of cigarettes. He flashed a homemade ID so the clerk could say it wasn't his fault if the sheriff took an interest. He spent the rest of the afternoon leaning against the back wall, smoking his pack, and remembering his father for the last time. At 3:30, when school was getting out three blocks away, he went back into the gas station and bought a dozen eggs. He cracked four of the eggs in his hands and let the yolks fall to the tar, where they sizzled and fried. They were yellow like congealed snot or thick sleep in your eyes.

The gas station was on the north side of the latex factory, near the highway. Ross could not see the smoke, but felt it behind him, just over his shoulders like a scrutinizing giant. He could feel the factory workers making condoms, latex gloves, and balloons, stretching the material over metal molds shaped like long dildos and large, featureless hands, which stood out from rotating half-spheres in wild clusters. There were people who said the town smelled wrong. If this was so, or had ever been, he couldn't find the scent anymore.

There were and always had been little white squares of paper on all of the pumps, over the credit card slots, with notes that said they were temporarily out of order, and the customer would have to go inside, with cash.

Some of the other kids came to smoke and talk about themselves. Not Diana, who was, apart from her association with Ross, one of the good kids. She was planning to go to college, probably with her sister, and Ross was supposed to come along and live with them. Of course that would mean leaving Floyd. Now that Hal was dead, this was easy to imagine, and it seemed very simple.

His uncle Warren drove by and waved through his window. His face had a certain kind of glow that Ross thought he recognized.

When he was at the gas station Ross Reed liked to be called Double-R. He pulled wild moustache hairs from his lip and twisted them between his fingers. Everything smelled like gas and rotten egg.

The other teenagers talked about school work they hadn't done, or had done poorly. Hal Reed was not explicitly mentioned, and already Floyd's youths found it easy to discuss other things, sometimes including who they thought should be killed next. There were no explicit criteria, though there must have been some shared understanding about who deserved to live, as conversation quickly coalesced around certain people, though none were specifically named.

Then it was dark. The air went sweet and sticky like it was all laced with soda syrup. Ross bought himself another pack of cigarettes. He couldn't smoke through this one so fast—he was nearly out of cash, and he was thinking of seeing a movie with Diana. He rounded up three other people, some of whom he might have called friends, and they went to egg Fat Steve's house with what was left of his dozen.

While they egged his house, which happened sometimes, Fat Steve dug a hole in his back yard. He laid a shoe box down inside. It was like he was burying his penis. He felt numb and weird between his legs. If this was a seed, he wondered, what kind of plant would it grow?

Ross Reed came home to find Diana was gone, and so were her sister and parents. There was a cold Totino's pizza on the counter, mostly eaten. The post-it note beside it said, "Had to go out. We'll be back before late. Feel free to use the computer."

Ross went up to the second story and into the master bedroom, from which he could see the town hall. Most of the cars were gathered there in the parking lot like bodies in graves, and the windows were lit up yellow like construction paper cut-outs. If there was smoke in the sky—and there must have been—it was impossible to see against the night. He understood why he had not been invited, and was glad not to be there.

A week passed. There was another meeting.

It was easy and simple for Floyd to agree that John Taylor would have to be killed. It was needless to talk about why. John, who had seen the necessity of Mr. Reed's death, but expressed neutrality as a personal matter, was also neutral concerning his own life, and thus allowed to attend the meeting. The most rousing speech was made by Ross Reed, who was himself scheduled to be murdered within the week by Mr. Taylor, though officially he did not know this. Without pointing to the character flaws of him on trial, or his sins, or even his name, Reed alluded to them all, and in so doing summoned such a feeling of loathing and pity in Floyd that none could deny the necessity of what they would do later, while John was asleep.

"What is it to kill another human being," said Ross, "if not to destroy yourself?" He paced the center of the hall. He was not wearing his leather jacket, only his best Iron Maiden T, which rode up on his gut with each wild motion of his arms. "What is it to own the weapon, but to plan the act? How is planning another person's destruction unlike undertaking it yourself?" He turned now to look at his mother. "In short," he spat, "what's the difference?"

He repeated himself: "What's the difference?"

At their next meeting they would talk of Fat Steve, who might come or might not, and would not change or challenge the outcome. Theirs was a reasonable community, and careful, and when something needed doing they did not shy from the task. It was agreed that they would not go too far, that most of them could go on living—but given their perfection of the method with Hal Reed, and the goodness of the outcome, it was certain that they would do with other miscreants and slugs as they had done with him, and that Floyd would be better off for it. The important thing was that they were scrupulous, discerning, and the process democratic.

The widow Reed told her children to come to the table. She poured Dominic a glass of milk and filled Doreen's sippy cup with apple juice. "Kids," she called again, "come on. It's your favorite."

"Just a second, Mom," called Dominic, from the living room.

Mrs. Reed laid out three plates, two sets of silverware, and Doreen's plastic airplane spoon. She put the spaghetti pot next to the children's origami Thanksgiving centerpiece, which was one year old and still resembled a turkey. She stirred the meatballs in, breaking them into bite-sized chunks with the serving spoon.

She checked the night through the open blinds. She flicked them closed. Things were quiet here without Mr. Reed and his son. She felt old tonight, and counted out the years she would have left if she still had half her life, and counted out the years if she had used two thirds. Her fingers were tight and swollen from all the old rings she still wore. They still stank of the liquid wrench she had used to pry those rings off.

It would be three years before she could change her name without it looking suspicious. It would be several more before she could annul the marriage, because legally her husband would never die. It had only been three weeks and the children no longer asked after their father.

Mrs. Reed went into the living room. "Slowpokes," she said, "what's your mischief?"

Doreen stood naked in the center of the room, simple and easy as a candle's flame. Her arms were stiff at her side and her eyes focused on something just beyond the walls of their home. "She's taken off her clothes again," said Dominic. They were scattered all around the room.

"I can see that," said the widow Reed. Dominic was pulling her underpants up her legs.

"Sometimes she can be so ignorant," he said. It was the family euphemism. He meant she was being retarded again. He was not supposed to say it that way—was not supposed to blame her, under any circumstances, for what was God's handiwork.

When Doreen was dressed they would gather at the dinner table. Dominic would feed Doreen with his own silverware while she made the airplane spoon fly. Mrs. Reed would tell them all about her day, and the jokes she heard at work, and Dominic would smile knowingly at her, as if they shared something.

As for Mr. Reed's heart, that was his widow's business.

PLAYING HOUSE

by Sarah Scoles

✳   ✳   ✳

Every night, Sam and I can hear our downstairs neighbors fighting. They fight about whether cooked green beans should crunch or not, whether inadequate pre-washing has led the dishwasher to produce speckled plates after its cleaning cycle or not, whether red wine can ever really go with fish or not, and whether it is possible to track down all the pieces of their relationship and superglue them together again. Or not.

"The problem is that I'm only willing to pay for Elmer's glue, and that just won't cut it this time," says the woman.

"Well, maybe if you'd invested more in the first place, we wouldn't need to buy any glue at all. You never think in the long-term," says the man.

"Is that why I planned out our future for us? You didn't follow the plan, because you want to put your full efforts into 'helping the community' and can't be bothered with good jobs or quality time with me. What does 'community' even mean? What if we had a child?"

"Jesus Christ, how can you talk about having a child when we're like this?"

Every night, the sounds of conflict eventually dampen, in the way that springs bounce less and less and less and less. Some nights, the verbal abuse fades into creaking wood and hospitable grunting. This, oddly, seems less intimate than arguments.

Sam and I lie on our respective sides of the bed reading like respectable couples do before sleeping. She puts her book down and stares at its cover.

"I kissed Kara Novak on Halloween," she says. Her hands are holding the comforter against her mouth. "We were twelve. I didn't even know I knew she was pretty. She was a witch, go figure."

If I stay quiet long enough, she will say more. Given a little silence, she usually decides that her dream-quick thoughts are worth verbalizing.

"I thought that I was so big, you know? I thought that I knew things, almost every thing. I thought, We're almost grown up. And not because we'd kissed. No. We'd kissed in the first place because we were almost grown up. A few more inches, some menstrual cycles. That's all," she says. "Kara's married now."

"I'm sorry," I say.

Some people move easily forward along their timelines, hardly considering what is to the left of them. And some people have timelines that are all collapsed and curled, so that what is to the right squirms up and smashes what's to the left, or what's here now: Sometimes when Sam is twenty-nine she's actually five and wobbling down Beech Avenue on her first two-wheeler, and sometimes she's twelve and dressing up for Halloween and feeling nervous without knowing why, and sometimes she's only twenty-nine again and understanding why but wanting to be just twenty-nine, nothing else. This is something Sam and I have in common.

"It's called Intrusive Recollection Disorder," Sam told me once. "It's a technical term. But it's only clinical if it causes 'persistent and marked distress.'"

"Well, does it?" I asked.

"Who wants to be twelve again, Emily?" she said.

"In my seventh-grade yearbook," she says now, "Kara just wrote Halloween. No signature. Just Halloween, with a little curlicue underneath."

"That's pretty clever for a twelve-year-old."

"I told you," she said. "We were all grown up."

When I was twelve years old, I told Elaine Taylor that I would build her a rocket.

"I'm going to build us a rocket," I said to her when we were wandering around a construction site in Kingsbridge Heights, our incomplete neighborhood. "So we can get away from here."

She was standing at the top of a set of stairs that ended there, at the top. They were thus stairs in the purest form, fulfilling only their goal: to go up. Light from a streetlamp came through the second-story window and hit the right half of her face. It was as if she were the moon, the lamp the sun, and I the earthbound observer, looking up at her first quarter phase.

"Why do we need to get away from here?" she asked. Only I knew.

She hopped down the steps and was soon in the darkness with me. Moments always moved like this when I was around her: one second high and bright, the next shadowy and grounded.

"I mean, why not, right?" I said. "If we were on a rocket, your mom wouldn't be wondering where we were right now. Because we'd be on a rocket."

I fingered the beam next to me, being careful to keep my hand away from the insulation. My mother had warned me about insulation. "It's made of tiny particles that get under your skin," she said. "You'll itch, but they won't come out, so you'll keep itching."

"You're projecting," Elaine said, a verb she'd learned from her mother. "Your mother is wondering where we are right now, even though she doesn't even have a reason to think we left my house."

"Well, maybe I'll just build myself a rocket, then," I said, hurt, as I often was around Elaine, because I took every word she said as either an acceptance or a rejection of my personhood.

"You can't leave me behind," she said. "You can't."

"I could so," I said, because I wouldn't.

Elaine ran back up the stairs and surveyed the undivided house, which was really just a rectangle that happened to be protected from the elements. The space could have become anything.

"This could be our launch pad," she said.

"Definitely," I said, though it would have made a terrible launch pad, given that crashing through the half-roof would have been an inefficient use of fuel. But it was important to me that Elaine think she was right until she forgot what she'd said, so that when I contradicted her, she wouldn't even know. She sat down on the landing and moved her hand toward the pink, exposed wall.

"Don't touch that," I said. "You'll get hurt."

"Let me make my own mistakes," she said, another theft from her mother, but still she pulled her hand back, making the light shift across her finger bones.

Mine didn't stick out enough to make shadows, though sometimes I pulled the skin tight across them to see what I would look like if I were more like Elaine.

"Thanks for letting me sleep over at your house," I said.

She was my best friend—I didn't need to thank her.

"You're welcome," she said. "Let's get back before the bogeyman gets us."

We already said "bogeyman" like it was a joke, not something to worry over our shoulders about. We had some sense of what was true and what was false, as if life were a test we were preparing to pass. False: Life is a test. True: No one in this town was going to build a rocketship, although if Elaine had asked me seriously, in all seriousness I would have said, "I have already bought the parts on eBay with my mom's credit card." The pragmatism of that imagined statement, though, meant that I was already tethered to the sharp edge of the real world.

We were, that night, on the brink. The brink of many things, really: of finding ourselves turning into real people, of finding out that we couldn't just nose around no-trespassing zones, of finding hairs beneath our zippers, of finding that our creative powers were fading. At a certain point, after all, people become incapable of saying, "You be a unicorn, and I'll be a dinosaur, and we'll just spend an hour doing that."

"Watch this," Elaine said, as she jumped from the middle of the staircase. "I'm a bird."

"Now you tell me something," Sam says. "Something about when you were little."

"How little?" I ask. "What age?"

"Well, I just did twelve. So twelve."

"Um," I say. "Hm. Give me a minute."

She does. She puts her hand on my clavicle and her head on my chest, and she mouths all the numbers from one-one-thousand to sixty-one-thousand. Her breath barely breaks across my skin.

"You know what?" I say. "I don't think anything happened to me when I was twelve."

She sits up, pressing her hand down into my collarbone for support. This is what support feels like: pressure, not entirely unpleasant, but capable of breaking bones.

"What do you mean nothing happened?" she says. "It's seventh grade, the worst year of everyone's life in the entire world, and you're telling me nothing happened."

I pull on her earlobe to make her face come down and kiss me, but she dislodges herself and stands up at the edge of the bed, crossing her arms over the Barney the Dinosaur t-shirt I gave her the first year we were together.

"I don't understand why, after all this time, you don't think you can confide in me," she says. "Look, I know you were a nerd, so it's not like whatever you say is going to surprise me and make me say, 'Oh, really, this is my cohabitating partner? I had no idea she was such a loser. I'd better pack my things, but not any stuff she touched, because there'll be cooties.'"

"It's not that," I say.

When I was twelve, I used to think, "When I look back on this time, I won't remember the Law of Cosines, and I won't remember what my History of the Americas textbook looks like, and I won't remember how many minutes were between the class bells. When I look back on this time, I will remember a person, that person." I think the same thing about now and Sam.

I move to pat the bed, to motion for Sam to come back. At the same time that my hand hits the mattress, there is an outburst from upstairs, and the synchronicity causes me to think I've made something terrible happen.

The upstairs woman, punctuating her words with the banging of cupboards, says, "I don't know why I wasted my goddamn time on you. You can't even admit that you were wrong about the grocery bags. You don't even listen to me when I say what I'm saying."

The man: "Maybe I would listen to you if some worthwhile words were coming out of your mouth. But all I hear is a factory of queen bees buzzing around inside your face."

"See," she says, "that doesn't even make any sense. I can't be with someone who can't even make a sensical sentence."

Sam, who has been standing silent next to our bed, gets back in and winds herself around me.

"I'm sorry," she says.

"Me too," I say.

When we leave to get coffee the next morning, all the neighbors' furniture is on the front porch, so dense we can hardly get through.

Please take this memoribilia, says a Sharpied sign.

"I want that bureau," Sam says. "It's quirky."

Elaine was the first seventh grader to become weird. I was, therefore, the second. She began stringing neon beads together and wearing them, 60s-style, across her forehead. She dragged a Wite-Out pen across her backpack, calling up unevenly thirded peace signs and clauses like "circuses are cruel to elephants" and "socialism lives."

I bought *Utopia* and tried to slip its lines into casual conversation.

"Look at Mike Bixon following Carey around," Elaine said. "It's pathetic. He'd do whatever she said, even if it involved knives."

"Reason directs us to keep our minds as free from passion and as cheerful as we can," I replied.

"Yes," Elaine said, still fixated on the chase. "Absolutely."

My mother's trips to the thrift store, formerly embarrassing, now seemed the perfect opportunities to find articles of clothing that would alert people to the fact that I was an individual.

When I wore a Mickey Mouse dress with a layered skirt, Mike Bixon said, "Isn't that a dress for children?"

I said, "It's ironic."

Elaine, always just close enough, shut her locker. "You just don't get subtlety, Mike." She turned to me. She always did, eventually. "You look really individual right now," she said. "I think the ironic child is a grown-up look."

We thought we wanted to be grown-ups, but we actually wanted to be teenagers. Who else would, like I did, Sharpie the word "idealist" onto a pair of cutoff shorts from the blue-tag men's section of the Salvation Army?

"Teenagers," my mother said one weekday when I had already spent an hour on the phone with Elaine. "Didn't you spend all day with her?"

"We're in different math classes," I said. "Elaine," I said into the mouthpiece, "are there any Emilies in your geometry?"

"Emily Smith is there," she said.

"No," I said. "I mean any mes. Any people who are your new Emily."

"Never," she said.

I pulled my German Army-style button-down tight across my planed chest.

"Let's take some of this furniture back inside," I say to Sam. "We wouldn't want someone to steal our potential new possessions."

"Really?" Sam says as if I have never contributed anything so great. "I want this, too." She points to a vintage vinyl chair.

"That's all yours," I say. "This is mine." I point to a creamy, hard-carved end table.

"And this is mine," she says, touching an oak nightstand.

"I claim this one."

We stake our territory. We stake out all new furniture, nicer than any we could get on our own. Neither of us, though, says, "We want this one. This one for us." We are already dividing it, so we won't have to later.

After we lug the furniture inside, it takes over the living room, and each piece waits for one of us to give it a new home.

"It's kind of creepy, isn't it?" Sam says, surveying. "Having the spoils of their war in our place? It seems like bad luck."

"No, it's fine," I say, because I'm not sure it will be. I have learned that a large part of a successful relationship is saying most emphatically that things will be okay when you know least certainly that they will be. I say, "That was upstairs; this is downstairs. Everything will be different. All this means is that we'll sleep better because they won't be slamming any of this stuff around."

I used to put myself to sleep by imagining Elaine passing out. In my night-time daydreams, she became faint and withered toward the floor. I—what a hero—caught her before she spilled her brain-blood all over the speckled tile. She always collapsed in the Earth/Space Science classrooms at Kingsbridge Heights Middle School.

I laid her on a lab table and, always prepared for the catastrophes I made up, pulled an already warmed washcloth from my pocket.

"It's all right," I said, and it was.

"Sh, don't speak," I said and put my finger to her lips.

When she fell asleep, which she always did, she twitched her fingers like Morse Code. This was the only way I could save her.

I did feel bad about mentally harming her just so that I could make everything better, but I assuaged my guilt by remembering that my imagination, like everyone's imagination at age twelve, was beginning to fail.

Imagination fades gradually, so that you don't even notice until one day you can't really picture yourself as someone who is on an extravehicular spacewalk. Then it starts to sputter, and there are some days when you can't go anywhere at all.

Then it stalls out. There's a spark now and then, under the right conditions, but you are reluctant to fuel up, reluctant to give yourself over to even that kind of delusion.

I comforted myself with the knowledge that at least the misfortune I gave Elaine wasn't as vivid as it would have been were I eight or nine. The clamminess of her palms was less clam-like, the transfer of momentum from her falling body to my non-bony hands less mathematically significant, and the sound of my voice less like my own than they would have been had I been so perverse in my younger years.

"And this is the living room," we hear our super say, later that afternoon. "There are 1.5 baths and 1.5 bedrooms. There are seven windows and three sinks."

"Excuse me," says a new woman's voice. "What is a half bedroom?"

"Christ," says Sam, who is sitting on her new vinyl chair. "They're showing that apartment already? People move on so fast."

"Sometimes," I say.

"Christ," says Sam, more quietly. She turns her head to the left, away from me, and bites her lower lip and closes her eyes, as if her thin eyelids can change the fact that she's crying, or that I can see it. She is unsteady when she gets up to walk to our room.

Faint, I think.

"Hey," Elaine said when she called me the next morning, in real life, not the least bit impaired or in need of repair. "You going to school?"

"Am I going to school?" I repeated. "What kind of a question is that?"

"I was just thinking you could tell your mom you were going to school, and then we could go to, I don't know, the launch pad, or something."

"I wouldn't have to tell my mom I was going to school," I said. "She tends to assume I'm following the law. School is the law."

"Is that a yes?" she asked.

"You realize, don't you, that you're putting peer pressure all over me."

"My mom says that that's the most effective way to get anyone to do anything," Elaine said. "I used to think that 'peers' meant 'teenagers,' but that's not true."

"I have a math test," I said, because I didn't.

"Well, maybe I'll just build the rocket myself," Elaine said.

"See you at school," I said, and I would. The empty house, without me, would be boring, and not launch-pad-like in the slightest.

At school, I found Elaine by her locker, 115, where she was talking to Mike Bixon. Mike Bixon had never been so near her before. He was leaning against 114 like he'd taken a class in leaning.

"Hey, Em," Elaine said. "Mike is here."

"Yeah," I said. "Hi, Mike."

"Hello, Emily," he said. Because he didn't straighten up, this felt like an intimate moment.

"What's up?" Elaine asked, like she was asking for our interaction to have a point, which it had never needed before.

I couldn't think of one. "Nothing," I said.

"Mike was just asking me if I wanted to skip," she said.

He nodded as if his verification were necessary.

"I thought we were going to that place," I said. "You know, our place." Elaine shut her locker and spun the dial. "You have a math test," she said. "Remember?"

"Canceled," I said. "It's canceled."

"You guys have a place?" Mike asked.

"Yes," I said. "A clubhouse, kind of."

"Aren't clubhouses for kids?" he asked.

"It's not like that," Elaine said.

Sam doesn't faint. I can't make her. In the bedroom, she's sitting on top of her new nightstand instead of our bed.

"It's so quiet up there," she says, looking at the ceiling. I imagine her gaze piercing through, up all the way to the sky. "We're all alone."

I touch the edge of the nightstand, making my fingertips barely press against her thigh. "They're still with us," I say.

We are both facing the door, both just looking, and we don't say anything for a long time.

"Do you ever miss Kara Novak?" I ask. "Has there ever been another Kara Novak?"

Elaine and I left school and walked to the construction site, which was less than a mile away, the middle school being part of as well as named after our neighborhood. In the daytime, it was harder to pretend that the structure could have become anything. You could already see where it was going, even though it wasn't there yet.

I realized for the first time that just by drawing a boundary, you could create something new. This is this; that is that. I imagined the first people to build a house, and what they told each other. This is safe; that is dangerous. This is warm; that is cold. This is together; that is alone. With a few bare materials, a whole concept was created: inside. Here is inside; there is outside. In this half-formed place, though, the distinctions were blurred.

"I've been thinking about it," Elaine said, "and I think that leaving in a rocketship makes sense." She went to a pile of bricks and began laying them down next to each other, then on top of each other. "This can be the living quarters," she said. "It'll look like home, but it will be better."

As we piled the rest of the bricks into a flyable living room, we kept silent. Speech, its reality, would have contaminated what was happening. Speech would have made us realize that this would never go anywhere. This was heavy. It would have no lift, no matter how many fins we superglued to it. Besides, people would laugh.

But there were no people and no words, and we didn't need to think about the fins or the guidance system or the aerodynamics of the nose cone or whether we would use a liquid or nuclear propulsion system: Logistics were in the future. Right then, we were only concerned with the payload—ourselves—and not how we would move forward or what path we would take.

"Em," Elaine said, "you're bleeding."

I looked everywhere else before I looked between my legs, where a slow stain was spreading. I didn't yet know that my body wasn't something I should be embarrassed about, that it would do what it wanted when it wanted, that it would want what it wanted when it wanted to.

I didn't know any of that. I was only twelve. I was only sitting next to a pile of bricks and asking a girl to leave with me in that pile of bricks and almost believing that I—we—could go to space, and truly believing that when we got there everything would be different, not knowing yet that "space" and "Earth" are not totally distinct, that the atmosphere's particles become less and less and less dense, that the Earth just fades and that there is no line saying "this is space and that is Earth," and not yet knowing that even if I managed to move past any particles that could be considered atmospheric, I would always, no matter how far I moved in time and space, would always feel the Earth's gravitational pull. It might be miniscule, but it would be there, calculable, a reminder.

"This is horrible," I said. "There is nothing more horrible than this." I touched the inside thigh of my jeans and wiped the red evidence onto the concrete floor.

"It matches the bricks," Elaine said. She smiled without opening her mouth, and then she turned her head away. She climbed into our living quarters, which now had walls up to our undeveloped hips, her finger bones flexing out so that there was almost nothing between them and the air. "Come on," she said. "It's time to get out of here."

Inside the rocketship that neither of us would say was not a rocketship, we could see only the sky, each other, and the boundaries keeping us together. She touched my leg, where the seeping blood was at the lowest point. Even though it was only a fingertip, I felt warm, insulated. It seemed like she was saving me from something. Exposure, maybe. Or the whole world, though that seemed dramatic, even to a twelve-year-old.

"You're a woman now," Elaine said.

"No," I said. "I'm not going to leave you behind."

Sam continues to look at the door. I get up and close it, even though there's no one outside to hear us.

"I don't know about Kara Novak," she says. "Everything was different then. I didn't know what was happening, so I couldn't know what wouldn't."

I walk over and lean my hip against the bed. "I want to tell you something about seventh grade," I say.

She gives me just enough silence.

"Do you ever think back on things you've done," I say, "things that you'd never do now, and feel like they're in a dream, like maybe you never really did them in the first place and you just imagined them, but they're so vivid that you know they're real, and they're so strange that you couldn't make them up, and you want to think the person whose eyes you're looking through when you remember them isn't you, or isn't you anymore, but really you know that that person is still there inside you?"

Sam says: "Yes."

"When I was twelve, right after I got my period, when I was sleeping over at Elaine Taylor's house, I put ketchup on a pair of her jeans while she was sleeping, and then I told her she should wear them to school."

Elaine, trusting my opinion, wore them. Mike Bixon was the first to see.

"Ewww," he said. "Elaine can make babies now."

"Everyone pointed at her," I say to Sam. "They said, 'Baby maker, baby maker, baby maker.'"

I grabbed Elaine's hand, and we ran to the Earth/Space Science building's bathroom, and I used scratchy, public-school paper towels to wick her tears away, and she stood in a stall in her underwear while I washed the stain out, which was much easier than it would have been if the stain had actually been blood.

"When there was only a wet spot left," I say to Sam, "I knocked on her stall, and we stood there next to the toilet and blew on her jeans until they dried."

"It will be all right," I said to Elaine. "You're a woman now. We're both women now."

I'm crying a little, and Sam gets up from the nightstand and presses us back into the bed, and we are together there on top of everything, in spite of everything. I close my eyes and pretend our bed is something that can leave, something that can go out the door or through the roof.

"It's all right," Sam says. "It's okay."

NONFICTION

NONFICTION

MIGRATION

By Kelsea Habecker

✳   ✳   ✳

Author's note: For five years I lived in the Arctic, on the northern slope of the globe. I lived a calendar of winter. I went north to be a teacher in a remote and isolated Inupiaq Eskimo village in north- western Alaska, on the shore of the Arctic Ocean.

Migration

When you travel to the Alaskan Arctic—a three-hour flight from Anchorage—you see no imprint of civilization. No lights, no development. You pass over the Arctic Circle at 66 degrees latitude. Of course nothing delineates it except a gradual absence of trees, which can't grow above the Arctic Circle; there's not enough daylight, not enough heat.

To your right—east—is the snow-covered tundra of northern Alaska, and beyond the tun- dra loom the icy peaks of the Brooks Range. To your left—west—is the Arctic Ocean, which is frozen—or should be—for nine months each year, and beyond that is the Russian Far East. On clear days, you can see Russia. That is, when the sky is clear and the ground is free of snow, you can make out the fine line on the horizon that is the edge of Russia's land mass. In winter, when the waves freeze to bridge the two continents, it's all just one endless expanse of ice.

Notice what happens now: You'll lose all perspective. Without any of the familiar points of reference—trees, buildings—your mind suddenly can't even discern how low to the earth you're flying. What's your position? How can you tell?

You lose yourself in the hum of the propellers and the enormous chiseled silence beneath you. All you see are endless undulations and gradations of white.

The atmosphere becomes one continuous loop without boundaries, a circle of space holding you in.

Or setting you free.

Unmoored

The light looks exactly the same in morning as at four o'clock in the afternoon as at midnight. Our superimposed time structure feels very flimsy. And so night is arbitrary and sleep becomes a series of hallucinations. I rest, I wake, the light is the same; I rest and wake some more and it is the same. And then, somehow it is time to get up. Or maybe it is time to go back to sleep. Or maybe I slept through the day and it is night again. Perhaps I haven't slept at all.

Cold That Burns

Some days when she is walking home from school on the coldest, windiest days, she will want to lie down with the chill, with the heaviness of the cold pressed up against her. Snow rises in the current like smoke and she is the only fire. She can't see the road, just a dim light ahead of her she hopes is home. Her goggles fog over. Really, she must sit. On this drift. Crawl inside this curl of sculpted snow. Only the wind exists. Only this cold that burns her up. Only this slowing body, this drowse. She drops to her knees, feels polished ice under them. Sleep is a great drift blowing over her. That window ahead glows. She is a dog, curling tightly in the snow.

Try You

"This is the heart. These are the eggs."

Claudia, a wizened elder, sat at the tiny turquoise table in the preschool classroom in the village school, a resplendent silver salmon spread out on the table in front of her, pointing out to my students important parts in the fish. A half dozen dark heads hovered over as my four-year-old students leaned in for a closer look. She showed them how to remove the glimmering scales, how to slice the flesh with the curved blade of her *ulu*. Using a portable griddle, she showed them how to cook the fish, and then we all ate it dipped in seal oil, a thick, slightly sweet oil rendered from the blubber of seals. Earlier in the fall, when the weather was still good, another elder took us to the beach to show us how the line nets were used to catch fish.

I invited elders to come into my classroom to teach traditional customs and skills. Some of my students got these lessons at home, but some didn't. Either way, it was a selfish move: I wanted to learn these things myself.

Tillie came to teach us how to make dancing gloves. Shaped like mittens, these gloves have tiny bells sewn along the top edge, as if at the tip of each finger. When they're worn for dancing traditional Inupiaq dances, the bells tinkle—a sound that is believed to welcome the animal spirits to return for the dance. We made our gloves out of felt and rickrack rather than fur. I wrote each student's name in magic marker on the back of each pair of gloves and passed them out when other elders came in to teach us dancing.

For each dancing practice, I'd stack up most of the chairs and tables in one corner of the room and push the slide and play equipment back into another corner. One row of chairs was lined up against the back wall for the several elder men to sit on as they drummed for us. The large, flat drum bellies were taut with the skin of bearded seals. In between the songs they beat out, the men took breaks to splash water onto the drum bellies to keep them soft. They beat on them with rigid strips of baleen.

The girls and I bobbed in place and lilted our arms slowly back and forth, as if we were gently swirling water, in the women's style of dancing, while the boys stomped their feet, leaning slightly forward with their torsos as if they were about to push a heavy object. Sometimes when I didn't have the motions right, an elder would instruct me, guide my limbs through the move. "Try you," she'd say, and watch to make sure I had it right. We all chanted monotonously and gutturally. *"A ya ya. A ya ya."* Later, we'd perform our dance together at the school's Christmas program. I loved moving in unison with my students and the village elders, held by an ancient rhythm, singing in a language I didn't understand.

How To Be Buried Alive

One afternoon in December it will begin to snow. And it will keep snowing. You'll walk out your door and you'll greet a thick curtain of snow—snow thick as batter, snow whipped up all around you into stiff peaks like meringue but tall as trees. The snow is relentless, falls and won't be stopped. It gives up against anything it can. The days go blind with its billions of tiny gestures that fall like an erasure of anything but drift. The air thickens with it, draws in like a net.

You'll walk around in a bubble of white. Everything else is muffled. No sound beyond the soft, padding swish of each step, and sometimes you'll think that what you're actually hearing is the shifting, loosening motions of joints and muscles from within your own body, which has also filled with snow.

Held

When we're all in the gym dancing, it's like a fur pouch—like I'm held in the belly of something. The men hold their damp drums over their laps, taut hoops of skin they beat with the strip of baleen. The steady, rhythmic beat is a pulse beneath the guttural, throttling sound of their singing. The women are bending their knees, head upright, arms outstretched, surfing this pulse. Men pound their feet into the floor, thrusting their arms out or down, fighting back, pushing against. Someone calls like walrus, someone else invokes a harpoon.

And it's as if the golden gym floor were the ice. As if the banners hanging from the ceiling to celebrate victorious basketball seasons were hides to celebrate victorious hunts. As if we didn't arrive to this village by plane but on foot, across the sea that used to be land. As if ten thousand years ago was yesterday. As if drugs and drink never arrived. As if time never warped or snagged or hung slack.

I don't have the movements right. Someone comes along beside me, shows me how to sway.

As They Fell

He hunched over a guitar. She hunched over a notebook. He pounded drums. She pounded verbs. He poured it into a song. She ladled stew into bowls, sometimes salmon, sometimes halibut or char. They put together puzzles on the living room floor. They put together their bodies on the living room floor, candles piled on the window sills. She made quilts. He made strides. He made mistakes. She made excuses. They watched the snow fall. He made cookies. She chiseled a poem. They had dinner guests, who lined up their boots in the hall. There were many conversations. You should have seen the pile of tea bags in the sink. You should have seen the mess. You should have seen the drifts of snow that built up on their windows before he'd head out with a broom. You should have seen the kids from the school, standing on drifts to peer into their windows. You should have seen them, jumping off the roof into the drifts. You should have heard their screams as they fell.

THREE CARDBOARD GODS

By Josh Wilker

✶   ✶   ✶

Author's Note: I started writing about my childhood baseball cards a little over a decade ago out of desperation. I didn't have a job, and my money was running out, and the novel I purported to be working on was dying of pretentiousness and exhaustion. Writing about baseball cards didn't solve any of those problems. But there was some life in it, at least. Over the years it has grown into a practice of sorts, or maybe it's a hobby, like building ships in bottles, who knows, but either way it seems to help keep me from completely unraveling. The cards, those faulty unpredictable conduits to a long-gone childhood and a rangy colorful world that's otherwise inaccessible to me in my everyday life, remain a mystery to me. They make me think of Fuckhead's words near the end of "Emergency," Denis Johnson's story about aimlessness and visions in the 1970s: *That world! These days it's been erased and they've rolled it up like a scroll and put it away somewhere. Yes, I can touch it with my fingers. But where is it?*

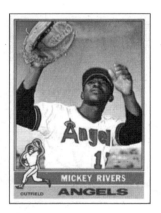

Mickey Rivers, 1976

By the time I came into possession of this 1976 card of Mickey Rivers bracing for the impact of a falling piano, he had been traded to the Yankees along with Ed Figueroa in exchange for Bobby Bonds. I guess you could say that the falling piano was the fate of continuing to toil with the Angels. Mickey Rivers darted away and let Bobby Bonds take the hit. Rivers lasted three and a half seasons with the Yankees, and in each of his three full seasons the Yankees played in the World Series, winning it in 1977 and 1978. Rivers got plenty of credit for that run, in part because of a lack of understanding in the baseball world at that time that the most important element in scoring runs is getting on base. Rivers was considered the dynamic catalyst of the Yankees' offensive attack because he generally produced a high batting average and stole bases. However, despite batting at the top of one of the better lineups in the league, Rivers never topped 100 runs scored for a season for the Yankees (and in two of his three seasons he didn't even get close), an outgrowth of his inability or perhaps unwillingness to draw walks. The sportswriters of the day didn't notice this deficiency, voting him third in league MVP balloting in 1976, eleventh in 1977, and (most incredibly of all, considering his .265 batting average and .302 on-base percentage that year, numbers that were inferior that season to those of, for example, Duane Kuiper, Bob Bailor, and Mario Guerrero) twenty-fifth in 1978.

The other night ESPN Classic replayed the game that got Rivers and the Yankees to the first of the three straight World Series: the fifth game of the 1976 American League championship series with the Royals. Before the famed riot-sparking home run by Chris Chambliss in the bottom of the ninth, Rivers keyed an early rally by slapping a base hit into centerfield. I'd forgotten how unusual Rivers looked and moved.

"What's wrong with him?" my wife asked.

We were watching him strut-limp back to first after rounding the bag. He seemed like he'd been assembled in a rush from spare parts, long bow legs springing from a tiny torso, a weird jaunty lean to his body, as if he was suffering from a running cramp. His mouth was motoring.

"He was a character," was all I could say to my wife by way of explanation.

While my ill will toward the Yankees hasn't abated since I was a kid (with the possible exception of the benign Steve Balboni years), I do find that time, along with that always questionable eroder of clarity, nostalgia, has allowed me to become less specifically resentful of some of the Yankee players on the 1970s teams. I loathed Mickey Rivers, for example, mainly for the possibly apocryphal parts he played in two terrible Red Sox moments (somewhere, somehow, I got the idea that A: he teamed up with Graig Nettles to separate Bill Lee's shoulder during a 1976 brawl, and B: in a late October game two years later, the 163rd contest for the two teams playing, he produced and passed along a bat of dubiously powerful qualities to one weak-hitting Yankees shortstop just after said shortstop had broken his own bat and just before he popped an improbable home run over the Green Monster). Now, however, I can't help but get a chuckle out of Mickey Rivers. My ten-year-old self would glare at me as a traitor for saying this, but the 1970s would have been a little poorer without a guy willing to comment on the physical appearance of another major leaguer (Danny Napoleon) by saying, "He's so ugly, when you walked by him, your pants wrinkled. He made fly balls curve foul."

Don DeMola, 1975

In 1970, at the age of seventeen, Don DeMola won the *Carl Yastrzemski Award*, given to the best high school baseball player in Suffolk County, Long Island. The Yankees drafted him and shipped him to their Rookie League farm club in Johnson City, Tennessee, the first of three minor league stops in two years before the Yankees released him in April of 1972. This 1975 card doesn't offer any reasons for this decision, which is illustrated by the use in the 1972 line in DeMola's career major and minor league record by the always mysterious stat-less listing: Not In Organized Ball.

It took exactly nine months beyond the reach of numbers, like some kind of second embryonic passage, before Don was signed in January 1973 by the Montreal Expos. Back among the organized, Don sped up through the Expos system and within a couple years reached the big leagues and made it onto a baseball card, this 1975 offering, his first and second-to-last cardboard incarnation, which references Don's rare skill: "Don's best pitch is a fastball which 'smokes.'" His minor and major league strikeout totals, which in most years hovered near the elite one-strikeout-per-inning mark, also attest to the wonders inside the seemingly normal arm he holds out toward the viewer on the front of the card. His small smile and the reaching arm ending in a loose fist make Don DeMola seem like a friendly, generous guy, someone who wants to share a handful of M&Ms with you.

Others among the upper echelon of smoke-throwers do not generally give off such an approachable aura, but Don DeMola seemed like somebody who wouldn't mind if you just called him up one day to chat. This approachability, if it ever was fiction and not fact, has become a reality in the present, at least in terms of Don DeMola's online presence. On Don DeMola's website, you can contact Don, who proudly identifies himself as a Montreal Expos pitcher, to receive baseball skills instruction. Also, if you live in Suffolk County, you can have Don come over to your house to install an entertainment system. And that's not all. When arm trouble curtailed Don's career as a flamethrowing major leaguer, Don went into the fur business, and this facet of his life is also represented on his website in the form of an offer by Don to get you up to speed on the most effective strategies in the fur-buying and fur-care game. Finally, Don offers tips on how to get rich and live your dream life. "I'd like to share a few secrets with you," Don says. "Simple truths that have helped many people create a life of wealth, freedom and abundance."

Dick McAuliffe, 1974

Here's the featured player on the only glove in my childhood home with a signature embedded in it. It belonged to my brother. I always found this signature and the glove itself a little mysterious, because at almost exactly the same time I started coming awake to baseball, Dick McAuliffe was disappearing. It gave my brother's glove a somehow disquieting connection to the distant past. Dick McAuliffe was not completely unknown to me but was instead a weird, unsettling flickering in my consciousness. I had this 1974 card of Dick McAuliffe and no others, but the card and my other few cards from 1974 (the year of my first shallow foray into buying packs of cards) always seemed out of place with the rest of my cards, in part because there were so few of them in my collection and in part because most of the players shown on them still seemed to be rooted in an earlier, more cleancut era than the one that exploded through the more colorful cards that Topps featured for the remainder of the decade. I'm attracted to the classy understatement of the 1974 cards now, but when I was a kid I think I was a little creeped out by them, as if they were akin to one of those shadowy, toyless rooms at your grandparents' house that no one really hangs around in anymore. If you ever ended up alone in one of those rooms you'd linger for a little while just to kind of scare yourself a bit, standing there on a self-made dare and looking at the dusty antique lamp and the leather-bound books and the black and white photos of your uncles as crewcutted little Rockwellian boys with melancholy eyes, but then before long you'd go sprinting back downstairs to where everyone was sitting around eating cheese and crackers and intermittently monitoring a football game that no one really cared about. This is the primary function of sports, isn't it? To serve as comforting background chatter when you race in from dark quiet rooms with your heart pounding? Anyway, the 1974 cards were like those dark quiet rooms to me, sort of, or at least some of them were, like this Dick McAuliffe card. Who was Dick McAuliffe and what was he doing on my favorite team and on my brother's glove? And where did he go? And why had I never heard about him anywhere despite the long run of good seasons listed on the back of his card?

We're all just passing through.

All images © The Topps Company, Inc.

BARRACUDA APE

STRANGE BUT TRUE

COW with 2 FACES

'PASTURE' WILDEST DREAM!

MEAH
S. Kulick

23 foot PYTHON

LEASED TO
Spring Star
ENTERPRISES INC
NEWARK DEL.

TROPIC
TERROR

RUSHVILLE, IN, 1994

WEST BERLIN, 1978

TWO HEADED CALF-INDIANA STATE FAIR, 1984

FLYING BOBS-INDIANA STATE FAIR, 1984

ELEPHANT SNACKS-INDIANA STATE FAIR, 1984

TENTS-INDIANA STATE FAIR, 1984

SIDE SHOW–INDIANA STATE FAIR, 1984

SIDE SHOW BANNERS 2-INDIANA STATE FAIR, 1984

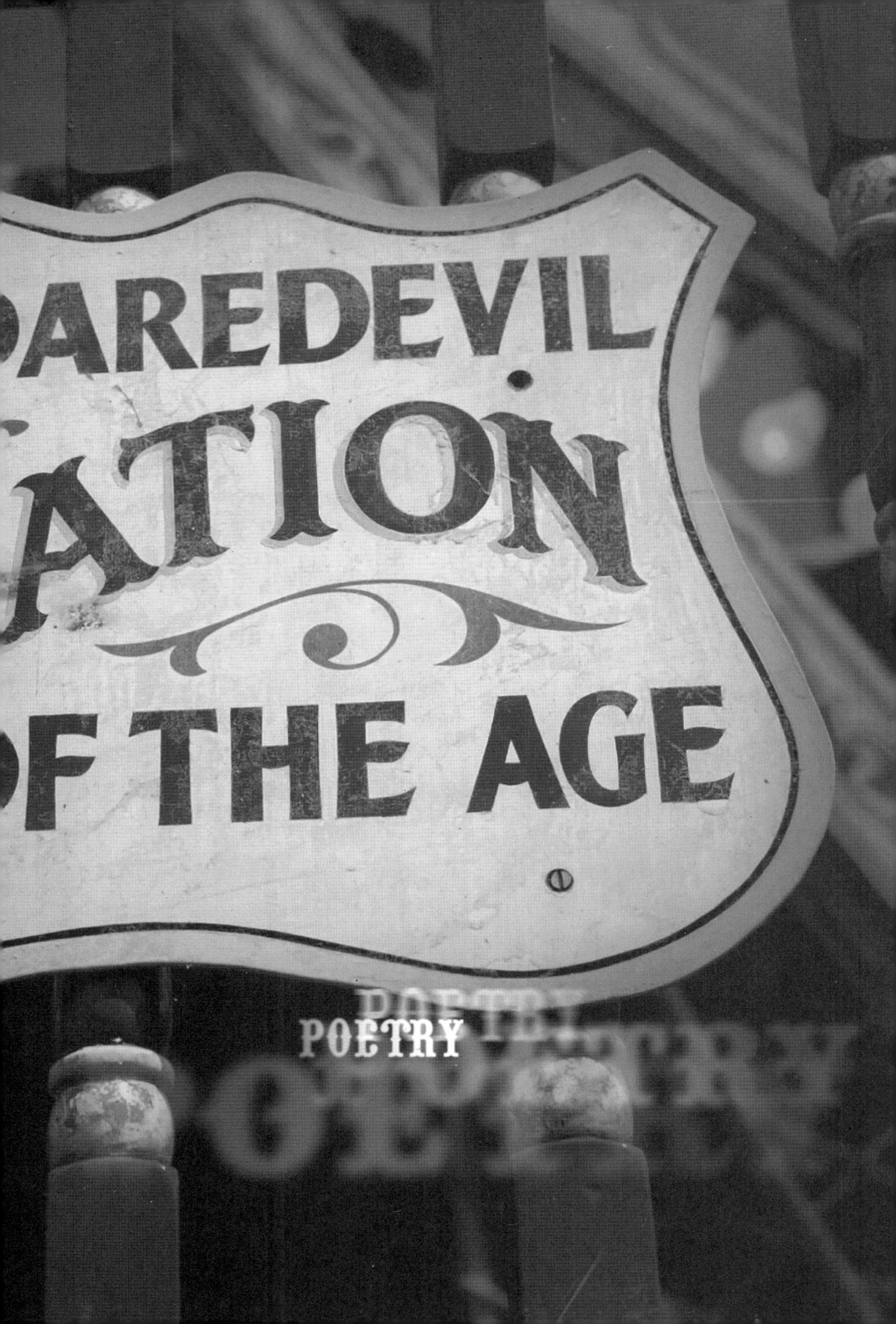

POETRY

SAM AND LULU AT THE VERY END OF THE WORLD

By Aubrey Ryan

They talk in lowered voices about ash. Lulu says it falls
like lashes on her face; she comes in from the yard all streaked

with grey. Sam jokes: snowday. Every morning he trips
from their bed and peeks out the curtain and fakes a gasp: O Lu-

lu-lu—I'll bet you a snowday. At the end of the world, every bet
is a good one. Lulu's hair in the morning is a lazy, blow-dried

tiger. She used to run her hair down Sam's belly, and his cock
would bob and bob. She'd lay down her body. She'd lay

between his legs, and he'd take her hair in his fist and spread it
all across his chest and neck and mouth. He thought it was a crop

of something gathered from the ground, and something threshed.
At the end of the world, the sky is a pot of dishwater. The sun

is so tired. Sam dares Lulu to blow the sun out—just the breeze
from her whistle would do it. He nuzzles her neck and says: you

could whistle down the sun, O Baby Lu. They go out for a Sunday
Morning Walk. In the dark, the ash looks blue-jean blue; they wade

up to their thighs. Sam lists Lulu's face to her: one little freckled
nose. One curly eyebrow hair, twanging in the wind. Two cheeks

with gold beneath. He says: your eyes are blue-jean
blue. She says: O Sam. If I had fire, I'd light myself up.

FURROW AND PLOW

By Aubrey Ryan

She likes that he watches her in class, then follows her
home down the farm road and all the way
outside of town. He acts like he's got the bit in his mouth
and she likes that too. She surprises herself
by screaming as he pushes her down, surprises herself
and stops. Birds settle back on their posts;
he lifts her skirt by the side of the road. There is gravel
between her back and the ground, and later
she will find tiny bruises like seeds where rock fixed to skin
and she didn't feel it, was thinking of changing
into jeans, of her mother in the fields and how the plow
cuts through dirt. On her way home
it's dark. The neighbor woman on her porch
watches under the light, moths in a reckless halo
above her head. She sees the girl's legs, bare against
black fields, shakes her head no, no
and makes a chirp with her tongue. She wants to tell the girl
to comb her hair and stand up straight.
It's so much nicer to look pretty—stop walking
like something's pinning you down, plowing you under.

STABLE

By Mark Petrie

That summer night in Fort Collins,
you looked like an 18 wheeler
on an Oklahoma interstate, big
and shaky as hell.

You spun across the porch
in your blue jeans and boots
like a ballerina

with cinderblock feet,
kicking rocking chairs
and ousting moths,

sending all the insects
running for cover,
and in one dangerous motion,

you pumped up the volume
on the little black speakers,
opened the mini-fridge,
and beered yourself.

I asked how you'd vote,
asked what star that one was
and to tell the jail story again,

and then when the sky became maroon,
asked if you preferred horses or dogs
and you chose horses,

which came as a surprise.
I hadn't known you yet,
as the galloping sunset type.

But then you said, rising
from your lawn chair,
But you ride stallions;
I, a mare,

as if I fed you fish heads in the basement,
as if we'd never even tried the fox trot,
as if I hadn't bought the beer
slipping from your hand.

ORGASM

By David LaBounty

my nine year old
asked me what
an orgasm is

and I was
absent for
the answer

I was typing
words on the
screen while
he was watching
another

so he asked me again

he asked me,
dad, what's an orgasm?

and I found
shelter in
my absence
and said,
I didn't know

and he said,
yes you do, you know everything

I shrugged my
shoulders and
left my absence
but only
for a moment
the way one
leaves the
umbrella
to barely
touch the rain

I turned my
eyes to the
ceiling
and said,

an orgasm
is the
tool that
god uses
to keep
creation
moving,
kind of
like the
way the
earth opens
just enough
to swallow
the seed
dropped
by the tree

my son looked
at me and said,

dad, I don't think
that's what it is

MY FIRST LOVE
ASKS ME TO STOP WRITING ABOUT HIM

By Elizabeth Wade

Your daughter sounds out Seuss, knows all the words

of *Hop on Pop*. I learned in Montessori

that words had ancestors. They flocked like birds

on paper wings, their nests the baggies we

secured in pockets, used for daily drills.

My favorite patriarch was "it," begetter

of targets hit with schoolboy's spit. I filled

my tongue with offspring—glitter, kitttens—letters

that opened worlds. In time I met the clan's

black sheep, from zit to misfit. (I met you,

and mother called me smitten.) Love, I understand

wanting to shield your child, but who

succeeds? She'll find the others soon enough—

from clitoris to bitch and bullshit—outcasts,

eccentric aunts and uncles, banished, loved,

just out of sight, but lurking close, held fast.

GOLDFINCHES

By Tasha Cotter

The Goldfinches never asked for the seed bag I tied to the tree. They come and go now, resembling very large, ecstatic bumblebees. I wonder if they recognize the way they escape each other. Do they arrive only to discover the song of the other left hanging in the air? Does life get disrupted by ghost? They remind me of some elementary hands being raised, each holding its breath, an answer for everything. These birds sense the mystery of a gone friend, but they can find each other after the initial loss. Maybe they can even do this against a very great wind.

THE MAILMAN

By Dana Kroos

I am in love

  with the mailman.

   I know that it is a

   cliché, but

    I can't help it.

    I love his sense

     of routine and commitment,

     his tracks in the snow,

      the rubber band with which

      he binds

       my bills and catalogues

       together.

              He is not

               obstructed by phone calls,

               appointments, traffic, road

               construction or Big Wheels

               scattered across his path;

               does not feel obliged to make

               small talk; and when the dog

               barks furiously he maintains

               a Zen silence.

It is true,

  I have never seen him, but

    I imagine that he has large

      hands and delicate fingers for

        slipping all of those letters into

          boxes. I fantasize that one day

            he will save me from all of this

              chaos. I would like to put

                myself in a stack with the

                  outgoing mail so that he can

                    pick me up.

CLEVELAND, OHIO, 1964

By Tara Mae Mulroy

The automobile plants

ensure the snow

falls like ash,

clumps like thick spiderwebs

in the drainage gulleys,

in the eyes of the manhole covers.

The town is aging;

most of the young women leave

in search of men

without gnarled thumbs,

blackened fingers,

a mild deafness sure

to grow worse.

Each year,

another graduated class:

clean-collared boys

needing jobs

sign up at the plant.

Soon, they all walk

home together in the evenings,

silted to their bones.

My mother and her four sisters,

pale blue-eyed, blond-haired women,

too fresh to have shocks

of gray at their temples,

look as delicate and lovely

as crocuses emerging from snow.

INTERVIEWS

THE PHILOSOPHY OF SPACE

An Interview with Jonathan Lethem

The work of Jonathan Lethem could fill a bookshelf. His novels include Fortress of Solitude, Motherless Brooklyn *and, most recently,* Chronic City. *Lethem has also penned two collections of nonfiction, three collections of short stories, and the graphic novel* Omega the Unknown. *In 2005 Lethem was awarded the MacArthur Fellowship, and in 2011 he will begin his tenure as the Roy E. Disney Professor of Creative Writing at Pomona College. Lethem recently spoke at Butler University as part of the Vivian S. Delbrook Visiting Writers series, after which he sat down to speak with Booth's Alex Mattingly.*

Alex Mattingly: *When you were starting out, looking for places to publish, did you have an idea of what kind of writer you wanted to be?*

Jonathan Lethem: I did, but that idea changed constantly based on something new I'd learn about myself from writing, or something new I'd glimpse about the world of publishing. So yes, I had what I felt was a strong idea, but it was a very mercurial one at the same time. What I really had was a strong impulse to assume the role of the writer in some way, and I was waiting for the world to say yes to that.

When my first novel was published, it was a bit of a Rorschach test. Some people thought it was a postmodern pastiche, some people thought it was an out-and-out dystopian novel, and some people were sure it was a crime novel because it introduced a detective and because there were clues in the book and a solution at the end. They were sure I was going to write about that detective over and over again. So I got in this business of gratifying and also disappointing expectations very early on.

It was great fun to try on these different roles. For me, it was exciting to keep messing with expectations. I like being slippery and problematic.

AM: Amnesia Moon, *your second novel, which was sort of a strange collection of dystopian fantasies, was very different from* Gun, With Occasional Music. *I read somewhere that it actually began from several short stories you'd written.*

JL: It was partly a salvage operation. I had these failed short stories that began to relate themselves in my mind. They all exhibited these same impulses—I felt compelled to destroy the world again and again. I started to wonder, what am I trying to accomplish here? Why do I want to imagine everything in ruins? And I thought that maybe these unfulfilled apocalyptic stories could themselves be put in relation to one another, where the question that was interesting to me was, why do I keep doing this?

It was about characters who are dreaming the world into destruction, and why they feel they have to do that. It's a very homely construction, and I wonder sometimes how it would strike me if I reread it. Some of my earliest published writing ended up engulfed in that book—there's stuff written by an eighteen year old in there. The fact that it's still in print and sitting among my other books is almost an act of impersonation. It's like a kid in a Halloween costume. On stilts.

AM: *You've described* Chronic City *as a dystopian novel as well.*

JL: It's the kind of book I was trying to write when I wrote *Amnesia Moon*, but which I didn't have any of the equipment to do. It's the kind of book I once thought I would always be writing, consisting of characters enmeshed in reality meltdowns and paranoid decon-structions of everyday life. I loved that so much when I first encountered writers doing it, I valorized it so totally that my dream was to be that kind of writer exclusively. Of course, I turned out to have all sorts of other agendas that snuck up on me, but in Chronic City it's like I got back to the primary job, my initial assignment.

AM: *Do you see any of that with the book you're working on now? You've described it as being set against the collapse of the ideals of Communism, and it seems that the characters must be dealing with their own private dystopias.*

JL: It's there but in a totally different kind of way in my thinking about the real life political nightmare of the American Left in the twentieth century, which is a kind of paranoid dystopia that was enacted. Half the communist cells in America consisted of three real communists and two FBI agents leading the charge. Half the communist activity that was detectable in America, at a certain point, was probably created by FBI agents. It is its own insane game of masquerade and paranoia, but also with this unbelievably powerful core of human learning and despair of wanting to transform the world and having that spirit crushed so utterly in so many ways.

It's not so different, but it's sourced in personal memory for me and in factual research into the era, the fifties and sixties. But in a certain way, helplessly, it's the same kind of project again.

AM: *Can you talk about your approach for a collaborative piece like* Omega the Unknown, *or the book with Carter Schultz,* Kafka Americana?

JL: With both those projects, the conditions of their creation were so specific . . . with Carter, we had been thinking and talking about this joke that became much more than a joke, that there was something about Franz Kafka and Frank Capra, apart from their names, that was in dialogue and needed to be unearthed. So we drew this idea out of the air between us, and if we were going to do it justice it would have to be a piece of genuine collaborative writing. Of course, it also had a reflexivity in it, because it was a collaboration about the idea of collaboration between two sensibilities. We were two writers with different strengths and different leanings, writing about two artists with different strengths and different leanings. The hope was that maybe we could be the antidote to the other's weaknesses rather than cancelling out each other's strengths. But I just can't imagine those exact circumstances coming about around any other thing.

Omega the Unknown was collaborative too, but in some ways much more awkward and in slow motion. It was actually an involuntary collaboration, imposed on the other creator, Steve Gerber. It also came at a time when I was thinking a lot about intertextuality and multiple-authored works and how, while the art form I'd chosen didn't have a particularly strong tradition of collaboration, there were other art forms like pop music or Hollywood film or the superhero comic book that were fundamentally collaborative. So I was excited about that. I wanted to see if I could enter into this position, be the writer of a comic book who could never claim for a minute that everything on the page was my responsibility or origination, and instead celebrate this weird, bastard form.

AM: *Did you approach Marvel with an interest in the character, or did they approach you?*
JL: They invited me to do something with some character of theirs. I think they were expecting me to pick Spider-Man or somebody famous, the idea being that anyone given the keys to the castle of their intellectual property would want to choose one of these mighty pieces of property. But instead it was like I came in and ignored all the treasure and instead noticed this ashtray that someone's twelve-year-old made in school and said, "I want that!" One of the guys I talked to in the initial meeting didn't even remember the character.

AM: *Were you into this character as a kid?*
JL: I loved him as a kid, and I'd always fantasized about what the story might have become if he'd been popular enough to be continued. There's a certain beauty in ruins, and *Omega the Unknown* was a ruined story. It only existed for ten issues, and even those had been compromised—the first writer, Gerber, had been taken off the book for a couple of issues. So it was a fragment, and I began to imagine what the fragment would look like if it were completed.

AM: *Gerber was pretty unusual for his time—he created* Howard the Duck, *for instance.*
JL: He was a very strange writer, and very much ahead of his time for comic books. He was doing stuff that anticipated the graphic novel boom, things like *Watchmen* or *The Dark Knight Returns*, these literary retellings of superhero myths. He was doing that before anyone had any idea that there was an audience for that, or could even understand what he was up to. He was twenty years ahead of his time, at least.

AM: *With* Omega the Unknown, *were there issues on the shelf while you were still writing it, or did you have it pretty well scripted out in advance?*

JL: I wanted to understand what I was doing and get command of it before I let the first issue get out. What I did was a ten-issue sequence, and in fact there were issues published before I'd written the last issue, but I'd gotten a grip on the thing. I wasn't working as much by the seat of my pants as a "real" comic-book writer would have been. I was working so much slower, it was humiliating when I think about it. Those guys were writing seven of those comic books a month in their heyday, and I was taking three or four months over each issue. Marvel must have thought they had the most astonishing prima donna on their hands.

AM: *Did you work from an outline with something like that?*

JL: I never like to work from outlines. Sometimes I resort to it, in certain situations, most often when someone needs evidence of the fact I know what I'm doing, and then I'll some-times grudgingly scrape out a few pages of plans. But in this case, I did it from my own sense of security. I didn't do heavy outlining, but very scant indications, just so I could trust that I was going somewhere.

AM: *With a book like* Motherless Brooklyn *or* Gun, With Occasional Music, *where the mystery element is so strong and there have to be clues along the way, would you use an outline in that case, or do you feel your way along more intuitively?*

JL: I was very audacious about working without plans. With the two crime stories, I had to have a solution in mind, and feel my way towards this revelation. There's one part of your brain that's working backwards when you try to write a crime story with any kind of traditional resolution, and each of those does have a version of that. They're trick resolutions, but that's actually traditional in most cases. So I had to consciously plot backwards from a solution, but I didn't do that with a lot of notecards or charts or diagrams. As it happened I did it all in my head.

AM: *Who are you reading now?*

JL: There's a core group of names that I've dropped so often it would probably be humiliating to me if you Googled and revealed it, but they're my constellation of formative influences, so I do think about them all the time, helplessly. They help organize the way I think about storytelling, and even more than storytelling they've laid down track in my brain for how I think about experience, consciousness. Kafka, Orwell, Philip K. Dick, Shirley Jackson, and so on. And then I expanded and started piling other kinds of influence on top of that.

And some of those layers are very formative too, such as when I discovered Italo Calvino, or Don DeLillo in my early twenties. Anything subsequent to that can be wildly exciting, but I'm not eligible to be reprogrammed. No influence will ever compare quite to some of those.

But in recent years I've been consciously in the thrall of Iris Murdoch, Christina Stead, Philip Roth, James Salter, J. G. Ballard, all at different times and sometimes in different combinations. Those are the writers that are prominent enough in my mind I would never be surprised if someone pointed them out. And then there are others that I'm conscious of, but wouldn't be obvious to other people. Some of them are very foundational writers—I was reading a lot of Henry James in the years up to the writing of *Chronic City,* and I don't think anyone would call it Jamesian. But I was absorbing a lot of his version of social arrangements in fiction, and I can see imprinting itself on the results of the book I was writing. Similarly, Charles Dickens is in *Fortress of Solitude*, but there'd be no reason for anyone to remark on it. Partly because Dickens is such a fundamental influence on fiction per se that to be influenced by him is just to say you're a novelist. Whether you read Dickens or not, he's part of what you do. He's part of the basic language.

AM: *What's your actual process like? When you sit down at the computer or the writing desk, what happens next?*

JL: Well, the answer's pretty much in the question—I sit down at the computer, I sit down at the writing desk. The only rule I keep is to work every day, because I strongly believe in the power of remaining subconsciously immersed in the work. The same thing that makes writers problematic spouses, that they're always a little bit thinking about their project, is to me impossible not to desire. I want to always be half-writing as I fall asleep and as I wake up. Because then I work better—I stay attached to the work. I'm not a very fast writer, but I'm committed to the idea of putting together a shelf of books. I've always believed that the writers I've loved most, it's not that they were prolific or speed-demons, but they kept at it and rewarded their readers' curiosity with a lot to read and explore. I'd always be very frustrated when I found a writer I loved and then found out they'd only written one other book. I've always wanted to be able to delve and consume, and so I want to be able to offer that.

The way to write a lot, if you're not fast, is to write every day, to be the tortoise and not the hare. I've tried to do that faithfully, to trudge every day through some paragraphs. For me, a good day is a page and a half of fiction. Once in a while I'll get on a tear and leave three or four pages behind, but I don't rely on that by any means. I'm happy if I get my page or two.

AM: *Do you work on multiple projects at once? Like, if you're working on a novel, will you also have short stories going?*

JL: It ends up being that way, but you're not really writing more than one thing at a time, you're just switching back and forth. And it's costly. When you're doing that switching, energy is lost, so I try not to. I'm often backed into it by promises I've made to myself or someone else, or life plans changing slightly. Books get interrupted in favor of this or that short thing, but the best of all is to do one thing until it's done.

AM: *At what point do you decide something is ready to show someone else?*

JL: There's one type of showing that I often do when something is not ready. At some point medium-early in a project I need to throw a lifeline out from my own anxieties, so I get someone to read it to say "You're onto something, now get back to work." So there's one type of reading that has to do with a book not being ready, but with me needing a pat on the back. But after that, I don't really like to show unfinished work. I like to get it to where I think it's going to knock people out of their shoes, and then deliver it, make it a fait accompli.

AM: *How do you develop that internal set of tools to see problems in your own work?*

JL: It's a corner you turn, and it happens usually in the course of workshopping or writer's group or some even less formal version of finding devoted early readers that you begin to see through a potential reader's eyes, and you can be honest with yourself about how much of your original intention was achieved on the page. It's never instantaneous—there are lots of scenes I've written where I was sure I carried it off brilliantly the first time through, and that feeling persists as a kind of obscuring of what's really on the page. And then the time comes when I read it and I see, oh, seventy-five percent of my intention is there. Then I grumble and go back to make it right.

AM: *Do you revise daily?*

JL: I do end up reworking stuff every time I write, as well as writing new stuff every time I write. Nowadays that's mostly how I work. So in a sense, where once upon a time I'd have written a fast first draft and then a full second draft, I now have a slower pace through the first time, but it might be described as a kind of first and second draft combined. Then comes the setting-aside, and reconsideration, and a genuine, full revision. But the computer has changed the way everyone writes.

I'm a living bridge to this other time. I wrote my first three novels on typewriters. So a second draft was a draft—you rolled a fresh sheet of paper into the machine, and made new contact with every word. Every word and every decision had to pass again through your fingers to make it into the second draft. Well, that's a very strong learning tool. Sometimes I will ask my writing students to print out a draft and delete the file. Put the draft on your desk and open a new document and make your draft a draft. Rewrite the whole thing. Look at the page and ask, does this sentence deserve to go from this pile of paper back onto my computer? And I'm sure that anyone who's ever followed my advice has had great breakthroughs, but probably no one ever does.

AM: *Would you recommend the same thing with short stories?*

JL: Sure. If you're afraid of doing it for a novel, do it for a short story. You'll learn from totally tearing it down and building from the ground up.

AM: *I'm kind of reeling a little now, because it makes me wonder what might be lost by computers. It must completely change the way fiction is made.*

JL: I think it changes a lot. I don't mean that the best books or the most realized writing is in some essential way different than it would have been without computers. The end result is probably fairly similar. But the way people are getting where they're going has fundamentally changed because of the fact that your text is committed in this endlessly mutable, watery medium, where you can fidget around with it all the time. With typewriters, if you typed a paragraph with a ribbon and ink, then it was typed. You had a few really clumsy options. You could use white out, you could go XXX for a few sentences, or you could pull out a pen and write words above the typewritten font. It was like you were carving in a physical substance.

I revised one of my books with scissors and glue. I would cut paragraphs out of the paper, and sometimes sentences. I would have these ribbons of words I would be pasting onto the page in different places. But now we carve in air. We carve in ether. It makes some things much easier, but it makes other things invisible. There are things that are never confronted or encountered because you're not handling them in a more material way. You can wave your hand and just make them fly through the air.

AM: *When you're writing, do you start with characters in mind?*

JL: I usually have simultaneous and wedded inklings of characters and problems, a situation or milieu. The characters don't just exist the way a costume designer draws a character on the page, in white space. Usually to be interested in the character you're already connecting them to some situation or dynamic involving other characters.

AM: *Fortress of Solitude* *starts in third person and then goes into first person. The reader gets a different feel for the character that way. Was that the point?*

JL: For better or worse it was always the plan—it was how I saw the book from the outset. The first half would be omniscient and multi-vocal. You'd get to meet a lot of different characters through third person subjective, and you would only know the primary character in those terms and see him in his world. And then there would be this harshness of the experiences of having his world fall away, and you and he would be stranded together in adulthood. I wanted to create something structural in the book that was analogous to the giant gulf created between childhood and adulthood, which was one of my subjects in the book. So the shift was a way to create a distressing pothole in the middle that you had to jump over in order to continue with Dylan as a character.

And he's distressing to meet in first person. He's mean and small-hearted.

AM: *Was that difficult to write?*

JL: That whole book was exhilarating to write, because I was working over my head the whole time. The plan seemed audacious to me, but I felt at the time that I was ready to make this incredible thing come to life, and that I was doing it, even as I wrote the most painful material … whatever else it was, it was also exhilarating. The overwhelming feeling was of empowering myself to give names to things that didn't have names and to put my imprimatur on all this chaos of experience and longing and shame and confusion that had been out of control until I took command of it.

AM: *When you say "give names to things," you're not talking just socially, but also personally?*

JL: All of the above. The whole footing of that project was to be as overt and extensive in naming the unnamable, talking about the shameful or the unspoken stuff of that life that I was a part of in Brooklyn. I wanted it to be a book about embarrassment, and I wanted it to be embarrassing to read. I wanted it to feel, by the end, that something extensively secret had been extensively unveiled.

AM: *What made you, in a book like that, decide to bring in the element of the ring?*

JL: There was never any question. The structure of your question suggests that there was this ground of realism, and that I brought in this other thing, this disrupting, surprising element, but to me they arrived together. It was always one idea. The lens of the super heroic powers, as ludicrous and second-hand as they might seem to be—that was the focusing element that made the entire thing come to life.

I suppose looking at it in retrospect I would otherwise have been in the realm of nonfiction. I think people underrate that, when they read the book. They don't realize how much the uncanny element in the book is intensifying their experience of what they see as realism, that it's actually all one thing. Because otherwise it's very anecdotal, very sociological, very centrifugal material—it's not emboldened into metaphor. It's not fiction without the magic.

AM: *Chronic City has that feel as well. There are people leading these seemingly normal lives that keep being interrupted by the bizarre. Is it fair to say these two books were dealing with the same idea of the unnamable?*

JL: I think it's a very different ration and distribution of the same kind of fundamental urge I have to reveal the presence of the uncanny in everyday experience. It's difficult to persuade anyone that it's safe to talk about, so mostly we don't, but we're still saddled with it.

AM: *Do you think that's something kids are more equipped to deal with?*

JL: I don't think anyone's equipped to deal with it, but kids may be more apt to seek its expression. Part of adult life, at least in non-mystical cultures, is stemming the impulse to express the presence of the dream-life, the irrational.

AM: *This is sort of a half-baked thought, but—*

JL: That's okay, we're in a half-baked area here.

AM: *(laughs) Do you think there's something culturally telling about the popularity of superhero movies and graphic novels?*

JL: Sure, and it doesn't limit itself to superheroes. The world is right now overrun with zombies and vampires. And in another place it's overrun with angels. This stuff can be packaged and sold in extremely banal ways. But it wouldn't have any hold on the subconscious imagination if it wasn't anchored in the anxious apprehension that life has more to it than meets the eye, that consciousness is stranger than prosaic reality. The problem of being and the problem of consciousness overruns its container, which is everyday experience.

AM: *Is that something fiction is especially equipped to deal with?*

JL: I'm tempted to give you the exact same reply—nothing is equipped to deal with it (laughs). I sound very pontifical and authoritative because I'm trying to answer your questions scrupulously, but I'm not doing anything more than gesturing in the direction of my own peculiar inklings. I don't have access to a secret understanding of anything. I'm just framing questions in storytelling that are exciting to try to get on the page. My friend John Kessel wants his tombstone to read, "He didn't know, but he had an inkling." And it's good enough to have an inkling.

AM: *Is that part of the impulse to write for you, to make gestures toward this unknown thing?*

JL: One of the great banal and true clichés about what storytelling does, besides enmesh us in vicarious experience and delight, is also to assuage our existential loneliness. So of course this gesture of making someone else feel as strange as I feel, even for an instant, can be immensely consoling to believe I've managed. And sometimes it's very obvious and simple things that go unnamed, and after they're named you can say, "Why didn't anyone point to that before?" Other things you gesture toward, give a momentary name, and people feel the relief flood in, but an instant later it's unnamed again. But that doesn't mean the exchange didn't occur. Those things are just more elusive.

I'm very proud when I give something a permanent and simple name, even if it's just in this microscopic area of experience. *Motherless Brooklyn* kind of does that, I think, in that way that we all kind of feel Tourettic. I'm the guy who got to give that its name. That's easy, afterwards, to quantify and remark upon.

My friend Maureen is a philosopher, and she says that she learned at some point that there is an infinity of philosophical space, and the great philosophers have gone into that infinity, that void, and filled in some little area of understanding. And then someone else will go into another quadrant and fill in another little area. Once you arrive, if you're not at the very birth of philosophy, you can point to two spots and pick a zone between them, maybe fill that in yourself. That's all I'm ever hoping to do. That description seems perfectly lovely to me.

Some of the stuff that I'm prone to try to name is distinguished by its unnamability. That's what I'm getting at in *Chronic City*—the power of permanent inexplicability, in our experiences of our social lives, in our political selves, in our assuming of roles in everyday life. There is a permanent gap between what we're asked to do, the script we're handed, and the actor secretly behind the script. That's why it's about an actor who doesn't even know he's been handed a script, because I'm trying to name this unnameable space between our essential, disturbed yearning and the social enactment of adequate personhood (laughs). Sorry, now we're way out in philosophical space.

AM: *I know you need to catch a plane, but do you mind if I ask you one last question?*
JL: No, if you get us out of this bleak vacuum we're in here . . .

AM: *What excites you about the future of writing and publishing?*
JL: I don't have any overview. I'm just coping like everyone else. Authors are habitually asked this now, whether it's going to be okay or if the Kindle is going to kill us, but I was thinking about the way new mediums change and how when the dust settles they always wind up funkier and more fallible than they might seem when they're first approaching. Film was going to kill radio and theater, but they changed and adapted and made room for film. And then television was going to kill film, but now they're all here.

One of the things that's going to change is book culture, and by that I mean the culture that connects physically with books, which is going to be reinscribed and damaged by the arrival of electronic reading. Because I think the book has a very deep, resonant place in human culture. Rooms full of books, physical objects made of certain kinds of substance—this resonance is going to be magnified now because of a certain kind of threat. The meaning of the object is heightened, and as a great lover of that object and its traditions, I think that's kind of cool.

THE VAN HALEN BROWN SOUND

An Interview with George Saunders

✳   ✳   ✳

George Saunders is a fiction writer and essayist whose work has appeared in The New Yorker, *McSweeney's, Harper's, and GQ, earning him the National Magazine Award for fiction in 1994, 1996, 2000, and 2004. He is also responsible for several acclaimed short story collections, including* CivilWarLand in Bad Decline, *a finalist for the 1996 PEN/Hemingway Award, and* In Persuasion Nation, *a finalist for The Story Prize in 2007. On his way to becoming a professor at Syracuse University, Saunders worked as a technical writer and geophysical engineer, a member of an oil exploration crew in Sumatra, and a knuckle-puller in a Texas slaughterhouse.*

In February 2011, Saunders was a writer-in-residence at Butler University. Chris Speckman, a contributing editor for Booth, sat down with Saunders to discuss biking on the Erie Canal, the Van Halen brown sound, and Ben Franklin playing Nintendo Wii.

Chris Speckman: *You've held down a variety of occupations other than author and teacher. How much have these "outsider" experiences influenced your writing?*

George Saunders: Early on in life, it allowed me to see to a lot of places I wouldn't have been able to get into. My first job was on an oil crew in Indonesia. There were all sorts of scandalous things going on. If I went back there as a journalist, they would have tidied it up. It gave me access to specialized experiences.

CS: *Did these experiences push you toward writing?*

GS: Kind of, because I was so inept at it. I felt pain at the thought of a life of engineering. I worried I would be bad at my job for the rest of my life.

The other thing that it taught me was that in engineering, if you do the problem nine times and it's wrong, it's still wrong, and you don't get any credit for having tried it. When I switched to writing, there was a lot of that idea. I did twenty drafts already. It still sucks. Therefore, you're not done. There's not a sense of shame or entitlement. You do as many drafts as you need. That really was helpful, transplanting that idea of scientific rigor to literary rigor.

CS: *Do you think aspiring novelists stand to benefit from getting a taste of the world outside of creative writing and academia?*

GS: There are exceptions to every rule, but I've noticed that if two people come in equally talented, and one has been out in the world for three years and the other has come from undergrad, the first one has better luck. The one who just came from undergrad will often feel like, "I know my chops are as good. Why are my stories not being received as well?" She hasn't found anything to subjugate her chops to.

You never know, though. We're reading applications (from the Syracuse Creative Writing MFA program) now. There hasn't been one application of the five hundred that didn't have some talent. What you see is that there are some people who are lacking urgency—they're undergrads. My baseline advice is to go out and do something for three or four years, and when you can't stand it any more, then you come back.

CS: *When did you first take an interest in fiction and consider a career as a writer?*

GS: It happened about twelve years apart. My interest in fiction came early and was full-bodied. When I was in third grade, a nun gave me *Johnny Tremain* by Esther Forbes, and I just loved it. She was a real stylist. You could tell that it was sweated over, and there was a lot of her on each page. I had a real visceral reaction of pleasure to that, but I didn't know what to do with it. It didn't occur to me I would want to be a writer. I just enjoyed the book.

And then many, many years later, after engineering school, when I was working in Sumatra, I was reading Kerouac or something, and I got the impulse. Somebody did this. I'm not stupid, and I'm having some pretty cool experiences, does it make sense that I could maybe do it? For whatever complicated reasons, it didn't occur to me to do it until much, much later in the game.

CS: *I read that before the stories in* CivilWarLand in Bad Decline *were published, you were content writing on the side without worrying about the ultimate fate of your work. What compelled you to keep at writing even when you didn't have much to show for it?*

GS: It felt like it was the only way out. My wife and I had two kids at that point. I was thirtyish and working a job. I could see that it wasn't the worst life, but I could also see that it was going to get pretty tedious. It was a little bit like the bliss of exhaustion. I'd been through the MFA program, the rollercoaster of praise and complaint, and I got out and had nothing to show for it. Another two or three years passed and I couldn't get anything that I wrote to make sense, even to me. It's like a relationship where you try and try and try and it doesn't work. At some point, you just go, "Fuck it." And in that energy of saying, "Fuck it," your true inclinations are then free to play a little bit. At that point, I thought, "Obviously, I'm not a child prodigy." It's almost like I tried so hard to do what I thought would get me success. Well, that didn't work. Alright, why not just do what you like? If you fail, then you're in the same place that you were in before.

I remember I was actually riding my bike to work at the time along the Erie Canal, and it was such a pleasurable thing to just go "Nobody knows I'm writing. Nobody's waiting for anything. I'm just riding my bike, and today I hope to do a paragraph." It was sweet. It was really, really fun.

CS: *Did you ever entertain the idea of giving up writing and moving on to something entirely different?*

GS: Not really. But there was a time when I got so hungry for power, any kind of power. At work, I didn't have it. And I was a musician, so I thought, "Maybe I'm barking up the wrong tree." So I played a couple of open mic nights, and then I thought, "Maybe I'm a comedian instead." There was definitely a feeling of this is not paying off. But I knew from having been a musician and having done stand-up that at the end of the day it was kind of writing or nothing. That was the thing I felt the most articulate about and that I had the strongest opinions on. That is actually something that I teach to my students: trust strong opinions. If you have a strong opinion about something, that's good—that's like a light on top of your helmet. The scary places in writing are when you don't have an opinion. Is it getting better or worse? I can't tell. That's hell.

CS: *How do you come up with the unusual subjects and settings that have become a hallmark of your fiction?*

GS: For me, I learned early to keep the playing field as small as possible. I try not to do a lot of thinking beforehand about theme or any of that stuff. Just give me one paragraph that's got a little bit of energy, for whatever reason. Hopefully, you don't really know why. It just has a little bit of jangly energy. If I have an idea that was spontaneous like that, immediately some conceptual part of me says, "Oh, that's good. What does it mean? Why does it matter?" To me, that was a death sentence. Whenever I would think that, the story would always go off into a ditch, the ditch of being too predictable, the ditch of being preachy. So what I learned to do is just say, "OK, look. If you can write one paragraph that doesn't suck and that has a little bit of ambient energy, and then just refine it—poke around at it, make it a little better—eventually it will sprout a little tendril, usually a very natural one: curiosity." Why did he say that? How does she respond to that? Where are they? Then you just very cautiously go, "Let's find out," and you do the next thing. In a perfect world, it's like a seed crystal—it just grows outwards. And you might not know what it means, but it's grown spontaneously. Like a relationship. When you meet this person, you don't know where it's going, but if you follow the natural energy, you look up and three years later, you've got a kid. If you didn't falsify the energy, then that kid makes sense. It's that kind of process. I never think, "I need a bizarre idea." It's just, "Does this core idea interest me?" OK, then start. Trust that your process will force some meaning out of it.

CS: *So you don't consider the mind of George Saunders to be a dark, twisted place?*

GS: I don't think my mind is particularly dark, but it might be. If I say to you, "Imagine a terrible thing that could happen right now," you could do it. Everybody has the capability of negative imagination. That isn't so hard. So why do my stories seem to be darker than most? Is it because I have a dark inclination in my imagination? Maybe. Is it because when I have that impulse, I don't block it? Could be that. But the thing I've concluded is what Flannery O'Connor said, that a writer can choose what he writes about, but he can't choose what he makes live. I've noticed that if I go dark, there's energy.

It's like if you were a musician and all the songs you played in a minor key were really good. Does that mean you're sad? No, I don't think so. It's a mystery to me. And I'm struggling with it. I don't mind being dark, but I don't want to be habitually knee-jerk dark.

CS: *During your reading last night you mentioned that you want to bring more light to your work. How do you plan to do this?*

GS: Light is a funny term. I don't necessarily mean happiness. But I like the idea of writing that has a broad stance so that any phenomenon could be voiced in that style.

For example, one time I was walking through Rockefeller Center in New York, just minding my own business. And there's a really high-end chocolate shop in there. I looked over at it, and I saw a beautiful Christmas window display. And my heart kind of rose like when you're a kid and it's Christmas vacation. And I thought, "Wow, that's interesting. I wonder if I could write that." I thought I could do justice to that moment, but my inclination would then be that an icicle would have to come down and kill the guy (who is looking at the display). I thought that was interesting. Dickens could write that scene and let it stand. Why is it that moment isn't quite at home in my fiction? I don't know the answer to that. When I say more light, I'm asking if my prose style is big enough to accommodate actual phenomenon. Why would I have to have a shrunken vision of the world? It doesn't mean that the stories will get less weird. I'm just trying to push the walls of the room out a bit.

CS: *Many of your stories, most notably* The Brief and Frightening Reign of Phil, *might be considered fables or parables. Do you have a message in mind when you start writing something like* Reign of Phil?

GS: When you start to tell a story, there's the apparent topic of the story. I used to live on the south side of Chicago and that's a rough part of town. And you go, "OK, this is a story about how rough the town is." If it's only about that, I think at the end you feel a little let down. We both understand that's a gateway to something hopefully deeper that happens.

Like with *Reign of Phil*, I think anybody reading that will go, "Well, it's a fable about world politics." And when I started it, I thought, "I'm going to do a riff on genocide." But every message that's in there is pretty obvious: be kind, don't kill people. So it's almost like using that as an excuse to do what I think is the real work of the book, which is to be funny, to make weird images, to make good sentences.

I think often people who ask me about my work are asking about the surface politics of it, which is there. But for me, ninety-nine percent of the energy is the stuff that's going on to the side.

CS: *I want to talk a little bit about your book of essays,* The Braindead Megaphone. *In the title essay, you say the Iraq War was a "literary failure" because of the way it was recorded and covered by the media. If the contemporary news cycle is failing us, who do you think people should turn to for information and guidance?*

GS: I'm always a little bit queasy about questions that are so big because I don't really know. In that essay, the idea is that when a person turns to another person for counsel or comfort or information, if that other person has not much of an agenda besides truth and has had sufficient time to put together whatever he is putting together, then the information that comes from that person is more heartfelt and truthful.

Our set-up is that you get information from someone with a big-ass agenda who is doing shit really quickly to advance his own program. So it's rickety. If that's the only place we have to look to, it makes us stupid. But if you turn to Tolstoy, you're getting a bigger sounding board. For me, I turn to novelists, good essayists, playwrights.

CS: *Do you think more writers and intellectuals should step up and voice their opinions on important issues?*

GS: I do think so, but I can't really defend thinking that because it is what it is. But I did feel after 9/11 you saw the number of random assholes who were happy to step up to a big microphone and not only make pronunciations, but lead troops. I thought, "Why is it that the smartest and most compassionate people I know—my poet and fiction writer friends—why is it that we are so reticent to do that?"

But now I'm not sure if that was the right thing. I put myself into a different role for a while. I was writing essays more and political satires and going on TV and stuff. And, in retrospect, I don't think that's a good fit for me, but who knows? The people I know who are the brightest and the most well-informed and the most curious are not the people that you see on TV. Those people are marginalized, whether self-marginalized or marginalized by the culture. That's dysfunctional. If you had a family and the smartest, most articulate, curious, compassionate people were kept in the basement, and moronic Uncle Craig spoke for everyone, you would think, "This house isn't running very well."

CS: *What drew you to writing essays? What did you get out of trying something different for a while?*

GS: It's lifeblood. You have to. I can say now that I don't want to do that. But at the time, that's what I was really feeling. Part of the thing is that no one has infinite talent—well, maybe Shakespeare did or Tolstoy. Most of us have a little wedge of cheese for talent, and it's the work of a lifetime to try to keep working without being repetitive. For me, one of the risks is knowing what I do so well that I just keep doing it. You have to push yourself out, and when you push yourself out, you're going to blunder off the reservation sometimes. And that's fine. You have to.

I saw Vonnegut one time. Someone asked him which book is his favorite. And he said, "You know, for me it's like you were skiing on a hill by yourself all day, and at dusk you look up and you go, 'That's where I was at 10 o'clock this morning. And that's me at 3.' You were just exerting your energy in the way that felt appropriate at that time." And I love that. It shows in his work—that sort of freedom and experimentation. And it's a form of ego puncturing because instead of saying, "I must write the perfect novel," you're saying, "Fuck it. I'm going to write something that's interesting and fun right now. In a year, it might be stupid. So what?"

CS: *In the essay you wrote about Vonnegut, you talk about truly successful stories being the ones that change the reader and not necessarily any of the characters. How do you go about having this kind of effect on your readers?*

GS: It's a funny kind of paradox because, when I had that realization, it actually freed me up from those kind of concerns. I'll try to explain. It seems to me like if you say, "I'm entering into a sacred compact with you, reader, that I promise not to condescend to you, I'm going to treat you like you're as intelligent and attentive as I am," then you're taking yourself out of a manipulative relationship with your reader, and you're brothers. You're walking into this thing together. That means, if you can surprise and satisfy yourself in the process, you can know that your brother is feeling the same thing because you're joined at the shoulder. You don't have to worry about anything other than your own reaction to your own piece as you're rereading it, trusting that if you can keep yourself interested, you can keep your reader interested. If you do it the other way around and think that your reader is stupid and that you need to jerk him around, he's going to feel that. And also, you'll find that you're not smart enough to stay ahead of your reader that far. You're going to be telegraphing things all over the place.

If you're too sure of what you're doing, the reader is way ahead of you. But you can use it the other way, too. I call it the "motorcycle-sidecar theory." If the writer is doing his job right, he's driving the motorcycle, and the reader is right there. When I go left, you feel me going left. If you're writing a bad story, that sidecar is like six miles away, and there's no connection between the two.

CS: *In the same essay, you mention that "humor is what happens when we're told the truth quicker and more directly than we're used to it." And in other interviews, I've heard you talk about the value of improvising as you write. Do you see any parallels between your writing and any of the popular TV comedies that take advantage of improvisation, like "Curb Your Enthusiasm" or "The Office"?*

GS: You see a great show like "Arrested Development" or "30 Rock", and you think "Wow." In the same way that photography changed painting, I think this changes fiction. Suddenly, you go, "You're not going to get much funnier than 'The Office'." So when you're writing fiction, you have to say, "OK, what do we have time and space to do that they can't?" It's definitely informed my work to see those shows and how funny they are.

CS: *Do you consider yourself to be a funny guy? How do you approach writing humor?*

GS: It works best when I'm not thinking of it as funny. For me, the nature of humor in fiction is often just taking something old and making it seem new. Let's say a guy goes into a mall. When you go to write that scene, you have an incredible weight on you, which is the nine million times people in movies and other stories have been in malls. So even though walking into the mall is a totally fresh phenomenon for us if we go there now, you have the burden of what has been done before. Therefore, if you need him in the mall, then you've got to make it new in some way. For me, one of the ways is to actually look at the energy of that and say "What's been excluded from fiction in the past?"

Here's a corny example. I heard a comedian do a joke once about how when two people are in an elevator and somebody farts, everyone knows who did it. That's a funny moment: being on the elevator with a little gas. We've all been there. But I don't see it in a lot of fiction. So that's an inherently funny moment, not because it's a joke, but because it's so true. Some of my stories have these internal monologues. If you could look at your thoughts in a given moment, they're hilarious. And I don't think it's just me. The humor I like is more organic, where it comes out of the situation and you're not forcing the joke. If someone said to me, "Write something funny," I would be like, "Oh, don't say that." If someone said, "Have great sex with me," you'd be like, "Wait, don't say that. I will, but don't say that."

CS: *Many of your stories take place in the future, exploring dystopian possibilities. Do you expect the future to look anything like the way it is depicted in some of your stories?*

GS: No. I put them in what looks like the future just to give myself a few more degrees of freedom. Just based on having lived fifty years, I guarantee no one can predict the future. I always think of them as being what-if scenarios. What if there was a Civil War theme park? What would it look like? It's not at all saying there will be or there should be or there can't be.

I think that's the mysterious thing: why is that interesting to people? If once upon a time there were two star-crossed lovers in fair Verona, why do we give a shit? Were there or weren't there? But somehow when someone makes up a story, it does have interest to us, even if the basis of the story is totally not viable. Like in *The Metamorphosis*, when Gregor Samsa wakes up to find that he's been transformed into a giant bug, what's interesting is that nobody ever stops after the first sentence and goes "bullshit." They go, "Oh, really?"

CS: *So you don't see something like commercialism as a threat to society in the future?*

GS: I'm kind of worried about it the way that you probably are. Yeah, it could suck. But, on the other hand, there's a great story that I've told a million times. Tolstoy was walking around with this writer Maxim Gorky, and they saw these young Cossacks coming. Tolstoy goes on a rant about how obnoxious these guys are and how disgusting their military instinct is. And as soon as the guys pass, he goes, "On the other hand, those guys are so manly and so strong." I think that's basically the attitude I aspire to, to say, "Yes, our culture is so over-commercial-ized and degrading and materialistic, and it reduces the individual. That is true. Also, have you seen my iPhone? It is so cool."

I think anybody has those impulses. You take any issue. Let's say abortion. I want you to passionately explain to me why it's absolutely essential to keep that right. You could do it. And you could probably supply examples from your life. Now, go to the other side of the table and give me a passionate reason why it's an outrage. If you allow yourself, you can do that, too. I think in a funny way the novelist or the fiction writer has this really cool job, which is to nurture that ability in himself to see things multiple ways. Normally, your role in life is to choose one side and get behind it. In our job, we get to say "on the other hand" constantly.

So for me, with the future, it's like, probably things will be fucked up, but they will also probably be beautiful. It's just like right now. You imagine if Ben Franklin came here: "Oh, you've made a mess of everything." "But Ben, have you ever played Wii?" And he would freak out. He would love it.

CS: *I really appreciate your newest story, "Escape from Spiderhead" (published in The New Yorker in December 2010), for the way it distills people down to their most primal urges—sort of a literary version of the game "Marry, Fuck, Kill." It seems as if most of your characters are in*

151

tune with their most basic impulses. Did this notion serve as the inspiration for "Spiderhead"? Is this something you hold true?

GS: That's the way the story turned out. I don't know if that's the way I feel. I was always really interested in the idea that we could someday have an anti-depressant that actually works, which I don't know if we do now. But if you and I got the flu right now, the world would change. It would literally change before our eyes. It would be a shitty place, and we would hate it, and it would be hard to get back to our cars, and so on. So I was always interested in this idea that it's not the case that you're in the world and good things or bad things happen. It's that you are your mind, and your mind is malleable, and depending on the condition of that mind at any place, the world literally changes outside. So I thought if we get a much more sophisticated understanding of the brain in the future, which I'm sure we will, we're going to have a much more sophisticated ability to manipulate it.

Like when I can say to you, "You're a little shy. I can fix that." And I literally can. Now, it's called Adderall. But if I could do that with a great deal of precision, would you want me to? If I could make myself magically less anxious, which I've always wanted, would I do it? OK, do it—who are you now?

CS: *You considered writing "Escape from Spiderhead" as a novel. Was that difficult for you to abandon that aspiration and turn it into a short story?*

GS: Sure it was. And I've done this before, and I know the syndrome, which is: "It's not a novel, dumbass." "I know, I know." Then three days later: "Well, it seems like it kind of is." But that's OK. It's good to hope. But it's also good not to mistake your dog for a horse. Sometimes it's part of the process to exhaust every corridor. I had up to one hundred sixty pages, and it really shut down at twenty.

CS: *How difficult was it for you to scrap that much text?*

GS: Actually, it's bitter. But then it's fun. Then it's kind of like, "Oh, I'm that serious about writing." Faulkner said, "Cut your darlings." Watch this, Bill. One of the things that I've realized is that we're much more fecund than we think we are. We can create endlessly. To have eighty pages of typing that I throw away, big fucking deal. I could type eighty pages again. That attitude I think is essential for a writer. Because if you think that you've just pooped gold, you're in trouble because you're going to protect it too much. I can create pretty much at the drop of a hat, so let me have a double standard: I want it to be beautiful and creative and wonderful and useful. Then you can get in my story. And that's actually hard.

You know it isn't the case that we always feel infinitely creative. But I had someone in Hollywood tell me that in a script the requirement for a scene to exist is that it be entertaining in and of itself and essential to the forward movement. Which is interesting. I've felt that. You have some material that's pretty funny or good or whatever it is, but it's just sitting out there in Purposeless Land. As soon as you import it into an essential part of the story, it lights up. I think once you've had that experience, it's a little bit addictive. You don't really want to settle for anything less than that. If you have to cut eighty pages, so be it.

CS: *I think, especially as a beginning writer without maybe the awareness that, "Yeah, I can write something this good again," I have a tendency to overwrite and underedit. Do you find this is true of most of your students? How do you wean them off it?*

GS: It's not overwriting. It's overclinging to what you've done, even if the thing is not helping you. It's kind of like if you went on a date and you had a plan that at 7:30, you were going to praise her clothes no matter what. Well, at some point, if the evening's going differently, you have to lose your plan, or else you're being a baby. I think that the hardest thing to say is "I know you've spent three months on this. I hear ya. I've done it myself. But let's just face it that the juncture on page twelve isn't working for you. Does the story have anything else to tell you?" Actually, to me, that's the most exciting part of it. It's kind of like a small laboratory for training yourself in non-clinging. It's easy to say, but I had a fit of crying in my beer this weekend because I had to cut another sixty pages of something else. But that's the game I think.

I will say that I don't think that's the game for everybody. There are some writers I know who don't do it that way. I know one very famous writer, a very good writer, who told me he just doesn't do much revision. He knows what he's going to write that day. He sits down and does it. And he stops. He can predict his output months in advance, and he's good. This is just my particular set of neuroses.

CS: *Self-editing involves more than just cutting. What's your approach? Do you labor over a sentence until you get it right? Or do you write in spurts and then keep revisiting it?*

GS: Both. The boilerplate is that I'll have printed something out the night before, and I'll kind of delay, delay, and then just sit down and read it with a red pen in my hand. At that point, I talk about where I start getting sloppy and then I start editing or adding. At some point when I've gone a certain number of pages, I'll go back in and put it in again and print it out again. I just keep doing that. That's the theory. But I don't really have a system.

The one thing I try to do is work when interested. Actually, I'm always interested—I could write right now. But if I have three projects going on, I try to gravitate towards the one that makes me happiest at the moment. When there's that tedious feeling, I usually make mistakes in that mode. If I'm not feeling some joy, the rational mind takes over, and you've reduced something complex into a two-dimensional thing.

CS: *How do you know when you're done with a story and it's ready to send out?*

GS: That's the million-dollar question. It's different for everybody. But for me, there's just a feeling. I remember hearing Eddie Van Halen one time, and they asked him about his sound, and he said, "We just mix it until we get the brown sound, man." And I'm like, "The brown sound? What the fuck does that mean?" But now I know what he means. There's a certain tightness to it. For me, it's kind of like doing that thing I described where you're reading it as if you haven't read it before, and there's a feeling of inevitability. You get to a section and you go, "Yeah, I accept that. That happened." As you're reading, it's all real to you. It feels true and real and there's enough precise energy going on that you get that sidecar feeling. Then at some point, you get to the point where it's not in that state, and you feel it. That's where you have to start again. The whole process is to push that line farther and farther back. It's kind of an intuitive feeling.

CS: *Even as an established author, does it still feel cool for you to see your work published in The New Yorker and other major magazines?*

GS: Cooler than ever, actually. I think maybe when you're young you don't appreciate it as much. It's a little bit like being on a hunt. I've got this story now that I've been working on forever. It has been my adversary for many years. It's a nice feeling to go, "I can wait as long as you can. We're in this together. Let's see if we can finish you." It's very satisfying and deeply fun.

As you get older, you realize that it was not actually a given that you would have a writing career. And it was not a given that you would have an audience. And it's not a given that you always will. I didn't write anything worth reading until I hit about thirty. And I assume that light will go off at some point. I think it's good to be grateful.

CS: *How does it feel to have passionate fans of your work? Why do you think your writing has caught on?*

GS: I don't know the answer to the second part. Maybe it's just ignorance or cultural decline. But it's deeply rewarding. I just had breakfast with a Lutheran reading group in town here, and they were such intelligent, nice men. The thought that before I ever met them they were reading something that I had written and taken it seriously is very humbling. I love it.

I saw Toby Wolff, who was my teacher for a time, when he came back to Syracuse and someone said, "If you weren't a writer, what would you be?" And he's the most articulate person in the world, and you could see him kind of going "wow." And he just said, "Sad." It's a really great job because it calls you to be an increasingly more alert person throughout your life. Even at the point in your life when you're getting old, there's still no reason in the world why you can't communicate to younger people. It's an incredible growth opportunity because you have to keep going back into the fire, into a place that's really scary or interesting to you. What a great opportunity to be getting older and not have that part of your life be rote or habitual. You get to keep coming back to basically a twenty one-year-old place in your own psyche in a certain way.

CS: *Right, every day is something different.*

GS: That's the disorienting thing about what we do, and I know that you've felt this. You write something on Wednesday, and it's perfect. You finally did it. Wow. And you go out and have a good time. And you go back Thursday morning and read it, and it's not perfect anymore. So when were you right, Wednesday or Thursday? The answer is neither—come back Friday. I think for some people, that's troubling, and it is for me sometimes. You think, "My God, I'm fifty-two years old—don't I know what I'm doing yet." But part of the job is to be comfortable with that feeling of uncertainty, which is very invigorating.

CS: *When I heard you read "Victory Lap" (published in The New Yorker in October 2009) last night, the story jumped out at me more than it did when I read it in print, mostly because of the energy you brought to the characters. Do you typically enjoy readings?*

GS: I really look forward to these readings. I've probably read that story twenty times now, but it's always different. It makes me nervous, but I like the feeling of getting up there in front of three hundred strangers. In that story, you can't be shy. So it's really funny because you go to dinner (with people who will be at the reading), and you're nervous. You make polite small talk. Then you go, "Fuck, in twenty minutes I'm going to be up in front of these same people doing eight different voices."

There's a feedback loop. You're not just writing to read it, but maybe you've been reminded of what connection feels like—that you're not just writing for yourself or to be clever, you're actually writing to reach out to that guy right there who maybe is a little skeptical. There was a guy at the reading yesterday who was sitting in the front. He was very skeptical And I kept watching him. I'm not sure, but at least for a moment I saw him suddenly lean in. So it's the idea that when you're sitting in your writing room, you actually are trying to connect.

Readings are fun. But there's also a danger in it. Most places where you read, there's what I call "laugh inflation." So if someone goes up and says even a stupid thing, people laugh. In a reading situation, you're getting twenty percent more laughs than you would actually get. People are generous. It's a social thing.

CS: *It's kind of a contract—I want to be here, so I'm going to laugh. It's like how Steve Martin quit stand-up because people would laugh at whatever he said, no matter what.*

GS: That's right. If you do it too much, then you start counting on that laugh inflation, and your focus drifts a little bit. You're looking for the next laugh line, and when you're writing you shouldn't be doing that. To read a piece like that, where basically the laughs stop at a certain point, it goes pretty dead. The first time I read it, I thought I bombed. My wife said, "What are you talking about?" I said, "There were no laughs." She said, "Well, it's not funny after a certain point in the story."

There's a quality of attention that people have that is just as valuable. There's a program in Boston where you go to read another writer's work. I read this story called "We Didn't" by Stuart Dybek. It's a brilliant, funny, beautiful piece of writing. But it's just different. He's a beautiful lyrical writer. So the rhythm of it is different because there's not the kind of pulse of punchlines that there is in my work. I was reading it, and I had this realization that I was getting a completely different energy from the audience. I looked up, and they were just riveted. It was really interesting to see that an audience can pay attention to you in a lot of different ways.

CS: *Do you think using humor is one of the better ways to reach an audience?*

GS: Yes, if it's natural for you, that's right. It's like meat tenderizing. In that story, when you start out with the girl and you're laughing kind of affectionately for her even though she's an exaggeration, she becomes somewhat real. And she has a characteristic, which is her optimism. Then you leave her and go to the boy, and he's funny and ridiculous and exaggerated, but he's got this quality of being stage managed by his parents. So even though those qualities were created in a kind of cartoonish way, they're there. And then that gives you a lot to work with. Suddenly that girl, she's not just words—she's a girl. And if something happens to her, you don't like that.

CS: *You become invested in those characters.*

GS: I think that's exactly it. The thing is, we often think as writers that the process of getting someone invested is intellectual. But I think it can be done through all kinds of tricky ways. If you think about a movie, you see a guy walking up the street towards you in an opening shot, and you're invested. Why? You can get there in a lot of different ways. Humor for me is one way to do it. But I think everybody has to find their own.

CS: *Is there a certain amount of time that you dedicate to writing and reading every day?*

GS: I get up in the morning, and I take the dog on a walk. Usually on the walk, I'm getting kind of excited about getting back in there. I've noticed that if I have an excitement about living and if I sort of acknowledge my innate need for attention, then I get excited. Let me do something that will get the world's attention—that'll be fun. I'm guessing that's an impulse that all writers have. But for most of us, it seems a little sleazy, but actually I think it's all right.

So I walk the dog and head back to the house. By that time, it's fun, and I have some coffee. And I block out from 9 in the morning to 3. It's a little bit flexible, and I'll do errands during that time. But it's basically to say, "This is assumed writing time. We'll see how it goes." As I get older, I'm becoming more and more of a workaholic, so usually it's just me in there from 9 to 3 and then trying to come back at the end of the night.

It's a great life. The only kind of bittersweet thing is that you start to realize how long it takes you to finish things, and you go, "Oh, so there are not actually infinite books in the quiver." Which also focuses you. Let's say that you get really lucky and you live to one hundred twenty. Well, for me that's still only about six more books. You've learned about the limitations of your talent. But you've also learned that you have some. So you try to figure out how to use that in a responsible way in the time you have left. And it's really kind of fun.

CS: *Do you feel any pressure to finish a novel? Are there any other forms you'd like to take on?*

GS: I would love to write a novel because I think the short story and novel are really different. There are things that I used to love about reading that I don't get to in my own work—the kind of big-picture stuff. But I also know, going back to what we talked about, that doesn't mean I should do it. I would also like to have a record out. Well, no. I'm certainly thinking about trying a novel, but I know from the past that if you do something because you think you ought to, it might not be so good. My real aspiration is to just go deeper. With stories like "Victory Lap" and "Escape from Spiderhead," it's really fun to have surprised yourself and gotten more out of the material than you thought you would.

To write something that you read to people and they like it, that's deep, and it's not to be taken for granted. So if in fact in my life I get to do that x number of more times, that's great. It's not a given. I try to keep that in mind. Of course, we have an aspirational energy that says, "Now I'm going to write an operetta." But even if you could just keep doing what you're doing a little better until you were eighty, that would be great. That's where I try to keep my head.

CS: *Did you always want to be a teacher?*

GS: I think really early on I wasn't interested. I thought, "You're teaching because you haven't gotten your big nut yet." And then, when I was in grad school, it was sort of assumed that was the aspiration—if you got lucky enough to publish a book, you get a teaching job, and you kind of endure it and neglect your students. But then once I started doing it, I really loved it. It helps me as a writer. It helps me as a person.

Like any responsible teacher of writing, I'm always wrestling with the idea of what can you actually do for a person. At our program, this year we had almost five hundred applications for six spots. You could literally sit there and stare at the people, and they would get better. Or you could just leave—it doesn't matter. Part of it is like the Hippocratic oath; you just don't do any harm. They're all really self-motivated and brilliant and all that. So then it's not really about teaching. I think it's always about trying to teach them talent management because they're already incredibly talented.

In that way, you can sometimes coach. You see someone block, and you can kind of intuit why they are. And maybe in some opportune moment, you just give them a little poke or recommend reading or give them a really intense line edit. But it's definitely possible to take those incredibly talented people and throw open a gate every once in a while. For sure. No question about it. You'd have to be kind of a dunce to not do it, I think. If you have a thoroughbred horse, open the gate. That's all you do, basically. If you don't open it, they're probably going to jump over the fence anyway.

CS: *I see what you're saying. For me, grad school has been less about specific instruction and more about the overall experience of being part of a writing community.*

GS: That's right. The reason is, if you have that desire and that curiosity, you owe it to yourself to expend the energy to see about it. It's actually funny. From this end of the thing, you see how much of it has to do with what a person is born with. Hard work? Yeah. But there are people who are very hard-working who don't succeed. It's not a given.

Long before I went to grad school, I was in Chicago, and I was really struggling on a lot of levels. I knew I wanted to write, but I didn't like to write. I wanted to have written. So I cooked up this plan that I wanted to go to El Salvador because there was a war going on. I thought, "That's what I need—some really cool experience." So I was studying Spanish on my own and was going to go down to El Salvador. I stopped by to see my friend, and he wasn't there, but his father was there. His dad was a really nice older guy who had six or seven kids and had driven a truck in Chicago his whole life. I'd never talked to him as a person—he was just a dad. So we talked a little bit, and I told him about this dream to be a writer and go to El Salvador. I expected him to kind of mock me about it. And he said, "If that's your dream, you should do it. If you don't do it, you know who you're going to blame?" I said, "Yeah, myself." And he said, "Bullshit. You're going to blame your wife and kids when you get older."

With writers, if you have this idea that you want to be writer, you better work with it now, in a situation of relative ease, if possible. After that, it's not up to you. But at least you'll know you took a swing at it.

CS: *What's the best piece of advice you have for aspiring writers?*

GS: It's sort of anti-advice. When I was a young writer, so much of my energy was worry energy. Like what should I write about? I'd like to be Kerouac, but I also like Faulkner, so can I be a combo? Should I set my stories in my hometown? That kind of thing—these decisions that you make. I think that's probably necessary, but also, I have found that so many of those questions get subsumed and almost invalidated if you just work enough.

I think Robert Frost said it one time to a grad student: "Don't worry. Work." There's something a little facile about that, but also kind of true. It's like if you were saying, "Now, we're going to drive to San Francisco this afternoon. Should we stop in Utah?" Well, you can worry about it, but if you keep going, you'll find out that by the time you actually get to Utah, the car's breaking down, and you can't get to California. Or you meet a girl on the way, and you spend twenty years with her. Until you get there, the worry is a bit extraneous. Same thing with the big question any young writer has: "Do I have it?" You don't know. And your teachers don't know. I have brilliant students here, but I could not predict, even in the third year, who is going to break out. In a certain way, the only thing to do is get in there every day and throw energy at the problem. And in that wonderful way that worthy problems have, it will be very satisfied by the energy, and a whole new set of questions will be generated that you can then answer the same way—through work. I think if I could go back and talk to myself at twenty-six, I'd say, "You know what? It's fine if you want to obsess about these things, but make sure that you're putting in your six hours a day, and you'll see that the questions will become quite irrelevant by the fifth day of that. You'll answer them on the fly."

COMICS AND MISCELLANY

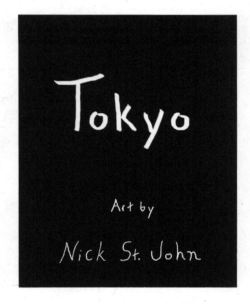

Tokyo

Art by

Nick St. John

NINE POSSIBLE OBSERVATIONS TO CONSIDER

By Michael Bazzett

✳ ✳ ✳

1. The sound a bluejay makes, if it were a color, would not be blue. It would be the color of something torn open.

2. The ubiquity of dust.

3. Two men enter a room. One asserts time is an invention; the other claims it as a discovery. They stare into one another's eyes. The exact length of this pause has yet to be determined.

4. Roughly half of all food is discarded, leading observers to conclude that we could, if necessary, live on the moon.

5. It is a truth universally acknowledged that absolutes are not to be trusted. Fortunately, plans are underway to etch this into the cornerstones of public buildings.

6. Throughout history, each individual has found the fact of his or her impending demise to be implausible. Most believed they were special. This secret was held closely to their chests. It apparently makes a dry, rattling sound when knocked loose.

7. Punctuation matters: the penis, mightier than the sword?

8. In modern parlance, we have one word for snow. Native peoples, however, had dozens of words for money, including bones, clams, bread, trees, meat, shells, and coca leaves, which, ironically, produce the aforementioned snow.

9. It is not possible to consider the next observation.

10. Directions can be difficult to follow. The authorities are aware of this and have convened a committee to propose solutions. Internal politics are slowing the process, however. As in all things, it is a question of cultivating the proper discipline.

Vampire Story

Written by

Zeynep Alpaslan

Art by

Nick St. John

He Brings Exotic Flowers
From Eastern Countries

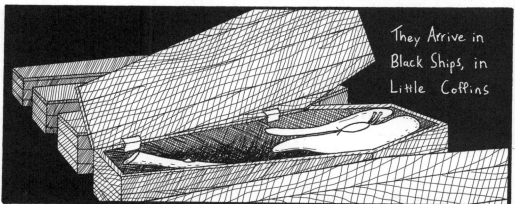

They Arrive in
Black Ships, in
Little Coffins

He Plants Them at Night

CONTRIBUTORS

ZEYNEP ALPASLAN lives and works in Istanbul, Turkey.

✳   ✳   ✳

MICHAEL BAZZETT's poems have appeared in journals such as *West Branch*, *Green Mountains Review*, *Best New Poets*, *Diagram*, and *The National Poetry Review*. He was the winner of the 2008 Bechtel Prize from Teachers & Writers Collaborative and was recently nominated for a Pushcart Prize. New poems are forthcoming in *Beloit Poetry Journal*, *Bateau*, *The Los Angeles Review* and *Sentence*. He lives in Minneapolis with his wife and two children.

✳   ✳   ✳

RYAN BOUDINOT is the author of *Blueprints of the Afterlife* (Grove/Atlantic, 2012); *Misconception* (Grove/Atlantic, 2009), a finalist for the PEN-USA literary award; and *The Littlest Hitler* (Counterpoint, 2006). He teaches at Goddard College and Richard Hugo House.

✳   ✳   ✳

DALE BERNSTEIN has worked with some of the world's great photographers, including Irving Penn, Richard Avedon, Horst P. Horst, Arnold Newman, and Robert Mapplethorpe. Born in New York, he has operated his own commercial studio in the Midwest for twenty years. His work has appeared in several galleries, including the George Eastman House in 2001, and he has published articles and photography in *View Camera Magazine*, *PHOTOVISION*, and the *Graphis Photography Annual*. His book, *Collodion Travelogue*, is available through Blurb.com.

TASHA COTTER's work has appeared or is forthcoming in *The Rumpus*, *Contrary Magazine*, and elsewhere. Her fiction was recently nominated for a storySouth Million Writers award, and her poetry has been nominated for *Best of the Net Anthology 2011*. You can find her online at www.tashacotter.com.

✳   ✳   ✳

KEVIN DUCEY lives in Madison, Wisconsin. His book of poems, *Rhinoceros*, is available from Copper Canyon Press. His fiction, nonfiction, and poetry have appeared in *Exquisite Corpse*, *Crazyhorse*, *Sonora Review*, *AGNI*, *Hotel Amerika*, *The Pinch*, *Beloit Poetry Journal*, and other places.

✳   ✳   ✳

SHERRIE FLICK is author of the flash fiction chapbook *I Call This Flirting* (Flume) and the novel *Reconsidering Happiness* (Bison Books). Her work appears in the Norton anthologies *Flash Fiction Forward* and *New Sudden Fiction* as well as *The Rose Metal Press Field Guide to Writing Flash Fiction*. A recipient of a Pennsylvania Council on the Arts grant, she lives in Pittsburgh where she teaches in the MFA program at Chatham University and works as a freelance writer and editor. You can find her online at www.sherrieflick.com.

✳   ✳   ✳

KATHLEEN FOUNDS has a BA from Stanford and an MFA from Syracuse. She has worked as a drop-out prevention counselor at a South Texas middle school, organized an after-school program ("The Inner Beauty Parlor") for teen girls in inner-city Syracuse, and taught English and creative writing at a technical school in the Ohio cornfields. "The Un-Game" is a chapter from her novel-in-stories, When Mystical Creatures Attack!

JESSE GOOLSBY's writings have appeared in *Epoch*, *The Literary Review*, Alaska *Quarterly Review*, *Harpur Palate*, *The Greensboro Review*, and *The Journal*. He is the recipient of the John Gardner Memorial Prize for Fiction and the Richard Bausch Short Fiction Prize. He is a fiction editor at *War, Literature & the Arts*.

❋   ❋   ❋

KELSEA HABECKER is a writer, poet, and teacher. Her first book of poetry, *Hollow Out*, was published by New Rivers Press in October 2008. She has received grants and fellowships from the Santa Fe Art Institute, the Virginia Center for Creative Arts, and New York's Saltonstall Foundation. She was a finalist for the 2003 Ruth Lilly Fellowship in poetry. She received her MFA in poetry from Bennington Writing Seminars and her BA from Randolph-Macon Woman's College. She teaches creative writing through Empire State College. She currently lives in Anchorage, Alaska.

❋   ❋   ❋

DANA KROOS received an MFA in fiction writing from New Mexico State University. Her fiction and poetry have appeared in *Glimmer Train*, *The Superstition Review*, *The Florida Review*, *Minnesota Monthly* and others. She also holds an MFA in ceramics from the Rhode Island School of Design. Currently she resides in Las Cruces, New Mexico, where she teaches creative writing and art at Alma d'arte High School and English at New Mexico State University.

❋   ❋   ❋

DAVID LABOUNTY has held jobs as a miner, a mechanic, a reporter, and a salesman. His work has appeared in *Rattle*, *The Los Angeles Review*, *Night Train*, the *New Plains Review* and several other journals. He is the author of the novel *Affluenza*. He lives in Michigan.

KIRSTY LOGAN lives in Glasgow, Scotland, where she writes fiction, edits a literary magazine, teaches creative writing, and reviews books. She is currently working on her first novel, Rust and Stardust, and a short story collection, The Rental Heart and Other Fairytales. Her short fiction has been published in around eighty anthologies and literary magazines and has been broadcast on BBC Radio 4. She has a semicolon tattooed on her toe. Say hello at kirstylogan.com.

✳   ✳   ✳

ALEX MATTINGLY completed his MFA at Butler University. He has previously published interviews with Joe R. Lansdale and Matt Fraction, and his fiction has appeared in *Annalemma*, *Joyland*, and *3 AM*. He lives in Indianapolis.

✳   ✳   ✳

MIKE MEGINNIS has fiction, poetry, and essays published or forthcoming in *The Lifted Brow*, *Hobart*, *The Collagist*, *elimae*, *Smokelong Quarterly*, *kill author*, *The Contemporary Review of Fiction*, and others. He co-edits *Uncanny Valley* (uncannyvalleymag.com) with his wife, Tracy Bowling.

✳   ✳   ✳

TARA MAE MULROY is an MFA candidate in poetry at the University of Memphis. She is currently the managing editor for *The Pinch*. She has work published or forthcoming in *Connotation Press*, *The Los Angeles Review*, *The Southern Women's Review*, *The Meadow*, and others. She can be reached by e-mail at maetador@gmail.com.

✳   ✳   ✳

MARK PETRIE grew up in Arizona but currently resides in New Orleans. He is a graduate student at the University of New Orleans, where he studies poetics and literature under the guidance of several talented and experienced professors. He enjoys playing basketball, cooking, and annoying his cat.

AUBREY RYAN holds an MFA from Northern Michigan University, where she served as an editor for *Passages North*. Her work has appeared most recently in *DIAGRAM*, *Pebble Lake Review*, and *The Dirty Napkin*. She lives in Iowa.

NICK ST. JOHN is a writer, artist, and forklift operator living in San Francisco.

SARAH SCOLES is a writer and astronomy educator/outreacher working in West Virginia. She recently completed an MFA at Cornell University. Other short stories can be found or will soon be found in the *Alaska Quarterly Review*, *DIAGRAM*, *Fringe Magazine*, and *Eastown Fiction*.

CHRIS SPECKMAN is a former journalist and the author of several unpublished short stories. He is pursuing an MFA at Butler University, where he serves as the graduate assistant for the Writing in the Schools project, a cooperative effort involving the creative writing program and Shortridge High School designed to help young minds develop and cultivate a passion for the written word.

ELIZABETH WADE holds degrees from Davidson College and the University of Alabama. Her poetry and prose appear in such journals as *Kenyon Review Online*, *AGNI*, *Oxford American*, and *The Rumpus*.

JOSH WILKER studied writing at Johnson State College and Vermont College and is the author of the 2010 book *Cardboard Gods*. He lives in Chicago and, virtually, at http://cardboardgods.net.

The Theology of Justin Martyr

Erwin R Goodenough

BIBLIOLIFE

THE THEOLOGY

OF

JUSTIN MARTYR

ERWIN R. GOODENOUGH

B. D., D. PHIL (OXON)

VERLAG FROMMANNSCHE BUCHHANDLUNG

(WALTER BIEDERMANN)

JENA 1923

TO MY PARENTS
IN LOVING GRATITUDE

PREFACE

A word of explanation is due for the inclusion of the two chapters of Introduction The desirability of defining one's point of view and terminology before beginning upon a discussion of the Theology of Justin Martyr is increasingly demonstrated as one glances through the literature which has been written upon him. The great interest in Justin is his transitional position. In his writings are to be found for the first time in Christian literature many conceptions and phrases which later theologians used to great effect. But granted that Justin's writings contain philosophic elements which the Synoptics do not, one must still ascertain the source or sources whence these bits have been drawn, before their true meaning or the significance of their use for the character of second century Christianity can be understood. Such a search is impossible without a previous understanding as to the character of the thinking which preceeded and surrounded Justin in the Greek world, but unfortunately much of the criticism of Justin has been conducted without definition, and too often without understanding, of the development of Greek thought. The same may be said of Judaism. It is customary to contrast Judaistic with Hellenistic Christianity, as though the terms Judaistic and Hellenistic were mutually exclusive, and had not for centuries been united in a school which men still do not know whether better to call Judaistic Hellenism or Hellenistic Judaism. Here again, it was felt, only misunderstanding could have resulted from an attempt to discuss Justin's relation with Judaism without a preliminary statement of the author's point of view.

The references are for the most part self-explanatory, except perhaps for one device which has been introduced to combine brevity with immediate accessibility of full titles when a title is to be found in the Bibliography, reference is given by the title number, for example Bib 313. In that case the title will be found at once by turning to number 313 of the Bibliography. References are given to Justin's writings by chapter, and section as divided in all editions of the Apologies and Dialogue later than Otto, together with the page and letter of the edition of Morellus as given in the margin of Otto's third edition. References to Philo are given by sections in the edition of Cohn and Wendland, to which is added in parentheses the pagination of Mangey as found in the margin of Cohn and Wendland.

My sincere thanks for his help in revising the proofs are due my dear friend Theodore M Hatfield, Esq., of Lincoln College, Oxford.

Alassio, Italy, March 1, 1923.

E. R. G.

CONTENTS

		Page
Introduction	.	1
I The Philosophic Environment of Justin Martyr		1
II Judaism		33
A Palestinian Judaism		33
B Hellenistic Judaism		40
The Theology of Justin Martyr		57
I Justin's Life	.	57
II. Justin's Writings		78
A The First Apology		80
B The Second Apology		84
C. The Dialogue with Trypho		87
XII Justin's Apologetic .		101
IV God		123
V The Logos	. .	139
A The Personal Existence of a Second God		141
B The Origin of the Logos		147
C. The Nature of the Logos	.	155
D Cosmic Significance of the Logos		159
E. Titles Applied to the Logos	.	168
F. Conclusion		173
VI. The Holy Spirit and the Lower Powers		176
A The Holy Spirit .	.	176
B The Lower Powers		189
VII The Created World		206
A Matter .		206
B Man		211
C Sin		226
VIII Christ		232
IX Redemption and the Christian Life		250
X Eschatology		279
Conclusion		292
Bibliography		295

INTRODUCTION

THE PHILOSOPHIC ENVIRONMENT
OF JUSTIN MARTYR

The aim of the early Greek Philosophers was to find some central principle in the confused multiplicity of existence. They marked the beginning of the Greek Philosophic movement, because the philosopher is essentially characterized by his desire to view life as an ordered whole, rather than as a succession of disjointed phenomena, and it was these early thinkers who for the first time, at least in the west, attempted to explain the world as a unity. The first suggestions were crudely materialistic. All things are one, it was thought, in the sense that all things are manifestations under varied forms of some single material element. Each of the four elements was suggested as this primal element by a different philosopher (solid, γῆ, disguised under the form of atomistic theories), with the impression that each of the other three elements could be derived from the one primal element by the process of rarification and condensation made familiar in the easy changes of water into a solid or a gas. Our fragments from these very early thinkers are so scanty that we do not know in how great detail they attempted to work out their conceptions. It is likewise impossible to state finally that the primal element was ever regarded by them as more than a vague material substrate, the source and power of whose operation was not questioned at all. But it seems probable that even the earliest thinkers regarded their single element as more than the material principle of unity in the world,

for from a surprising number of them, considering the
scantness of our fragments, a passage has survived in
which the primal form of matter is called θεός   Of the
many theories proposed to explain the meaning of this
θεός it seems that the simple interpretation is the best,
that which understands these first attempts at philosophic
systems not as mere materialisms but as pantheistic
materialisms.   That is, before the vastness of the conception of the world as fundamentally homogeneous would
inevitably have sprung up a sense of reverence which knew
no other way of expressing itself than to assert the divinity
of the All. But it was an instinctively pantheistic materialism. not an expressly pantheistic system, which the
earliest philosophers taught. An interesting illustration is
to be found in the advance of Xenophanes upon Anaximines.
Anaximines had said that the primordial element was air.
and Anaximines had himself called air Θεός.[1]   Xenophanes
seems to have followed Anaximines in his assumption of air
as the primordial element, but he called the world God,
a living, breathing thing,[2] and in doing so Xenophanes
represents a very definite advance over the vagueness of
the earliest use of θεός as applied to the primal material
element.

It is a matter of serious dispute whether Heraclitus
did or did not advance measurably beyond a vague pantheistic tendency. The primal element of Heraclitus was
fire, by which he probably understood intensely hot and
greatly rarified mist or aether. But the difficulty in connection with Heraclitus lies in several ambiguous passages
where he speaks of Logos   Since the time of the Stoics
the traditional interpretation of these passages has been
that by "Logos" Heraclitus meant "all-pervading Reason".
and that this Logos was to be identified with primordial
fire in the sense that fire was more than the material principle of the universe and the source of all things existing,
but that it was also intelligent, and that its omnipresence

---

[1] Diels: Die Fragmente der Vorsokratiker, 3. Aufl 1912 I.
24 (Anaximines A. 10).

[2] Arist Met. A. 5. 986. b. 10 et al.

meant an omnipresent and cosmic intelligence and reasoning force. This traditional interpretation, as will be seen, corresponds in general with the teaching of the Stoics, and represents Heraclitus, briefly, as a Stoic before the Stoa That the Stoics were deeply indebted to Heraclitus cannot be doubted, but on that very account their testimony, as to the Logos of Heraclitus must be treated with all the more caution, for the Stoics were never content at purely eclectic appropriations from the older philosophers, but by their avowed practice of "accommodating" (συνοικειοῦν), they tried to represent all their predecessors of note as teachers of Stoic principles. The Stoics insisted that they followed • Heraclitus not only in their choice of an ultimate material element, but in regarding that element as identical with a universal Logos.[1] The verbal similarity between Heraclitus' Logos and the Logos of Stoicism made his doctrine so easy a subject for accommodation that their testimony as to what he taught has no independent value It is hard to understand how Zeller, fully understanding the practice of the Stoics in accommodating, could say that the doctrine of Heraclitus must be understood in Stoic terms.[2] The difficulty with accepting the Stoic view of Heraclitus is that while his fragments are intelligible as the Stoics read them, yet they can be read equally intelligibly in quite another sense. Thus the two latest antagonists in the discussion, Burnet,[3] and Adam,[4] each advance plausible arguments for opposing interpretations, but neither advances conclusive arguments. Adam defends the traditional interpretation, while Burnet asserts that Heraclitus meant by Logos only his own message to mankind, much as the word "Report" is used in Isaiah 53. 1. The fact seems to be that the evidence we now possess will never warrant a conclusive opinion on the subject, and that it is equally daring to say of Heraclitus either that he did or did not teach a "Logos Doctrine".

[1] Sext Math. VII. 127 ff.
[2] Philosophie der Griechen I ii (6 Aufl 1920) 840 n 3 Engl Tr : Presocratic Philosophers, II. 43, n 1
[3] Early Greek Philosophers 3d Ed. p. 133 ff.
[4] The Vitality of Platonism, Camb 1911 p 76 ff. Essay, The Logos in Heracleitus.

More important than the doctrine of Heraclitus, as an early antecedent of the Logos Doctrine, was the teaching of Anaxagoras, who tried to reconcile the contradictions of the world about him by the introduction of a primordial νοῦς [1] He conceived of the world as the combination of a large group of opposites,[2] which were at first mingled together in hopeless confusion. Out of this chaos νοῦς separated the opposites, and then combined them again in such a way as to produce the phenomenal world. "All things were mingled together, then mind came and ordered them"[3] Anaxagoras was fundamentally dualistic in contrast with the world in which all things are compounds he predicated the νοῦς whose nature is uncompounded Here is the dualism of God and the world which was continued in most of the greater philosophies of Greece, and which, strengthened by a similar dualism from Judaism, went on into Christian theology The νοῦς, according to Anaxagoras, is essentially unlike all other things, and yet it is not infinitely removed from the world, but dwells in all living creatures [4] Anaxagoras represents a distinct advance upon the other early philosophers of Greece, and did much to shape the doctrine that later was called Logos, for with him the early and vague θεός was beginning to take on the attribute of Reason, and, as Reason, to occupy an important position in an explanation of the Universe

But it was exactly in the matter of the importance attached to the νοῦς that Plato and Aristotle [5] found fault with Anaxagoras Plato said, and Aristotle echoed him, that he had hoped to find in Anaxagoras a more satisfactory

---

[1] Arist. (Met A iii 984 b. 18) says that Anaxagoras learned of the νοῦς from Hermotimus the Clazomenian, but nothing is known of Hermotimus beyond this statement of Aristotle Cf Zeller I ii (1920) 1267 n 2, Engl Tr. Presoc Phil II 365 n 1

[2] Arist. Met I' 1012 a 26.

[3] Diog. Laert II iii 6 (Rit et Prel. 153) πάντα χρήματα ἦν ὁμοῦ· εἶτα νοῦς ἐλθὼν αὐτὰ διεκόσμησεν Cf. Arist Met Λ 1069 b 21.

[4] Arist De Anima A 404 b 3 Here so real is the all pervasiveness of the Anaxagorean νοῦς that Aristotle parallels it to his own ψυχή theory.

[5] Plato Phaedo 97 c ff Arist Met A 985 a 18

explanation of the world than the other materialists had given But he found that Anaxagoras used the νοῦς only when the operation of material forces proved an inadequate explanation of some phenomenon, so that Anaxagoras, like his predecessors and contemporaries, did not meet Plato's and Aristotle's needs But if the νοῦς of Anaxagoras was inadequately developed, at least Anaxagoras gave direction to a tendency to conceive of reality as a dualism between an all ruling, all pervading and all shaping Intelligence on the one hand, and an inert mass, usually called Matter on the other. The next great step was taken by Plato.[1]

While drawing heavily upon Socratic general definitions and the Pythagorean doctrine of number, the Platonic doctrine of Forms seems to have been a new departure in human thought. But brilliant a departure as it was, it is an entirely inadequate philosophic system in the form in which Plato first stated it in the Phaedo and Republic. Aristotle's criticisms of the Forms, based fundamentally upon the following three points, have never been successfully controverted.

1. If the Forms are separate entities it is easy to show that there must be a greater number of them than of pheno-

---

[1] Three fragments from other early writers seem like valuable material for understanding the development of the Logos doctrine. They are :

a) Leucippos (Stob Ecl. 1. 160 R P. 195 b). Λεύκιππος πάντα κατ' ἀνάγκην, τὴν δ' αὐτὴν ὑπάρχειν εἱμαρμένην. λέγει γὰρ ἐν τῷ Περὶ νοῦ · οὐδὲν χρῆμα μάτην γίνεται, ἀλλὰ πάντα ἐκ λόγου τε καὶ ὑπ' ἀνάγκης.

b) Empedocles (from Arist. Met A 993 a. 17 cf. De Part. Anim A. 642 a. 18) · Ἐμπεδοκλῆς ὀστοῦν τῷ λόγῳ φησὶν εἶναι.

c) Epicharmus (frag. 57 2, 3, Diels).

ἔστιν ἀνθρώπῳ λογισμός, ἔστι καὶ θεῖος λόγος ·

ὁ δέ γε τἀνθρώπου πέφυκεν ἀπό γε τοῦ θείου λόγου.

But the same comment is fairly to be made upon each. In each case there are no further fragments to justify assuming any philosophic conception of a Logos. Had there been any such doctrine the chances are overwhelming that a specific tradition and further fragments to that effect would have been preserved. In the absence of such testimony the only safe course is to admit that we have no justification for expanding these isolated fragments into a philosophic system

mena Consequently the philosopher is still presented with
a hopeless multiplicity to organize and explain, and indeed
is in greater perplexity to account for the manifold Forms
than for phenomena without them

2 The Forms as beings separable from Phenomena
are bound to lead to infinite regress, the most hopeless of
all possible contingencies For if a separable Form is
necessary to account for any two things which resemble
each other, then a third Form is necessary to account for
the resemblance between the Form and the phenomenon
partaking in it That is Two men resemble each other
because they each partake in a common Form, Humanity.
But Humanity and an individual man' also resemble each
other, and can do so, according to Plato's reasoning, only
by both partaking in a third kind of Man, a third Form.
The third then calls for a fourth Man by its resemblance
to the second, etc , ad infinitum The argument is called
"The Third Man", and is a very fair extension of the
reasoning of the Platonism of the earlier Dialogues

3 The third objection to the Forms is that, granted a
world of Forms in which matter participates, the Forms
are still completely incapable of producing a world of
phenomena because Plato ascribed to the Forms no
activity They are represented as passive Matter partakes
in them, but they have no initiative to join themselves to
Matter Hence they are useless, if they do exist, for the
philosopher must supplement them with some efficient
cause which will act to bring Matter and the Forms together On the other hand, if such an efficient cause has
been assumed, the Forms themselves become altogether
superfluous

But Aristotle is criticizing not the Plato of the Parmenides, Politicus, and Philebus, but the Plato of the
Phaedo and of the Republic, with the Timaeus as somewhat
transitional For Plato himself, after he had written his
earlier works, criticized his former doctrine of the Forms
on much the same grounds as Aristotle, and while he uses
the Forms thereafter, they no longer occupy the same important place in his system, nor seem to have the same
character, which they had in the earlier Dialogues Plato's

later metaphysic is very puzzling, partly because of its obscure nature, and partly because he alludes to it in only occasional and very slight passages In the Parmenides[1] he saw that separable Forms, whether as essences, thoughts, or patterns, lead to infinite regress of Forms (the "Third Man" argument), and at the same time he saw that to distinguish fundamentally between the nature of the Forms and the nature of phenomena is to introduce manifold difficulties, for there can be no intercourse between the qualified and the absolute This argument pointed out the deficiency which Aristotle later suggested, when he demonstrated that in order for the Forms, as Plato described them in his earlier works, to be able to affect Matter there must be in addition to them an Efficient Cause An Efficient cause, then, Plato was driven to assume, and it is precisely the Efficient Cause which most distinguishes the later from the earlier Plato

Plato found his efficient principle by developing a conception which had already appeared in the writings of the earlier philosophers, that of the Divine νοῦς. He seems to begin at the point where he alleges that Anaxagoras failed,[2] namely with the attempt to give the νοῦς consistent reality The first important passage is found in the Timaeus,[3] where God as Creator, who up to that point has been called θεός is suddenly called νοῦς. But the same conception of the νοῦς is expressed more philosophically in the Philebus[4] where the νοῦς is represented as the efficient principle in the universe There are four great divisions of reality, says Plato: 1 The Unlimited, τὸ ἄπειρον. This corresponds to τὸ μὴ ὄν, Not-Being, which Plato in other passages identifies with Matter. 2 The Limit, τὸ πέρας The meaning of the Limit is much disputed, but it appears to be simply a modification of his older doctrine of Forms. The Limit is τὸ ὄν 3 The Combination of the first two, that is, the world as we see it, which is neither un-

---

[1] 128 e —136 a
[2] Phaedo 97. c. 1f
[3] Timaeus 39 e Cf. Crat 396 b 3, 400 a. 8, 416 b 10 —d 10; Phil 28 e 7, Laws X 891 e 4 ff; XII 966 e 4 ff
[4] Phil 29 b 3 —31 a 10.

qualified Not-Being nor unqualified Being, but which lies between the two in the realm of Becoming 4. The One who affected the combination, or νοῦς.

In contrast with the division of reality in the Republic[1] two great changes appear in this later analysis. The first is the change in the character of the Forms. Either they have been omitted altogether, or are, as has been suggested, to be discovered very much altered in the Limit. They are no longer treated as separable realities, but have once for all been combined with Matter, and are now to be found only in the combination of Matter and Form, that is in the world of phenomena This was precisely Aristotle's position. He did not at all deny reality to the Forms, but rather said that the only reality in a given thing lay in its Form[2] Formless Matter was τὸ μὴ ὄν. What Aristotle could not accept was the conception of the Forms as found in a separable Intelligible World, and it was precisely that Ideal World which Aristotle later rejected, which Plato seems to have abandoned in this passage. Plato and Aristotle alike finally represented that the Forms are not separable, but exist only in connection with material objects.

The second change is found in the new importance of νοῦς, which is conceived as the Efficient Principle in combining Matter and Form, and at the same time as Universal Intelligence. As Universal Intelligence, νοῦς permeates all things, and by its special indwelling different phenomena become intelligent Zeller's intrepretation of the νοῦς is the usual one.[3] He represents it as the equivalent of the Idea of the Good in the old sense of that term, that is as the culminating Form of the hierarchy of separable Forms But Plato is clearly treating νοῦς as a third principle, different alike from both the Forms and Matter, and as such able to combine and control both.

Plato describes the νοῦς by saying that the Supreme Intelligence is eternally associated with a ψυχή, for no νοῦς

---

[1] 509. d. ff.

[2] Met. Z 3.

[3] Philosophie der Griechen II. 1. (1922) 691 ff, 709 ff.

can exist apart from a ψυχή. [1] Therefore he concludes
that there is in the nature of Zeus a βασιλικὴ ψυχή, and a
βασιλικὸς νοῦς. This ψυχὴ—νοῦς—θεός is indifferently denoted
by Plato by any one of the three terms It permeates all
things. The creation of the Animus Mundi in the Timaeus
is familiar,[2] but Aristotle is probably true to Plato's
thinking when he says that this Animus Mundi is a νοῦς.[3]
For the assertion is substantiated by a passage in the Politicus, where Plato explains that τὸ πᾶν. the Universe, is said
to have been given φρόνησις (= νοῦς) by Him who created
it [4] But since we know from the Timaeus and Philebus
that the Creator was also νοῦς, we have here two νόες, or
more properly one νοῦς which permeates into the Universe
and imparts itself to it Similarly Plato mentions a single
νοῦς wich is present in all the stars,[5] evidently a further
permeation or self impartation of the one νοῦς. In the Philebus [6] Plato contrasts the νοῦς θεῖος with the νοῦς ἐμός or the
human νοῦς, but a closer examination shows that the contrast is one not of kind but of degree Our νοῦς is still the
divine νοῦς, but in us is hampered because of its close
contiguity with Matter Thomas Aquinas, quoting from
Themistius, likens Plato's conception of νοῦς to the sun
and its light The νοῦς θεῖος of Plato would be the sun,
our νόες would be rays from that single source of Light.[7]
The comparison is helpful but not completely accurate For

[1] Philebus 30 d 1—3.
[2] Timaeus 34 b
[3] De Anima A 407 a 3
[4] 269. d 1
[5] Laws XII 966 d 9, 967 d 8.
[6] 22 c 5 cf 28 c 7 where νοῦς is called king of heaven
and earth, but where Socrates suggests that this conception is
commonly held only because thereby Man feels himself elevated
in importance Two inferences from this statement are important:
1 that a νοῦς doctrine was fairly widely held. 2 that it meant
to those who held it that in some sense they were, as sharers in
the νοῦς, rulers of the Universe, so that the νοῦς must have been
understood as emanative The human νοῦς and the divine must
have been regarded as one

[7] Aquinas: De Unitate Intellectus, in Opuscula Philosophica
et Theologica, ed by A. Michael de Maria, S J, Tiferini Tiberini
1886 Vol I 470

in a real sense Plato would have said that we have within us the source of light. Our ἡγεμονικόν, or the chief division of our souls,[1] is divine in its nature as well as in its origin It is God in us. Whether in God, the World, the Stars, or in men, all νοῦς is one All are parts without division of the Divine Mind Our minds are God's mind In so far as our minds can rise above the material, we are able to think God's thoughts

Plato uses νοῦς or φρόνησις for the supreme intelligence, never λόγος. Logos in Plato always means expression or explanation[2] One of the indications that the Epinomis is later than Plato is the expression in 986 c, where λόγος ὁ πάντων θειότοτης is recorded as creating the world, or as arranging it in visible form, an activity which Plato always ascribes to νοῦς or θεός. Thus to speak of a Logos doctrine in Plato, as is frequently done, is as misleading as it is inaccurate For it obscures the fact that we must find Plato's contributions to the later Logos doctrine in his remarks about the νοῦς.

Aristotle was a true Platonist though an outspoken opponent of the men who, succeeding Plato in the Academy, were unable to follow his deeper thoughts, and who were running Platonism into absurdity Aristotle is closely akin to Plato in his conception of God, though his statements on the subject are so incomplete as to leave room for great diversity of interpretation on many important points From the few passages where deity is described it seems quite clear that its significance to Aristotle was chiefly that it served as a limit to what would otherwise have been an infinite regress of causation For Aristotle, like all Greeks, abhorred an infinite regress[3] The infinite regress in this case appeared by the fact that everything in motion has been set in motion by something else in motion, and that by something else, etc ad infin To stop this infinite series he assumed a divine principle, which, like Plato and Anaxa-

[1] Laws XII 963 a 8
[2] See the definitions in Theaet 291 c 7 ff
[3] In Met α 994. b 14 Aristotle states that the mind can only function upon a limited subject it cannot operate at all with an infinite series

goras, he called νοῦς, and which he defined as itself unmoved and completely at rest, but able while remaining
stationary to impart motion to something else. But how
can these things be? Aristotle's explanation of how the
divine νοῦς could impart motion to inert matter without
itself moving is one of his most remarkable passages.[1]
The νοῦς he explained, is so perfect that its perfection inspires in matter a desire to be like it. The desire is so
strong that matter spontaneously moves itself towards the
νοῦς, is drawn by it. So a beautiful woman attracts others
to move toward her by the power of her own beauty without
necessarily being herself moved. Before this attraction took
place matter was only potentially existent. But in the
primal motion it began to take on form, and in so far
as it has achieved form matter may said really to
exist.

Such is the operation of the First Cause. As to the
nature of the divine νοῦς Aristotle says several things,
but leaves us still in mystery. First, this νοῦς must be
actual mind, ἐνεργείᾳ, not potential mind, δυνάμει.[2] This fact
is assumed to stop another infinite regress. Aristotle thinks
in terms of every actuality as coming from a potentiality,
and of every potentiality as from an actuality. He, took
very seriously the problem lightly expressed in the modern
riddle about the hen and the egg. Did potentiality ultimately
develop from actuality, or actuality from potentiality? Such
a proposition, once having begun to revolve in the mind
with no way to stop it, was torture to a Greek thinker.
He must get through to some solution; he could not leave
it in the air. Aristotle arbitrarily settled the question by
asserting that the starting point must have been an actuality.
Accordingly he assumed a Cosmic Primal Actuality, which
he identified with νοῦς, the Unmoved Mover, asserting that
as ultimate Mind it must be actual Mind, not potential
Mind. But what is actual mind as distinguished from
potential? Actual mind is mind that is thinking, potential
mind is something that is capable of thinking, but is

[1] Met. Λ. 7.
[2] Met. Λ. 6

not thinking. Therefore the Divine Mind, as actual, must be thinking. But what does it think?

The Divine Mind, answers Aristotle,[1] thinks its own thoughts, not of anything outside itself. Here it is easy to show that Aristotle has started an endless chain. For the thought which was the object of thought must have been a thought about something, and if the Divine Mind is self contained, the second thought must have been a thought of a third thought, which involves a fourth and an infinite series of thoughts, or a meaningless circle of thoughts. But Aristotle nowhere recognizes this difficulty, and contents himself with saying that a mind can have its own thoughts as an object of thought. But ingenious as such an explanation is, it is not permanently satisfactory, and it must be admitted that Aristotle has rather avoided than answered the problem of the activity of the Divine Mind

Aristotle clearly meant to leave the Divine νοῦς as absolute But when he speaks of the human νοῦς he comes dangerously near to a doctrine of permeation like that of Plato For in describing the human mind, Aristotle says that there are present in human beings two minds, one kind a capacity, δυνάμει, and the other an actuality, ἐνεργείᾳ. The first is pure passivity, a blank sheet of paper which is part of the body and soul and perishes with them But the second is apparently a spark of divinity, or of the Divine Mind.[2] Like the cosmic νοῦς, of Anaxagoras, the higher νοῦς in man, according to Aristotle, is pure and unmixed with the rest of his constitution. It is essentially active, so much so that it is in no sense passive but always active. Hence it can receive no impressions, has no memory Its function is to act upon the lower mind and impress conceptions upon it It is itself deathless and eternal, and comes into its own only when removed from the restrictions of the body It is the only part of man that survives his death and it does so without memory.

[1] Met Λ. 9
[2] Aristotle does not say this but he speaks of the higher mind in man in such a way as to justify this inference. See de anima II. 2. 413 b. 24—29 See also Zeller II ii (1921). p. 372 n. 6. (Engl Tr. Aristotle I 404 n. 2)

as of itself it has no memory We are here very close to
a doctrine of the undivided indwelling of the divine νοῦς.
Aristotle does not himself expressly teach such a doctrine,
but he comes so close to doing so that it is difficult to
stop with him, even if one does not care to go further
and reduce the whole to pantheism Aristotle's doctrine is
indeed sufficiently suggestive of pantheism to have had
various expressly pantheistic philosophers refer to him as
their authority [1] There are several paths of argument which
Aristotle began upon but did not follow out, which need
only slight extension to lead to pantheism Thus not only
that the higher soul or νοῦς of man is an undivided part
of the Divine νοῦς, but that all matter is at least infused
with νοῦς, if not identical with it, is clear from Aristotle's
description of the manner in which the original formless
matter, unmoved, inert, τὸ μὴ ὄν, came into its present condition where it possesses form and movement This process,
which has already been described, is based upon the
attractive power of the higher over the lower, and is
utterly meaningless unless intelligence of some kind is
allowed to formless matter, by which it could first recognize
the perfection of its antitype and hence be drawn to
imitate it On this basis both partake of νοῦς, or, one step
further, both are νοῦς; that is, pantheism is a quick and
easy inference from Aristotle's description, though Aristotle
was himself diametrically opposed to any such conclusion

In Anaxagoras, Plato, and Aristotle, a fairly consistent
dualism of God or νοῦς and matter had been sustained
But the Stoic tradition went back to the materialism of
the early philosophers, and developed the hint of pantheism
which they had disclosed in their use of θεός. The Stoics
followed Heraclitus in taking as their fundamental element

[1] Cf. the pantheistic interpretations of Aristotle by Aristocles
of Messene (See Zeller Eclectics, p 316, where he quotes from
Alexander Περὶ ψυχῆς p 144 a, 145 a, in the 2nd Cent after
Christ), and of Averroes and his followers as described in Thomas
Aquinas De Unitate Intellectus, and in M Horton· Die Haupt-
lehren des Averroes nach seiner Schrift Die Widerlegung des
Gazali, aus dem arabischen Originale ubersetzt und erlautert, Bonn
1913 A contrasting realistic interpretation was given by Alexander
of Aphrodisius, see Zeller· Eclectics, p 318 ff

fire, conceived of as hot aether or very rare mist, which they called πῦρ, or πνεῦμα interchangeably. They denied the existence of immaterial reality, except theoretically for a few conceptions such as time and space. In general all reality was thought of as material, because all things are made up of πνεῦμα. So even virtues, wisdom, emotions, impulses, as states of the πνεῦμα in us, are all material.[1] All things come from, nay are, a single element in various stages of condensation, and some day all will be reduced again to the primal form. In a very real sense all things are one. Among other things identified by the Stoics with this primal element was the deity. The primal fire is God, God is the fire. The conception is as far removed from personality as could be imagined. It is much more akin to the modern "energy" of science than to personality, and indeed the parallel between the Stoic πνεῦμα and modern "Energy" is illuminating if not, of course, everywhere perfect. The Stoics identified this πνεῦμα with Reason, the Logos. Πνεῦμα is rarified, dynamic matter which can think. Sometimes it is confusing to determine whether a Stoic writer is thinking in terms of all material as a manifestation of Reason, or of all Reason as by nature material. Probably the latter is true usually, for materialism is very strong in the Stoics. In any case when the Stoics used the terms πῦρ, πνεῦμα, λόγος, they were refering in each instance to the same fundamental material from which all things are made, a material which is by nature a reasoning force.

The mind of the individual man was conceived by the Stoics as being an especially pure form of the universal substance, very closely akin to its purest and most universal form. As the One Substance became condensed into liquid and solid, it was not in so admirable a condition as when it was in its original fiery gaseous state. Hence, while the Stoics theoretically denied any dualism between the Cosmic Intelligence and matter, yet they were convinced that the individual must live according to the higher

[1] See references as quoted in Zeller. Stoics, pp 120—124. notes.

rather than the lower part of his constitution, as the result
of which Stoic Ethic expressed himself commonly in
dualistic language But dualistic as the language often
became, the Stoics never admitted in theory the presence
of any dualism, for they ever insisted that all things are
some form of manifestation of the one material element.

A comparison of such a conception with the Platonic
is most interesting Plato and the Stoics alike thought
that all things are pervaded, not merely controlled, by
a single intelligence In each system all Mind is one, but
in the Platonic dualism the All Mind is by nature immaterial
and incapable of admixture with material But the Stoic
Logos, though very similar to the Platonic νοῦς, did not
distinguish between the material and the immaterial
Thought, like goodness and the other virtues, is material,
matter in its purest state, that of fire, is itself thoughtful
and thinking.

God with the Platonists and Aristotelians was fundamentally unchangeable The Stoics identified deity with
the fire of Heraclitus which was the synonym of change.
and which, taking every form, becomes all things Hence
in practical speech it was essential for the Stoics to speak
of the Logos by various names They called it "Fate"
when they thought of it as the unavoidable relentless
force of the universe, to conform to which is the highest
happiness of man In this they rather foreshadowed the
modern scientist who thinks of primal energy in terms
of relentless law Again the Stoics spoke of God or the
Logos as Zeus, Zen, or Athene, as they thought of the
deity in terms of its universality, its life-giving powers,
its leadership of all things; or as Hera, Hephaestus, Poseidon,
or Demeter, according as it was thought of as in the air,
in fire, in water, or in the earth [1] Similarly, says Diogenes,
they thought of it in terms of many other names, but
in any case it was the One that was meant, and no Stoic
thought of the various names as meaning more than aspects
of the one deity Indeed with no loss of unity of conception,

[1] Diogenes VII 147 (Rit et Prel. 513) Apparently Diogenes'
Stoic source distinguished between the two forms of the same name
Zeus and Zen for the purpose of interpretation

the multiplicity of manifestation of the Logos was often
expressed by the plural Logoi

Of the various uses of the term Logos by the Stoics,
none has been more frequently misunderstood than the
phrase λόγος σπερματικός or λόγοι σπερματικοί. M Puech[1]
has done a real service in recalling the true doctrine of
the Stoics upon this point to the attention of theologians,
for the more detailed exposition of the subject by Heinze[2]
has apparently not received the attention it deserves
Λόγος σπερματικός was in Stoic physics a biological term
to account for the persistence of types and groups from one
generation to another. Theoretically the Stoics were, as
M Puech points out, complete "nominalists". Each
individual phenomenon they regarded as the ultimate
existence, classes and orders were only convenient fictions
with no independent reality of their own And yet nomin-
alism cannot avoid facing the problems presented by the
facts of the persistence not only of types, but even of
what are apparently individual peculiarities For example,
though the Stoics denied the existence of a type dog, and
only recognized individual dogs, yet they saw dogs continuing to beget dogs, indeed spaniels to reproduce spaniels,
while even marking and other individual peculiarities were
to be traced from generation to generation

The Stoics explained this survival of type and of individual traits in successive generations by means of the term
λόγος σπερματικός, which should be translated "spermatic
principle" According to the Stoics there is in each plant
and animal a center, located in animals in the heart,
from which the πνεῦμα flows out into all the body. As
it flows out through the eyes, it is the sense of sight,
through the ears, of hearing, through the voice, it is
the power of speech, through the sexual organs, it is the
germinal element in the sperma[3] The female has a
similar flow from her πνεῦμα, and it is from the union

[1] (Bibl 334) pp 315 ff

[2] Die Lehre vom Logos in der griechischen Philosophie,
Oldenburg 1872

[3] Rit et Prel 509 a

of these two pneumatic principles that the new offspring comes into being. The "pneuma" or "gaseous flow" is a co-ingredient with the "damp" to make the complete seed,[1] but it is this pneumatic ingredient in the seed which alone carries on the type, and which alone was signified by the term λόγος σπερματικός. The spermatic logos was thus a physical conception, not merely material as all Stoic conceptions were ultimately material, but it was a material thing with a definitely material function. Because of the fact that the senses and the powers of expression were likewise conceived of as outflowings of the pneuma, the λόγοι σπερματικοί were properly made co-ordinate with the senses and power of speech in the division of the human constitution [2]

But what greatly complicates the comparative simplicity of this conception is that the Stoics used the spermatic logos for similes and metaphors of all kinds, and particularly in cosmological descriptions and in attempts at accommodating Greek myths. The term spermatic Logos was applied figuratively to God, for example, in the passage of Diogenes Laertes VII 134—137.[3] Here the original state of all things is described under the figure of the spermatic fluid as made up, while still being a mist, of two elements, the active and passive. The passive element was damp, the active a gaseous permeation of the damp, whose action within the damp caused the beginnings of the formation of the world by the separation of the four elements. But this statement was intended by the Stoics to be taken figuratively, and not as a statement of fact. Τοῦτον σπερματικὸν λόγον ὄντα τοῦ κόσμου is a metaphor, and no indication that the Stoics properly associated the term with any cosmological principle. The author is simply using a biological figure in a cosmological exposition. Such figurative use of the biological term is by no means uncommon with the earlier Stoics,[4] and

[1] Eus Pr. Ev. XV. xx
[2] See Plac. IV. 4. 4 (Dox. 390). Rit et Prel 509, Diog VII 157 Rit. et Prel. 500. a
[3] Rit. et Prel. 493
[4] See also Plac. I 7, 33 (Dox. 305) Rit. et Prel 494

probably became conventionalized For even so early as
Chrysippus we find an explanation of the obscene pictures
of the loves of Zeus and Hera, that these represent the
infusion of spermatic logoi into matter in order to bring
about the formation of the world.[1] But such a passage
can by no means be used as representing the true thought
of Stoicism, in which God and matter were always ultimately One, though this One contained in itself both
active and passive qualities The Stoics were not careful
metaphysicians, and in ordinary writing were content
to be bewilderingly loose in the use of terms The easy
lapse into a dualistic manner of speech already mentioned
was increasingly common as Stoicism became older and
more popular, particularly in the ethical passages, and
in the interpretation of myths. As Platonism and Stoicism
crossed and recrossed each other's paths, traces of Platonic
dualism are increasingly common in Stoicism, until so
complete a change had taken place that whereas the
older Stoics, in allegorizing myths, had made Zeus equivalent to the Logos, in the first Century after Christ Cornutus asserted that the type of the Logos was the Phallic
Hermes, the fertilizing offshoot and messenger of Zeus [2]
That is, Cornutus was content to think of the Logos, not
as a term interchangeable for God, Fate, or the original
material substrate, but as a secondary mediatory God, or
at least as a distinction of function in the Deity. When
the same identification of Hermes and the spermatic Logos
is later made by Porphyry,[3] the environment is much
more harmonious, for such a conception of the Logos
was exactly that of later Platonism, as will shortly appear.
Losely then, as the term spermatic Logos was later used,
there seems no ground for believing that in strictly Stoic
thought the spermatic Logos ever lost its proper biological
signification, or that the Stoics, uninfluenced by Platonism,
ever thought of a cosmological entity by that name.

[1] Orig. contra Cels IV 48 (Arnim. II 1074) I am not
certain that Origen has correctly assigned this interpretation. He
may be quoting a much later Stoic
[2] Ch. XVI. p 20 ff from Lebreton (Bibl 163) p. 312.
[3] Eus Prep Ev. III xi. 42 (114 d).

Another pair of terms which has sometimes been confused with a conception of a δεύτερος θεός are ὁ λόγος ἐνδιάθετος and ὁ λόγος προφορικός. The Stoic use of these terms was, as Zeller has pointed out, Aristotelian,[1] though it was a case of Aristotle's giving technicalities to a distinction which Plato had already pointed out[2]. The terms were logical technicalities used to distinguish between thought in the mind and thought expressed verbally. On the basis of this distinction, the two departments of Logic were made, first the study of vocal expression, such as singing, elecution, etc., and second the study of mental sciences proper. It is as logical technicalities in precisely the same sense that the terms are used by the Platonist Albinus in the Second Contury after Christ[3]

The later philosophers of Greece and Rome were divided into many schools, but no attempt can be made in this brief sketch to describe all of them. The Epicureans and Skeptics contributed little if anything to Christian thought and were usually set aside by Christians as men not worthy to be called philosophers. For the other schools, Platonist, Aristotelian, Pythagorean, a spirit of eclecticism was so strong in all, that it is often difficult to say, for example, whether a passage is Platonic with Pythagorean elements, or Pythagorean with Platonic elements. These two schools had different disciplinary programs, as Justin shows,[4] but fundamentally they were very close to each other. The Pythagoreans clothed their thought in so technical a language that careful discipline in science and mathematics would alone have made their writings intelligible to students. But what they meant by their "numbers", was very similar to what the later Platonists meant by then "ideas". The Aristotelians seem also to have been deeply influenced by Platonism, but taught chiefly logic and science, though Alexander of Aphrodisius, at the beginning of the third Century after Christ, was teaching

---

[1] Zeller. Stoics p 72. n. 1. Cf Arist Anal Post I 10 70.
[2] Theaet 189 e; Soph 263. e.
[3] Albinus - Introd. to the Plat Dialogues, c 2. (Ed Freudenthal p 322 line 20 ff.)
[4] Dial 2 3 (219 A).

a strictly Aristotelian philosophy, and even was carrying
Aristotelianism into a particularism which Aristotle had
never advocated.

For the purpose of this brief review only one school,
the later Platonic, needs any detailed examination, for in
matters metaphysical it was the philosophic school which
most influenced Christianity. The riper conceptions of
Plato were surprisingly neglected and misunderstood by
his followers. The Republic, Phaedo, Phaedrus, and
Timaeus, especially the latter, were the standard books
from which Platonism seems to have been taught and
studied, and consequently Inseparable Ideas and the Ideal
World, which it has been shown we have reason to think
Plato himself later disregarded, if he did not actually reject,
were retained as the distinguishing doctrines of Platonism.
The Timaeus, a book cryptic enough to please the growing
love of mystical cosmological schemes and myths for
expressing philosophical conceptions, had come to be the
chief treasure of the Academy. But while the followers of
Plato neglected the deeper doctrines of their master, they
stood distinguished among the philosophers of their day for
their interest in metaphysics, which they followed with
such passion that they were led into profound mystical
aspirations.

Platonism never lost its fundamental dualism, and it
was this dualism which kept the Academy and the Stoa
distinct in spite of the constant tendency of philosophers
of both schools to borrow from each other. God and the
Ideal World stood in eternal contradistinction to the
material world. The Platonists never seemed to have personalized in Zoroastrian fashion this antithesis to deity.
Matter seemed only to be a great filthy morass, into which
the souls of men would inevitably be sucked because of the
material element in the human constitution, if by
aspiration and philosophy they did not rise above their
material nature into union with God. Justin says that the
supreme object of the Platonism of his day was to get the
vision of God.[1] The highest part of man, his Reason,

---

[1] Dial. 2. 6 (221 D)

was one with the divine Reason, and could save itself from
pollution and destruction in matter only by rising to reunite
itself with the All-Reason. God and the νοῦς seem in
Academic as in Stoic writings to have been used usually
interchangeably, though the late Platonic νοῦς was often
used in distinction from Θεός to represent God in relation
with the world, as over against God the Absolute. The
Academic God was always the Absolute, but his νοῦς, not
a separate person by any means, but a distinct attribute of
God, bridged the gap between God and the world, so that
deity in matter, that is the formal element in what
otherwise would have been formless matter, was the divine
νοῦς, though God proper was utterly removed from and
above the material.

Perhaps the simplest way to give a picture of second
century Platonism will be to describe the teaching of a
typical Platonist of the time. The philosopher Albinus
commends himself pre-eminently for that purpose, for while
we possess from most of the second century Academicians
only a few fragments, there are preserved from Albinus,
besides fragments, two treatises. One of these is entitled
ΑΛΒΙΝΟΥ εἰσαγωγὴ εἰς τοὺς Πλάτωνος διαλόγους, the other
ΑΛΚΙΝΟΟΥ διδασκαλικὸς τῶν Πλάτωνος δογμάτων, but both have
been satisfactorily proved by Freudenthal[1] to belong to
the single philosopher Albinus. The second of the two
treatises sets forth in systematic form the doctrines of Plato
for a beginner's use. The pupil is supposed to turn to the
Dialogues themselves from this intoduction, which probably
is a very fair representation of the light in which the
dialogues were interpreted to prospective Platonists of the
day. The teaching in the Academy at that time was by
no means fixed, and the amount of Stoicism and Aristotelianism intermixed into the Platonic substrate would vary
widely with the different teachers So Eusebius has perser-
ved from Atticus, a Platonist of the same period, a vigorous
protest against the tendency of Academicians to borrow
Aristotelian conceptions, though Zeller has pointed out

[1] J. Freudenthal: Der Platoniker Albinos und der falsche
Alkinoos. Berlin 1871. In his: Hellenistische Studien, Heft 3

marked traces of Stoicism in Atticus himself.[1] On the whole, however, Albinus seems to be a very typical Platonist of the time

Albinus is dated by the fact that Galen, in a very credible passage, tells us that about the year 152 he studied under Albinus in Smyrna, where Albinus was held in high regard.[2] Albinus wrote also a greatly esteemed abstract in nine or ten books of the lectures of his teacher Gaius, which cannot now be found, but which Freudenthal shows to have been extant so recently as 1667.[3]

The first notable point in the extant writings of Albinus is that both treatises are written in a strictly Aristotelian style The argument is developed throughout by definition and deduction, division and sub-division, while the language and sentence formation are distinctly those of Aristotle. Similarly Albinus' thought is saturated with Peripatetic conceptions. He describes God primarily as ὁ πρῶτος νοῦς, which he makes equivalent to ὁ πρῶτος θεός [4]

This Primal Intelligence ever thinks, in truly Aristotelian fashion, ἑαυτὸν καὶ τὰ ἑαυτοῦ νοήματα, an activity peculiar to Itself [5] The Deity is "eternal, unutterable (ἄρρητος), self-sufficient, eternally perfect " It is "divinity, substantive in nature (οὐσιότης), truth, symmetry, good . . . . . It is good since It makes all things actual as far as possible, and as such is cause of all good, It is beautiful because Its form is by nature perfect and symmetrical, truth, because It is the beginning of all truth as the sun is of all light; Father, in that It is the cause of all things, and has ordered the Heavenly Mind (τὸν οὐράνιον νοῦν), and the World Soul in accordance with Itself and Its thoughts." But these, says Albinus, must not be considered as attributes in the sense that the Deity is compounded; for Deity is pre-eminently

---

[1] Zeller III. 1 839.   Engl. Tr.: Eclectics, p. 343

[2] Freudenthal p. 242

[3] The two treatises still extant are printed in the sixth volume of Hermann's Plato, pp. 147—189; Freudenthal has edited carefully the treatise preserved under the name of Albinus, in the above mentioned monograph pp 322—326.

[4] X (ed Hermann) p 164 line 18, 23

[5] X p. 164. line 25

Unity The Deity is ὄρρητος in that It is comprehensible by the mind alone, and cannot be described, for It has neither class, form, nor distinction (γένος, εἶδος, διαφορά). Freudenthal[1] sees in this latter point an important advance toward the Neo-Platonic doctrine of the indescribable character of God which was expressed by Plotinus: καὶ γὰρ λέγομεν ὃ μὴ ἐστιν, ὃ δέ ἐστιν οὐ λέγομεν.[2] Deity transcends all distinctions, even moral distinctions Thus to say that It is good is as inaccurate as to say that It is evil, says Albinus, basing his argument on the Platonic doctrine that for anything to be good or bad it must be preceded by and partake in the Good or the Bad Deity cannot be good or bad because Deity precedes the Forms and is above them, hence cannot be qualified by participating in them Deity is good in the sense that It causes good to others, but in Itself is neither good nor bad Likewise It transcends both the possession or lack of quality, as well as the distinction between Same and Other Deity neither moves nor is moved, It is immaterial, does not occupy space, is unchangeable and unbegotten It is clear that Albinus has constructed a conception of an absolute God from Aristotelian and Platonic statements together The result is a Deity, much more clearly defined than the Deity of either, but very fairly in harmony with the few statements about Deity in the Philebus as well as with the Unmoved Mover, who is νοῦς. of Aristotle's Metaphysics

In the same passage Albinus goes on to describe three ways in which Deity can be apprehended by men[3] The first is by Abstraction from the sensible world, as one comes to conceive of a mathematical point by ascending from a surface to a line, and from a line to a point The second is by Analogy, comparing the Primal Mind, for example, to the sun by which we are able to see, though the sun is not itself the sense of sight. So the Primal Mind by enlightening the truth furnishes knowledge and the object of knowledge to man's soul, though It is not Itself the faculty of knowledge in man By such analogies, one may come

[1] p 287 n. 1
[2] Enn V. 3 14
[3] X 165 line 13 ff

to understand and comprehend the Deity. The third process is by Generalization of the specific qualities of individual objects So, Albinus illustrates, one rises from a perception of beauty in bodily objects to a conception of beauty in the soul, thence to beauty in actions and laws, and thence to a conception of Beauty itself, τὸ πολὺ πέλαγος τοῦ καλοῦ.[1] It is hard to see how this method differs essentially from the first method, that of Abstraction, unless the process of Abstraction is to deal exclusively with mathematical symbols, the Pythagorean method, while the other is to deal with general qualities as found in common objects. On that basis the process of Abstraction would be an essentially intellectual process, the other primarily a mystical ladder, much more popular with ordinary people. We shall find that it is this last method which Justin seems to have been using as a Platonist, when he was enchanted, as he says, by the contemplation of Forms and of general conceptions, and hoped soon to rise to the contemplation of God Himself. Both Albinus and Justin show that God in Platonism was conceived of as higher than the Universal Good, the Idea of the Good. One had to rise above all Universals to find Deity, not merely rise to the highest Universal.

The Deity is thus sufficiently abstracted from all things terrestrial. Its connection with the Cosmos is described as mediated by lower deities, the highest of which is ὁ νοῦς τοῦ σύμπαντος οὐρανοῦ.[2] This νοῦς is not the Primal νοῦς the First Cause. Νοῦς, Albinus says, is better than ψυχή; and νοῦς, actually thinking of all things at the same time and eternally (ὁ κατ' ἐνέργειαν πάντα νοῶν καὶ ἅμα καὶ ἀεί), is better than potential νοῦς, while the Cause of this actual universal intelligence is still better than that which is caused. The Cause is ὁ πρῶτος νοῦς, and that caused is the mind of the whole heavens, which consequently is a mind thinking actively of all things simultaneously and eternally, as distinguished from the Primal Mind which thinks only Itself and Its own thoughts The thoughts of the Heavenly Mind are apparently the Forms of the early Plato. When

[1] Cf Plato, Symposium 210. d. (Freudenthal p. 286).
[2] X 164 line 23

Albinus descends from the Heavenly Mind to the World Soul, he has obviously in mind the passage of the Philebus already discussed in which Plato says that νοῦς is not conceivable apart from a ψυχή, so that if there is a βασιλικὸς νοῦς there must be also a βασιλικὴ ψυχή. Albinus identifies the βασιλικὴ ψυχή of the Philebus with the ψυχὴ τοῦ κόσμου of the Timaeus However, although Albinus joins the βασιλικὸς νοῦς, which he calls the Heavenly Mind, with the World Soul, the union may not have been eternal, for the existence of the World Soul began in its present form from an act of creation, while the activity of the Heavenly Mind seems to have been eternal, though not so eternal as not itself to have been caused by the Primal Mind of Deity. The relative times of generation are very confusing, for Albinus gives no account of the origin of the Heavenly Mind. The World Soul, however, is eternal in a certain sense Albinus becomes very mystical when he speaks of the first ordering of the World, because he is working from a presupposition of the eternity of matter, and yet does not, for some reason, wish to express the doctrine explicitly He insists upon the eternity of the World, and then hastens to say that he does not mean the world in its present form There was never a time in which the World did not exist, yet the World was begotten, eternally begotten, if you will Similarly the Soul of the World always existed. God had only to awaken it and order it (κατακοσμεῖ), and give it its νοῦς. The world as consisting of σῶμα and ψυχή is a living thing (ζῶον), and is eternal in both its σῶμα and ψυχή. though God had to order both before the world as we know it existed Albinus probably, in Aristotelian language, would have agreed that in the eternal material substrate there existed the potentiality of both World Body and World Soul, potentialities which became actualities when the World Body was ordered, and when the World Soul was ordered and awakened as from a deep sleep The World Soul was at the same time made intelligent by being united with the Heavenly Mind. The united Soul-Mind of the universe had now but to look to its own thoughts to find the Ideas and Forms which constitute the Ideal World

The next step in creation was to make the World Body

by ordering matter, which had theretofore been an un-ordered chaos First the four elements were separated out, then Deity made the world, only begotten (μονογενῆ τὸν κόσμον),[1] using up the totality of matter (ἐκ τῆς πάσης ὅλης).[2] In describing the process of creation Albinus uses the geo-metrical and arithmetical language of the Timaeus, and from the same source states that the different parts of the universe, the stars, spheres, planets, are intelligent living beings, gods.[3] The Soul-Mind was now put into the World Body, so that the World, as constituted of soul and body, is itself a living being (ζῷον) while by virtue of the Heavenly Mind in the World Soul, the World is also endowed with the power of thought (νοερόν).

But one more act remained to Deity in creation, that of making the lower gods and demons, "whom one should call 'begotten gods'," [4] to be found in all the elements To these was entrusted the formation and rule of the sublunary world. They took as their patterns the Intelligible World, but gave form to individual objects on earth by causing these objects not to partake of the Eternal Forms, but to imitate them The forms in the individual objects are quite distinct from the Eternal Forms, and perish with the objects. Τὰ νοητά, says Albinus,[5] are of two sorts, first αἱ ἰδέαι (by which he meant the Separable and Eternal Forms), and second τὰ εἴδη which are inseparable in matter. Albi-nus is not unique in making this distinction between εἴδη and ἰδέαι, for Seneca had already used it, and it was prob-ably one of the usual ways of attempting to reconcile the early Platonic theory of Separable Forms with Aristotle's assertions that form is the inseparable concomitant of in-dividual phenomena [6] But Albinus is not consistent in his later use of these terms.[7]

[1] XI p 167 line 11
[2] XI p 167 line 33
[3] XIV p 171 line 11.
[4] XV p 171. line 13
[5] IV p 155 line 34
[6] See Zeller II i (1922) 658 Anm 2 Engl Tr Plato, p 238 n 32
[7] V p 157 line 10 Here εἴδη includes both kinds of forms

Of the constitution of man Albinus teaches like Plato that the human body is the creation of the lower deities out of the four elements, of which they borrowed certain parts on the understanding that the loan was to be repaid. They put the parts of the elements together with invisible nails, and so made a single unified body [1] The higher part of the soul of man they did not make, for they received it after it had been sent down from the first God [2] This part of the soul had been prepared by Deity in the same mixing bowl in which the World Soul had been composed,[3] so that the human soul and the World Soul were of similar natures [4] However, the lower gods did not put the soul into the body as they received it from Deity, for Albinus says that they created two mortal soul parts which they combined with the immortal soul The first part of the soul is thus essentially different from the other two parts, called will and desire, since they are both in the realm of the impressionable, παθητικόν, and are to be found in animals, while the higher part is the reasoning force in man (τὸ λογιστικόν). Albinus feels that reason in the highest sense has no kinship with passivity or impressionability, but is pure activity The lower and higher parts of the soul are so utterly unlike that it would mean incessant warfare if they were situated in the same parts of the body, so that the creating gods separated the parts of the soul, put the highest part into the head where it would be safely isolated, and the two lower parts into the chest and abdomen respectively Albinus is of course perfectly Platonic in his division of the soul and distribution of the parts in the head and body, but he goes beyond Plato in the contrast between the παθητικόν and the

---

[1] XVII p 172 line 17 ff. οἱ δὲ θεοὶ ἔπλασαν μὲν προηγου-μένως τὸν ἄνθρωπον ἐκ γῆς καὶ πυρὸς καὶ ἀέρος καὶ ὕδατος μοίρας τίνας δανειζόμενοι εἰς ἀπόδοσιν, συνθέντος δὲ ἀοράτοις γόμφοις ἕν τι σῶμα ἐργασάμενοι, a paraphrase of Tim 42 e ff Albinus continues to borrow from the same source to describe the con-stitution of the various parts of the body

[2] XVII p 172 line 20, XXIII p 176 line 8

[3] Following Timaeus 41 d

[4] XXV p 178 line 15 ff

λογιστικόν. For while Plato admits the utter dissimilarity of the two, he nowhere hints at a fundamental antagonism. Plato taught that the lower part is rebellious and needs to be repressed by the higher, and that the higher is put into the safe isolation of the head to preserve its purity, but he gives no indication that the two are kept apart because their mere juxtaposition would mean warfare [1] The distinction is a fine one, but is indication of the contemporary tendency to cheapen all the parts of man except the divine and immortal part of the soul Plato, while teaching the complete superiority of the highest part of the soul, taught at the same time that the soul was best nourished and developed when all its parts were functioning normally. But the Platonists of Albinus' time tended to forget the sane balance of their master in an all engrossing desire for mystical experience.

Albinus comes very near to introducing the double νοῦς of Aristotle when he discusses the various sorts of mental activity possible to man.[2] The power of judgment, ἡ κρίσις, is double, consisting of the active force which does the judging, which he calls ὁ ἐν ἡμῖν νοῦς, and the natural organ or implement of judgment, by using which the νοῦς acts, and which is itself called ὁ λόγος φυσικός. There are two kinds of reason, or logos. the first is possible only to God, for it is in every way inerrant and incomprehensible, but the second, which is possible to man, is also inerrant in its knowledge of facts.[3] But the human logos is also of two kinds, that which is concerned with Intelligible Things (τὰ νοητά), and that which is concerned with sensible things (τὰ αἰσθητά), of which the first is knowledge proper (ἐπιστημή, or, νόησις), and the other opinion (δόξα). Albinus thus distinguishes between the νοῦς active and the logos passive, for the logos is active only as the νοῦς acts through it, and is itself only an ὄργανον. The distinction is not merely that of Plato between knowledge and opinion, for

---

[1] Tim. 69 c ff

[2] IV pp. 154—156.

[3] κατὰ τὴν τῶν πραγμάτων γνῶσιν ἀδιάψευστος IV p 154 line 19

the logos deals with both δόξα and ἐπιστημή, but its motive force is not in itself but in the νοῦς. But knowledge, as contrasted with opinion, is still of two kinds, that possible to be gained in the body, and that possible of acquisition only for disembodied souls For when the soul is disembodied, the mind, by means of the logos, can have a vision of the Primary Intelligibles, by which Albinus meant the Separable Forms He lays considerable stress upon the fact that the mind does not judge of or apprehend the Primary Intelligibles apart from Logos [1] The two must function together, or neither is of any use, even in the disembodied vision of Primary Intelligibles The second kind of knowledge is that which apprehends the Secondary Intelligibles, by which he means the inseparable forms as found in material objects To this second knowledge he assigns the Stoic term φυσικὴ ἔννοια. It springs, he says, from a latent knowledge of the Primary Intelligibles which the soul, by a process analogous to memory though not accurately so called, has carried on into its incarnate state [2] It is to be inferred from what Albinus says that during the incarnation the νοῦς by means of the logos can hope adequately to comprehend only the lower inseparable forms

The mixture of Aristotelian and Platonic elements with Stoic terminology in this passage on the human mind hardly needs elucidation. When Albinus speaks of the latent knowledge of Universals one feels the influence of Aristotle; when he uses the word "memory" to account for the presence of this latent knowledge and bases all upon a pre-incarnate existence of the soul, he is indubitably Platonic It is clear that Albinus conceived of the higher human soul which was sent down from the First Deity to the lower creating gods as constituted of two parts, the νοῦς, the active intelligent force, and the logos or passive instrument of the νοῦς. The logos is by no means the material brain, for by it νοῦς thinks during its pre-incarnate existence. The logos seems to be in a sense the ψυχή of

[1] IV. p 156 line 4 ff.
[2] IV p 155 line 24 νόησίς τις οὖσα ἐναποκειμένη τῇ ψυχῇ.

the νοῦς, and was probably what Plato had in mind when he said that νοῦς could not exist apart from a ψυχή. The logos also corresponds in many points to the lower νοῦς of Aristotle, except that Aristotle connected the lower νοῦς inseparably with the body, and said that the lower νοῦς and body perished together. Albinus' doctrine seems to have drawn upon Aristotle for the functions of the active and passive νόες, or νοῦς and logos as he called them, but he remained Platonic in assuming the immortality of both

In his descriptions of the pre-existence of the soul, of its destiny at death, of its re-incarnation in women or lower animals in case of its failure to prove worthy of restoration to its former place and state in the stars, Albinus follows the Timaeus very closely, and need not be elucidated It has been clearly shown by Freudenthal[1] that Albinus in his logic and ethic follows Aristotle and the Stoics much more than he does Plato, though he uses Platonic passages to illustrate the doctrines of the other schools One feels on the whole that Albinus is more than half way from Plato to the Neo-Platonists His philosophy is much more mystical than that of Plato, though not yet so mystical as that of Plotinus To him the human body still is a reputable part of the human constitution, to be improved by exercise and training, but it has been pointed out that the importance of bodily training is much less real in Albinus' mind than in Plato's He has made more vivid than Plato the existence of the Heavenly Mind and the World Soul, and yet these conceptions were advanced still further in the next century Like the Neo-Platonists he is strongly eclectic He does not say, as did they, that Plato and Aristotle taught the same philosophy, but he feels perfectly free to use Aristotelian conceptions whenever they can contribute to his system Yet he has no criteria for borrowing Since he does not admit frankly that Aristotle and Plato are in his mind teaching the same doctrine, he makes no attempt seriously to combine them, but merely draws upon

[1] p 278 ff

Aristotle when he feels disposed to do so Another Platonist might draw more, another less, while the capricious admixture of Pythagorean and Stoic conceptions must have varied greatly among his contemporaries His philosophy in inspiration and motive is frankly mystical He defines philosophy as ' the aspiration for wisdom, or the loosing and wrenching of the soul away from the body, when we turn ourselves to the Intelligible and the true Existences".[1] His pupils must have found in his teaching chiefly a training in mysticism The passages in which Albinus treats of the constitution of the world are so extensively and literally taken from the Timaeus, that one wonders whether he understood the descriptions of his master, and was not simply rounding out his own system by borrowed statements largely unintelligible even to himself. Of his metaphysical conceptions, those of the soul of man, of the World Soul, and of the Heavenly Mind most seemed to bear the impress of his own thinking, and these he consequently would most sharply have impressed upon the minds of his pupils Superficial dabblers in his system would have received the impression of a mystical doctrine in which they would first learn about the Heavenly Mind and World Soul, understanding that these were both transcended by the Absolute They would then have understood that their own souls were akin to or a part of this Universal Mind-Soul, and would have enlivened the whole by speculation upon pre-existence and metempsychosis It is precisely such a Platonism which we shall find described by Justin Martyr.

An attempt at depicting the philosophical situation in the world at Justin's time would, however, be completely inaccurate if it stopped at trying to reconstruct the close metaphysical thinking of the schools. For there has probably never been an age when philosophy was so familiar a topic for the street corner and barber shop as during this decadent period of Greek Philosophy Everyone could readily talk the philosophical jargon of his day, so that no normal child would have grown up in a

[1] I p 152. line 2

Greek city (including the cities of Greek culture throughout
the eastern part of the Mediterranean basin), without
acquiring the vocabulary of, and accustoming himself to
taking a part in, popular philosophical discussions.

But if such ignorant and untrained people were freely
talking of philosophy and the philosophic schools, it must
not be supposed that the discussions were not thoroughly
ignorant. The superstition and unchecked fancy of ignorance
together with an utterly uncritical use of suggestions from
the mythologies and religions of foreign travellers, produced
harangues in the name of philosophic schools which must
have been completely contrary to the aims and conceptions
with which the schools were founded. To satisfy the desires
of such people, and incidentally to profit by the large fees
they were ready to pay for short terms of easy instruction
which would enable them to boast of specialized philosophic training, the leaders of the schools themselves
taught "exoteric" doctrines, or philosophy for the unphilosophical, which took the form largely of cosmological
myths and accounts of creation, with rudimentary instruction in mysticism and ethical theory. The urge to mysticism,
together with the popular craze for cosmological myths
had opened the door wide for the mystery religions of
the East. These had added their large mythical elements
to the Greek traditions, while both were supplemented
by the fabricated myths of the philosophers.

It is not to be wondered at that in such an atmosphere
the Divine Νοῦς or Logos, as defined by the philosophers,
became, like all abstractions, personalities in a sort of
philosophical theogony, which graduated down to the most
insignificant demons. Such was the popular philosophical
environment of Justin, a welter of crude superstitions
expressed in myth and in snatches of philosophical terminology. At the same time a few higher spirits were
trying to keep pure the better traditions of philosophy,
while at least the leaders of the Platonic and Pythagorean
schools were driven by a profound desire to find peace
in a mystical communion with God.

CHAPTER II

JUDAISM

At the time of the origin of Christianity Judaism had long been developing on two distinct lines which may perhaps be called Judaism proper and Hellenistic Judaism None of the terms used for these two schools of Judaism adequately describes them Geographical terms such as Palestinian and Alexandrian have a connotation of localism by which the actual developments were not at all limited Of the two types of Judaism one had its center in Palestine, the other in Alexandria, but the first was also present very strongly among the Jews throughout the Dispersion, while the Jews whose Judaism was affected to a greater or less degree by Hellenistic speculation were present in appreciable numbers even in Palestine itself. Nor were the two developments mutually exclusive. True Jews, however deeply influenced by heathenism, always had at least a genuine regard for the Law, while Greek terminology is to be found even in the earliest tradition of the Tannaim But though the two tendencies were not mutually exclusive, they represented attitudes of mind fundamentally different from each other

A PALESTINIAN JUDAISM

Palestinian Judaism, or Judaism proper, was primarily characterized by its legalism and by the clarity and simplicity of its religious impulses, as well as by its intensely personal relationship with God.

It has been seen that when the Greeks were at their best they were scientists and their Deity was the Absolute, or in any case utterly impersonal But when the Jews

were at their best they were loving children of a kind
Father, to serve Whom was life's supreme joy because of
the intense reality of His personal existence, and the
vividness of their faith. The Jewish instinct for monotheism
by the time of Jesus had long been fundamental and
distinctive. The Greek philosophers strove to reduce all
things to Unity under a single ultimate First Cause which
they called among other names God, but at the same
time they never scrupled to talk of lower beings as gods
in a sense very much above the nature of the ordinary
demons and powers. The Jews recognised angels and
demons of all kinds about them, to be sure, but so far
as we know they gave to none of them sufficient prestige
so that they should be worshipped. Worship belonged to
the one God alone. The Jewish schoolmen went further
and denied the independent existence of angels, saying
that all celestial beings were merely rays from the glory
of God. These rays were of two kinds, the passing and
the permanent.[1] The temporary or transient angels came
forth each day afresh in great multitudes, sang songs of
praise to God, and then perished or were recalled into
the glory whence they had come. Justin probably represented a good Jewish tradition about the permanent angels
when he said that they were rays from the glory of God
which it was the will of God not to recall.[2] Bentwich
has pointed out that the Jews regarded the permanent
angels not as independent existences but as personifications
of the one God in his dealings with the world.[3]

Similarly the personifications of Memra, Torah, and Wisdom, like the Bath Kol and Shechina, were never conceived
of by the Jews as minor deities, if the Jews ever thought
of them as actual personalities at all. The Jewish love for
heavenly descriptions was even stronger than the Greek
as the Semite has always been pre-eminently a visionary
who told abstractions in concrete language. So in the

[1] Ferdinand Weber: Judische Theologie auf Grund des Talmud
und verwandten Schriften. Leipzig 1897. p. 166.

[2] Dialogue 128. 3. 4 (358 B, C) see below pp. 189 ff.

[3] Norman Bentwich. Philo Judaeus of Alexandria. Philadelphia
1910. pp. 141 ff.

early references to Wisdom, for example, as found in the Canonical books of the Old Testament, nothing more than Semitic imagery and literary personification can legitimately be inferred.[1] That the Jews at the time when the best Psalms were being written actually thought of a mediatory deity or person as necessary to link the world with a transcendent God, would need far more evidence than exists to make credible. Perhaps by Jesus' time, certainly by a century later, the Rabbis were influenced by Greek-Jewish Wisdom speculation to develop the Wisdom personification in the eighth chapter of Proverbs into what is apparently intended as a separate person. But if a Wisdom personality was later intended, it never constituted an important element in the essential teachings of the Judaism of the Schools. Wisdom was highly important, as will appear, in Hellenistic Judaism, but had little importance in the Palestinian Judaism of Jesus time. Indeed the importance ascribed to Wisdom and similar conceptions is one of the distinguishing differences between the two types of judaism. Similarly, highly figurative as the language in the Talmud grew about the Torah, Schechter is quite right in insisting that no personalization of the Torah was ever seriously intended by the Rabbis.[2]

The monotheism of Palestinian Judaism was thus never broken by any conception of lower intermediary deities. The prejudice against minor deities, indeed, had come to be one of the most deeply rooted of all Jewish religious instincts, so that the representation of Jesus as possessing divine character in any sense was in Jewish eyes the fundamental heresy of Christianity.

Christians have rarely done justice to Judaism in its legalistic aspects. For those not trained in a legalistic religion, the Law would seem to crush all spontaneous expression of religious impulses. This difficulty has been

[1] Cf Ernst Sellin. Die Spuren griechischer Philosophie im Alten Testament Leipzig 1905 pp. 17, 18. Sellin's dissertation is an answer to M Friedlander: Griechische Philosophie im Alten Testament Berlin 1904

[2] Some Aspects of Rabbinical Theology, in Jewish Quarterly Review VIII. 9.

immeasurably enlarged by the invectives of Jesus against the Pharisees, and the protests of St. Paul against the inadequacy of legalism. But both Jesus and St. Paul were addressing people who understood the circumstances perfectly. Jesus especially would have been understood by his hearers as condemning corrupt Pharisaism, rather than the Pharisees as a class. As in the case of all earnest reformers, their denunciations give a very distorted impression of the system underlying the abuses they are attacking, so that unless checked by the remains of Judaism itself their statements incline to be misleading.[1] The testimony of Judaism itself as to the spiritual value of legalism is of an entirely different character. The Jews thought of God in positive and definite terms, and believed that His will and pleasure for the conduct of men went into the most intimate details of every day life. There was a right and wrong way to do everything. This right and wrong way God had revealed to the Jews in the Law as their supreme mark of distinction, for once in its possession they alone were in a position adequately to know and to do the will of God. To the true Jew, and probably to most Jews, the observances of the Law were hourly reminders of the goodness of God who had so far honored Israel as to reveal this His divine way of living to them. The motive of obedience to the Law was not fear but grateful love.

It was upon this foundation of spiritual enthusiasm for the Law that the scholarship of Rabbinism was built, for to a pious Jew no higher scholarship was conceivable than that which could explain in ever increasing minutiae how the Law of God could be applied to the most detailed incidents of life. So when the Jewish Schoolmen multiplied the great number of precepts and by-laws by casuistery they had no idea, nor had pious Jews, that a burden was being increased. Rather did it seem to all that the joy of observance was being extended. Each

---

[1] Schürer is an outstanding instance of a great scholar who allowed the invectives of Jesus and Paul against the Pharisees and legalism completely to warp his understanding of Rabbinical Literature.

new definition was a new revelation in the sense that it increased the scope of an old revelation

Palestinian Judaism was however sharply split within itself between the learned and the ignorant. There was no hereditary caste system in Palestine expect the High Priestly circle, but there was the sharpest distinction between a peasant and a scholar.[1] The ordinary people seem to have been in many cases deeply pious, to have attended the feasts at Jerusalem whenever possible, and to have had a genuine reverence for the Law But the small training which the synagogue school gave to every Jewish boy, even though helped out by the weekly sermon of the synagogue, kept the masses, the Am Ha-ares, in only the most rudimentary touch with the legal code These people envied and reverenced the leisure and learning of the scribes which enabled them to know the Law in its detail, and regarded such a condition as the most happy a human being could enjoy But for people with heavy common work to do no such life was possible. The attitude still survives occasionally among orthodox Jews. The writer will never forget hearing a young Jewish truckman speak of those who had leisure and opportunity to study and observe the will of God He, he wistfully said, had no time for such practices At night he was too tired to study He had to disregard fasts because his heavy work demanded nourishing food But life and hope for Heaven must seem entirely different to one privileged to spend his time in religious study

The dividing line between learned and ignorant was sharpened by the fact that the scholastic definitions of the Law were made by professional legal scholars who had their own needs in mind much more than the conditions of hard working people Further, intercourse between a clean Jew and an unclean Jew was proscribed and carefully avoided by the meticulous, and since it was a safe assumption that a working man had done in ignorance something

[1] See the valuable note by Professor G F Moore. The Am Ha-Ares and the Haberim, in Jackson and Lake The Beginnings of Christianity, I i London 1920 App E pp 436—445

that made him unclean, the avoidance of ordinary people
by the professional religious classes must early have become a permanent habit. This was however perfectly
understood and approved by all classes. The doors of the
rabbinical schools were always open to sons of these unclean masses, and many of the greatest Rabbis, notably
Akiba, came from such an origin. But once in the inner
circle a man must live the life of the inner circle or
automatically, by his uncleanness, necessitate his ejection.

No greater mistake could be made, however, than to
suppose that these associations of learned and careful
observers of the Law were made up exclusively of self-
righteous hypocrites. The literature which this group built
up through the centuries, while difficult for Christians to
understand, is yet one of the greatest and deepest religious
expressions in human history. It would be impossible that
such a circle of scholars, with its social prestige among the
Jews, should not have attracted many unworthy men, but
that it did so is no reflection upon the ideals, motives, and
value of the schools.

In general, the distinctive spirit of Palestinian Judaism
was its loyalty and love to the one personal God, and its
conviction that in the Law it possessed a verbally inspired
revelation of the will of God. God was to be pleased, the
Jews were convinced, by the minute observances of His
commands, and in performing this office devout Jews
carried into every department of their lives all the spiritual
uplift of a divinely appointed cultus. Strict Jews never
had any sympathy with the half proselytes, "God fearers",
so numerous in the Dispersion, who thought to get benefit
from the pious spirit of Judaism without assuming the
obligation of the Law. Rabbi Jose said that such would be
laughed to scorn by God in the Messianic Age, if they
claimed any share in the portion of true Jews[1] As
Dr Abrahams has recently pointed out,[2] to carry into

[1] Abodah zarah 3 b From J Klausner: Die messianischen
Vorstellungen des judischen Volkes im Zeitalter der Tannaisten
Berlin, 1904. pp 83 ff.

[2] Studies in Pharisaism and the Gospels, First Series Camb
1917 Preface, p vii

Judaism the Pauline distinction between spirit and letter is completely to misunderstand Judaism, because in "orthodox" tradition Judaism has never had the slightest recognition for such a distinction. When God had given the letter, it was not for man to stop to distinguish between the letter and the spirit The Jew found profound spirituality in the fulfillment of the letter

But simple as the fundamental spirit of Judaism was, it was complicated by being a religion of expectation, and was still more complicated in Jesus' time by the fact that instead of the original expectation which hoped only for prosperity for the Jewish race, now the newly substantiated belief in a personal survival of death was developing many speculative attempts to explain how all Jews, alive or dead, could share in the coming Age With some the national element of the expectation was stressed, so that they looked for an Age in which Israel should be the ruler of the physical world Others looked for a time when all the world would accept the obligation of the Law and become Jews At the same time different and contradictory ideas of a resurrection or resurrections were being explained in such a way as to make all men sharers in the Age to come, true Jews in its blessedness, the others in its horrors Always expressing their intense patriotism in love of liberty and ambition to rule others, the spirit of the Jews was at the exploding point in Jesus' time because of their holy hatred of Roman aggression The focus of discontent was not Jerusalem but Galilee. The Jewish rulers in Jerusalem were educated men who were faring very comfortably as heads of the Jewish cultus But the less sophisticated Galileans boiled with a fanatic desire for rebellion which was the hourly concern of the Roman rulers as well as of the leading Jews in Jerusalem

It was in such an environment of simple piety, of religion which was expressing itself fundamentally in an effort to please a beloved Father in the conduct of life, and of a patriotism which was enflamed and fevered to the point of delirious vision, that Christianity was born When exaggerated patriotism, as is usually the case, had utterly ruined the object of its loyalty, the Christianity

which had tried like its Master to remain a part of the
Jewish national religion rapidly dwindled into insigni-
ficance By Justin Martyr's day, as Harnack points out,[1]
the appeal of Jewish legalism to Christianity had lost all
its force; the Dialogue with Trypho is not a genuine discussion, but the monologue of a victor It is in the realm
of Hellenistic Judaism that this change becomes intelligible.

B. HELLENISTIC JUDAISM

The spirit and problems of the Jews in the Dispersion
in places where their contact with Greek thought had been
at all close were entirely different from those in Palestine.
They found themselves in the situation of having a religious
ideal which in their environment was utterly incapable of
fulfillment, even when the will to do so was not complicated
by the lure of many ideas of the people about them   In
strange countries then as now Jews tended to form colonies
in which a social life could be created that would rule out
all unnecessary contact with the impure Gentiles, and in
which they could help each other observe the Law. But
their success was only partial; for Judaism no longer seemed
to them to be the uniquely correct teaching about God.
The ordinary Palestinian Jew, in little contact with other
religions, maintained his Judaism almost unchallenged. But
the Jews in Alexandria, Tarsus, or Ephesus heard men
talking metaphysics and describing cosmological schemes
on all sides, and were attracted by many of the heathen
conceptions in spite of themselves. It was not long that
Jews were thus exposed before a gradual but persistent
protest of syncretism had begun   The early demand for a
Greek translation of the Old Testament which resulted
in the Septuagint meant that the Jewish language had so
far lost its hold that at least a large body of Jews could
not understand the original. That is they were a Greek
speaking, rather than a Hebrew sepaking people, who had
apparently lost all language tradition of their own, and
were familiar only with the language of the Gentile world
about them.

[1] (Bibl 395) p 92

The literature of Hellenistic Judaism came thus to have
a double foundation. In theory Hellenistic Jews thought
themselves orthodox, and were intensely proud of their
racial inheritance of legalism, but apologetic and personal
interest constantly impelled them toward a philosophic
adaptation of Judaism to the thinking of the Gentile world,
and in the process many Jewish conceptions were radically
changed The Jews in the Dispersion grew into the cosmic
sense of the Greeks. The highest achievment of Old Testament prophetic monotheism had been to declare that Je-
hovah was the one God of all men, while the conception
that He ruled the physical universe was taken for granted
and given little thought But when a Jew met the scientific
Greek whose leaders had been inspired to speculation
chiefly by the problem of the unification of cosmic phenomena, he found that while the God of his fathers met
his religious needs, yet his religion had no scientific tradition at all, and needed a great deal of interpreting in terms
of Greek thought to meet the interesting questions which
his neighbors were discussing The sense of the inadequacy
of Judaism for science may well have come very gradually,
and approaches toward a re-interpretation of Judaism may
have been made quite unconsciously, but nevertheless the
adaptation of Judaism to its environment in centers of
Greek culture was profoundly significant

     One of the first important changes must have been
in the direction of a more cosmic conception of God The
Jewish worshipper held to his God the Father, but the new
Jewish thinker, usually the same man as the worshipper,
began to put God ever farther back toward transcendent-
alism and the Absolute. The simple and utterly un-
scientific myths of creation in the first two chapters of
Genesis were "adapted" to the theories of the Stoics and
Platonists, while the Wisdom of Proverbs was identified with the cosmic force which we have seen the philosophers were calling either νοῦς, or λογος or ψυχὴ τοῦ κόσμου.
There is not space in this connection to trace the doctrine
of Wisdom in detail as it developed in Judaism In Sirach
a long stride appears already to have been taken, for when
the writer says that he wishes to explain to the "lovers

of learning' how the Hebrew scriptures may meet their
needs, and ultimately suggests the solution in the identification of Wisdom and Law, he implies that Wisdom had
already become a philosophic term useful for those interested in Greek thought.[1] At the same time Law was
approaching the Stoic νόμος, which was a manifestation or
aspect of the Logos, so that Law had also clearly become
more universal a conception than the precepts of the Mosaic Code. The philosophic character of Sophia, as found
in the Wisdom of Solomon, is quite indisputable. It is a
matter of dispute how deeply read in Greek philosophy its
author could have been, but that he uses σοφία, λόγος, θεός,
ψυχή, πνεῦμα, τὰ πάντα, etc., in truly Greek meanings is
patent. In the Wisdom of Solomon God appears, especially
in the first ten chapters, to be transcendent. He created
the world in the presence and with the help of Wisdom,
which thereafter extends through and permeates the Universe; by Her presence the order of Creation is preserved.[2]
Wisdom is called interchangeably σοφία, πνεῦμα σοφίας, λόγος,
and ἀτμὶς τῆς τοῦ θεοῦ δυνάμεως.[3] At one time Wisdom
seems Herself to be πνεῦμα,[4] at other times, and more consistently, Wisdom contains a πνεῦμα, by which the author
seems to mean that phase of Wisdom which can be imparted to others.[5] The author says he has been granted
the πνεῦμα σοφίας, which seems here to be a free and
special gift. Wisdom is universally present, but the impart-
ing of the πνεῦμα σοφίας implies a unique empowering with
the faculty of reason. The author does not try to connect
this in any consistent way with a doctrine of human psychology. While usually the personality of Wisdom is clearly
implied,[6] occasionally the author uses figures of speech
utterly incompatible with a personal conception, as for

---

[1] Sirach, Prologue, and xxiv 22 ff. See also Friedlander,
Griechische Philosophie im A. T., p 166, and Holtzmann, as quoted
in Friedlander, p 175—176.

[2] Wisd. vii 24, viii 1.

[3] Wisd. vii 25.

[4] Wisd 1 6.

[5] Wisd vii 22.

[6] e g ix. 4 etc

example when he speaks of Wisdom as a "clear effluence
of the power of the Almighty, and effulgence from everlasting light, an unspotted mirror of the working of God,
and image of his goodness" [1] The author is Platonic in
passages, as when he speaks of building the temple in
imitation of the "holy tabernacle which thou hast prepared
from the beginning," [2] and in his doctrine of the pre-
existence of souls, and the relative defiling power of different bodies [3] On the other hand he is strongly Jewish in
identifying Wisdom with the Jewish Law [4] The writer seems
indeed to be no philosopher, but to be interested in claiming
philosophy for the service of Judaism by identifying the
νοῦς-λόγος doctrines of philosophy with the poetic Wisdom
of the Jews, which he does by describing Wisdom in all
the catch words of philosophy which he can muster and
apply. The Book of Wisdom has none of the earmarks
of being a pioneer. The few fragments preserved from
Aristobulus and Aristaeus may well represent original speculation, but speculation is not a characteristic of the Book
of Wisdom It is a book of devotion and aspiration such as
could only have come from a man whose convictions had far
outrun the stage of speculation, while it could only have
been received by people who took for granted the doctrines
upon which it is based. It is pre-eminently a religious book.
Not a trace of argument or demonstration mars the mystical
song of prayer and praise to God and Wisdom. Its date is
uncertain. Probably Holmes is right in putting it in the
last fifty years before Christ, it is almost certainly pre-
Pauline, if not pre-Philonic. [5] But the book clearly indicates
that at whatever time it was written, so universal a belief in
Wisdom as a cosmic force and personality obtained, that
a book of devotion based upon it could be written and soon
widely accepted among the Jews of the Dispersion.

[1] Wisdom vii 25, 26. Holmes translation in Charles: Apo-
crypha and Pseudep

   [2] Wisdom ix 8

   [3] Wisdom viii 20

   [4] Wisdom vi 18

   [5] In Charles Apoc and Pseudep. p 521, cf p. 526

The great Jewish philosopher Philo is thus no unique
figure in Jewish theology, nor can he be taken as attempting
de novo to bridge the gap between Hellenism and Judaism
His allegorical method and doctrine of the dependance of
Greek philosophers upon Moses are already found in Aristobulus;[1] his identification of Wisdom with the cosmic
λόγος or νοῦς of the Greeks was a popular by-word; and his
choice of Platonism as the best Greek philosophy, with
many borrowings from Aristotelian and Stoic schools,
appears in his predecessors, though Aristobulus was traditionally a Peripatetic[2] But Philo is the only philosopher
of Judaism whose writings we possess in any detail, and
consequently the only one whose system we can hope to
reconstruct He was far deeper a philosopher than most
Hellenistic Jews, and probably refined Hellenistic Judaism
on many points far beyond the reach of its ordinary
followers But fundamentally Philo's point of view was
typically that of his school

Some Jews went much further than Philo in that they
discredited the Law for the greater glorification of Philosophy. A trace of their point of view is still to be found
in Philo's "De Migratione Abrahami,"[3] where he mentions
people who are not content with the race which loves God,
but must try to live according to both human and divine
standards. Philo never once allowed himself to admit any
inadequacy in the Law He insisted that all truth could be
found in the Law when read in its deeper significance, and
because he thus retained the legal tradition, even though
he departed in many doctrines from the teachings of the
Palestinian Jews, he represents a truly Jewish mode of
thought. Because of the importance of Hellenistic Judaism
for an understanding of the doctrines of Justin Martyr,
and because of the representative character of Philo's

[1] Euseb. Prep. Ev. VIII. x p 376 b ff , XIII. xii p 664 a ff
[2] Euseb Prep. Ev. VIII. ix p 375 d
[3] 158 (I. 461). See also 89 (I. 450). For fuller discussion
of such sects see Friedländer: Synagoge und Kirche, pp 70—121.
Friedländer sees in these sects precursors, if not actual founders
of Gnosticism See also Friedländer: Der vorchristliche judische
Gnosticismus

writings, it will be no digression to attempt very briefly to describe the metaphysical principles upon which Philo based his system

That Philo was personally much influenced by Persian speculation is highly improbable though the early Wisdom conception of Judaism may well have been inspired from such a source [1] Philo is pre-eminently an eclectic Greek in his thinking, and a Jew in his piety He was trying to do what few people have done so well, to join, in some degree of consistency, his philosophy with his religious impulses To him the Judaism of the synagogue, or rather of the Old Testament, with its myths was intellectual child's play, while the speculations and sporadic mysticism of the philosophic cults utterly failed to satisfy his genuine religious genius It is quite correct to think of him as a Greek philosopher who was trying to express Greek ideas in terms of Old Testament mythology But it is just as important to understand that to him the mythology was more than an interesting survival With Jewish mythology there came to Philo its strong presentation of a God who was at once fully God and yet vividly realized The problem of distinguishing between Philo the metaphysician and Philo the mystic is often very difficult But the distinction must always be born in mind if one wants to discover what was the metaphysical system of Philo

In general it is safe to say that Philo returned to the dualism of Plato between Deity and Matter As Plato sometimes suggests that Deity is Absolute, the highest of all, to be seen only imperfectly in a mystic union which transcends all Matter, so Philo has his passages where God is similarly represented Nothing could be more explicitly a reference to the Absolute than some of Philo's statements

God is not a composition, nor is He combined out of many ingredients, but is unmixed with anything else   . So God is ordered according to the One and the Monad, or rather the Monad is ordered after the Fashion of the one God." [2]

---

[1] Cf The False Philonean Logos, by Prof Lawrence Mills

[2] Leg Al II 2, 3 (I 66, 67) ὁ δὲ θεὸς οὐ σύγκριμα οὐδὲ ἐκ πολλῶν συνεστώς, ἀλλ᾽ ἀμιγὴς ἄλλῳ..... τέτακται οὖν ὁ θεὸς κατὰ τὸ ἓν καὶ τὴν μονάδα, μᾶλλον δὲ ἡ μονὰς κατὰ τὸν ἕνα θεόν.

God is inaccessible by direct approach. Our reason breaks
down before it comes to Him in His purity [1] Such passages could easily be multiplied Unquestionably Philo
claimed for his God all that is gained by making Him the
Absolute But if much is gained by conceiving of God as
the Absolute, much is also lost, and Philo in the eclectic
spirit of his day did not plan to let any good thing be lost.
In contrast to the Absolute, in many passages God is represented as immanent in almost the Stoic sense   For
example he says: ἡ γὰρ τῶν ὅλων ψυχὴ ὁ θεός ἐστι κατὰ ἔννοιαν.[2]
Again he says that God is to be likened to gold because
it is incorruptible, but particularly because it is malleable.[3]
God is malleable because He extends into and permeates
all things, is πλήρης ὅλη δι' ὅλων.   The eye of the living
God is itself the source of a supersensual light which per-
vades all things [4]

In this last figure is found much more nearly Philo's
true conception of God because it makes room for both
transcendence and immanence By this figure God Himself
is far off in the remoteness of the Absolute, while in all
things is the light which radiates from Him It is the
same figure as that we found Aquinas using to describe
the conception of Plato, but it is as inadequate in Philo's
hands to describe his own conception, as in Aquinas' to
describe the thought of Plato For while it is true that
Philo regards the immanent aspect of God as in a sense
inferior to the transcendent, yet there is no division between
the two, and both are God Himself The immanent deity
is true deity, not merely an emanation from deity. Philo
urges that men be not content with finding God in
immanence, but that they go back to God, the transcendent.
However they should do so only because a stream in purest

[1] De Posteri Caini 168 (I 258) Cf De Opif Mundi 8 (I 2).
where God is ὁ τῶν ὅλων νοῦς, the Mind of the Universe, unmixed
with anything else, and superior to virtue, knowledge, and to the
highest Platonic Forms

[2] Leg Al I 91 (I 62)

[3] Quis rer div Haer 217 (I 503)

[4] De Cherubim 97 (I 156) Cf below p 148 ff

at its source; the distinction is one of degree of purity not of nature

Philo's favorite name for the true God in immanence is Logos The term is in constant use in all his writings and assumes an astonishing variety of meanings By Philo the mystic it is even called a second God, which is all of deity the mass of men can hope to know although the wise and perfect, as Moses, get visions of the First [1] Philo's first description of the Logos, cosmologically speaking, is in a passage in which he identifies it with the Ideal World of the earlier Plato [2] God created this Intelligible World, the κόσμος νοητός the Logos This then acted as the formal cause in the creation of the sensible world [3] How the Logos can thus act as the formal cause Philo typifies by a seal [4] Shapeless Matter is impressed with the form of the Logos, and thereby is made into a κόσμος αίσθητός.[5] But though Philo frequently uses this figure, it by no means exhausts his thought of the action of the Logos upon the material world For he declares that the Logos was made by God to be the cohesive force of the Universe [6] It permeates all Matter and thus supports the world from falling

Philo is consistent in at least one thing He nowhere to my knowledge lapses into pantheism, for he is always thinking in terms of unreconciled dualism When God planned Creation, always Matter was at hand for Him to use God and Matter are fundamentally contrasting conceptions to Philo God has shaped Matter, created the phenomenal world out of it, but nowhere does Philo

[1] Leg Al III 207 (I 128)

[2] De Opif Mundi 24 (I 5) cf Horovitz, J., "Das platonische Νοητὸν Ζῷον und der philosophische Κόσμος Νοητός' Marburg 1900

[3] In De Cherubim 124 ff Philo describes the four causes 1 τὸ αἴτιον (τὸ ὑφ' οὖ), equals ὁ δημιουργός, equals ὁ θεός, 2 the material cause, the four elements, 3 the instrumental cause, equals τὸ ὄργανον, equals τὸ δι' οὖ, equals ὁ τοῦ θεοῦ λόγος, 4 the final cause, τὸ δι' ὅ, the goodness of God

[4] De Opif Mundi 25 (I 5).

[5] De Plant 3 (I 329)

[6] De Plant 8, 9 (I. 331)

identify Deity with Matter as did the Stoics, or assert that God created Matter The Logos permeates all things, without being mixed with the material of the world [1]

But as in the Stoic and Platonic systems, so in Philo the human mind is an especial expression and representation of God Philo describes two minds in the human constitution in almost Aristotelian terms [2] The first is a created mind, and goes with the body as part of the material constitution It is purely passive, the treasury of impressions But the higher mind is God in us [3] οἶκον οὖν ἐπίγειον τὴν ὁράτον ψυχὴν τοῦ ὁράτου θεοῦ [4] This divine element has been given to man as a gift.[5] Ἀπόσπασμα ἦν οὐ διαιρετόν. it is an extension, not a partition [6] Because of its peculiar relationship with divinity the higher human νοῦς is not properly human, but divine, so that the most heinous sin a man can commit is intellectual pride, which means giving himself rather than God the credit for anything that he does or thinks [7] By means of his kinship with Deity he can conceive of the Intelligibles, and even of God,[8] for that, as in Phaedo, is an act of memory [9]

As the mind is an integral part of God, part without partition, so its existence is continued only as it keeps

---

[1] Cf here Wisd vii 24 ff

[2] Quod Deus sit immut 41—50 (I 278 ff . Cf Leg Al I 32 (I 50)

[3] De Opif Mundi 135 (I. 32) γεγενῆσθαι γὰρ τὸ μὲν σῶμα χοῦν τοῦ τεχνίτου λαβόντος καὶ μορφὴν ἀνθρωπίνην ἐξ αὐτοῦ διαπλάσαντος, τὴν δὲ ψυχὴν ἀπ' οὐδενὸς γενητοῦ τὸ παράπαν, ἀλλ' ἐκ τοῦ πατρὸς καὶ ἡγεμόνος τῶν πάντων· ὁ γὰρ ἐνεφύσησεν, οὐδὲν ἦν ἕτερον ἢ πνεῦμα θεῖον ἀπὸ τῆς μακαρίας καὶ εὐδαίμονος φύσεως ἐκείνης ἀποικίαν τὴν ἐνθάδε στειλάμενον ἐπ' ὠφελείᾳ τοῦ γένους ἡμῶν, ἵν' εἰ καὶ θνητόν ἐστι κατὰ τὴν ὁρατὴν μερίδα, κατὰ γοῦν τὴν ἀόρατον ἀθανατίζηται Cf. Quod det pot. insid. 22, 23 (I. 195)

[1] De Cherub 101 (I 157), cf De Plant 18 (I 332)

[5] De Opif Mundi 66 (I 15) ᾧ νοῦν ἐξαίρετον ἐδωρεῖτο, cf De Plant 42 (I 336)

[6] Quod det pot insid 90 (I. 209) Τέμνεται γὰρ οὐδὲν τοῦ θείου κατ' ἀπάρτησιν, ἀλλὰ μόνον ἐκτείνεται.

[7] De Cherubim 71 (I 152)

[8] De Opif. Mundi 53 (I. 12) ὅπερ γὰρ νοῦς ἐν ψυχῇ, τοῦτ' ὀφθαλμὸς ἐν σώματι βλέπει γὰρ ἑκάτερος, ὁ μὲν τὰ νοητά, ὁ δὲ τὰ αἰσθητά , cf. Leg Al I 37 ff (I 50 ff)

[9] De Plant 129 (I 348)

itself clean from material pollution. It must continue to be
turned toward God, and must keep firm control of the
lower part of the soul Philo follows Plato in dividing the
soul into three parts,[1] and frequently brings in the figure
from the Phaedrus of the higher part of the soul acting
as charioteer driving the two lower parts[2] The good of
the flesh is irrational pleasure, but the good of the soul
and of the entire man is ὁ νοῦς τῶν ὅλων, ὁ θεός.[3] Men are to
pray to God that He will dwell within them, and by so
doing raise their minds above the earth and join them with
the heavens.[4] Philo's frequent passages describing the
achievement of mystical illumination and unity are among
the finest in the literature of mysticism.[5] Indeed like most
true mystics, in some passages he goes far towards denying
the reality of individuality,[6] and towards suggesting that
death means the collapse of our material bodies and the
reabsorption of the higher mind into God whence it came.

But this higher part of our constitution will return
to God only if we keep it pure. The body dies, Philo
says,[7] when the ψυχή leaves it, the ψυχή when the λογισμός
leaves it, the λογισμός when ἀρετή leaves it. And in another
passage he describes the death of the soul in sin.[8] When God said
that the soul which sins should "die the death", He meant
that in falling into sin the soul would cease to live in
its true character, would really die as a divinely constituted
being. Philo has no hope for resurrection after such a

[1] Leg Al I. 70 (I. 57). Though Philo is here more like
Albinus than Plato.
[2] Leg Al I. 73 (I. 58)
[3] De Gigant 40 (I. 268).
[4] De Sobr. 64 (I. 402), cf Leg Al. III. 29 (I. 93).
[5] e g De Opif. Mundi 69 ff. (I. 16); De Gigant 47 (I. 269).
[6] De Cherub 114 (I. 159). πόθεν δὲ ἦλθεν ἡ ψυχή, ποῖ δε
χωρήσει, πόσον δὲ χρόνον ἡμῖν ὁμοδίαιτος ἔσται; τίς δέ ἐστι τὴν
οὐσίαν, ἔχομεν εἰπεῖν; πότε δὲ καὶ ἐκτησάμεθα αὐτήν; πρὸ γενέσεως;
ἀλλ᾽ οὐχ ὑπήρχομεν· μετὰ τὸν θάνατον; ἀλλ᾽ οὐκ ἐσόμεθα οἱ μετὰ
σωμάτων σύγκριτοι ποιοί, ἀλλ᾽ εἰς παλιγγενεσίαν ὁρμήσομεν οἱ μετὰ
ἀσωμάτων σύγκριτοι ποιοί But see the entire section
[7] Quod det. pot. insid. 141 (I. 218).
[8] Leg. Al I. 105 (I 64)

death, as St Paul has in Christ To Philo the lapsing of the soul into sin is the supreme tragedy of existence

Such very briefly seems to be the metaphysical scheme of Philo He enriches every detail with abundant imagery and speaks upon each point now philosophically and now mystically in so inexact a way that few details of his system are not in some passage contradicted. But theoretically he is a pure monotheist, a pure dualist, with a strong belief in the fact that all spiritual and mental forces in the world are One

It has already been pointed out that while Philo believes the immanent God to be the highest God, the only God, God. yet his supreme reverence is for God as transcendent, apart from any relation with the world It is thus on the whole his custom to speak of God in emanation by the distinct title ὁ τοῦ θεοῦ λόγος, or simply ὁ λόγος. But by no means is this his consistent practice. There is hardly a function which Philo assigns to the Logos which he does not also assign to God He often describes the Logos as the Demiurge, apparently distinct from God, but it is most common to find God spoken of as Creator [1] The Logos is often described as an intermediate, and in one place is called a hostage, neither created nor uncreated, guaranteeing to God that man will not rebel, to man that God will not desert him But God is Himself called σωτήρ.[2] It has been stated that God created the Intelligible World which was the Logos, but in another passage Philo represents the Logos as the means by which the Intelligible World was created [3] The only way in which any consistency can be found in Philo is to understand that while God in emanation is often apparently distinguished from God the Absolute, and as such is described in many different rhetorical passages in irreconcilable terms, yet Philo by all the terms alike means that God in relation with the world, and God in

[1] De Post Caini 157 (I 255); 175 (I 259), De Ebriet 30 (I 361)

[2] De Post Caini 156 (I. 255).

[3] Leg Al I 21 (I 47)

Himself, are the same. God transcendent, ὁ Θεός, and God immanent, ὁ λόγος, are one and the same God. There is therefore no room whatever in the Philonian Logos for independent personality. The Logos is the supreme Deity in relationships. Philo's Deity though absolute is personal, and the Logos, as one aspect of Deity, shares in the personality of Deity, but it has no personality of its own distinct from the personality of God. When Philo speaks as a mystic the Logos seems frequently to be personal, but when he speaks as a metaphysician Deity is always one and indivisible, and the Logos has no personality of its own.

Similarly in the case of δυνάμεις and ἄγγελοι. Philo is fond of describing the attributes of God under these terms, and frequently his language is so suggestive of personalization that Kennedy still clings to the misapprehension that Philo attributed to them independent existence and reality.[1] And yet in one passage Philo states explicitly that angels and all such beings are simply God's way of revealing Himself.[2] When we think we have seen an angel, he says, we have seen God Himself in the form in which He chose at that time to be made visible. Hence it would appear that in Philo's metaphysics there is only one Divine Person, and strictly speaking no minor deities at all.

But like the popular philosophizing of the Greeks, the tendency of the Semitic mind, because of its instinctive concreteness in thought and expression, would be to personalize cosmic forces. When Greek philosophers could speak of a νοῦς or ψυχή or Logos impersonally, the Jewish instinct would be to describe them in elaborate anthropomorphic and personal language. As a result when Philo speaks other than as a Greek metaphysician, scientific conceptions appear much more personal than in strict Greek writings. And yet an equally strong Jewish motive, that of the preservation of monotheism at all costs, necessitated the theoretic

[1] H. A. A. Kennedy: Philo's Contribution to Religion. pp. 163 ff.
[2] De Somniis I. 232 (I. 655).

denial of personality to any divinity but the One, so that the personality and impersonality of the Logos, bewilderingly alternated in Philo, must have been far worse confused in popular Hellenistic Judaism. It is this obligation to preserve the unity of the divine nature even while going so far as to affirm the separate personalities of the Divine Beings which marks the Christian metaphysics of Justin and his successors as having its root primarily in Hellenistic Judaism rather than in Hellenism itself.

The distinction between Judaism in its Palestinian and Hellenistic developments has perhaps been made sufficiently clear. Palestinian Judaism believed in a personal God the Father whose will had been expressed in the Law. Cosmic problems received only the most sketchy treatment, and probably in cases where such problems were raised at all it is safe to presume a Greek inspiration. Hellenistic Judaism tried to be scientific and to think of Deity in terms adequate for a scientific mind, while it took over the Greek scheme of a mediatory principle to unite the Absolute Deity with the Universe. Also Palestinian Judaism adhered to its belief in man as made of both soul and body, and asserted that neither soul nor body could have existence apart from the other. Thus in Palestine belief in a continuation of life after death logically took the form of a doctrine of the resurrection of the body, according to which the soul at death went to Sheol or Hades in a state of semi-consciousness, in which it could neither be said to exist nor not to exist. At the appointed time it was again restored to life in the full sense by being reunited to the body. But in Hellenistic Judaism the hope was much more for immortality in the Greek sense, by which the soul is conceived of as relieved from bondage at death so that it can return to God, or go to Heaven, immeasurably benefited by its freedom from the defilement of the body. So did the two currents of Judaism drift far apart on both the doctrines of God and of man.

In their understanding of the distinction between Jew and Gentile, we have reason to believe that the two schools of Judaism were also quite unlike. The Palestinian

Jew would have no recognition for one who did not keep
the Law He was an unclean dog Business of course
necessitated dealing with Gentiles, but no true Palestinian
Jew would have recognized that a Gentile had any religious
rights or privileges unless he became a Jew But in the
Dispersion, much as Hebrews might group themselves
together for mutual help in keeping the Law, and deeply
as its observances must have stirred their religious natures,
still the code of Judaism must generally have been indeed
a "burden" So impossible was it to keep the Law out of
Palestine that a member of the Rabbinical group in Jerusalem automatically lost his standing upon leaving the
country.[1] Information about life in the Dispersion is sadly
incomplete, but passages in Josephus and Acts, as well
as the spirit of the writers of Alexandria, indicate a
Judaism in the Dispersion which had even in its worship
long been making strides toward meeting Gentiles half
way The Synagogues had their nuclei of extreme Jews
who possessed the undisputed right to speak for the
congregation, but most of them also had their groups,
and apparently their large groups, of half-proselytes, 'God
fearers", who admired the monotheism and moral sturdiness
of the Jews, and who wished to identify themselves with
that part of Judaism, but who had not sufficient regard
for the Jewish Law in itself to comply with its first
rite in circumcision The significance of the situation for
judging the Judaism of the Dispersion is not that Judaism
had an attraction for Gentiles, but that these Gentiles
were so far tolerated and encouraged as even to be allowed
to attend the Synagogues in company with full Jews.
The strict Jews themselves held in theory that God could
be pleased only by the rigorous observance of the Law,
but so baffling and unattainable was their ideal in a
heathen environment that they quietly made room at their
side for those who wanted to worship with them, whether
they attempted the observance of the Law or not. The
practice had no inconveniences until Pauline Christianity

[1] See G F Moore· Am-Haares and the Haberim, p 142,
n 4

came forward offering all the advantages of Judaistic monotheism and morality, and indeed claiming to be the true Judaism, but explicitly asserting the inconsequential character of the Law Such a gospel must have been enormously attractive to the "God fearers", because it offered them a pure worship of God in which they could have full and unqualified participation. However once the theory of the strict Jews as to the nature and authority of the Law had been openly challenged, the slack line had to be drawn tight, and the practice of encouraging such half proselytes had inevitably to give place, as we have seen, to a fierce denunciation by the Rabbis of all people who wanted the benefits of Judaism without its legal obligations.

The Hellenistic Jewish character of St. Paul's thought and writings is strikingly clear. That St Paul, a man of Tarsus, who understood no word of Hebrew, who made no claim to Rabbinical training in any of his writings, in spite of the advantage such prestige would have given him in the controversy reflected in the Epistle to the Galatians, and who on the contrary was steeped in the ideas and fixed in the point of view of Greek Judaism, was actually a trained disciple of Gamaliel is impossible to believe. The author of the seventh chapter of Romans was a deeply conscientious Jew who found observance of the Law impossible in a Greek city He was fanatically intolerant of any trace of blasphemy in Jerusalem, because in his struggle to be a Jew in the Dispersion, Jerusalem as a place of perfect religious atmosphere was idealized to him as it could never have been to one familiar with all sides of life in the Holy City His Gospel, which he received from no man, was a conception of Christ as a divine personality, revealed in the incarnation, and described in a mingling of the Philonic Heavenly Man, Wisdom, Nomos, Logos The Epistle to the Galatians, with its theory of a spiritual Israel, as illustrated by the eclectic character of the line of descent through Abraham and Isaac, only carries Philo's treatise on Nobility one step further than Philo himself cared to do. St Paul fairly made his choice. Where Philo had philosophized about the superiority of the Heavenly

Ideal Law, Man, Logos, but did not dare himself, except
in moments of exalted mysticism, to cut loose from the
physical worship of God as prescribed in the Torah, St. Paul
found such a reality in Christ that he fearlessly proclaimed
the sufficiency of the Spirit, and threatened the loss of
all the benefits of the spiritual Christ to those who were
so weak in faith that they wanted still to retain both
the Law of the Flesh and the Law of the Spirit. It was
St. Paul who made the tremendous discovery of the
identity of Christ the man of history with the Logos of
Hellenistic Judaism He does not use the word "Logos"
for Christ, to be sure, but no attendant of a Diaspora
Synagogue could have mistaken the meaning of such
statements as those of Paul when he wrote. Χριστὸν θεοῦ
δύναμιν καὶ θεοῦ σοφίαν:[1] and that characteristic passage
beginning ὅς ἐστιν εἰκὼν τοῦ θεοῦ τοῦ ὀοράτου.[2] In such a
case, speculation as to whether Philo's writings were a
literary source for St Paul's Epistles is entirely of secondary
importance, though it seems that the similarity between
Galatians, the ninth chapter of Romans, and the treatise
of Philo on Nobility already mentioned is in itself almost
adequate proof that St. Paul had read at least some parts
of the Philonic corpus But more important is it to understand that whereas the first stage of Christianity had
apparently been conducted on the basis of, and in the
atmosphere of, Palestinian Judaism. St Paul claimed
the person of Christ as the solution of the problems
of Hellenistic Judaism The contrast between Hellenistic
and Palestinian Judaism could not be more adequately
represented than that between St Paul's allegorical account,
for example, of the veil of Moses, and the parable of
the Prodigal Son The one is as idiomatic of the philosophic
adaptations of awkward passages of Scripture, as the other
is true to type of the Haggada of the Tannaim

    Christianity thus almost from its incipiency had two
interpretations, both Judaistic, but utterly different in
character from each other If there ever was a violent

[1] I Cor 1 24
[2] Col 1 15 ff

and prolonged conflict between the two schools of Christianity it has left astonishingly little trace. The solution eventually was a compromise between the two which was apparently early begun, but which it took many years of Christian thought to complete. From this point of view Justin's writings are most valuable testimony, for, as will be seen in the course of the following discussion, they preserve the two traditions still strikingly intact.

THE THEOLOGY OF JUSTIN MARTYR

CHAPTER I

JUSTIN'S LIFE

Justin Martyr was born, by his own record,[1] at Flavia Neapolis in the Roman Province of Syria Palaestina, by which name the Roman Province of Judaea was called after the great rebellion and fall of Jerusalem under Hadrian Flavia Neapolis, the modern Nablous, was one of the colonies founded as Greek cities by the wise imperialists of the day, but was not organized until A D 70 The city was situated in Samaria, near ancient Sichem where was Jacob's well Justin does not give any decisive information about his race He says that his father's name was Priscus, a Latin name, his grandfather's Bacchius, a Greek name, and on the basis of these names it is usually assumed that his ancestors were Greek or Roman colonists in the new city The evidence for his ancestry is, however, confusing He definitely calls himself in one passage a member of the Samaritan race,[2] but he nowhere seems to have had any Samaritan training, so that if his blood was Samaritan he was to all appearance bred a heathen From Dialogue 28 we learn that Justin was uncircumcized, so that whether Samaritan or Greek, he was certainly not a Jew

In the second chapter of the Dialogue Justin tells of a determination to learn philosophy which drove him from school to school in search of the truth He says that he

[1] Ap I 1 (53 C)
[2] Dial 120 6 (349 C). Cf Epiphanius Adv Haer. 46 1. Epiphanius may not represent testimony independent of the Dial

first attached himself to a Stoic philosopher, and stayed with him some time (how long Justin does not say), but left him because the master was teaching him nothing about God, and had confessedly put such knowledge among the non-essentials Justin says that he turned quickly to a Peripatetic of great pretensions But the disciple of Aristotle, after a few days instruction, requested his pupil for a fee, a demand which aroused Justin's suspicions that the man was an impostor, and prompted him to leave the school at once. His next attempt was with a Pythagorean, a man of great reputation with himself as well as with others But this man insisted at the first interview that it was useless to come to him for instruction in philosophy unless Justin had already trained his mind in abstract thinking by the mastery of music, astronomy, and geometry, so that when Justin confessed his ignorance of these preliminary disciplines he was peremptorily dismissed. Justin was disappointed at thus being rejected by a man who had impressed him as having what he was seeking, but felt pressed for time and did not think it feasible to learn the Pythagorean preliminaries In his perplexity he thought he found a way out in Platonism. Here was what he had been seeking He was ushered at once into acquaintance with immaterial conceptions and the world of Ideas, and was so rapidly growing in his mystical hold upon these that he hoped soon to come to the goal of Platonism and experience the vision of God. It was at this point that his attention was called to the Christians

This most interesting account of Justin's philosophical quest has always been taken literally by his commentators, although the story of the conversion to Christianity which immediately follows it has long been regarded by many scholars as an idealization of Justin's actual experiences. The fact is, however, that the two narratives are one, unbroken by any transition, and that the chances are very probable that Justin's adventures in the philosophic schools are as ideal as his conversation with the old man which introduced him to Christianity. Justin, in the entire passage, is dramatizing the relations between Christianity and philosophy, and has here adopted the familiar convention

of relating someone's adventures in passing from school to
school, and finally to the Christian school, in order to
criticize each school by the adventures related Helm has
recently pointed out a remarkable parallel between this
account of Justin and Lucian's Menippus or Necromancy
cc 4—6, a contemporary piece of writing [1] Here Menippus describes himself as having gone through several schools
of philosophy, and as having given them all up because
their mutual contradictions convinced him that none could
speak with authority [2] Some of the verbal similarities
which Helm points out between Justin and Lucian are
striking They show no interdependence, but only the
conventionalization of the literary form The same form,
probably borrowed from the Greeks, is used by the Tannaim to describe the three rabbinic types of true proselytes,
Githro, Naaman, and Rahab, who go "through all heathen
cults and schools without finding peace They find their
first rest and peace in the haven of the Bible and the
Prophets, because the sacred word alone can insure peace
of soul and knowledge of God " [3]

But if Justin is using here a conventionalized form, he
is using no less conventionalized criticisms of the schools.
His criticism of the Stoics was that they had not sufficient
interest in metaphysics, but the Stoic indifference to metaphysics has always been proverbial It is only with the
greatest difficulty that we reconstruct the metaphysical
background of the Stoics at all, because their indifference
and neglect of that aspect of philosophy was so universal
that we have little to build upon, while contradictions are
everywhere common Pfattisch suggests that Justin's difficulty with his Stoic teacher may have been the fact that
he had tried to find in Stoicism a personal God, and was
not content with ordinary Stoic pantheism [4] But no such
explanation is necessary The Stoics were mostly teachers
of ethic and of logic, and as a rule had no interest in

[1] Helm "Lucian und Menipp" pp 40 ff
[2] Cf Ap I. 4 8 (55 C), 7. 3 (56 D), 26 6 (70 B)
[3] Goldfahn (Bibl 389) p 52
[4] (Bibl 385) p 9

speculating about the nature of even their pantheistic deity
When they spoke of conforming to fate or nature they
were content to leave these terms largely undefined Justin's experience in the Stoic schools was thus not necessarily a personal incident, but only reflects a commonplace
criticism of the school as a whole

Similarly in the Aristotelian's greed for money is to
be recognized a most typical contemporary criticism. Information is very explicit that at this time nothing was
more common than the wearing of a philosopher's cloak
by ignorant impostors who made thereby a good living,[1]
while Atticus, the Platonic contemporary of Justin, shows
vividly a spirit among the Platonists of the day to suspend
friendly borrowings from the Peripatetics, and to inveigh
in tirades against their morals.[2] Nothing would be more
natural then than for Justin with his Platonic sympathies
to join the Academic reproach against Aristotelian morals
by representing his peripatetic teacher as a mercenary
impostor.

The criticism of the Pythagorean school is likewise
perfectly general and typical and does not suggest a personal experience in the least. Lucian laughs at the Pythagoreans, one of whom he calls an arithmetician, astro-
nomer, trickster, geometrician, musician, and magician.[3] In
general the attitude of most men toward the Pythagoreans
is well summed up by Justin, that the Pythagoreans were
profound men but so walled in by technical scholarship
that a popular scholar could get little from them

When Justin comes to speak of Platonism he speaks
much more in detail and shows here as throughout his
writings that he has at least dabbled in Platonic doctrines.
In general then it appears that Justin tells in the form of
his personal experiences in the philosophic schools only his
criticisms of those schools and accordingly at this point
it may be well to inquire what is the testimony of the body

[1] See the collection of references in Trollope (Bibl 28) p 10 n. 22.

[2] See Euseb. Pr. ev. XV 4, 5

[3] Vit Auct Ch. 27, from Trollope (Bibl 28) p 11 n 28.

of his writings as to the extent of his knowledge of Greek
philosophy

Of the fundamentals of Stoicism Justin appears on the
whole to have little grasp   He speaks of the hopelessness
of the Stoic doctrine of metempsychosis and cycles from
any teleological or individualistic point of view,[1] and of
the contradiction between Stoic monism and fatalism on
the one hand, and Stoic ethic on the other[2] He knows
that the various Stoic departments of instruction are called
Logoi[3] On the other hand Justin makes the popular
error of including Heraclitus among the Stoics[4] He
likewise states that according to the Stoics God is Himself
to be consumed in the final conflagration,[5] whereby he
shows his ignorance of the first principle of Stoic pantheism   For according to the Stoics God was identified
with the fire which would ultimately take all things back
into itself   In popular Stoicism it has been seen that the
dualistic tendency of Stoic ethics was allowed to fraternize
with Platonic metaphysical dualism so far as to distinguish
between God and fire, which thus became the ultimate
state of all matter   Various attempts have been made to
establish an immediate connection between Justin's Spermatic Logos and the Stoic teaching, but without success
as will be shown later[6] Justin's Stoic references are those
of the ordinary conversation of untrained men of the time,
and show no trace of his having made any study of Stoicism
at all

Justin's references to Platonism are, as has been said,
much more detailed   He calls himself a former Platonist[7]
Socrates and Plato were two of his favorite heroes, the life
and death of Socrates had especially made a profound
impression upon him   Parallels to Plato can frequently be
found in the Apologies and Dialogus, but that they come

[1] Dial 1 4 (217 E, 218 A)
[2] Ap II 7 8, 9 (46 A, B)   See Blunt in loco
[3] Ibid.
[4] Ap II 8 1 (46 C)
[5] Ap. I 20 2 (66 C)
[6] See below pp 161 ff
[7] Ap II 12 1 (50 A)

direct from Plato's writings is by no means sure. For
example in Ap. I. 68. 2 (99 C) Justin writes ὅ φίλον τῷ
θεῷ τοῦτο γενέσθω, which Otto suggests[1] is closely paral-
leled in Plato's Crito 43 D, Apol. Soc. 19 A, and Phaedr.
246 D. But the parallel is in no case close enough to suggest direct influence in view of the fact that in Stoic and
Christian, as well as in Platonic, circles the idea of submitting to the will of God was so common that such
phraseology must have been on everyone's lips. The source
of the expression, if a direct source must be assumed, is
with equal probability assigned to Mat. xxvi. 42 or Acts
xxi. 14 by Pfattisch.[2]

Yet Justin had probably something more than a street
philosopher's knowledge of Platonism. He may have
read the Apology, Phaedo, Republic, and Timaeus, for
with each of these he has a verbal parallel sufficiently close
to suggest literary acquaintance with the master.[3] But
traces of no further Platonic books can be found with confidence in Justin's writings. Indeed such references to
Plato as that to the νοῦς βασιλικός[4] are a fair indication
that at least he had never read the Philebus. For whereas
in Justin the human ψυχή is called a part of the νοῦς
βασιλικός, in Plato it is the νοῦς ἐμός, not the ψυχή, which is
compared and joined with νοῦς βασιλικός. Justin certainly
learned of the νοῦς βασιλικός outside the Philebus. It is
easy to fancy parallels between Plato and Justin, as for
instance to see in Justin's description of the degeneration
of the philosophic schools from the master philosophers
who founded them,[5] a reflection of the degeneration of
succeeding generations from the truly philosophic type of
man, the ideal citizen of Plato's Republic. But actually the
evidence that Plato had any appreciable direct influence

[1] Otto in loco, followed by Blunt in loco.

[2] (Bibl. 44) in loco.

[3] Cf. e.g. Ap. I. 8. 1 (57 A) Apol. Soc. 30 d., Dial 3. 3
(220 B) Phaedo 85 c, d ; Ap. II. 10. 6 (48 D) Rep. II. 377 ff,
X. 595 ff, Ap. II. 10. 6 (48 E) Tim. 28 c, Ap. I 60. 1 (92 E)
Tim. 36 b, c

[4] Dial 4. 2 (221 E); cf. Plato Philebus 22 c. 5, 6.

[5] Dial 2. 2 (218 D.

upon Justin is not forthcoming, so that Dr Holland was
right in suggesting that it was quite typical of Justin's
understanding of Plato's text, when Justin interprets as a
prophetic type of the Cross the statement of Plato in the
Timaeus that the soul of the world was placed in the
universe in the form of a Greek Chi.[1] Indeed Geffken
denies to Justin any Platonic training whatever [2]

The sort of system which Justin knew by the name
of Platonism he has expounded in part in the discussion
with the Old Man which immediately follows the narrative
of his supposed adventures in the different schools of philosophy. For it was while he was carried away with
Platonism, and was seeking lonely places in which to carry
on the mystic exercises whereby he soon hoped to get a
vision of God, that one day, he says, he met in the course
of his solitary walks an Old Man who turned out to be a
Christian. They fell into a discussion about philosophy
during which the Old Man completely shattered the confidence of Justin in Platonism, and then represented to him
so forcibly the superiority of Christianity that Justin soon
thereafter became a Christian Various attempts have been
made at identifying the Old Man,[3] but there is no reason
for supposing that Justin's account is not a fiction, and that
the Old Man is not merely an ideal figure. Hubík points out
that Eusebius did not treat the introduction to the Dialogue
as an historical document, and that he entirely disregards the
Old Man incident, because he had apparently a good independent tradition for the conversion of Justin [4] But if
not historical, the passage is of great value as showing
Justin's idea of the doctrines of Platonism, and hence for
revealing the true nature of the Platonism whose traces
might be found in Justin's theology.

Philosophy is defined as ἐπιστήμη τοῦ ὄντος καὶ τοῦ
ἀληθοῦς ἐπίγνωσις which must be translated, "the knowledge of the existing One and the understanding of the

[1] Holland (Bibl. 153) p. 584. See Ap. I 60 1 (92 E), cf.
Plato Tim. 36 b, c.
[2] (Bibl 205).
[3] See Semisch (Bibl. 118) I. 9. n. 1.
[4] (Bibl 209) pp. 297, 298.

Truth "[1] Here is the first distinction between Justin's
Platonism and Plato, for while Justin is in this section obviously drawing in general upon conceptions to be found
in the Phaedo, yet Plato in the Phaedo speaks of τὰ ὄντα,
Justin of τὸ ὄν. The change is not an insignificant one, for
τὸ ὄντα meant to Plato a scientific field of inquiry, while
τὸ ὄν to Justin meant simply God, the goal of Mysticism
Justin shortly after this definition of philosophy speaks in
truly mystical language of τὸ ὄν as visible to the purified
eye of man Τὸ ὄν is an indescribable Something which
comes suddenly into properly prepared minds because of
their kinship to it and desire for the vision [2] The Old Man
promptly rejoins by asking what is man's kinship with God,
thereby showing that it is God and no other that Justin
means by τὸ ὄν Philosophy then is to Justin knowledge
about God, or knowledge of God, as the end of philosophy
is the vision of God and growing like unto God [3] Of interest
in science in the larger sense there seems no trace in
Justin's Platonism Ἐπιστήμη and σοφία are in Justin filled
with the popular mystical connotation of the day

The Old Man asks Justin, after his definition of Philosophy as knowledge τοῦ ὄντος to define τὸ ὄν.[4] Justin
answers at once that it is that which is fixed eternally
in its nature and mode of being, and is the cause of existence to all things else, or in other words God.[5] The
aim of Justin is clearly to define the Absolute God of contemporary Platonism, in which the influence of the Aristotelian Unmoved Mover, the First Cause, is distinct Justin,
like Albinus, distinguishes between God and the νοῦς
βασιλικός, an expression in many ways coordinate with the

[1] Dial 3 4 (220 D)

[2] Dial 4 1 (221 C, D)

[3] Dial 2 6 (219 D), cf. Fragm XVIII (Otto; τέλος τῷ
φιλοσοφοῦντι ἡ πρὸς θεὸν ὁμοίωσις κατὰ τὸ δυνστόν.

[4] Mss here and all editors read θεόν for τὸ ὄν, except
Thirby with whom Aubé very properly agrees It is clear that
Justin is here using the two interchangeably, but the reading is
much smoother with τὸ ὄν than with θεόν.

[5] Dial 3 5 (220 E) τὸ κατὰ τὰ αὐτὰ καὶ ὡσαύτως αἰεὶ ἔχον
καὶ τοῦ εἶναι πᾶσι τοῖς ἄλλοις αἴτιον, τοῦτο δή ἐστιν ὁ θεός

Logos of Philo There is, according to Justin's Platonism,
the νοῦς βασιλικός which is the connecting link between all
living beings and God the source of life, but which itself
contemplates God in a perfection of mystical clarity which
our mysticism can only copy.[1] The νοῦς βασιλικός is the
universal mind of which all souls, both of men and
animals, are only parts,[2] the distinction between the souls
of men and animals is not one of nature, but is the result
of the relative hampering power of the different kinds of
bodies A soul in a dog's body is much more intimately
ensnared in matter than in a man's body, and hence is kept
from mysticism because it cannot rise above such an en-
cumbrance For mysticism in men is possible only according to the ability of a man to rise above the material
part of his nature into pure abstraction A few men are
able with difficulty to do so, but ordinary men and animals
are hopelessly tied down by the flesh. Justin's Platonism
is typical of the Platonism of his day in that it is founded
upon a dualism consisting of an Absolute God who is
pure existence, to whom is opposed dead and killing
matter, while the two are bridged by a third principle,
the νοῦς βασιλικός which projects the life of God into matter,
and so furnishes life to whatever lives in the world. Justin
says very little of the world of Ideas, only mentions that
he had been thrilled by the contemplation of them They
appear to have played no essential part in his system, and
were apparently carried over, as in Philo, only because
the familiar Platonic Dialogues made much of them The
Ideas would then probably with Justin, as with Philo
and Albinus, have been identified in some way with the
νοῦς βασιλικός, if he ever understood them sufficiently to
have had a theory about them at all. There can be little
doubt that the World Soul of the Timaeus was also identified by Justin as by Albinus with the νοῦς βασιλικός,
although in the Timaeus it is νοῦς which creates the ψυχή.
The νοῦς would then have been regarded by Justin as the

[1] Dial 4 2 (221 E)
[2] This confusion of the terms ψυχή and νοῦς is Justin's, and
is one of the many indications that he had had little close philosophic training.

sustaining, cohesive force in the universe, whose presence in the world prevented a relapse of matter into chaos, and whose especial presence in men furnished them with their higher powers.

But the Old Man is represented as finding in Justin's Platonic thinking a profound ambiguity in the matter of the nature of the human soul and of its relation to the νοῦς βασιλικός and to God He challenges Justin's position and a very interesting discussion ensues. From this point on Justin does not make it at all clear what of the theories suggested he intends to be understood as Platonic, and what as Christian. The Old Man is an ideal Christian who is able to meet Justin on his Platonic ground and lead him thence into Christianity, and it may be that Justin intends his original position on each point to represent Platonism, while the various corrections of his first statements may suggest the Christian improvement upon Platonic doctrines. But toward the end of the discussion occurs a complete break and change of ground, and this break seems the best point to take as the place of departure from Platonism to Christianity. Up to that point, then, the discussion may fairly be taken as concerned with various types of Platonism. It seems most likely that Justin intends in the argument to refute views from the Academy of his day which were incompatible with Christianity, in favor of a Platonism more to his purpose.

Justin's first anthropological position in the discussion, as has been seen, is that the ψυχή of man is divine and immortal,[1] and a part of the νοῦς βασιλικός,[2] and that all souls, whether of men or animals, are alike as all being parts of the νοῦς βασιλικός. As the νοῦς βασιλικός sees God, so the proper aim of all souls is to comprehend the Divine, but they are prevented from doing so by ethical

---

[1] For a similar doctrine see Severus in Euseb. Pr. Ev. XIII. xvii.

[2] Dial 4 2 (221 E. Justin has clearly in mind such a νοῦς βασιλικός as we have found in Albinus. It is notable here that there is no hint that the word μέρος in such a connection implies a division.

impurity Only the ethically pure can see God But Justin
is forced to change his point of view because animals are
certainly not ethically impure, so that he attempts to
explain that the nature of the bodies in which a soul may
be implanted may vary widely in hampering power Only
the human body is fine enough to enable. the soul to rise
above it. The Old Man here questions whether human
beings have bodies thus superior to the bodies of animals,
but does not press his question, because it is the human
soul he is most interested in understanding Justin assumes
that the human soul sees God while still in the body if
the man is ethically pure, although the vision is much more
perfect after death, while those who are unworthy are
condemned after death to be imprisoned in the bodies of
wild beasts. But since Justin admits that no permanent
advantage accrues to the soul in receiving either the vision
or punishment, because both are forgotten in the next
incarnation, the Old Man is allowed summarily to reject
two fundamental doctrines from Justin's first Platonic
views He denies the power of the soul to get an actual
vision of God, and rejects the doctrine of the incarnation
of human souls in animal bodies. The argument has thus
far not been particularly convincing The Old Man seems
to use practical expediency as an adequate philosophical
criterion, and from that test alone he has put aside
both doctrines He argues that it is useless to punish
people when they do not remember afterwards either
the fact or reason of their having been punished, and
concludes that such punishment because useless, cannot
exist. Similarly since according to Justin's own statement
one forgets the vision of God in the next incarnation, the
vision is likewise useless and hence non-existent The
appeal to expediency was evidently in that period of
decadent philosophizing considered a legitimate philosophical argument, for Zeller points out that expediency was
the ultimate basis of all Atticus' discussion, and that it
was on the basis of its practical results that Alexander
of Aphrodisius attacked the Stoic doctrine of fatalism [1]

[1] Zeller III 1 (1909) p 840, Engl Tr . Eclectics, pp 322
343—344. See also Alex. Aphrod De Fato XVI ff

This passage in Justin would not then appear so weak to Justin's contemporaries as to us

Chapter Five of the Dialogue returns to a discussion of the nature of the soul on the basis of new Platonic definitions. Some Platonists, says Justin, define the soul as immortal and hence unbegotten,[1] but Justin now represents a school of Platonism which does not agree with this. The Old Man, with Justin's consent, begins the second discussion by asserting the complete coordination of the world and the human soul, by which if the world is immortal and unbegotten, souls are likewise so, and if the world is not immortal, souls cannot be.[2] Some Platonists, says Justin, assert that the world is immortal and unbegotten. We have other evidence that his very Aristotelian doctrine was taught in the Academy. Proclus says that Albinus taught the eternity of the world.[3] Albinus himself says that while it is not right to think that there ever was a time in which the world was not, because it is entirely in process of generation, yet this very fact reveals some more original cause of its existence.[4] Severus tried to assume a middle position by saying, "in general the world is eternal, but this world which now exists and is so subject to change is begotten."[5] But Justin thinks that the correct Platonic doctrine does not teach the eternity of the world. Nothing immortal or unbegotten can be subject to such change and decay as constantly take place in the world. Hence the world, and with it the souls of men, must be mortal and begotten, and live only by the will of God. When God ceases to will that souls should live, they perish. The soul survives the body, those of the good being rewarded and never dying, while those of the evil are punished sufficiently and then cease to exist. There can be no plurality of unbegotten beings

[1] Severus would represent this Platonic point of view.

[2] On the co-ordination of souls and the world see Zeller III. i. 839. Anm. 2; Engl. Tr : Eclectics, 342. n 3

[3] Proclus in Tim. 67 c. (Ed. Diehl I. 219 2 ff.).

[4] Albinus: Introduction, p. 169.

[5] Proclus in Tim. 88 d (Ed. Diehl I 289. 7 ff.)

for God is uniquely the Unbegotten, a doctrine which he quite correctly says was held by Plato and Pythagoras [1]

The next step is most important, for it finds the solution of the problem of the relation of man to God by introducing into the soul a third principle, the πνεῦμα, which bears the same relation to the soul as the soul to the body. The soul as a created thing cannot be a living principle itself, but only can partake of life It partakes of life by having in itself a part of the ζωτικὸν πνεῦμα, a conception which is not defined, but which probably, as will shortly appear, takes the place in Justin's thinking of the μέρος τοῦ βασιλικοῦ νοῦ which he had recently defined as the soul The soul now appears to be a created thing, surviving the body, to be sure, but doomed to perish if it is not the will of God that the πνεῦμα abide with it If God withdraws the πνεῦμα from a soul, the soul ceases to exist, and at once relapses into that out of which it came, a statement whose meaning Justin does not explain.

Justin has thus far not left contemporary Platonism, though his solution of the problem of the nature of the soul is clearly influenced ultimately by the Aristotelian double νοῦς. Albinus has already illustrated to us the tendency of contemporary Platonism to sharpen Plato's distinction between the higher and lower parts of the soul by introducing Aristotle's double νοῦς, Similarly Atticus distinguished between the νοῦς and τὸ πνευματικὸν ὄχημα τῆς ψυχῆς, and ascribed immortality only to the νοῦς.[2] Porphyry slightly later represents a better tradition of Platonism, according to Proclus,[3] in teaching that the ὄχημα, while not immortal in its own right, survives the death of the body. Marcus Aurelius divided man into a trichotomy of σάρξ, πνεῦμα, and ἡγεμονικόν, in which the last principle is clearly an Intelligence [4]

In all these philosophers, the highest principle in man

[1] See Tim 41 a, b

[2] Proclus in Tim 311 a (Ed Diehl III. 234 9 ff)

[3] Ibid.

[4] Marc. Aurel. Commentar. 2, 4. p 13 from Lebreton (Bibl. 382) p 329.

was a νοῦς, and there is no reason to suppose that
Justin conceived of the ζωτικὸν πνεῦμα as merely a principle
of life, with no further function in the soul Expressed in
different language in different schools, the highest principle
in man was always a rational medium between man as
a created being and the Cosmic Intelligence. It was a
source and instrument of knowledge of the Eternal Verities,
whether these were conceived of as Forms or as Axioms
The ζωτικὸν πνεῦμα must have played a similar part in Justin's
scheme He does not say so, but it is entirely probable that
in addition to the ζωτικὸν πνεῦμα, itself a rational guide, he
conceived of a lower type of mind in the ψυχή proper,
which was the intellect dealing with sensible objects
according to whose guidance most men were content to
live But the human soul was in itself not especially exalted.
Justin had admitted the identity of nature of the souls
of men and of animals,[1] and had never seen fit to
contradict the statement as his thought developed in the
discussion with the Old Man And yet clearly, though
the ζωτικὸν πνεῦμα brings much of life and intellectual
light to the soul, the centre of personality is the soul
The πνεῦμα can be given or withdrawn at God's will It is
at best a borrowed thing. But the soul is the man, and
the object of endeavor is to make the soul come into
harmony with the life of the πνεῦμα. So will a man be worthy
of retaining the πνεῦμα. or in other words, of continuing
to exist

Thus far in the argument Justin has been only clearing
the air as to what he means by Platonism He is writing
from a Christian viewpoint, and is unquestionably choosing
those doctrines current in Platonic schools which will
best serve his purpose as a Christian Apologist He has
now but to turn the terms νοῦς and ζωτικὸν πνεῦμα into
Logos, and to assert the complete incarnation of the
ζωτικὸν πνεῦμα in Christ to have his Christian Logos doctrine in its fundamental aspects. It is impossible to say
from what Academic teachings Justin went over into Christianity, but he is perfectly accurate, according to our

[1] Dial 4 2 (221 E, 222 A)

evidence of the teaching of Platonists of his day, in insisting upon the system he has just outlined as being a fair statement of Platonism as he would have heard it expounded.

Of the circumstances of Justin's conversion from philosophy to Christianity little is actually known. The ideal story of his philosophic quest and discussion with the Old Man is continued from the point where the ζωτιχὸν πνεῦμα is admitted, by a very sudden shift to Christianity. Justin represents himself in Chapter Seven of the Dialogue as deeply perplexed He has allowed the Old Man to take the last step of the argument, in which the ζωτιχὸν πνεῦμα has been introduced and the relative unimportance of the human soul asserted. Justin now intimates that he is beyond his depth While it has been seen that there is no reason to believe, either from contemporary Platonism or from Justin's later doctrine, that Justin did not consider that he now had a firmer basis than ever for knowledge and mysticism, yet Justin makes himself appear as though thinking that if the ψυχή was not itself akin to the Divine he had no means of finding the Truth He abruptly asks the Old Man what way of finding the Truth is left The Old Man, likewise abandoning the advantage of the new description of the soul, immediately explains to Justin that the Prophets, more ancient than the philosophers, gave men the Truth because it had been revealed to them by the Holy Spirit, and that they had been followed by Christ, the supreme revelation of Truth He recommends to Justin a careful study of Christ and the Prophets, and goes away leaving Justin with a strange desire kindled in his heart to search out the new school of philosophy, Christianity. He straightway did so, he says, and soon adopted Christianity as his philosophy He concludes the remarkable story by saying that as a teacher in this his latest school, he now was wearing the Philosopher's cloak. "In this sense, and for these reasons, I am a philosopher."[1]

The Second Apology gives the only direct evidence

[1] Dial 8 2 (225 C).

we have as to Justin's conversion [1] There he states that
while still a Platonist he was attracted to investigate the
doctrines of Christianity by the moral integrity of the
Christians and their fearlessness before persecution Upon
examination he was convinced that Christian doctrines
were the pure Truth of which everything else is either
an inadequate imitation or a demonic perversion. There
is here no fundamental contradiction between the Apology
and the Dialogue, even taking the passage in the Dialogue
as a record of Justin's actual experiences It may well
have been that just at the time when his attention was
called to the Christians by some remarkable instance of
Christian fortitude during a persecution, he was in a
state of discouragement at the discovery of new teachings
in Platonism which he had found difficult to understand.
In any case it is perfectly plain throughout Justin's writings
that he considered Christianity as superior to philosophy,
not only because the Books of Moses were the direct
source of Plato's doctrines, but because in Christianity
Justin found relief from the necessity of seeking metaphysical knowledge through his own efforts. He consistently regarded philosophy as good so far as it went,
but as confusing, contradictory, and unsatisfying. Not by
the efforts of man's own reason, but through Revelation,
he insists, is the Truth to be had by men. And once in
possession of this Truth, all the ethical virtues, honesty,
courage, truthfulness, purity, self-control, follow spontaneously and inevitably.

Justin's quest, while probably not autobiographical in
detail, is thoroughly autobiographical in spirit He represents himself as seeking a short and easy way to a
foundation for mystic experience. It was a religious, not
an intellectual quest. He adopted Christianity at the end
because it was able to give satisfaction to a fundamentally
unphilosophic mind. Pythagoreanism was utterly too difficult Platonism was easier, but not easy when one penetrated
at all deeply into its teachings. But the necessity for
philosophic effort vanished in Christianity with its doctrine

[1] Ap. II. 12. 1, 2 (50 A, B); cf. 13. 1 (51 B).

of revelation. According to Justin the ordinary human mind is unable to find the truth by rational processes, and in Christianity does not try to do so. A Christian can exercise himself in cultus and mystical worship, completely at rest in an objective body of revelation, to question which is the height of impiety.[1] Justin was of the stuff that Christian saints are made of, because he could completely accept an external body of teaching, and unhampered by any philosophical inhibitions, could throw the whole force of his enthusiasm and mystical fervour into the single task of living and teaching the Truth. Not great penetration but great conviction makes for sainthood, and it is conviction rather than penetration which we shall find characteristic of Justin's temper and writings

There is no reason to suppose that Justin has been guilty of a serious hysteron-proteron in putting the writings of the Prophets among the causes and inspirations of his conversion. Justin's age was intensely eager for the mysterious, and found great delight in the allegorical explanation of cryptic language of all sorts. Especially did the mystic urge of the time seek to find expression through oracles, secret passwords, and myths. The appeal to prophecy which now seems to us as the weakest sort of apologetic, exactly met the prevailing taste of the day, and was a powerful weapon against the opponents of Christianity. Justin could seriously challenge the heathen, "That the Prophets were inspired by none other than the Divine Logos, even you, as I fancy, will grant."[2] Accordingly the incessant use of prophecy, together with the love of elaborate and fanciful exegesis which seems a great barrier to the understanding of the early Fathers today, was the most forcible presentation of Christianity to an age with a morbid love for the unusual and marvellous. Semisch[3] points out that Tatian, Theophilus of Antioch, and Hilary, all definitely attributed their conversion

---

[1] For the use of this idea in Justin's Apologetic see below p 110 ff

[2] Ap I. 33. 9 (75 D).

[3] (Bibl 118) I 14 Anm 1.

to the peculiar appeal of Old Testament prophecy, and
Justin who thought it worth while to rest the bulk of the
defence for Christianity with heathens as well as with
Jews upon the prophetic argument, may well have been
induced to do so because he had been attracted to
Christianity by prophecy himself.

Of Justin's life as a Christian we know unfortunately
very little. Tradition, begun in the "Martyrdom" and
carried on by Eusebius and the later church writers,
represents him after his conversion as having dedicated
his life to Christian propaganda, and the spirit revealed
in the Apologies and the Dialogue completely harmonizes
with such a tradition. With the Cynic Criscus (Greek,
Criscens) he says he had an open dispute of so violent
a character that he expected the hatred of Criscus sooner
or later to bring about his death[1] Trypho is made to say
that Justin is obviously a man of wide experience in
controversy on the points they are discussing,[2] while
Justin himself says that he is accustomed to answer the
questions and objections of all people of all nations
who want to examine Christian doctrines with him[3]
According to the "Martyrdom", Justin seems to have
conducted a sort of school of Christian doctrine "I live
above one Martinus, at the Timiotinian Bath . . . . if
anyone wished to come to me, I communicated to him
the doctrines of the Truth." At the end of the Dialogue
Justin appears to be on the point of sailing, though
whence, whither, or why is not told[4] As the first word
about the sailing comes from Trypho, there must have
been some earlier conversation on the subject in a lost
section of the Dialogue, very likely in the opening remarks
of the second day's discussion In the "Martyrdom" Justin
is reported as saying that he has twice lived in Rome,
so that usually it has been thought that Justin held the
Dialogue in Ephesus (following Eusebius)[5] on the eve

[1] Ap 11 3 1 ff. (46 E ff).
[2] Dial 50 1 (269 C).
[3] Dial 64. 2 (287 D)
[4] Dial 142 1, 3 (371 C, D).
[5] Eusebius H E IV 18 6.

of his second departure for Rome. But there is no
evidence for such an assumption. The martyrdom of
Justin is very well attested Tatian,[1] Irenaeus,[2] and
Eusebius,[3] mention his martyrdom explicitly, while Tertullian[4] calls him "Martyr". The very early record of
the martyrdom of Justin with others has rarely been
challenged as a genuine account of the death of the
Apologist. Its verbal accuracy cannot of course be relied
upon, but its utter simplicity, together with its harmony
with the character of Justin as revealed in his writings,
make so strong a presumption in its favour that the lack
of external evidence for its genuineness is rightly disregarded. The "Martyrdom" tells that Justin and others
were brought up before Rusticus the Roman prefect in
accordance with a new law which was particularly directed
against the Christians to force them to offer sacrifice to
the gods They refused to comply with this law and
opened a brief parley defending their action. Justin said
that after an attempt to learn all doctrines he had
accepted Christianity as the one true doctrine Christianity
he explained as the worship of the God of the Christians,
who is One from the beginning, fashioner of all creation
visible and invisible, as well as the worship of Jesus
Christ, God's Son, who after having been foretold by
the Prophets became a member of the human race, a
herald of salvation, and teacher of beautiful doctrines.
Justin said that he could not, as a man, speak worthily
of Christ, because to do so required special revelation such
as was recorded in the prophecies. Rusticus, who seems
to have been bored at the prospect of a sermon, abruptly
changed the subject by trying to get information about
Christian meetings and headquarters, but he met with very
little success Justin told of the meeting at the house of
Martinus, but said that Christians had no temples because
their God could be worshipped by anyone anywhere. He
denies outright knowledge of any other meeting place. The

[1] Orat. c. Gr. 19. 1
[2] Adv. Haer I 26 1 (Harvey I. 220).
[3] H E IV. 16 1 ff
[4] Adv Valent. V

fact that a company was brought in together for trial, and
that all were most evasive about information as to Christian
meeting places other than the one at the house of Martinus,
suggests that the company may have represented the fruits
of a raid upon this house. Rusticus soon found that while
each man was eager to confess being a Christian, yet
none would give any useful information. He accordingly
cut short the trial by calling upon them for a last time to
sacrifice to the gods, and upon their refusal pronounced
sentence of decapitation, which was executed at once.
Other Christians later went to the place of execution and
secretly removed the bodies to a place suitable for Holy
Martyrs.

The literature upon the chronology of Justin is very
extensive, but Harnack's [1] summary of the evidence and
conclusions have been in the main unaffected by later
criticism. The evidence for the chronology of Justin's
writings will be discussed later. For Justin's general dates
a starting point must be made with the martyrdom. Four
pieces of evidences are to be considered

1. Eusebius, though he said that Justin owed his death
to Criscus under Pius, yet dated Justin's death in the
Chronicon in the year 2,168 (2,170), and said in the H. E.
(IV. 16. 7 ff.) that Justin died under Marcus Aurelius. That
Justin's death occured under Marcus Aurelius, Harnack
justly concluded was Eusebius' true tradition.

2. The Chronicon Paschale puts the death of Justin
in the year 165

3. The "Martyrdom" puts Justin's death under Rusticus, whose period of office fell between 163—167.

4. Epiphanius also puts Justin's death under Rusticus,
and Harnack thinks Epiphanius is using evidence independent of the "Martyrdom". [2]

Harnack therefore properly concludes that Justin's
death must have fallen between 163 and 167, and that
the tradition of the Chronicon Paschale, 165, is perhaps
exact

---

[1] (Bibl. 182).   II. i. 274—284
[2] Adv. Haer. 46 1.

Epiphanius in the same passage states that the death of Justin occurred when the martyr was thirty years old, a statement which Harnack, like many of his predecessors, interprets as meaning thirty years after Justin's conversion to Christianity Harnack therefore thinks that Justin was converted about the year 133, but this date cannot be taken as having at all the same certainty as the date of Justin's death The statement of Epiphanius is much too ambiguous to be sufficient evidence in itself for dating Justin's conversion Zahn[1] has tried to demonstrate that the Dialogue, while composed later, was actually held in Ephesus about the year 135, which would of course necessitate putting Justin's conversion at least a few years earlier. But it does not seem that Zahn has made a case for any historic character for the discussion with Trypho, and consequently the historical references in the conversation recorded (as to the Bar Cochba War) cannot be taken as a date in Justin's own life There is nothing inherently improbable in the idea that Justin was actually converted between 130 and 135, but there is certainly no adequate evidence to prove that the date should not be five or ten years earlier or later. Aside from his extant writings, which apparently, as will be seen, fall in the decade from 150 to 160, Justin's death is the only incident of his career which can with any confidence be dated

[1] (Bibl 155) p. 50

CHAPTER II

JUSTIN'S WRITINGS

Justin Martyr has been one of the outstanding Christian authorities since his own generation, and it is natural that many forgeries and anonymous writings should traditionally have been ascribed to him. Justin's actual literary activity was probably quite extensive. He himself mentions a treatise against all heresies,[1] and Irenaeus reports a special treatise by Justin against Marcion.[2] Eusebius is our earliest informant that Justin, in addition to two Apologies and the Dialogue, wrote treatises "On the Soul", "On the Unity of God", an "Address to the Greeks" which particularly concerned itself with demonology, and some sort of psalter or hymn book of whose contents we know nothing.[3] Photius adds to the list a treatise "On Nature", and a general "Refutation on the chief reproaches against Christianity "[4]

A fairly large corpus of writings has been preserved in Justin's name, whose titles are as follows:

1. Apology for the Christians addressed to Antoninus Pius[5]

2. Apology for the Christians addressed to the Roman Senate[6]

---

[1] Ap. I. 26. 8 (70 C).
[2] Adv. Haer IV. xi. 2 (Harvey II 158).
[3] H. E. IV. 11, 18.
[4] Bibl. cod. 125, see also 95
[5] Ἀπολογία ὑπὲρ Χριστιανῶν πρὸς Ἀντωνῖνον τὸν Εὐσεβῆ.
[6] Ἀπολογία ὑπὲρ Χριστιανῶν πρὸς τὴν Ῥωμαίων Σύγκλητον.

3. Dialogue with Trypho the Jew.[1]
4 Address to the Greeks.[2]
5. Hortatory Address to the Greeks [3]
6 On the Unity of God [4]
7 To Diognetus [5]
8. A fragment on the Resurrection.[6]
9. Exposition of the True Faith.[7]
10. Letter to Zenas and Serenus [8]
11. Refutation of certain Aristotelian Doctrines.[9]
12. Questions and Answers to the Orthodox.[10]
13. Christian Questions asked of the Greeks.[11]

Of these only the two Apologies and the Dialogue can be accepted as genuine. Some include the "Fragment on the Resurrection", on the ground that it might legitimately be regarded as an elaboration of ideas expressed in the genuine writings But the stylistic impediments to accepting the Fragment seem insurmountable. Justin's expository method as shown in the Apologies and Dialogue is anything but ordered and compact But the author of the fragment on the Resurrection proceeds from premise to conclusion in so neat a consecutiveness that it is hard to conceive how Justin could have produced it The arguments in defence of the other pseudo-Justinian writings are all unconvincing and have been so thoroughly dealt with as to need no exposition here.[12]

---

[1] Πρὸς Τρύφωνα Ἰουδαῖον Διάλογος.
[2] Πρὸς Ἕλληνας.
[3] Λόγος παραινετικὸς πρὸς Ἕλληνας.
[4] Περὶ Μοναρχίας.
[5] Πρὸς Διόγνητον.
[6] Περὶ Ἀναστάσεως.
[7] Ἔκθεσις τῆς ὀρθῆς πίστεως.
[8] Ζήνᾳ καὶ Σερήνῳ.
[9] Ἀνατροπὴ δογμάτων τινῶν Ἀριστοτελικῶν.
[10] Ἀποκρίσεις πρὸς τοὺς ὀρθοδόξους περὶ τινῶν ἀναγκαίων Ζητημάτων.
[11] Ἐρωτήσεις Χριστιανικαὶ πρὸς τοὺς Ἕλληνας.
[12] Semisch (Bibl. 118) I 58—176 accepted the Fragment on the Resurrection and the Hortatory Address to the Greeks. Contrary, see Bardenhewer (Bibl 186) I 211—249, Harnack (Bibl 182) I. 99—114, and (Bibl 173) 130—175.

The text of the three genuine works is based almost
entirely upon a single manuscript, Paris 450, written in
1364, which contains most of the writings mentioned above
as still preserved under Justin's name. Though incomplete,
the text of the Dialogue seems much more reliable than
the text of the Apology. The only check we have upon
the readings of this manuscript are the few passages where
Justin has been quoted by other ancient writers, and an
important fragment from the First Apology (Chapters 65
to 67), which has independent tradition in Codex Otto-
bonianus Graecus CCLXXIV, of the Fifteenth Century,
in the Vatican Library at Rome

A THE FIRST APOLOGY

In the manuscript Paris 450, the shorter Apology with
the title "Addressed to the Roman Senate" appears before
the longer Apology addressed to Antoninus, and such was
the order of printing in the first two editions of Justin's
works. But the longer Apology is probably the earlier
because it is apparently quoted in the shorter, so that the
order is now always reversed, and the longer known as the
First Apology.

The First Apology dates itself with sufficient accuracy.[1] It is addressed to the Emperor Antoninus Pius,
together with his son Verissimus the Philosopher, and
Lucius the Philosopher, etc. Verissimus is obviously Marcus Aurelius whose philosophical reputation began about
the same time as his co-regency, 147. Lucius must be
Lucius Cejonius Aelius Amelius Commodus who was not
born until 130, and who would hardly have been addressed as a philosopher at least until he was eighteen or
twenty years of age, while he first entered into a position
of political prominence about 153 when he became a
member of the Senate.[2] Harnack[3] is inclined to give

[1] The best discussions of the date of the First Apology are
Veil (Bibl. 80) pp. xxviii—xxxii; Harnack (Bibl. 182) II. i. 275—281.
Blunt (Bibl. 43) pp. xlvii—l, has summed up the evidence in brief.

[2] Veil (Bibl. 80) p. xxx.

[3] Harnack (Bibl. 182) II. i. 277.

more importance to Justin's statement[1] that he is writing
150 years after the birth of Christ than the statement would
warrant, for Harnack denies that this figure can be even
ten years out of the way But though some of Harnack's
arguments are strained, his conclusion that the Apology is
to be dated a few years after 150, or approximately 152
to 154, to which conclusion Veil had already come (153
to 155), received striking confirmation in a discovery by
Kenyon in a Greek papyrus in the British Museum.[2]
Justin mentions in the Apology[3] that a petition had
recently been given to Felix, Governor of Alexandria.
Kenyon has identified this Felix as the successor of Marcus
Petronius Honoratus Honoratus was beginning his gover-
norship in 148, and Felix was succeeded by M Sempronius
Liberalis in 154, so that from this papyrus Felix would
probably have held office 150 or 151—154. Another papyrus definitely gives Felix's date of accession as 151.[4]
Since Justin's mention of the petition implies a very recent
event, it is probable that he was writing about 154 or 155,
and this date is now accepted as approximately correct.

There seems to have been no special emergency which
inspired Justin to write the First Apology, as we shall see
was clearly the case with the Second Apology. No reference is made to any significant events of the immediate
past as at all unusual At the time when the Apology was
written the Christian community was temporarily being
ignored, although the law still condemned the faith, and
Christians knew that any social unrest was likely to turn the
grim attention of the governors towards them. Their apprehensions were soon justified under Marcus Aurelius,
while in the years of comparative quiet before this great
movement against them their precarious position was kept
vividly before their minds by frequent minor sallies and
local disaffections which resulted fatally for faithful individuals in various parts of the Empire. Justin seems to

[1] Ap. I 46. 1 (83 B).
[2] Kenyon (Bibl 244) p. 98. See also (Bibl 245).
[3] Ap. I 29. 3 (71 E).
[4] Grenfell and Hunt: The Oxyrhynchus Papyri, London
1899 II 162 ff.

have been taking advantage of this period of comparative
security to register his protest against the general situation.
Puech has suggested that Justin naively expected not only
that his Apology would be read by the Royal Personages
addressed, as well as by the Senate, but that his arguments
would appeal to them as so conclusive that they would
order the Apology's wide publication and the immediate
alteration of official policy toward Christianity.[1] But
Heinisch is much nearer the truth when he says that the
practice of addressing apologetic epistles to a ruler was
taken over from Hellenistic Judaism, and that in neither
Christianity nor Judaism was it ever supposed that the
august personages addressed would read the apology.
Rather was the ambitious dedication put on the work in
order to give it dignity in the eyes of the public for
which it was really designed, ordinary non - Christian
people.[2]

The Apology falls into two main divisions of unequal
length In the first twelve chapters Justin states his Apology proper by refuting current anti-Christian slanders. Justin deals with three main points, first the fact that the
mere confession of Christianity is a crime so grievous that
no specific charges of lawlessness are necessary to justify
the death penalty (cc 4, 5); and second and third the
charges of atheism and immorality which he treats together
(cc 6—12) He flatly denies the truth of the rumours of
Christian immorality and lawlessness He insists that any
Christian who can be proved guilty of such conduct as is
generally charged against the faithful is unworthy of the
name he bears, and urges that he be given not the slightest
mercy It is true that the crimes slanderously alleged
against the Christians are the daily and open practice of a
large part of their accusers, but the Christians do not plead
this point They only urge that the acceptance of the
Christian doctrine, which stands for the highest morality,
be not taken by those who do not understand its teachings
as in itself a proof of moral degradation The Christians

[1] (Bibl 334) p. 5
[2] (Bibl 394) p. 18.

worship God whom they know in truth, and it is not they but their idolatrous accusers who are atheists. Furthermore Christians are not to be feared as political plotters, for the eyes of the faithful are not upon an earthly human kingdom, else they would try to save their lives, but upon the Divine Kingdom which is with God.

Short as this first division of the Apology has been, Justin asserts that he is confident that he has written enough to ensure a change of policy from any intelligent judge, but that still it will not be amiss to state clearly the real facts of Christianity Christians, Justin goes on to say, are monotheists who worship first God, then according to His secondary rank, Jesus Christ, and then according to his tertiary rank, the Prophetic Spirit (c. 13). Thereupon he devotes the major part of the Apology to explaining first the moral power of Christ's teachings (cc. 14—20), and then the relation of Christ, as the Logos, to God (cc. 21—60). Here, amidst many digressions, Justin argues for the divine character of Jesus Christ from the fact that Christ has been prophesied from earliest times by those whose unusual relationships with God gave them special insight into the Truth. To these prophetic descriptions the founder of the Christian Faith exactly corresponded The effective power of the teaching and person of Christ in elevating the moral tone of those who accept the Faith is demonstrated by the exalted character of the Christian cultus, especially in Baptism and the Eucharist (cc. 61—67). The Apology closes with an affirmation of conviction that the innocence of the Christians has been convincingly demonstrated: there is no need for Justin to quote a neglected precedent for toleration. The Christians can rise above these lower appeals and stand upon the justness of their own cause so fearlessly as to threaten the Governors of Rome with the future punishment of the willfully perverse if they persist in their hatred of the only true religion. The Christians themselves are in the hands of God and need only say, "The will of God be done" (c. 68). Nevertheless Justin does quote the legal precedent, a letter from Hadrian and Antoninus concerning the Christians which he has apparently misunderstood.

Various attempts have been made to find in the First Apology a more elaborate plan Wehofer tried to fit the Apology to the classic form of an oration,[1] and his thesis, while generally rejected, has been revived in slightly modified form by Jene[2] Similarly Hubik[3] and Pfattisch,[4] while rejecting Wehofer's thesis, have tried to outline the Apology according to a single unifying principle, but their attempts have rightly met with no greater approval than Wehofer's.[5] For it is only by violence to the obvious facts that the writings of Justin can be regarded as developed in detail according to a systematized plan Justin clearly knew in general what he wanted to say when he began upon a piece of writing, but he could not have produced documents so "rambling and fanciful, abounding in digressions, repetitions, and parentheses"[6] as are the Apologies and Dialogue, had he either begun with a careful outline, or systematically revised his work when he had finished writing.

B THE SECOND APOLOGY

The document commonly known as the Second Apology presents a much more difficult literary problem The chapters which we now have are obviously a fragment, for there is no introductory address, and the first sentence begins abruptly with a "but".[7] Critics have come almost to unity on the Second Apology in describing it as an Appendix or Postscript written because of an unfortunate incident which occurred shortly after the completion of the First Apology,[8] when a disaffected pagan, whose wife had turned Christian, had caused the execution of two Christians at the command of Urbicus, the Prefect Justin

[1] (Bibl 202), cf Rauschen (Bibl 203), and Geffcken (Bibl 205).
[2] (Bibl 210).
[3] (Bibl 209) pp 60 — 137.
[4] Pfattisch (Bibl 385) pp 131 — 182
[5] Christ (Bibl. 185) p 1029 Anm 5
[6] Blunt (Bibl 43) p xi
[7] Bardenhewer (Bibl 186) p 216.
[8] e g Veil, Harnack, Bardenhewer. Goodspeed (Bibl 45) entitles the Second Apology "Appendix".

thinks that he is himself in danger from such a pagan in the person of the Cynic Crescens. The Second Apology opens with an account of this incident, at the close of which Justin goes on to elaborate a few points which he had mentioned in his First Apology, particularly in connection with the Logos doctrine. Into his description of the Logos Justin now for the first time introduces the term "spermatic", and says that reason as found in men is a fragment from the entire Spermatic Logos. In the course of the brief document he at least twice refers to something he has said before,[1] but the passages referred to are both lacking in the Second Apology. They can, however, be identified with tolerable satisfaction in the First Apology,[2] and this fact has given rise to the theory that our Second Apology is only an appendix to the First Apology which has somehow come to be preserved as a separate document.

General as is the satisfaction with the Appendix theory it is by no means unchallenged, and is open to serious objections One of the starting points of the theory is the report by Eusebius that he has two Apologies from Justin, one addressed to Antoninus, the other to the Senate.[3] But Eusebius quotes from our Second Apology, saying that he is quoting the First,[4] while he has quotations from our First Apology as well. This has been seized upon by critics as the origin of the separation of the Appendix from its original position, on the supposition that since Eusebius mentioned two Apologies, some copyist wanted to provide two, and did so by copying the Appendix as a separate work. The real Second Apology which Eusebius mentioned, it is explained, is now lost, and our First and Second Apologies together were the First Apology of Eusebius. This explanation is more ingenious than satisfying, and has been rejected by several critics whose grounds for doing so were quite different from

[1] Ap. II. 4. 2 (43 D), cf Ap. I. 10. 1 (58 B); Ap. II 6 5 (45 A), cf. Ap. I 23. 2 (68 C), and 63. 10, 16 (96 A, D).

[2] See preceding note.

[3] H E IV. 11. 11

[4] H. E. IV 17. 1

each other Schwartz would reject the dedication from the First Apology as an interpolation, and put the Second Apology as the introduction to the First, representing neither document as an afterthought, but the two as a single unit, produced from a single inspiration.[1] Christ[2] inclines to agree with Schwartz, but Schwartz's theory leaves in the air the references in the Second Apology to what has already been said. Grundl has attempted a fantastic division of the Second Apology into two documents, the first of which is the original protest against the violence of Urbicus, into which have been interpolated chapters 4—10, and 14, the product of a convert to Christianity from Alexandrian Judaism.[3] But this theory has been adequately refuted by Emmerich.[4] Recently Hubík[5] has attempted to prove that the Second Apology was written in answer to the speech against the Christians by M. Cornelius Fronto, which very shortly afterward provoked the writing of the Dialogue of Minucius Felix in the Octavius, and from which alone Fronto's speech can be known. This would necessitate the dating of the Apology at least a few years into the reign of Marcus Aurelius (Hubík estimates 165), and accounts for the strong innovation of Stoic terminology. For the attack upon Christianity was being conducted chiefly by Stoics, and Justin was anxious to meet them upon their own grounds. As to the argument from the quotation of the Second Apology as the First by Eusebius, Hubík ingeniously points out that Eusebius might well have been quoting from a manuscript in which our Second Apology came before the First as it does in Paris 450, for Eusebius never confuses the two when he distinguishes them by their dedications.[6] Hubík weakens his case by trying to carry his theory too far, in attempting to represent a demonstration of probability as a demonstration of fact. As a demonstration of probability

[1] (Bibl. 206)
[2] (Bibl. 185) p 1029
[3] (Bibl 198)
[4] (Bibl 201)
[5] (Bibl 209)
[6] Ibid Appendix I   Except possibly in H E IV 7 5

Hubík's theory appears to have been accepted two years later by La Grange when he says that there seems to have been a long interval between the writing of the two Apologies, and that the Second Apology was written in the reign of Marcus Aurelius.[1] If our Second Apology is treated as fragment of a longer work, the references which now seem to look to the First Apology may well have had their source in the lost part of the Second, for it is only to be expected that if the Second Apology was itself a long document Justin would have repeated much that he had said in his former writings. It may indeed be true that it is just because of the general similarity of the two that only that part of the Second Apology has been preserved which was actually of value as supplementary to the First. But we are here in the realm of pure conjecture. Hubík can probably not be said to have proved all he started out to prove, but he has greatly weakened the sense of satisfaction attendant upon the "Appendix" theory, or any theory which tries to represent the two Apologies as originally one

C THE DIALOGUE WITH TRYPHO

The Dialogue with Trypho, while by no means a neglected piece of writing, has not attracted so much attention nor provoked so much discussion as the Apologies. The reason for this comparative neglect is not hard to find. The piece is nearly as long as the four Gospels combined, and as a whole is so astonishingly dull that to a general theological reader it can by no means have the same attraction as the Apologies.

But that the Dialogue is a genuine production of Justin's can hardly be doubted. The last attack against its genuineness, made in a posthumous fragment by Preuschen,[2] only demonstrated how few and weak were the arguments which could be adduced against it. The

---

[1] (Bibl 167) p. 70 La Grange does not quote Hubík, but includes him in his bibliography, and obviously has him in mind

[2] (Bibl 231). Preuschen has been satisfactorily answered by Fonck (Bibl 232)

document bears all the peculiarities of Justin's style, quotes from the First Apology, is cited by Eusebius as Justin's, so that the proof against it would have to be very strong indeed to warrant its rejection. The inspiration of the recurrent attempts to reject it is that Justin on several minor points of theology might seem to have different opinions in the Dialogue from those expressed in the Apologies. Lange distinguished between the background of the Dialogue and that of the Apologies, asserting that the latter rested upon Platonism, the former upon the philosophy of Hellenistic Judaism [1] But it will appear that Lange has made a false distinction and that there is as much reason to see Hellenistic Judaism in the Apologies as in the Dialogue. In the Apologies Justin says that worship is accorded to the Holy Spirit as a Divinity, while in the Dialogue Justin in one passage apparently limits divine character to two Persons, the Father and the Son.[2] In the Dialogue alone is found the conception of "Dispensation" and of "Chiliasm", in it the approach to the problem of the Deity of Christ is quite different, and results in apparent inconsistencies of detail. But all of these differences can readily be explained on the basis of the difference in purpose and method between the Apologies and the Dialogue, and constitute no indictment of the genuineness of the Dialogue.

The date of the Dialogue is not to be determined with great nicety. The First Apology is alluded to,[3] which necessitates a later date than that decided upon for the First Apology, 153—155. but there is no reason for assigning it to one year rather than another between the writing of the Apology and Justin's death.

In Platonic fashion Justin begins the Dialogue by setting the stage. In his philosopher's cloak he is walking one day by the Xystus when he is saluted by Trypho the Jew and his companions. Courtesies soon deepen into an exposition by Justin of the nature of the true philosophy,

---

[1] Lange (Bibl 219) from von Engelhardt (Bibl. 313) p. 26.
[2] Cf Ap. I. 6 2 (56 C); Dial 56 15 (277 C).
[3] Dial 120 6 (349 C)

in describing which Justin uses the fiction of a quest through various schools and the ultimate discovery of the Truth by conversing with the Old Man and by studying the prophets.[1] The Truth, he found, was Christianity. Trypho answers this narrative by saying that Justin had far better have remained a Platonist, for whereas formerly he had been engaged in a noble quest for God, now he had abandoned the quest to repose confidence in the human doctrines of Christianity.[2] He urges compliance with the Law as the true way to serve God, for the Christians have invented a Christ for themselves in whom there is no salvation. This statement, which Hubík well calls the theme of Trypho,[3] is answered by the theme of Justin, a complete denial of the alleged mistaken character of Christianity and a proposal to prove the truth and power of the Christian belief.[4] The proof which follows falls into three main divisions. The first division (cc 11—31) treats of the nature and obligation of the Mosaic Law, which Justin insists was given the Jews as a sign of reproach. Justification was possible even before the institution of circumcision, and has always been quite independent of Jewish legalism. Though God undoubtedly gave the Law, justification throughout Jewish history has been a matter of moral integrity and purity of heart, not a matter of legal observance. The second division (cc 32—110) discusses the nature, history, and significance of Jesus Christ, demonstrating that he is the incarnation of that saving power which has been prophesied from the first by the Prophets in Judaism. This section is the most discouraging of the Dialogue because the chain of argument is repeatedly found only to be lost as Justin wanders from digression to digression. The testimony which Justin adduces is strictly scriptural; the philosophers are forgotten, and the entire case is rested upon exegesis of the Old Testament In the course of the section Justin deals with

---

[1] See above pp. 57 ff.
[2] Dial 8 3, 4 (225 D ff).
[3] (Bibl 209) p 28.
[4] Dial. 9. 1 (226 C).

the Incarnation and Crucifixion in particular, and discusses
the existence of the Second God, the possibility of the
Incarnation, the possibility of the Virgin birth, the divine
human character of Christ after His birth, the necessity
of the Crucifixion, and the Resurrection of Christ. Justin,
by basing all of these points upon the Old Testament,
gives the impression that Christ is not a novelty, but the
long anticipated consummation and revelation of the true
character of Judaism. Accordingly in the third division
(cc. 111—142) he insists that those who have followed and
will follow Christ are the True Israel, the children of
promise, the true successors of those Jews who found
justification in times past. He closes with an eloquent
exhortation to Trypho and his followers to accept the
Truth and become Christians.

The conception in the Dialogue is powerful, but the
execution is weak, for only by reading and re-reading does
the basic plan of the whole come to light. The traditional
opinion that the Dialogue is a record of an actual discussion [1]
can hardly be maintained That the arguments of Justin are
those generally used in such discussions is highly probable,
but the Dialogue seems far rather to be a collection of
all possible arguments than a report of a discussion in
which each argument was actually brought up as recorded.
Trypho is in many respects a straw man, who says the
right thing in the right place; he never seriously embarrasses
Justin by his replies, and is a tool in his hands.[2] Justin
frequently represents Trypho as making a show of protest
against the course of the argument, but these protests never
take the form of rejoinders at all awkward for Justin's
purposes. The tradition of ,the historic nature of the
Dialogue goes back to Eusebius who says that the Dialogue
was actually held at Ephesus,[3] a fact which Eusebius

[1] Best expounded by Donaldson (Bibl 143) p. 88 ff.

[2] See e g. Dial. 65. 1 ff (289 B ff.), where at the proper
moment Trypho brings up just the passage of prophecy which
Justin wanted at that juncture, and allows Justin to take it from
him and turn it against him without protest Justin frequently
uses such devices to attract especial attention to some Old Testament passage.

[3] H. E IV 18 6

probably took from the lost introduction to the Dialogue, and which hence would have been only a part of Justin's stage setting for the fictitious meeting. Such discussions may have been common, though it seems likely that they would have been of a more violent character than the one described. But to try to explain the incoherencies and repetitions of the Dialogue as being the result of extempore argument lasting two days, necessitates the unjustifiable assumption that Eusebius had independent testimony as to the circumstances of the composition of the Dialogue.

It is equally idle to speculate as to the identity of Trypho. Eusebius has in this also been the origin of an erroneous tradition, for he states that Trypho was one of the most famous Jews of the day,[1] and this statement has given rise to repeated attempts to identify Trypho with Rabbi Tarphon [2] Trypho may be the Greek form of Tarphon, so that the indentity is at first sight alluring,[3] but will not stand scrutiny. Rabbi Tarphon was one of the most bitter and violent of the anti-Christian Rabbis, whose disposition as revealed in his traditional sayings is utterly incompatible with his sitting two entire days as a mildly protesting but friendly antagonist of Justin. Tarphon hated the Christians so bitterly that he said that though it had cost his children's lives he would have burned books containing the name of God, if they were the blasphemous books of the Christians.[4] Further it is even impossible to say that Justin names the straw man in honor of Rabbi Tarphon whose name he had heard as a great opponent of Christianity, but of whose actual teachings he knew nothing,[5] for Trypho is never represented as a

[1] H. E IV 18 6

[2] e. g see Christ (Bibl. 185) p. 1030; Zöckler (Bibl 283) p 44, Harnack (Bibl 395) pp. 53 ff. Dr. Kidd speaks of "Trypho, a thin disguise, it may be, for Tarpho": History of the Church, Oxf. 1922, I 90. These are all based upon Schürer, Gesch Volk. Jud II³ 378, 555 ff.

[3] See Strack: Einleitung in Talmud und Midrasch 5 Aufl München 1921 S. 125, 126 Anm. 1.

[4] See Bacher, Aggada der Tannaiten, I (2 Aufl.) 351, and G F Moore. Def. of Jewish Canon, p 102

[5] With Zahn (Bibl 155) pp. 61 ff

Jewish Rabbi To be sure, Justin could not represent Trypho as speaking from a wider knowledge of Hebrew and Judaism than Justin himself possessed, but Trypho is throughout represented as being helplessly dependant for his ideas upon Jewish Rabbis, and is exhorted to declare his independence of their tyranny over his thinking and to examine the prophecies with an open mind. Had Justin had Rabbi Tarphon remotely in mind when he gave the name to his straw man, he must at least have represented him as a Rabbi, and not as a very dependant layman [1]

But if Trypho is not Rabbi Tarphon his point of view is by no means a figment of the imagination Straw man he may appear in that he cannot be identified with any historical character, and is obviously a tool in Justin's hands, but there is good reason to suppose that Trypho represents with extraordinary accuracy the attitude of many Jews of the time. Zahn has reviewed very carefully one aspect of Trypho's character, and come to the conclusion that Trypho was a Hellenistic Jew with philosophical training [2] Holland has not used the term Hellenistic, but has pointed out that Trypho is far from an ordinary Palestinian Jew in his eagerness for philosophy on account of the poverty of the Law in intellectual appeal, particularly on the matter of its philosophically inadequate conception of God [3] Trypho has read the Gospels, a thing strictly forbidden all Palestinian Jews, and is apparently open to conviction toward Christianity He professes to be no authority in Judaism, understands no Hebrew,[4] admits the Alexandrian doctrine of the double sense of Scripture, according to which only the hidden sense was accepted as

---

[1] Cf Dial 38 1, 2 (256 C, D), 94 4 (322 B), 137. 2 (366 D), 140 2 (369 C), 142 2 (371 C). The latest protest against identifying Trypho and Tarphon is made by A Lukyn Williams Tractate Berakoth, London 1921, p 6 n. 2

[2] Zahn (Bibl 155) pp. 54 ff , see also (Bibl 181) I 468

[3] (Bibl. 153) p 570 Dial 1. 3 (217 D, E)

[4] Dial 125 1 (354 A) Justin asks the etymology of the word Israel, and not a Jew in the company has a suggestion

the true meaning of a passage,[1] and, like the moderate,
Alexandrians who still held to a part of the Law, he
regarded the Law as amply fulfilled by circumcision, by
the observance of the Sabbath and the feast of the
new moon, and by care in washing after touching prohib-
ited things and after sexual intercourse.[2] He has no
objections to Justin's carrying him along to a denial of
the value of the Law,[3] to a more philosophic and mystical
conception of justification than that founded upon legalism,[4] and even seems to have no implacable prejudices
against believing in an intermediary and secondary Deity,
whose complete divine character is yet insisted upon.[5]
Trypho only parts from Justin on the possibility of the
incarnation of the Second Deity, and especially of that
incarnation's actually having taken place in Jesus. Cohn
goes so far as to call Trypho a Judaistic Hellene,[6] and
indeed Trypho in all these respects illustrates remarkably
what has been described as the point of view of the
Hellenized Jew. But Trypho's character and the problem
of Justin's acquaintance with Judaism are complicated
by the fact that Trypho's apparently casual comments
are remarkably accurate reproductions of the traditional
sayings of the Jewish Schoolmen. Trypho allows hope
of salvation to upright heathen,[7] which at first seems a
Hellenistic compromise, but which was actually a doctrine
of the Tannaim. Rabbi Joshua ben Chanonja taught, in
expounding Psalm ix. 18, that only the godless among
the Heathen are excluded (from eternal life), for there
is a large number of pious men even among the heathen
who will have a share in eternal life.[8] Trypho says that

[1] Dial. 90. 2 (317 C)
[2] Dial. 46. 2 (264 C).
[3] Dial. 67. 6 ff. (292 A ff.)
[4] Ibid.
[5] Dial. 60. 3 (283 B, C), 63. 1 (286 B). Harnack (Bibl. 395) p. 75 denies this, and the point is also missed by Freimann (Bibl. 230) p. 577
[6] Judaica. Festschrift fur Cohen. Berlin 1912. p. 331.
[7] Dial. 8. 3 (226 A).
[8] See Bacher I (2. Aufl.) p. 134, similar references in Gold-fahn (Bibl. 389 p. 54.

he is disobeying the injunctions of his teachers in holding communication with a Christian,[1] and such prohibitions are preserved in Babyl. Ab Sars. 17 a, 27 b: "Let no man have dealings with the Christians"[2] Trypho repudiates the divine character of the expected Messiah,[3] and with him agree all the Tannaim.[4] Trypho says that there must have been both God and an angel in the flaming bush,[5] which might be taken as a layman's understanding of the statement, "Everywhere where an Angel appears, the glory of God reveals itself; for it stands written (Exod. iii. 2), 'and an angel of God appeared to him in a flame of fire', whereupon it immediately continues, 'God called to him'".[6] Trypho is speaking according to Pharisaic tradition in ascribing Is. vii. 14 ff. to Hezekiah[7] One of Trypho's companions admits the inability of the Rabbis to explain how Moses could have been commanded to make the brazen serpent when to do so would involve the breaking of the Law against making images.[8] Goldfahn tries to show that the Rabbis had met this problem, and that Justin's reproach is unjust,[9] but his evidence quite misses Justin's point, and Justin is probably right in saying that the Rabbis had no answer to his argument. One only of Trypho's statements can not be justified by Judaistic tradition, namely that God had given the sun and moon to the heathen for gods, which seems directly contrary to the tradition. But here Trypho may represent

[1] Dial. 38. 1 (256 B).

[2] Goldfahn (Bibl. 389) p 106.

[3] Dial. 49. 1 (268 A).

[4] Klausner, J.: Die messianischen Vorstellungen des jüdischen Volkes im Zeitalter der Tannaiten Berlin 1904. p. 71. "There are p e r h a p s many indications of the divine nature of the Messiah in the later Midrashim; but in the authentic writings of the Tannaitic age no trace of such a thing is to be found"

[5] Dial 60. 1 (283 A).

[6] Exodus Rabba, end of Ch. 32 p. 135 d Goldfahn (Bibl. 389) p 113

[7] Dial. 67 1 (291 B), cf. Exodus Rabba Ch. 18 p. 103 d. Goldfahn (Bibl. 389) p. 146.

[8] Dial 94. 4 (322 B'.

[9] (Bibl. 389) p. 197

a doctrine which was later expressly rejected and contradicted, and so not preserved in the Midrash.[1]

Justin is thus by no means beating the air in his
discussion with Trypho. He has created in Trypho a Jew
who embodies the best of both schools of Judaism, one
who knows Scripture and the Rabbinic interpretations,
at least the Haggadic interpretations, and yet who has
all the open-mindedness and cosmic sense of the Hellenistic
Jews. As combining both elements, Trypho may well
claim to be an honest attempt on the part of Justin to
delineate the character of the ideal Jew It is useless
in such a case to scatter energy in an attempt to class
Trypho as either Palestinian or Hellenistic.[2]

It will further appear in the course of the exposition
of Justin's ideas that not only in drawing the character of
Trypho but throughout the Dialogue Justin shows the
most unexpected acquaintance with the details of Palestinian
Judaistic teaching.[3] Whence had Justin this knowledge?
The Pharisaic teaching was in Justin's time still entirely
oral, and Justin had no training in Hebrew which would
have enabled him to read the books had they been in
existence It is customary to explain Justin's knowledge of
Judaism from a statement of Trypho that he perceives that
Justin has had considerable experience in such dispute,[4]
from which statement it is concluded that it must have
been in these disputations with Jews that Justin had
gathered his information about Pharisaic exegesis. But
it seems much more likely that Justin had his information
from some written source or sources which he was using.
Certainly Justin is not creating a refutation of Judaism.
None of his main arguments is at all novel, with the ᐟ

[1] Dial. 55. 1 (274 B); cf. Goldfahn (Bibl. 389) p 109

[2] Harnack denies for him the character of a Hellenistic Jew,
and calls him a Rabbi (Bibl 395), p. 53, 90 Anm. 1

[3] For the most complete collection of parallels between the
Dial. and the Haggada see Goldfahn (Bibl. 389). Harnack (Bibl 395)
has only recast Goldfahn's material.

[4] Hubík (Bibl. 209) p. 3 Anm 6 deduces that Justin was
accustomed to dispute upon Christianity with Jews and others from
Dial. 50. 1 (269 C) and Dial 64 2 (287 D).

possible exception of the suggestion that the Law was a
reproach, a sign of God's displeasure put upon the Jews
because of their misbehaviour' His doctrines of the non-
essential character of the Law and circumcision for justification, based upon the experiences of Abraham and
his predecessors, and of the Christians as being the true
Israel, are as old as St Paul In spite of Justin's elaborate
use of Scripture he does not appear as a profound or
original student of the Old Testament, but rather leads
one to suspect that he has collected all the passages
which had ever been used against the Jews, and has
incorporated them into his own writing. He quotes one
Prophet in mistake for another in several passages, as
though he were using material with which he was not
thoroughly acquainted. These slips cannot be put down
as mere lapses of memory, because Justin from the great
length of his quotation is in all probability working from
a written source or sources We have ample evidence that
written disputes with the Jews and diatribes against them
were in exsitence long before Justin's time,[1] and the
Dialogue of Justin seems a compilation of material from
such documents, one of which might well have been a
written account of the teachings of the Jewish Rabbis
by a converted Rabbi, or possibly a Rabbinical anti-
Christian tract It may be that it was because Justin used
sources of different kinds that his completed portrait of
Trypho, and his arguments against him, are a composite
of Palestinian and Hellenistic elements The composite
nature of the material which constitutes the Dialogue,
however, makes it the more valuable as a picture of
Judaism and of the struggle between the two faiths

What was the purpose which Justin had in mind when
he wrote the Dialogue? The treatise was addressed to
one Marcus Pompey, for he is twice addressed in passing,[2]

[1] See Corssen (Bibl 224), Harnack, Texte und Untersuch
I. iii (1883), Hirzel (Bibl 228) Semisch (Bibl 118) II 44, 45
Anm 1 has an interesting collection of parallels between the ex-
egetical material of Justin and the letter of Barnabas See also very
important Dr Rendel Harris. Testimonies Cambr 1916—1950, passim
[2] Dial 8 3 (225 D), 141 5 (371 B).

but the dedication is lost, and with it possibly a key to
the purpose of the book as a whole. The discussion
occupied two days,[1] but the ending of the first day
and the beginning of the second are lost, while there
are repeated instances of references in the latter part
to passages in the earlier part which are no longer there.[2]
As we now have it, the Dialogue is in one unusually
long book, but it was probably in two books originally,
for chapter 82 is quoted in the Sacra Parallela of St. John
the Damascene as having been taken from the second
book.[3] Hirzel seems to think that Justin wrote the
Dialogue in a remote or very unsuccessful attempt to
imitate the Phaedrus, and that the reference to Marcus
Pompey is only a literary gesture.[4] Harnack on the
other hand assumes that there must have been a prologue,
and hints that the mutilations throughout the Dialogue
have not come about by chance,[5] but he does not suggest
the motive for mutilation. The Dialogue may have been
considerably longer and been abbreviated by a lazy scribe,
for it is clear that the κτλ which concludes many of
the quotations from Scripture is the work of such a
copyist.[6] Grube's suggestion that the Dialogue is an
"introduction into the correct understanding of the writings
of the Old Testament, designed for Christian readers" is
attractive, but still helps little in showing the connection
of the introduction with the body of the work.[7] That
the Dialogue was ultimately designed for propagandist

[1] Dial. 85. 4 (311 D), 92 5 (320 B). It is customary to
assume that the break between the first and second day occurred
in the obvious lacuna in Dial 74 3, 4 (300 A)

[2] See Dial 81 3 (308 A) συνήκαμεν; 105 4 (333 A). For
fuller discussion of the missing passages see Zahn (Bibl 155)
pp. 37—66 Otto's theory that the Dial. as we have it is sub-
stantially as it left Justin's hands finds no support to-day See
especially Otto (Bibl. 26) Dial. c. 74. n 7.

[3] Cf. Holl in Texte und Untersuchungen XX ii (1899)
p 34 from Bardenhewer (Bibl 186) p 227

[4] (Bibl 228).

[5] (Bibl 395) p. 47 n 3

[6] e g Dial. 56 2 (275 B)

[7] (Bibl 391) p 1

purposes amongst the Jews has been denied by Battifol[1] and Habík.[2] Bosse surmises from the dialogue form of writing that Marcus Pompey was a Platonist friend of Justin, but that in the course of the argument he was entirely forgotten by Justin, and that to understand the Dialogue not Marcus Pompey but Trypho must be considered as the person addressed.[3] Bosse is avoiding difficulties rather than solving them. Von Engelhardt attempts to explain the connection of the introduction with the body of the Dialogue by suggesting that Justin hoped at the outset to gain weight for his arguments in Jewish eyes by describing his conversion to Christianity as having resulted from reading the Prophets.[4] But if this was Justin's purpose in writing the introduction, he represents his hope as being singularly unfounded, for he gains no word of sympathy or commendation from Trypho for his interest in Jewish literature. Rather Trypho answers that Justin would have done far better to have abided by the philosophers than to have forsaken them as he did. The study of the Prophets is very pointedly not recommended. Feder says that the introduction is inconceivable as addressed to Palestinian Jews, and is only to be explained on the ground that the Dialogue was designed for Hellenistic Jews.[5] But Feder's suggestion, while a great advance in recognizing the true problem of the introduction, is still weak because he clings to the thought that the Dialogue is addressed to Jews of some sort, that is, that it is fundamentally a refutation of Judaism

The probability is strong that whoever Marcus Pompey was, he was at least not a Jew. Besides the strongly Roman character of the name, minor considerations point to his being a Gentile For Justin obviously is writing for someone unfamiliar with the Scriptures, as is made apparent by the fact that he always identifies the Minor

[1] In his preface to (Bibl. 162) p. xxiv
[2] (Bibl. 209) p. 207.
[3] (Bibl. 345) pp. 7, 8
[4] (Bibl. 313) p. 220.
[5] (Bibl. 350) p. 41.

Prophets at first quoting as "one of the twelve,"[1] and by the fact that his quotations from the Old Testament, originally probably considerably longer than now, would have been quite unnecessarily extended for one already familiar with the Scriptures, but would be interesting and essential to a heathen's understanding of the argument That Marcus Pompey was at least not a Jew is made probable by the fact that Justin brings charges of immorality against the Jews which are so palpably unfair as to be inconceivable in a document addressed to a Jewish friend, or designed as a model for use in converting Jews.[2]

Once the Dialogue is recognized as addressed to a man interested in philosophy and not as a record of a controversy, or a text book for controversy, against Judaism, the continuity of the introduction with the body of the Dialogue becomes clear It will be recalled that in the introduction Justin led the philosophical argument through to the final declaration that the highest part of man, his higher mind, is a fragment of the Universal Mind or Reason. But the fragment in us is in such a condition that its immediate apprehension of the Truth, which should be very clear, is actually much obscured, so that only by revelation of the Universal Reason in the inspired utterances of the Prophets, and pre-eminently in Jesus Christ, can it pierce the veil into the realm of Universal Truth and Reason. But how can the Prophets and the prophesied Christ claim such unique significance for revealing the Truth when Jews and Christians are in complete disagreement among themselves as to the meaning of this revelation? So long as the controversy between Jews and Christians is unsettled, revelation is at least as bewildering as the unassisted attempts of the human mind Accordingly the entire case for the superiority of revelation to philosophy must stand or fall with a proof that the writings of the Jews and the doctrines of the Christians are a unified production of the single Spirit of Inspiration and Revelation It is to prove precisely this that Justin writes the Dialogue

[1] e.g. Dial. 19 5 (236 E); 22. 1 (238 D); 109. 1 (336 A)
[2] e.g. Dial. 14. 2 (231 D); 134, 1 (363 D)

with Trypho to his friend Marcus Pompey Whoever
Marcus Pompey was, whether heathen or Christian, the continuity of the Dialogue as a demonstration of the unity
of Revelation, and hence of the superiority of Revelation
to heathen philosophy, is unaffected. The argument is
one most suitable to be addressed to a heathen, and such
Justin's "dearest friend" probably was Trypho is swayed
by the argument, but still clings to his faith in spite
of the fact that his defences have obviously all been
swept away. So must Marcus Pompey consider the Jews
In stubborn error they are holding to their own conception,
blind like Trypho to the clearest demonstration that the
revelation they cherish in the Prophets has had its culmination in the person and teaching of Jesus Christ
But the blindness of the Jews can be considered by no
fair minded heathen as an indictment of the light, nor
as an impediment to the Christians to prevent them from
using the Jewish Scriptures in spite of Jewish protests
The True Israel is a spiritual succession which since
the coming of Christ has been carried on not in the
Jewish race but in Christian hearts Accordingly the
Dialogue is Justin's demonstration that Revelation, shining
brightly from earliest times and glowing with glory in
Jesus Christ, is a path to God as luminous and hopeful
as the path of philosophy is obscure and despairing

CHAPTER III

JUSTIN'S APOLOGETIC

Apart from the reproaches of Judaism, Justin as a Christian Apologist had to deal with two sorts of attack upon Christianity. From the ethical and social point of view it was urged that the Christians were an immoral group whose practices made them enemies of wholesome society, and from the philosophical point of view the Christian doctrines were attacked as repugnant to all good sense. Rejection of the doctrines of Christianity would never of itself have lead to persecution in the tolerant Roman Empire, but when persecution had already arisen doctrinal reproaches served as additional justification for harsh measures An Apologist of the time must therefore meet the two counts, and meet them as more or less confused causes of a general hatred against Christianity. In the First Apology Justin seems to be trying to disentangle the two, and at the outset to clear away the social and ethical reproaches that he may thus be free to deal with Christianity as a system of thought and guide of life

In general the social and ethical charges were those brought in by the masses of people. As we understand them from Justin, they may be summarized under four heads First, it was alleged, Christians refused to accept their obligations in society as symbolized by Emperor worship Second, they were atheists, and consequently their presence in a community was apt to bring a visitation of wrath from the gods Third, the Christian community aroused suspicion by fact that it was made up almost entirely of people from the lowest classes, very largely of slaves. Then as now patriotic citizens were apprehensive of organizations which brought the slaves and servants of society into a close knit and secret organization, while suspicion on this count was the more awakened against Christianity by the fact that it was well known that Christians looked for a future Kingdom and a reorganization of society. Fourth, these secret meetings of the lowest order of society were reported to be attended by murderous and obscene orgies

Justin does not go into any detailed refutation of these popular charges. That the Christians refused to assume their social obligations, he flatly denies, and urges that though they can offer worship to God alone, Christians yet gladly recognize the sovereign rights of the Roman princes and pray for their guidance as rulers, while the Christians pay their taxes of all kinds more readily than any other group of people [1]

The charge of atheism was intimately bound up with the charge of social irresponsibility, because the refusal to worship the Emperor symbolized at once a rejection of what was considered the very minimum of religious observance, as well as a denial of obligation toward the government Justin says of the charge of atheism that it also is utterly unfounded The popular gods, he insists, have been very properly denied by all right thinking men from the time of Socrates, because though called gods they are only demons masquerading as gods, and are not gods Justin is willing to be classed with Socrates as an atheist in regard to such immoral deities But the Christians actually worship the true God, who, unlike the gods of popular worship, is free from all impurity, and is Himself the Father of righteousness and self-control and all other virtues And not only the One God, but also "we worship and adore the Son who came forth from Him and taught us these things, and the host of other good angels who follow and are made like to Him, and the Prophetic Spirit, a worship which we perform in reason and truth." [2]

---

[1] Ap I 17 entire.

[2] Ap. I 6 entire. For the credal significance of this statement which was primarily only of apologetic significance see below chapter VI

Again he denies any sacredness whatever to idols, and contrasts the worship of such man-made gods with the proper worship of the true God.[1]

The charge that the Christian communion is a dangerous political organization Justin also treats lightly. The kingdom for which Christians are looking and working cannot be a human kingdom, else the Christians would wish to live to have a share in it, and would not be so willing to die. But the Christian hope is for the Kingdom which is with God, entrance into which is conditioned by fidelity to the faith. As such the Christian organization, he implies, cannot be politically dangerous.[2] The fact that the Christian community is drawn largely from the lower strata of society, Justin urges, far from being a reproach, is actually a good sign, for it indicates that the Christians are teaching the true doctrines. Teachers of the truth, Justin points out, have always been persecuted and made unfortunate by the demons in proportion to the relative correctness of their doctrines[3] Consequently, he implies a group of unfortunate people gathered together, like the Christians, by some doctrine are more apt to be guardians of truth than a similar group from higher walks of life. Justin could hardly have expected this argument to have had much weight with any but the lower classes, and must have been aware that he was only inviting harsh measures against the Christians by a frank declaration of war against the upper classes

The charge that the Christian secret meetings were characterized by obscenities Justin heartily denies. The charges sound strangely inappropriate, he says, in the mouths of people who practice in shameless openness the obscenities which they charge against the Christians. Furthermore the people who circulate such stories of the Christian community utterly ignore the fact that the

[1] Ap I 9, 10 entire. In Ap. I 24 Justin points out that each religious group denies the gods of every other group, and asks why Christians may not have the same privilege.

[2] Ap. I. 11 entire.

[3] Ap II. 10; 7. 3 (45 D); Ap. I. 5. 3 (55 E ff.).

Christian ethic is by far the highest taught in any religious body. In the secret meetings this ethic is inculcated, rather than lost in such rites as the accusers describe. It is because of the persistent slanders against the morality of the Christian cultus that Justin devotes some space to an explanation of the high Christian standards of speech, thought, and conduct as taught by Christ [1]. Justin begs that any Christian who can be found guilty of evil deeds be condemned as an evil doer, but not as a Christian, for the Christian teaching is opposed to all evil practices [2]

In many of these arguments Justin has been profoundly helped by Jewish apologetic tradition which had had to meet the same, or nearly the same, slanders. Against the Jews, like the Christians, was brought forward their refusal to worship idols, and to do patriotic homage to the Emperor, while it was alleged of their cultus also that it was characterized by murderous and obscene orgies. The earlier Jewish apologetes had a slight advantage over the Christians on the matter of their refusal to worship the Emperor, because the Jews could point to the fact that a sacrifice was daily offered in the Temple for the Emperor.[3] But this argument was not ordinarily stressed, and if we may judge from Philo and Josephus the Jewish Apologetes based their defense usually, like Justin and the other Christian Apologetes, upon their group's high moral character and recognized qualities as peaceable and patriotic citizens.[4] Jewish Apologetic was singularly silent upon the matter of the Jewish Messianic hope. The silence is only explicable on the grounds that in the Diaspora the Messianic hope was so nebulous, if present at all, that attack on this score against the Jews had not yet been made. Not so the Christians. From the first they had proclaimed the imminent and catastrophic coming of the

[1] Ap I cc 12—17.
[2] Ap. I. 7. 4 (56 E)
[3] Josephus B. J. II 10. 4, c. Ap II 6
[4] Philo in Flacc. 48 (II 524); 87 ff. (II 530, 531). Josephus, c. Ap. II. 4, 5; Ant. XIV 10, XVI 6. On the Jewish Apologetic see especially Paul Kruger, Philo und Josephus als Apologeten des Judentums. Leipzig 1906

King of Kings, and they had, beginning from the
Crucifixion of their Lord, to meet a resulting storm of
indignation from all good people who very properly
abhorred the thought of change and revolution The
Christian answer, it has been seen, was not particularly
strong, and could not have been at all convincing Justin
said that the expected Kingdom was not a human kingdom
but was with God But he himself, as will appear, clearly
taught that the Kingdom was to be of this earth, and
was to involve a complete revolution of all human society
As a matter of fact there was no defence to be made of
such teaching in the eyes of complete outsiders. Certainly
Justin added little to the strength of the apologetic arguments against charges of immorality and social undesir-
ability to which he had fallen heir from Hellenistic Judaism

But besides these attacks against the Christian community as a social menace, Justin shows that the religious
views of the Christians were attacked for their inadequacy
as a system Christianity was accused of being a novel
innovation, was ignored or sneered at by philosophers as
beneath the notice of intelligent men, and it was this sort
of attack to which Justin chiefly devotes his attention.
The general scheme of his defence was first to deny the
novelty of Christianity by demonstrating its continuity with
Judaism,[1] then to show parallels between the teachings
of the Pentateuch and of the Greek philosophers, and then
boldly to assert, *post hoc ergo propter hoc,* that since Moses
antedated Socrates and Plato, any common ideas must
have been taken by the philosophers from the Jewish
Scriptures Granted thus the superior dignity of Christianity
over philosophy because it was the legitimate completion
of Judaism, the original source of knowledge of super-
mundane matters for all mankind, Justin takes a new course
and works from Christianity backwards again to philosophy
The system of Judaism achieved its long expected perfection
in the person and teaching of Jesus Christ, who was the
incarnation of that Spirit of Revelation which alone could

[1] It has been seen in Chapter II that the Dialogue is primarily
devoted to justifying this important part of the Christian claim.

guide the human mind to knowledge of the Truth. But this spirit of wisdom was present in every man as his highest intellect, so that not only does Christ represent the culmination of the prophecy of a single religion, even though that is the most ancient religion, but He is the incarnation of the Universal Intelligence which it has been the hopeless struggle of every philosopher to understand. The answer to the sneers of the philosophers that Christianity was not worthy of an intelligent man's consideration was thus the counter-attack that philosophy had failed, and that only in Christianity was the end of philosophy to be found.

In representing Christianity as the true philosophy Justin is again following Greek Jewish precedent, and it is interesting to see how far it could help him. The claim for Christianity that it was the culmination of Judaism was of course Christian, and is recognizably Pauline in origin.[1] But once this claim was granted Justin was justified in using to establish Christian prestige the arguments of Judaism for the superiority of Moses to Plato. Aristobulus had insisted that, before the Septuagint, there had existed another translation of the Old Testament which Plato and Pythagoras had used.[2] Artapanus represented Moses as the teacher of Orpheus.[3] Philo said that Heraclitus had his doctrine from Moses.[4] It was thus perfectly in accord with Greek-Jewish tradition for Justin to claim for the Sacred Book and teachings common to Judaism and Christianity that they were the source of much in Greek philosophy.

But the Greek Jewish Apologetic contributed yet another element to Justin's defence of Christianity, in suggesting to Justin the claim for his religion that it was the true philosophy. Philo's entire work is an attempt to

[1] For Christianity as the true Israel see below p. 117 ff.

[2] Euseb. Pr. Ev. XIII xii 1; VIII. x. 3. Cf. Zeller III. ii. 280 Anm 2.

[3] Euseb Pr. Ev. IX. xxvii ff.

[4] Quis Rer. div. her. 214 (I. 503); on this argument in Judaism see Semisch (Bibl 118) II. 170 Anm. 3; Kruger, op. cit. 20, 21.

represent the Pentateuch as a philosophical treatise. It is true that Philo is actually trying to find a reconciliation of Greek philosophy and the Pentateuch, and that he is obviously sacrificing the real teaching of the Jewish Scriptures in the interest of a Greek conceptions. But in himself Philo is convinced that the Old Testament is actually a philosophical document, and his object in writing is to demonstrate the thesis that the only true philosophy is to be found in the Jewish writings. Not only is this the burden of Philo's entire exegesis, but he twice explicitly mentions the worship and study of the Scriptures in the Synagogue as "philosophizing". In the first passage Philo says that on the Sabbath the Jews "give their time wholly to the study of philosophy, not studying that sort of philosophy which word-catchers and sophists seek to reduce to a system, men who do not blush to sell doctrines and explanations like any other commodity in the market, or eternally to use philosophy against philosophy (Ye Earth and Son); but the Jews give themselves to the study of the true philosophy (τῷ τῷ ὄντι φιλοσοφεῖν), which they make up of three parts, of volitions, of speech, and of actions, and harmonize them into one species (εἶδος) in order to possess and enjoy happiness."[1] Here the philosophy of the Synagogue appears to be predominately, if not exclusively, ethical. But in the second passage Philo's definition is broader. The Sabbath, he says, is devoted to "philophizing, that is on the one hand to devoting time to the investigation of the things of nature, and on the other to examining whether there has been anything impurely done on the preceding days," etc.[2] According to Philo, then, Judaism was a philosophy, immeasurably superior to the teachings of those professional philosophers who spent their time in paid instruction and in mutual disputations. That it was common for Judaism to regard itself as a philosophy is amply illustrated by Josephus, who seems not in the least to have understood Judaism in the philosophic sense of the Hellenistic Jews, but who had

[1] De vita Moses III. 211—212 (II. 167).
[2] De Decal. 98 (II. 197).

picked up the epithet "philosophy" for Judaism, and frequently used it.[1]

Feder overlooks the fact that Judaism in the Dispersion called itself the true philosophy, when he seeks in the mystery religions for Justin's inspiration for so describing Christianity.[2] There is no need to go so far afield. Converts from Hellenistic Judaism who regarded Christianity as a completion of their former faith must have asserted long before Justin's time that Christianity was the ultimate philosophy.

Justin supplements these Judaistic arguments by expounding three new apologetic propositions. First he claims that many pagan narratives, particularly the popular mythologies, are demonic and perverse imitations of stories truly set forth in the Hebrew Scriptures. The demons were especially active in parodying doctrines and incidents connected with the Incarnation. Second his theory of the Christian character of all truth, because Christ is the incarnation of the entire-Logos,—is quite new to Christianity.[3] Third he did Christian Apologetic an abiding service by distinguishing reason and revelation.

Justin's thesis with regard to the origin of mythological stories he himself states as follows: "The myths which the poets have made .... have been uttered, as we shall proceed to demonstrate, by the influence of the wicked demons, in order to deceive and lead astray the human race For having heard it proclaimed through the Prophets that the Christ was to come, and that the ungodly among men were to be punished by fire, they put forward many to be called sons of Jupiter, under the impression that they would be able to produce in men the idea that the things which were said with regard to Christ were mere marvellous tales, like the things which were said by the poets."[4] With this must be read Justin's statement that the gods

[1] Ant. I. 7 1, XV 10. 4, Bel. Jud. II. 8. 2, c. Ap. I. 10; cf Kruger p. 19.
[2] (Bibl. 350) pp 47 ff
[3] See below Chapters V and VIII
[4] Ap I. 54 1, 2 (89 A, B).

who committed the crimes recounted in the mythologies were not gods but "wicked and impious demons."[1] Such an aggressive Apologetic on the matter of mythology is so far as we know first suggested in Christian literature by Justin Aristides, writing but a few decades at most before Justin, has no hint of representing mythologies as the work of demons. He simply reproduces some of the arguments common to Xenophanes, Socrates, and Plato, that the gods as described in Hesiod and Homer are shown by their conduct to be utterly unfit for divine dignity and recognition Positive suggestion as to the real standing of these rejected deities Aristides has none[2] But the charge that the popular gods were actually demons is much older than Justin. Conybeare has called attention to the fact that the same teaching is to be met with in Dionysius of Halicarnassus (ii. 47) who died B. C. 7. "As R. Heinze truly remarks," says Conybeare, "the substitution by the Christians of evil demons for the ancient gods was suggested and grew out of the Greek philosophy itself."[3] Whence Justin himself had the suggestion it is impossible to say

Justin's second contribution to Christian Apologetic is more striking, though it seems never to have been accepted as a part of the orthodox defence of Christianity. Justin wished to do more than the Greek Jewish philosophy had attempted to do in accounting for the common element between his religion and some of the doctrines of his favourite philosophers Philo and the Greek Jews had asserted that Moses was the first philosopher, and that Plato, Socrates, and even Heraclitus had learned their great doctrines from him Therefore Judaism, as the school of Moses, was the true philosophy. But convenient as this argument was in justifying the claim for the antiquity of Christianity, it

---

[1] Ap. I. 5. 4 (56 B). Justin is here using the words ὀρθοὶ δαίμονες as "gods", κακοὶ καὶ ἀνόσιοι δαίμονες as "demons" His meaning is unmistakable though English equivalents are doubtful See the entire chapter

[2] See Aristides Apol. 8—13. For Justin's demonology see below Chapter VI.

[3] Conybeare (Bibl. 328) p. 113; cf. R Heinze, Xenocrates, p. 116.

after all left the distinctively Christian element in the air. Was not Christ still a novelty, and his doctrines the product of an unphilosophic mind? No, says Justin, for Christ was the total incarnation of that one Universal Mind which has always been found in minute fragments in every man, and which has been the source of whatever real knowledge any man has ever achieved. Christ is True Reason incarnate. Whoever has striven to lead a life according to reason, has lived according to Christ, and has been, however unconsciously, a Christian. Heraclitus, Socrates, Plato, were Christians because they regulated their lives by the Logos within them. Whatever is true in other philosophies, then, is Christian, for Christianity is the Truth. Christianity is not a novelty, it is as old as the universe, as old as Reason. It is the ultimate Knowledge toward which all philosophies have more or less falteringly been struggling. There is not the slightest discrepancy between Christianity and philosophy except in so far as Christianity achieves the goal which philosophy has never been able to reach.[1]

Upon the basis of this novel claim, Justin went on to distinguish reason and revelation in so clear a way as to have been a great service to Christian Apologetic of all time. We have already seen how Justin represented his conversion as a turning from the hopeless groping of reason to the full light of revelation. Man's higher mind is truly a part of the Universal Mind, but so small a part that man can grasp but very little of the truth, and is subject to a constant tendency to error If he is to know the truth, man must have it revealed to him The process of revelation will be more aptly discussed under Justin's anthropology,[2] but the fact of the distinction between reason and revelation is Justin's greatest contribution to Christian Apologetic The church early found it wise to ignore Justin's doctrine of the Universal Mind, and the Christian

[1] This is the argument of the second part of the Second Apology, as illustrated by the introduction to the Dial. See above Chapter I, and below Chapter VII

[2] See below Chapter VII, and p. 177 ff.

standing of Socrates. But orthodox tradition has ever since Justin's time attempted to hold to reason and yet decry it for revelation at the same time. Reason, it has been insisted, is a good thing, but rationalism is utterly unchristian. We can go only a little way by reason, if we can go any way at all. But the Christian must be prepared to believe certain dogmas which the reason cannot justify, or even may seem to contradict, for these dogmas are built upon truth revealed by God, and as such are not to be questioned. Whether this dogma has ultimately demanded a belief in the inspired infallibility of ecclessiastical tradition, or in the verbal inspiration of a Book which has revealed everything necessary to salvation, orthodox Christianity has always contrasted the weakness of reason with the fulness and security of revelation.

Thus ultimately secure in his revelation, Justin's Apologetic against doctrinal attack is triumphant. What intellectual rest he has found in Christianity he is confident every reasoning man will find as readily. But he who refuses to be enlightened and persists in doing a work of the demons by persecuting the Christians cannot escape the fires of Hell, though he be Emperor of all the Roman Empire. Justin's defence of the Christian doctrine becomes active propaganda. It is not toleration but recognition which he demands, and it is to instill conviction of the moral and metaphysical truth of Christianity that he is really striving.

It has been seen that Justin's defence of Christianity as a revelation of the truth was utterly meaningless apart from the continuity of Christianity with Judaism. Accordingly the Old Testament, even presumably for the Emperor's benefit, was examined much more carefully, and adduced much more frequently than the opinions of Greek philosophers or their schools. The Old Testament was Justin's Sacred Book, more authoritative than any record except possibly the sayings of Jesus Christ, and constituting even the foundation of authority for these. Justin's apologetic task, as he understood it, consisted almost entirely in finding in the Old Testament prophetic descriptions of the person and work of Christ. For he

believed that the representation of Christianity as the
fulfillment and completion of the mystical and ancient
books of the Old Testament was the strongest possible form
of presentation of the Faith to his generation. Accordingly
Justin's apologetic evidence is a series of allegorized passages from the Jewish Scriptures It will not, then, be a
digression in an inquiry into the nature and sources of
Justin's Apologetic to examine the character and origin of
this evidence

Two dogmas were essential to the validity of proof of
Christianity from the Old Testament. In the first place
the sacred character of the Old Testament must be
guaranteed by a dogma of its verbal infallibility. Such a
doctrine Justin fearlessly enunciates No passage can ever
be said to be in error, or in contradiction to another passage, he insists.[1] If an apparent discrepancy is pointed
out, Justin will not admit a contradiction, but will confess
inability to understand the passage, and will try to bring
to a similar point of view any person who has been so rash
as to conclude that the Scripture is in error In the second
place Justin must insure his right to read the Scriptures in
an allegorical sense rather than literally. It would have
been hopeless for him to try to find Christianity in the
Old Testament on the basis of a literal reading of the text
This right Justin assumes rather than claims. He protests
for example against reading the story of the brazen serpent
as though God had been teaching faith in such an object
The passage is utterly meaningless, he insists, unless it is
taken as a sign of the Crucifixion [2]

But Siegfried has demonstrated that there are several
other principles of exegesis according to which Justin is
reading the Old Testament: [3]

[1] Dial 65. 2 (289 B, C).
[2] Dial 91 4 (319 A, B), on Allegory in Justin, cf. Grube
(Bibl 391, 392)
[3] Siegfried (Bibl 390) pp. 337—339 The argument is there
given in more detail, with references to Philo and Justin. In still
greater detail is the chapter on "Hermeneutische Regeln" in Heinisch
(Bibl 394) pp. 69—125. But Heinisch is throughout worse than
careless in his treatment of his sources, and so while suggestive
must be used with great caution.

First, the Scriptures say nothing superfluous, repetitions, doublets, and the like, are significant. Second, the silences of Scripture are significant. Third, meanings of words determined by one passage are transferred to other passages; as for example the free application of the idea that a day of the Lord is a thousand years. Fourth, words are to be examined in all their possible senses. Fifth, numbers, objects, and names must also be regarded as symbols.

All· of these Siegfried shows to be common to Philo and Justin. All are distinctively Hellenistic canons of criticism. They are not, however, distinctively Hellenistic Jewish canons, and so far as the similarity of method is concerned, Justin might almost as well have learned them directly from the Stoic treatment of Homer as from the Alexandrian Jews. But not only does Justin use the methods and principles of exegesis which mark those writings of Greek Judaism which we now possess, but his explanations of individual verses are marked again and again with details of Philonic hermeneutics. The traces of Philonic ideas to be found in connection with Justin's theology will be mentioned in the course of the description of his different doctrines. Here it is only necessary to call attention to similarities in scattered details of interpretation.

Justin was certainly referring to a Philonic tradition, if not to a specific dissertation of Philo's, when he said that the Jewish teachers speculated upon the introduction of a second Alpha into Abraham's name, and of a second Rho into Sarah's name.[1] Only a Greek discussion could be based upon such a subject, for in the Hebrew text the change in the names is of course quite different. Philo, however, has an unusually detailed discussion of the significance of both the new letters [2] Another reference to a Greek Jewish tradition, is Justin's rejection of what he calls to Trypho a "heresy among you", namely the doctrine that the bodies of men were made by angels.[3] This doc-

[1] Dial. 113. 2 (340 B)
[2] De Mut. Nom. 57 ff. (I. 587 ff.).
[3] Dial. 62. 3 (285 D)

Goodenough, The Theology of Justin Martyr.

trine is taught by Philo,[1] though not in the same form,
for Philo assigns to the Powers the creation of the mortal
part of the soul It is clearly, however, to a Greek Judaism
affected by Platonism that Justin is referring. It can
likewise only be a reference to Philonic tradition, which
Justin makes in regard to the keeping of the Sabbath.
Justin says that the New Law prescribes every day to be
observed as a Sabbath, while the Jews think themselves
pious for remaining idle one day in seven.[2] Philo similarly insists that every day is a feast day according to the
Law [3] Heinemann has pointed out that Philo has here
in mind the Cynic-Stoic doctrine that the true feast is joy
in a complete state of virtue, such as is possible only for
God and a very few wise men.[4] Justin has lost the fulness
of the Philonic conception, but shows that he has a distant
echo of Philo when he goes on to say: "If there is any
perjured person or thief among you, let him cease to be so;
if any adulterer, let him repent; then he has kept the secret
and true Sabbaths of God."

But while no other explicit reference to the Hellenistic
interpretations of Scripture can be attributed to Justin,[5]
he is frequently echoing its exegesis. For example, in commenting upon the appearance of the three Men to Abraham,
Justin, like Philo, represents one of them as God and Lord
of the two others, who were angels.[6] Justin concludes
from the Scriptural passage that this God must have been
a messenger of, and hence other than, the First God. That
is, Justin uses the passages as a proof of the existence of a
Second God, whom he elsewhere calls the Logos of God.

---

[1] De Confus. ling. 179 (I. 432), De Fuga et Invent. 69
(I. 556).

[2] Dial. 12. 3 (229 C).

[3] De Special Leg II. 42 (De Septen. 3) (II. 278); cf. Heinisch (Bibl. 394) p. 250.

[4] Heinemann, n. in loco (Die Werke Philos von Alex. in
deutscher Uebersetzung. Breslau 1910. II 120 Anm 4).

[5] The passage in which Justin mentions the procession of the
Powers, Dial 128, is more in harmony with the Rabbinic than
Hellenistic Judaism. See below p. 190 ff.

[6] Dial. 56 passim.

Philo seems at first quite different in his conclusion, for he says in one passage that the two Powers who accompanied God on this occasion were His Goodness and His Ruler-ship,[1] in two other passages that they were His Creative and Ruling Powers,[2] while in the latter passages he goes on to a remarkable discussion of God, the Unity, appearing as Trinity. God, he says, (i. e. the Person who appeared to Abraham) was between these two Powers, and Philo makes it appear that the God who was between them was the highest God. Of the two Powers who here accompany God, the Good-Creative Power was to be called *God*, Philo explains, for it is by this that He made and arranged the universe, while the Ruling Power is to be called *Lord*. But on one occasion Philo speaks of a sudden burst of in-spiration which revealed to him that "in the One God who is truly existing there are two supreme and pre-eminent powers, Goodness and Authority. And by Goodness did He beget the world, by Authority does He rule over that which has been begotten. And the third which in the middle synthesizes the two is Logos; for by Logos is God both ruling and good."[3] That Philo got his inspiration for this interpretation from recalling the "three men" who appeared to Abraham, is most likely, since the two Powers named are in all cases the same Both are transcended by the Logos of God, and all, we know from elsewhere, are transcended by God Himself. Justin's statement now ap-pears in a fresh light. "The One of the three," he says, referring to the three Angels, "is Lord of the two Angels, and is the *God* and *Lord* who is subject to Him who is in the heavens."[4] Justin is unmistakably echoing the Philo-nic interpretation, though he rejects or misunderstands, or had never heard the more elaborate theories of Philo's doc-trine of the godhead.

Justin follows Philonic interpretation again when he discusses the polygamy of the Patriarchs. Philo had in-

[1] De Sacrif. Ab. et Caini 59 (I. 173).
[2] De Abrah. 121 ff (II. 19). Quaest. in Genes. IV 2
[3] De Cherub. 27 (I 143).
[4] Dial 56 22 (279 A)

sisted that Abraham, for example, did not beget children of three women for the sake of pleasure, but in order to propagate the race.[1] Justin similarly insists that the Patriarchs had many wives, "not to commit fornication but that a certain plan and all mysteries might be accomplished by them."[2]

The similarities and dissimilarities between Philo's theology and Justin's will be discussed with more advantage in connection with the individual doctrines. It may be well however to protest against too narrow a treatment of the evidence presented. Justin does not show trace of ever having made the writings of Philo a careful literary study. Extensive verbal parallels such as Heinisch has adduced between Clement of Alexandria and Philo cannot be found between Philo and Justin. But to dismiss the subject of the influence of Greek Judaism upon Justin's Christianity because of a lack of literary parallels between Justin and Philo, in the face of the obviously profound influence which Philonic conceptions and methods had upon Justin's theological manner and matter, is to beg the entire question. In his interpretation of the Old Testament, Justin is unmistakably a follower of Alexandrine tradition. On the basis of an allegorical treatment of the Septuagint he proposed finding a justification for his theology, and this thesis he demonstrated in a manner that can accurately be described as a weak reflection of Philonic exegesis.

But Justin's aim was something quite different from Philo's. Where Philo allegorized the Old Testament to justify his being a Greek metaphysician, Justin allegorized the same book to find continuity between Judaism and Christianity We shall see that on the metaphysical side, Justin's Christianity is, like his exegesis, a weak Philonic reflection and adaptation. Justin was not primarily a metaphysician but a Christian propagandist who sought evidence for believing that Christ, the Son of God, was born of a Virgin, and died according to God's plan, rose from the dead, and should come again to judge all men His traces

[1] De Nobilitate 207 (II. 441)
[2] Dial. 141. 4 (371 A), cf. 134. 2 (364 A).

of Philonic exegesis are thus naturally scattered. The astonishing fact is that in one so different in spirit and aim from Philo, so much that is recognizably Philonic is yet to be found.

An excellent illustration of Justin's echoing a Philonic thought is to be found in his last Apologetic argument, that is in his Apologetic against the reproaches of Judaism. Justin's Apologetic in answer to the criticisms of the Jews was fundamentally the same as that to the attacks of the heathen. In both cases he represented Christianity as the fullness and completion of what had been only partial before. Christianity was the True Philosophy over against philosophy, and it was the New or Eternal Law over against the Torah. In both cases Christianity was the final revelation of Truth, so that it was the same view of Christianity as the perfect revelation of God which constituted the foundation for Justin's defence against all attacks. But Justin's applications of this principle to the case of Judaism and to the case of heathenism were quite different. Justin's representation of Christianity as the completion of Judaism has already been mentioned in the analysis of the Dialogue. The argument is as follows

Judaism claims in its Law to have received a special revelation of the will of God. Jews cannot understand how Christians can profess a desire to serve God, can acknowledge the God of the Jewish Scriptures to be their God, and yet refuse to keep His Law. Many Jews were indeed ready to accept Christianity as a supplement to the Law, but could not see how the Gospel abrogated the Law. Justin's argument is only an expansion of the argument of St. Paul that Christ is the New Law, in whom all necessity for the Old Law is done away; that Christians are the true Spiritual Israel. Justin's argument is not exactly like St. Paul's however. He does not, in the first place, think so highly as St. Paul of the Old Law. To Justin the Jewish Law was not a schoolmaster, a training and preparation for Christianity but was a reproach, put upon the Jews because of their perversity and sin. It had never had anything to do with salvation. Man has never been saved on any other basis than his moral character.

But the Jews, more wicked than other men, refused to follow the light which can guide every man, and preferred to rebel and walk in the ways of wickedness Circumcision given to Abraham as the founder of the race was a prophetic sign of this future perversity, and indicated that God would cut them off from other nations for unique condemnation.[1] "To you alone was circumcision necessary, in order that the people may be no people, the nation no nation."[2] It is true that there was value to be found in the Law, but the Jews had ignored this helpful aspect of the Law, and completely misunderstood it. So the unleavened bread signified symbolically the doing away with the old deeds of wicked leaven, and the new leaven after the days of unleavened bread signified starting afresh upon a new conduct of life. But the Jews foolishly thought God was imputing value to the eating of one kind of food rather than another.[3] True sacramentalism, he insists in harmony with Philo and all the best Jewish tradition,[4] is not physical but spiritual.[5] Similarly the prohibition of certain food was enjoined in the Old Testament in order that in eating the Jews might have their thoughts brought back to God. But this spiritual significance of clean and unclean food was utterly ignored by the Jews in their thought that they were getting virtue in God's eyes in heedlessly fulfilling the letter of His Law.[6] Similarly in the case of the Sabbaths,[7] sacrifices and oblations,[8] and all other Laws; in themselves the Laws were valueless, "statutes

[1] Dial 16. 2 (234 A).
[2] Dial. 19. 5 (236 E).
[3] Dial 14. 3 (231 D, E).
[4] Philo's doctrine of feasts has already been mentioned. The significance of circumcision was to him the putting away of unrighteousness, not the tribal initiation (cf. Heinisch, Bibl 394, p. 270) The Passover meant the leaving of the life of sensation for that of reason (ibid. p. 250). Such Judaism had no answer when Christianity pressed the question, "Why then the external rite", and presented Christ as the New Law.
[5] Dial. 15. 1 (233 E).
[6] Dial 20 entire
[7] Dial. 21 1 (238 A); 12 3 (229 C)
[8] Dial. 22 1 (239 D).

which were not good, judgments whereby they shall not
live."¹ Salvation has never been dependent upon their
fulfillment Righteous men existed before the Law was
given, before even circumcision. But if God knew that
the Law would be thus misunderstood and abused or
ignored by the Jews, why did He give it to them? Justin
answers that the Jews were given the Law rather than
other people because God knew they would thus sin,
and was trying to adapt Himself to a people of such
extraordinary perversity ²

But God is unchanged There have always existed
"eternal righteous decrees",³ and it is according as one
lives by these, regardless of time or nationality, that he
may be saved. The test is universal, within or without
Judaism "Those who did that which was universally,
naturally, and eternally good are pleasing to God,"⁴
and will each be 'saved by his own righteousness."⁵
The immeasurable superiority of Christianity to Judaism
and heathenism alike lies in the fact that Christ is
Himself this "everlasting law and everlasting covenant."⁶
Christ is the New Law in a sense, but more correctly He is the the the Eternal Law.⁷ With His complete
revelation in the Incarnation a new epoch began. Men were
never saved by any other than Christ, for Christ is the
Eternal Law, and only as people have lived according to
it could they please God But now is salvation much easier,
for what before was hidden in the Old Law is now made
manifest in Christ. Justin has thus turned against the
Jews with the same method of attack which he used in
his theory of the partial validity of reason as contrasted
with the fulness of the Logos. Christ is complete Law
as He is complete Reason All is given in Him, who

¹ Dial 21. 4 (238 D); cf Ezek xx. 25
² Dial, 19 6 (237 A) ὅθεν ὁ θεὸς ἁρμοσάμενος πρὸς τὸν
λαὸν ἐκεῖνον.
³ Dial 28 4 (246 A) τὰ αἰώνια δίκαια
⁴ Dial 45 4 (263 E) τὰ καθόλου καὶ φύσει καὶ αἰώνια καλά.
⁵ Dial 45 3 (263 D)
⁶ Dial 43 1 (261 C)
⁷ See Windisch (Bibl 333) p 27, 28

transcends the Old Testament Laws as He transcends the philosophy of the schools. Christ is the eternally right Way for all men, as He is the Truth.

Justin is thinking of Law as a much more universal thing than a body of precepts, as in his doctrine of the Universal Logos he is thinking of more than the thought processes of God. Christ is the Right in the ethical realm, the principle of Truth in the metaphysical realm. Only as one conforms to or understands this one principle, whether approached from the point of view of ethics or metaphysics, is it possible to please God, or know Him, or above both, see Him.

The exaltation of the principle of Law as a frequently personified attribute of God is so familiar in Rabbinic Judaism as to need no comment.[1] But Philo understood this higher principle of Law, not in oriental personification, but as identical with what the Stoics meant by the Law of Nature, that is, as with the Stoics, as identical with the Logos.[2] A natural Law in the universe, the Philonic-Stoic Nomos is a moral law in man. According to Philo the precepts of the Jewish Law are Logoi, graceously given to help beginners on the right path. But the perfect man has risen above the need of precepts, because (Philo is now Platonic) his nature is entirely in accord with the universal Logos-Nomos.[3] The doctrine of St Paul of the passing of the need of precepts with the coming of the eternal principle of Law, which was the true dynamic and wisdom of God, in the person of Jesus Christ is thus much more in accord with Philo's interpretation of the Torah than with that of Rabbinic Judaism. For Rabbinic Judaism represented God in heaven as worthily occupied in embellishing the letters of the Mosaic code, i e. in glorifying the precepts as given. The tendency of philosophical Judaism was to interpret the Mosaic Law

---

[1] See Weber, Judische Theologie, pp 14 ff, 153, 157 ff Schechter, Some aspects of Rabbinic Theology. (Jewish Quarterly Review VIII p 9.

[2] De Migr Abr 130 (I. 456). νόμος δὲ οὐδὲν ἄρα ἢ λόγος θεῖος, κτλ.

[3] See Drummond, Philo, II 165 ff., 307—309

as a reflection, or imitation, of an eternal moral principle
When once a man has reached the eternal principle, the
precepts of the writen law seem superfluous and inferior.
The Epistle to the Hebrews is even more in harmony
with the point of view of philosophical Judaism in this
particular than is St. Paul Here Christ is an ideal Priest,
recognizably the Philonic Logos Priest, serving God in
an ideal world according to, and Himself constituting, a
Divine Law, of which the code of Judaism was but a
shadow [1] The writer to the Hebrews does not speak
so specifically of a contrast between the New and Old
Laws as St Paul and Justin, but the inference from
his words could only be that the Christians, as followers
of the Eternal Priest and Law, have no need of the
shadow The idea of Law as transcending precepts must
have been very popular with Jews in an environment where
observance of the precepts of the Jewish Code was
largely impossible The Christian attack against Rabbinic
Legalism, then, from its incipiency in St Paul, and as
found more developed in Justin, is conducted in the
atmosphere and uses the conceptions of Hellenistic Judaism.
As in the case of the Logos, the doctrine of the Eternal
Law only becomes peculiarly Christian when it asserts
the incarnation of the Eternal Law in the person of Jesus
Christ.

But granted this one step of Christianity, the consequences upon which Justin representatively insists are
inevitable, inevitable that is to those who are prepared
to accept the Alexandrian theory of the Mosaic Code
as a μίμησις of the Eternal Law.[2] Philo himself was too
consistent a Jew to assert that the real Israelites were
those who had risen above the Logoi into conformity
with the Logos But that was probably because he saw

[1] See Hebr viii 5; ix 11, 12, 23, 24, x 1 See Windisch's
note to Hebrews viii 5, with Philonic parallels, in Handbuch zum
Neuen Testament Tubingen 1913 p 68, also p 15.

[2] Philo does not so call the Mosaic Code expressly, but this
statement of his theory is quite fair to his other statements, and
is shown by the writer to the Hebrews to have been a familiar
conception See Hebr x 1

so very few, either in history or in his own circle of acquaintances, who had thus "passed beyond the Law of commandment and restraint,"[1] and Philo had no wish to rule out his beloved compatriots from their heritage as Israelites. But in a community which considered itself as having accessible for every man that Entire Law which made the partial Law obsolete,[2] a new group feeling would inevitably arise on the Pauline suggestion that the Christian communion was the true Israel. Justin's scorn of the history of Jewish observance of its law is naturally stronger than St. Paul's. The sense of superiority which Christians felt to the Jews had been sharpened by a century of controversy and amplification. It is only remarkable that Justin should still have been liberal enough to admit communion with the conservative party which even yet wanted to try to please God by being Christians and by keeping the precepts of the Jewish Law at the same time. He admits that such toleration is by no means the usual attitude taken by Christians, however, and will himself not allow these people to win the more philosophical Christians to their point of view.[3] For the Christians alone were the promises of the Old Covenant intended. What then, asked Trypho, are the faithful Jews of old not to be saved, and are we all cut off now from any heritage in the Holy Mount? The faithful of old, Justin answers, are saved because they were Christians in so far as they conformed to the Eternal Law. But now since that Eternal Law has been revealed in Christ salvation is hereafter possible only by becoming His disciples. All Jews who remain Jews are cut off from any share in the good time coming.[4] There is one door open for them as for all mankind, through Christ, the Eternal Logos-Law.

[1] Drummond, Philo II, 309.
[2] Dial. 11. 2 (228 B).
[3] Dial 47 1 ff (265 D ff.).
[4] See Dial. 25—30, 45, 46, 119, 120, 123, 124, 135, 137, 140.

CHAPTER IV

GOD

Early Christianity seems to have been for the most part uncritical about its doctrine of God. At its inception, Christianity had a wealth of devotional background in Palestinian Judaism, most of whose views primitive Christians found no cause to question, for they believed that they were Jews in the fullest sense, and that their particular doctrines about Christ were only the message of fulfillment which Jews had long been waiting to hear. As to the nature of God no change from Jewish tradition was dreamed of. Similarly in the Greek world, the Greek Christianity which was born of St. Paul inherited the religious attitudes and aspirations of the Synagogues of the Dispersion. Here again Christianity conceived itself only as changing the faith of its fathers in regard to the substitution of the new Christ-Law for the Torah, while it challenged otherwise as little as possible the Greek Jewish religion and metaphysics Even in its most elaborate expression, Greek Judaism had proposed no dogmas, and had achieved no consistent unification Theoretically its promoters were still orthodox Jews who could explain their beliefs in terms of Greek philosophy Devotionally even Philo was an orthodox Jew worshipping a personal loving God. For Hellenistic Judaism did not question the legitimacy of its worship by the implications of its theories of the nature of God It philosophized about an Absolute, but prayed to God the Father. Ordinary Greek Jews would only have understood the Jewish God of Abraham, while they would have used the philosophical phrases of the learned with the indiscrimination of unintelligence.

Early Greek Christianity had no incentive for going behind this careless mingling of devotion with philosophical jargon The devotional personal view of God, helped out by a few mysterious sounding phrases, is all that has ever been needed or desired by the mass of Christians. When Christianity was attacked by Jews or pagans, recourse was had of necessity to the philosophical terminology, which was then brought forward with more confidence than understanding, and given an emphasis utterly disproportionate to its real significance for their Faith Naturally in such a case the terminology shows no signs of having been applied with a careful eye to consistency or appropriateness But we shall see that with Justin the phrases and shreds of philosophical speculation about God are still recognizably a Christian adaptation of those of the Greek Jewish school, and show no trace of an immediate borrowing from the pages or even the traditions of the schools of Greece

When Justin is attempting thus to speak philosophically, the phase of Deity which he most emphasizes is the *Transcendence.* Justin particularly rejects the Stoic conception of immanence, in which God was conceived of as in a sense made up of the totality of material phenomena. God must not, he insists, be identified with the things which are "ever changing and altering and dissolving into the, same things."[1] On the contrary it is one of the chief distinguishing characteristics of God that He alone is *unchangeable* and *eternal.*[2] The Stoics had taken over much of Heraclitus' doctrine of eternal flux, and believed that the world as a whole, which was identical with Deity, must not be thought of as static, but as totally engaged in a great turning and changing which implied both motion in space and constant transformation of nature. Throughout Greek philosophy, κινέω and τρέπω have the double sense of spacial motion and of change of nature. The Stoics used these words in both senses in describing

[1] Ap II. 7. 9 (46 B). τρεπόμενα καὶ ἀλλοιούμενα καὶ ἀναλυόμενα εἰς τὰ αὐτὰ ἀεί.
[2] Ap I 13 4 (60 E). τὸν ἄτρεπτον καὶ ἀεὶ ὄντα θεόν.

the ultimate nature of God, and Justin answers the Stoics by denying both spacial motion and change of nature to God. God cannot "go up or go down, arrive anywhere, walk about, sleep or rise from sleeping, but remains in His own place, wherever that may be "[1] God is not only unmoved in space, but Justin goes further and denies that God is any sense spacially determined, whether by the universe as a whole or by a single place in the universe.[2] Spaciality he seems to conceive as having come into existence only at creation, for he argues against God's spaciality on the ground that a God who existed before creation could not have had spacial character.[3] Spaciality which itself first came into existence by God's creative act cannot be read back into the nature of God, and it is only with violence that we can associate any spacial objects or conceptions with God.[4] It is thus on the grounds of God's complete lack of spaciality, and of the corollary to this, His stability and freedom from any motion in space, that Justin attacks the Stoic identification of God and the world, and seeks to establish God's transcendence. Similarly in regard to the unchangeable nature of God, the other sense in which the words of motion would have been understood, Justin insists upon the eternal fixity of character of God His statement as a philosopher perfectly expresses his view as a Christian. God is τὸ κατὰ τὰ αὐτὸ καὶ ὡσαύτως ἀεὶ ἔχον [5]

Both the conception of the non-spacial character of God, and of the eternal unchangeableness of Deity had already been suggested in the Hellenistic-Judaistic books

[1] Dial. 127 1, 2 (356 D)

[2] Ibid

[3] Ibid

[4] This reasoning is purely Philonic Cf Conf Ling 136, 139 (I 425): "For who does not know that he who comes down must necessarily leave one place and occupy another? . . . . God generated space and location along with bodies, and we may not assert that the Maker is contained in any of the things produced . . . Accordingly all terms of motion involving change of place are inapplicable to God in His true nature "

[5] Dial 3 5 (220 E).

of the New Testament The non-spacial character of
God is clearly the philosophic thought behind the popular
language put into the mouth of Jesus in the Fourth Gospel,
when he denies to the Samaritan woman that God can
be associated exclusively either with the Temple at Jerusalem or with the mountain of Samaria, for God as a Spirit
is only to be worshipped in spirit and in truth [1] Likewise
the Hellenistic Jews to whom the Epistle to the Hebrews
was addressed understood perfectly that to say, "Jesus
Christ the same yesterday, today, and forever,"[2] was
precisely to say, "Jesus Christ, as unchangeable in nature,
is very God" Both the immovability and the unchangeableness of God are of course definitely asserted by Philo,[3]
and go back to the Aristotelian First Cause who was the
Unmoved Mover.

But although Justin denies spaciality to God, he is
naively driven by his denial of movement to God to assign
to Him *location*. In the passage already quoted Justin
speaks of God as "remaining in His place, wherever that
may be,"[4] and in another passage God is ὁ ὑπὲρ κόσμον θεός,
ὑπὲρ ὃν ἄλλος οὐκ ἔστι.[5] Justin makes no attempt at defining
the place of God, and refers to God sometimes as above the
heavens,[6] sometimes as in the heavens[7] Wherever God
is, it is some remote spot, so remote that it is not to be
conceived that He could appear among men. Justin's object
in securing the remote location of God is thus twofold, he
is trying to impress his readers with God's transcendence,
but particularly with a view to the impossibility of God's
being able to appear in theophanies.

[1] John iv. 21—24.
[2] Hebrews xiii 8.
[3] Cf collection of parallels in Siegfried (Bibl 390) pp 201 ff,
333. Drummond, Philo, II. 41—45. The conception was carried
on into Rabbinical Judaism. Weber, Judische Theologie, p. 149,
quotes Bereshith Rabba, c 68, "God is the place of the world,
and His world is not His place"
[4] Dial. 127. 1, 2 (356 D).
[5] Dial 60 5 (284 A)
[6] Dial 56. 1 (275 A); 60. 2 (283 B).
[7] Dial 127 5 (357 C); 129 1 (284 A).

Justin's argument on theophanies will be discussed
later.[1] Here it is only to be noticed that the basis of denial
to God of the power of appearing to men is not, as with
Plato, the unchangeable character of a perfect being, but
the fixity of His location. Philo uses both arguments
against theophanies,[2] and it is not an unjustified suspicion
that the argument from the fixed location of God is as
generically Jewish as the argument from the unchangeable
character of a perfect Being is generically Greek. For it is
notable that it is usually in connection with Old Testament
exegesis that Justin is prompted to assert the fixed heavenly
location of God, while an interesting quotation by Weber
from the Midrash upon the Song of Songs, viii 11, indicates that the Jewish inclination to locate God strictly in
the heavens was so strong that it lead the Rabbis at least
occasionally to conceive of the Torah as the personal
representative of God upon earth.[3] Philo is much more
philosophical than either Justin or the Palestinian Jews on
the matter of the location of God when he asserts that God
is His own place.[4] But both Justin and Philo are seriously
inconsistent in trying to combine the Jewish notion of a
location of God with the Greek denial of spaciality to God.
Philo says in one passage:[5] "God is called place, because
He contains all things, but is contained by none, . . . The
Divine, being contained by nothing, is necessarily its own
place . . . . God is at a distance from everthing created "
It is hardly necessary to look further for the source of
Justin's confusion of location and unspaciality in his doc-
trine of God. He is clearly following a Philonic tradition.

Justin denies that God is in any sense *composite.*
He says to Trypho that the Jewish teachers, when they

[1] See below Chapter V. pp. 142 ff.

[2] Ibid.

[3] Weber, Jüdische Theologie, p 16 "My Torah will I give
to the lower world, but I will dwell in the higher I will give my
daughter with her precepts to a city   .. but I remain with you
in the upper world."

[4] Leg. Al. I. 44 (I. 52). First stated in Christianity by
Theophil. ad Autolyc. II. 10.

[5] De Somniis I. 63—67 (I. 630), see entire passage.

interpret the theophanies of the Old Testament as actual appearances of God, must be wrong. God can have no hands, feet, fingers, nor soul, because He is not in any sense a composite Being [1] Here Justin means that God has not members, nor is He in human form, and yet Justin's mind seems not to be able to dispense with *form* entirely in conceiving of God In the Apology Justin denies that God has the form which makers of idols seem to think.[2] His objection is not against conceiving of God as having a form, for he says that God has an "ineffable glory and form" The sin of the idol makers is not that they are ignorant of the true form of God, but that they make their images in the form of demons, and describe these demonic forms as God's form In speaking of a form of God at all, however, Justin again betrays the popular origin and nature of his philosophic thought. Plato, as has been pointed out,[3] in his later life saw that to make God merely the highest form in a hierarchy of Forms was to lead into serious complications, and it is highly probable that in his later works Plato was thinking of God as transcending form entirely Such certainly was the doctrine of later Platonism, which tried to harmonize Aristotle and Plato The forms in Albinus,[4] as in Philo,[5] are rational projections from God in some way, but God is never Himself formal. But the formlessness of God is a point which might have been easily overlooked in popularizations of philosophy, and the thought of God as completely formless would have occurred only to one possessing a training in careful abstract thinking which there is little ground for ascribing to Justin.

Another favourite term by which Justin describes the transcendence of God and His difference from all other beings is *unbegotten*. It is notable that Justin consistently uses ἀγέννητος rather than ἀγένητος, though in some passages, notably in Dialogue 5 where Justin is discussing

[1] Dial 114. 3 (341 D)
[2] Ap. I 9 3 (57 E)
[3] Compare Introduction Chapter I. pp 5 ff
[4] Ibid
[5] Cf. Introduction Chapter II p 47

philosophy, the word ἀγέννητος is so inappropriate that Otto
thinks it is here and frequently in other passages a copyist's
error.[1] Ἀγένητος is the philosophical term applied to Deity
to express the fact that He has no beginning, and as such
is superior to the exigencies of change and decay to which
all other beings, having had a beginning, are subject. The
word ἀγένητος is used consistently in that sense in Greek
philosophy and Philo.[2] Ἀγέννητος, however, means unbegotten. It is much rarer as applied to the Ultimate than
the other, but is found in Aristotle as follows: "If there is
nothing eternal, neither can there be any coming into existence; for any real thing which comes into existence
necessarily pre-supposes some real thing from which it
came into existence, and the last term of such a series
must be unbegotten."[3] That is, this last term must have
an existence without exterior source, else we should have
one of the infinite series which, as has been seen, were
deeply repugnant to Aristotle. Ἀγένητος is a word of much
narrower significance than ἀγένητος. It means uncaused,
not brought into existence by or from anything outside
itself, and would be a perfectly correct title to apply to a
self-caused being. Ἀγέννητος, however, could only be applied
to something which has never had a beginning of any kind,
and is a much more expressive term than the other for
explaining the ultimate and eternal nature of God. Christianity found the term ἀγέννητος very useful in distinguishing
Christ the Son of God, from God the Father who was different from Christ in that He was unbegotten, uncaused in
any sense, while Christ was begotten. Ἀγένητος did not
commend itself in distinguishing the Son from the Father,
for to state that the Father was without beginning was to
imply that the Son had had a beginning, and hence to deny
His eternal character. But useful as the word is as a distinctive title when dealing with the problems of Christology,
ἀγέννητος is not the proper term to use as an antithesis to
ἀθάνατος, and it is because Justin uses it for all purposes, in

[1] See Otto (Bibl 26) Dial. Ch 5, n. 1
[2] Cf. De Sacrif. Abel et Caini, 57, 60 (I. 173, 174), Quis
rer div haer. 206 (I. 502).
[3] Metaph B. 4. 999 b 7 ff.

season and out of season, that Otto suspects the text in some passages where the word is obviously misapplied. The text however probably quite represents Justin's thought He has confused two words which sounded alike because he knew them largely from hearsay, and did not himself understand the distinction between them. The mistake in Justin's time was a common one, and is quite natural in a philosophic dilettante, but most unlikely to be committed by one who had any training in, or understanding of, Greek philosophy.[1]

The force of ἀγέννητος is further illustrated by the fact that Justin deduces God's *namelessness* as a corollary from the fact that He is unbegotten. The connection, which is not at first sight apparent, is founded upon the fact that in Justin's opinion a name, to be truly such, must have been given by a predecessor or maker of the person or thing named. We may call a person by any appelation (πρόσρησις) but only the name given by an elder is properly speaking the person's name. God as unbegotten came into existence from no external impulse, had no antecedents, and hence there was no one to give God a name.[2] "If anyone dares to say that there is a name he raves with a hopeless madness."[3] Thümer, who has attempted to see in the namelessness of God a direct reflection of Plato's own teachings, has fallen into error because he has ignored Justin's explicit reference of the namelessness to the unbegottenness of God, and understood the namelessness solely from Ap. I 61, where the namelessness and *unutterableness* of God are mentioned together.[4] Thümer argues that the unutterableness of God has been suggested to Justin by the Timaeus,[5] and that God is of course

---

[1] On the general confusion in regard to these two words in the early Christian theology see Lightfoot's note in his edition of the Apostolic Fathers, II. 1. (1885) 90—94

[2] Ap II 6 1 (49 D)

[3] Ap I. 61 11 (94 D)

[4] (Bibl. 380) p 7, followed by Pfattisch (Bibl. 385) p 20, and De Fay (Bibl. 381) p. 185.

[5] Tim. 28 c. τὸν μὲν οὖν ποιητὴν καὶ πατέρα τοῦδε τοῦ παντὸς . . . . . εἰς πάντας ἀδύνατον λέγειν.

nameless if He is unutterable. As a matter of fact the two passages of Justin in question [1] are remarkably like a passage in Philo,[2] where Philo urges, in commenting upon the incident of the burning bush, that God is unutterable and nameless. Any name by which we may speak of God is not a name but only an appelation (πρόσρησις), for a name properly so-called describes or limits the one named, while God has only revealed Himself to man as "the Existent", and is not more accurately to be described. Here is the origin of Justin's coupling of the unutterableness and namelessness of God. But Philo goes on to explain that names are a symbol of created things, wherefore God, as the eldest of all beings, and as such having no predecesor who could have created or begotten Him, is the nameless God. The close resemblance of Justin's reasoning to the argument of Philo is here obvious. Justin shows in another passage that he is aware of the association of the incident of the burning bush with the doctrine of the namelessness of God, for in commenting upon that incident he says, "All the Jews even now teach that the nameless God spake to Moses,"[3] a casual reference to an argument which he seems to assume will be familiar to his readers, and which was probably a stock bit of exegesis. A similar casual reference, unintelligible in itself, presupposing familiarity on the part of the reader with the reasoning to the namelessness of God from the fact that He had no predecessors, is to be found in the Syriac translation of Aristides: "He has no name, for anything that has a name is associated with the created."[4] While there is then no ground for supposing that Justin took the argument for God's namelessness direct from Philo, there is ample reason for assuming that the Philonic argument was a familiar part of the intelligent Christianity of the day.

[1] Ap II 6. 1 (49 D) and Ap I 61 11 (94 D).
[2] Philo, De Mutat Nom. 13 ff (I. 580, 581) This parallel was first suggested by Abbott (Bibl 454) p 569 Cf De Abrah 51 (II 8, 9); De Somniis I 230 (I. 655); De Vita Mos I 75, 76 (II. 92). See Cohort ad Gentil 20, 21 (19 B, C).
[3] Ap I 63 1 (95 C).
[4] C 1

The *unutterableness* of God, which was one of Justin's familiar points of emphasis in describing God, has already been mentioned. It appears in Justin as an unexplained epithet of God,[1] except when the unutterableness and namelessness are combined. The term is intended to indicate the conception that God is beyond the reach of human reason, and that what little we do know of Him is quite inexpressible. The word is frequently found in Philo, but Philo, probably himself recalling the Timaeus, conceived the unutterableness in a much more philosophic and mystical sense than Justin. Though our reason, Philo believed, breaks down in the search for God, the aspiration of the true seeker is met by a revelation of Deity given him by the Logos, but knowledge so received is in no sense an achievment of the seeker's own mind, and is quite uncommunicable. For God is beyond human reason either to grasp for one's self or to explain to others. Justin follows this train of thought at a distance. Human reason cannot apprehend Deity, Justin recognizes, and the true seeker must look to revelation to find the truth. But the revelation to which Justin looked for doctrinal instruction had been given objectively in the teachings of the Prophets and Christ. Justin does not recognize the obvious fact that a revelation given through such an objective medium was in the nature of the case largely "utterable". But Justin's motive for preserving this term for God from Hellenistic Judaism, in spite of its inconsistency with his doctrine of revelation, is clear. He was reverently impressed with the immense chasm between God and humanity, not to say God and His world. Immeasurably remote, unmoving, unchangeable, primal, unnamed, God was still beyond Justin's comprehension in spite of his over-confident boasts as to the pre-eminence and adequacy of the Christian revelation. His mind was too unphilosophical to permit him to conceive of God as the Absolute, as probably did Plato, Aristotle, Philo, and Plotinus. Justin's God was transcendent, but not Absolute. The terms which Greek Jewish

[1] Ap. I. 61. 11 (94 D), II. 10. 8 (49 A), 12. 4 (50 C), 13. 4 (51 C), Dial. 126. 2 (355 C), 127. 2, 4 (356 D, 357 B).

converts had introduced into Christianity to describe God.
Justin eagerly and uncritically accepted. The otherworldly
exaltation of the Christianity of Justin's day would have
been impossible if God had been conceived of as immanent
in the Stoic sense. A Stoic indifference may lift a few strong-
minded persons into a state of mind closely resembling
otherworldly exaltation, but no such popular movement as
Christianity could ever have been based upon such a coldly
intellectual foundation. But when God was conceived of
as personal and loving, and yet sublimely transcendent in
location and nature above the world of change, Christians,
with their hope through Christ, could face the vicissitudes
of fortune with a passionate scorn which at once puzzled
and amazed the pagan world. For the Christians were
confident that their souls were in the care of God, and so,
in a sense, like God were safe beyond the world of change
and suffering.

Justin did not by any means stop in the doctrine of
God with His transcendence. He could not consider God
as inactive, even though He was unmoved Aristotle had
made an indelible impression upon the thought of the
ancient world by his assertion that absolute existences which
had no activity were utterly useless and explained nothing.[1]
When Aristotle came to describe his own conception of
Deity he consistently insisted that this Deity must have
activity of some kind: the Primal Mind must not merely
be potential thought, but be actually thinking. Similarly
Philo in speaking of God's rest on the first Sabbath says:
"That which rests is one thing only, God. But by rest I do
not mean inaction since that which is by nature acting, that
which is the Cause of all things, can never desist from
doing that which is most excellent."[2] Justin reflects this
passage distantly when he says that God carries on the
same administration of the universe during the Sabbath as
during all other days.[3] The author of the Fourth Gospel
had already used the conception of the activity of God in

[1] See above p 11.
[2] De Cherubim 87 (I. 155). Cf Leg. Al I. 5 (I 44), from Abbot (Bibl. 454) p 576.
[3] Dial. 29 3 (246 E)

the expression, "My Father worketh hitherto and I work,"[1] but Justin is much closer here to Philo than to the Fourth Gospel. Justin says that as a philosopher he had defined God as the "Cause to all other things of their existence,"[2] and later uses the same term to describe the relation between God and the Second God. "God is the cause of His (the Second God's) power and of His being Lord and God."[3]

But as a Christian Justin more commonly expresses the activity of God in terms of the *creation* and *direction* of the universe, than of causality. That the world was made or begotten by God is a familiar conception found universally in mythologies, and introduced into Greek philosophy by Plato, if not by Anaxagoras. Judaism of course made much of the fact that its God was the creator and preserver of all things, and Justin was following predecessors of all schools in carrying on the doctrine. But he was forced by the teachings of the Gnostics to put unusual emphasis upon the fact that God is the Creator, for the Gnostics were insisting that the God of the Old Testament was in truth the Creator, but that the true God could have had no contact whatever with matter which they made synonymous with evil. They concluded that the God of the Old Testament, whom they commonly called the Fashioner (δημιουργός), was, as God of the world of matter, really the God of evil; at the same time they described the good God as absolutely transcendent, and as such as not only infinitely higher than the Demiurge but completely different in kind. Justin, whose intense desire was to demonstrate the unity between the Old and New Testaments, on the grounds that both were the expression of the same revealing Spirit, rejected this Gnostic account entirely, and insisted over and again that God was Himself the Creator, and that there was no higher God than the Creator.[4] Justin's theory of creation and of the relation

[1] John v. 17.
[2] Dial. 3. 5 (220 D); 4. 1 (221 D); 5. 6 (224 A)
[3] Dial. 129. 1 (358 D).
[4] Dial. 11. 1 (228 A); 60. 2 (283 B); 80. 4 (307 A); Ap. I. 16. 6 (63 D) on which last see notes by Veil and Blunt in loco.

of God to matter included the mediating activity of the Logos, and will be more fittingly discussed later.[1] Here it is only to be noticed that Justin never departs from the conception that the responsibility of God in creation is complete, and that in ordinary parlance God is spoken of as the personal Creator, as though the Logos had had no share in the process whatever.

God's active power and force are further described in His *omniscience*,[2] and *omnipotence*,[3] while His complete *autonomy* is defended in the assertion that the Stoics are utterly wrong in making God subject to fate.[4] God's action is free. Even the procession of the Logos, described in Greek philosophy as an emanation necessitated by the nature of God, is described by Justin as a free act of God's will, by which, as Duncker has pointed out, Justin goes further than any Greek writer to defend the freedom of God.[5] But how can a transcendent God keep such intimate contact with the world as to see, hear, and know all that takes place therein? Justin answers that God sees and hears all things not by eyes or ears but by δυνάμει ἀλέκτῳ [6] The passage at first tempts one to find in it some δύναμις doctrine of the sort increasingly popular in Greek philosophy at the time, but the phrase here seems to mean no more than a confession of ignorance Justin is confident equally that God sees and hears, and that He has no organ of sight or hearing. But by what power or faculty God then can hear and see Justin confesses in this phrase that he is not prepared to explain.

There is little reason to go back to Plato's Idea of the Good to account for the fact that God is represented by

Von Engelhardt (Bibl. 313) p 129 notes that Justin rarely speaks of God without describing Him by some such phrase as δημιουργὸς τοῦδε τοῦ παντός, ὁ ποιήσας τὰ πάντα. etc., but does not recognise the anti-gnostic inspiration of the repetition of these epithets.

[1] See Chapter V pp 161 ff
[2] On the omniscience of God see Semisch (Bibl 118) II 250
[3] Dial. 84 4 (310 E) πάντα δύνασθαι τὸν θεόν, ὅσα βούλεται.
[4] Ap II 7. 3 ff. (45 D); Ap. I 19. 5 (65 E, 66 A)
[5] (Bibl 339) p 22
[6] Dial 127 2 (357 A)

Justin as morally good and holy[1] The holiness of God
is originally a Jewish conception,[2] and the entire background of early Christianity, in Palestine and Hellenism, was
filled with the conception of God as a righteous God.
Nor is there any justification for denying to Justin's God
the kindly and loving interest in men which has always
been the Christian doctrine Justin, though not so extremely
as the Calvinists, was impressed more deeply by the majestic
aspects of Deity than by His loving providence, but several
passages indicate that he perfectly understood and fully
accepted the doctrine of God's loving and even sorrowing
solicitude for individuals as for humanity[3] Von Engelhardt has insisted that Justin knew nothing of God as love,
and that he completely disregarded this aspect of Deity,
alleging that Justin never understood the true message of
Christianity as to the nature of God, and never discarded
his Platonic conception of God as the Absolute[4] He
denies that Justin understood or accepted the personality
of God at all, or that Justin's theory of God admits of the
personal fellowship with God in Christ of which the Apostle
speaks Revelation, von Engelhardt says, opens the way
only to the addressing of the true God in prayer, and to
service of God "But God Himself remains far from the
world, and will be first approachable when man after death
has entered into the sphere of God as an immortal being."[5]
God is to Justin, as to the whole of heathendom, still always
and only a cosmic being (kosmisches Wesen).[6] Justin
thought of piety and righteousness, von Engelhardt continues, as knowledge about God and active imitation of God,
and such a conception "has sense and value only when God
is not a personality, love, and grace, but is the creating
Prime-Intelligence which man has to recognize, and is the
World-Law which man must fulfill"[7] It his hard to
follow such reasoning That Justin's sense of worship

[1] As, among others, does Pfättisch (Bibl 385 p 24
[2] Cf Craemer, O (Bibl 329) p 235
[3] Ap I 44 11 (83 B), 28 4 (71 C), Dial 1 4 (217 E, 218 A)
[4] (Bibl 313) passim, esp 231—241, 447 ff
[5] Ibid. p 240
[6] Ibid p 468.
[7] Ibid pp 482, 483

largely found expression in reverence, thirst for knowledge
of God, and a passion for imitation of God's virtues in his
own life, is perfectly true, but it is a long step from such a
worship to a denial of personality to God, and to an assertion that God is only a Cosmic Law which man must
fulfill. God was intensely personal to Justin, and the personality in his own thinking meant far more than the
catch-words of the Absolute which he had carried over
from Hellenistic Judaism in order to defend the existence
of the Second God, and to clothe Deity in a transcendent
majesty. In not recognizing the Christological motive for
much of Justin's emphasis upon the transcendence of God,
and in not perceiving how foreign to Justin's real thinking
were the implications of his terminology, von Engelhardt
has put enormously disproportionate emphasis upon Justin's
thought of an Absolute, and in carrying it to a denial of
God's personality, has reduced it to absurdity. Von Engelhardt on this point and throughout his important treatise is
laboring under a two-fold error First, to him original and
true Christianity means the Lutheran doctrine of Grace and
Justification by Faith, and because Justin does not expound
Christianity according to these catch-words, von Engelhardt attempts to rule him out of the true Christian succession. Second, von Engelhardt is far too eager to carry
Justin's terminology to a logical conclusion which Justin
himself never dreamed. We shall have occasion to speak
of von Engelhardt's interpretation of justification and grace
in Justin later. He could have contented himself with representing Justin's God as an Impersonal Absolute only by
ignoring Justin's Chrisological incentive and his awkwardness
in using the Absolute terminology, and the patent fact that
Justin speaks again and again of God in the most personal
language. Justin does frequently speak of the grace of
God through which we are saved,[1] of His love and
goodness to men[2] Men may be pleasing or not pleasing
to God, have fellowship with God, who persuades us and
leads us to faith, while it is our part to imitate His excellent

[1] Dial 32. 2 (249 D); 42 1 (260 D); 64 2 (287 D)
[2] Dial 43 2 (261 E) διὰ τὸ ἔλεος τὸ παρὰ τοῦ θεοῦ.
Dial. 107. 2 (334 D). ἐλεήμων ὁ θεὸς καὶ φιλάνθρωπός ἐστιν ἐπὶ
πάντας τοὺς μετατιθεμένους ἀπὸ τῆς κακίας ; cf Stählin (Bibl. 318) p. 37

qualities, His temperance, justice, and love to men [1] In such utterances we are very confident, Justin is not speaking by rote. He was consistently a loving child [2] of a kind Father, and shows no desire in any passage to strip God of all qualities and to make Him an impersonal Absolute. It is entirely misleading to enlarge upon the fact that Justin calls God ἀπαθής in a single passage,[3] inasmuch as God is throughout represented as stirred by emotions of many kinds

To understand Justin Martyr it is essential to bear in mind that his aim in all his teachings and writings was not philosophical or theoretical but practical and apologetic He was a missionary and not a professional philosopher, in spite of his wearing the philosopher's cloak He was not a philosopher first and a Christian afterwards, but a Christian first and always who used philosophical terminology of which he was not entirely master to defend his faith. The source of the doctrine of God seems sufficiently obvious His very inconsistencies are those of the Hellenistic Jews who had long been trying to do just what Justin was forced to attempt, to justify their faith by the help of philosophy. Like them Justin taught at one time that God was transcendent, unbegotten, impassive, perfect, self-contained, unmoved, unchanging, unnamed, the First Cause; at another time that He was the personal creator and sustainer of the universe, at another that He was the kind merciful Father who lead errant individuals into faith and saved them by His grace, or the dread God of righteousness whose final judgment awaited all men. Such a many-sided God was the God of the Wisdom Literature of the Hellenistic Jewish philosophers, and such a God Hellenistic Jews would have brought with them into Christianity. In spite of the fact that Justin does not carry transcendence into absoluteness, still his God is recognizably the God of Hellenistic Judaism

[1] Ap I 10 entire

[2] Ap II 13 4 (51 D

[3] Ap I 25 2 (69 B) where God is so called in contrast with the lustful gods of the heathen, and not given this as a generic title

CHAPTER V

THE LOGOS

In order to understand Justin's Logos and the early Christian Logos in general, it is most important to bear in mind the distinction between the impulse which produced the philosophic Logos doctrine, and the practical necessity which induced Christians very early to appropriate the term for their own use It has been seen that in Stoic circles 'Logos" was a word interchangeable with "God", and expressed the fact that the material All followed a reasonable course in its cycles of change. In dualistic circles of thought, where the tendency was increasingly to represent the Deity as the Absolute in order to free Him from all association with matter, the Reason of God, tending toward, but not yet properly having become, a separate personality, was that phase of God which connected God's otherwise Absolute nature with the world. Aristotle had conceived of an Absolute which had nothing in common with the world of change, and was unconnected with the world by any attribute or power But the νοῦς of Plato had not been thus transcendent, and certainly later Greek philosophers had felt the need of some Power of God which could create and direct the world The Logos then in all circles but the Stoic, and often apparently even in Stoicism, was a link of some kind which connected a transcendent Absolute with the world and humanity. The Logos came into general popularity because of the wide-spread desire to conceive of God as transcendent and yet immanent at the same time; the Logos as variously described in the Schools made possible such a twofold and contradictory conception of God. The term Logos in philosophy was not usually used as the title of a unique attribute of God, but rather as the most important single name among many applicable to the effulgent Power of God which reasonably had shaped and now governs the world

Christianity, however, began not with speculation but with a religious experience. In the person of the crucified and risen Christ it found a tremendous spiritual reality, so great that though Christ had taught men to worship not Himself but God, the early Christian community could not think of Him as an ordinary man But when Christians began to teach Christ as superhuman they immediately encountered opposition from Jews to whom it was the greatest possible blasphemy to teach more than one God It was in Hellenistic Jewish thinking that the problem was solved by the brilliant stroke of identifying Christ with the Logos. It has been seen that the man who made this identification possible was the Apostle Paul, although he, while clearly having the Greek doctrine in mind, for some reason avoided the word "Logos". The author of the Fourth Gospel found all the preparations made for the definite assertion that Jesus was the Logos made flesh. There is no reason to believe from the Gospel that the identification was then advanced as a novelty in Christian thought. It may thus be correct to say that the Christian approach to a Logos doctrine was from below, for its problem was how a definite and historical person could be represented as a cosmic deity. But the philosophic doctrine had been approached from above, and its problem had been to represent the transcendent Absolute as in some way in touch with the world Philosophy had never wanted a separate personality in its Logos doctrine, though as the doctrine became more popular and elaborate the tendency toward personality had been inevitable. But Christianity's central interest was precisely in the divine-human Personality.

In the writings of Justin we find the Christian Logos still in a very uncertain state. Feder is right in saying that the Logos is not fundamental for the theology of Justin, but that it is merely an explanation of the really Christian doctrine of the Son of God [1] It is clear that

[1] (Bibl 350) p. 154.

Justin has never had any interest in attempting to work
out a consistent Logos doctrine. It will be convenient
to use the term Logos to represent Justin's general doctrine
of the pre-incarnate Christ, and to speak of the incarnate
Logos as the Christ. This chapter on the Logos will
then treat only of the pre-incarnate Christ, while the
chapter on Christ will discuss the incarnate Logos. Justin
made no such distinction in terminology, and indeed in
the Dialogue prefers the term Second God or Christ
for the pre-incarnate Person. But on the understanding
that the distinction is not Justin's the division of matter
under the two terms will somewhat simplify the subject.

1. *THE PERSONAL EXISTENCE OF A SECOND GOD*

When Justin wishes to convert Trypho to Christianity,
the first essential is to prove to him the existence of the
Second God. There is no such necessity in the Apology
where Justin is addressing polytheists, for with them he has
only to assert the existence of the Logos, while proof is
needed solely to identify the historical Jesus with this
Logos[1] But in the Dialogue, which is a much more
thorough and idiomatic, though by no means a complete,
expression of Justin's Christianity, Justin is compelled to
prove the existence of a Second God. Herein the Dialogue
is different from the Philonic literature. Philo adduced
proof of the existence of God,[2] which Justin in no
passage felt called upon to do. Philo, on the other hand,
feels himself under no necessity of justifying his constant
appeal to the Logos, for he seems to assume that the
existence of the Logos is a corollary to the existence of

[1] The propriety of fully identifying the Logos of the Apologies with the Second God of the Dialogue has often been
questioned, but without justification. The Logos in His pre-incarnate
state is called Christ as well as Logos in the Apologies, Ap. I
62. 4 (95 B), while the Second God or Christ, in spite of Feder
(Bibl 350) p 154, is called the Logos in the Dialogue, e. g 61. 1
(284 B), 62. 1 (285 A). I therefore use the two sources interchangeably, in the conviction that only by combining the material
on the doctrine for the most part peculiar to each document can
an adequate view of Justin's Logos doctrine be obtained.

[2] See Drummond, Philo, II 3—6, 295, 296.

God. Such an assumption was possible to Philo for two reasons, first because he was writing in an environment where the Logos had for more than a century, at least, been proverbial, and second because he could always remove apparent inconsistencies with monotheism by treating the Logos impersonally. But with the Christians this escape was impossible, for it was precisely upon the personality of the Logos that their religious system was founded. In the Dialogue where the Jewish inheritance of Christianity stands out more clearly than in the Apology, the urge for monotheism is compelling, so that any mention of a Second Divine Personality demands the most careful justification.

Justin states his thesis thus: "I shall try to persuade you that there is and is said to be (in the Scriptures) a God and Lord besides the Creator of the universe, who is also called an Angel because He announces to men whatsoever the Creator of the universe wishes, but there is no other God higher than the Creator."[1] In the Apology, where the argument for the Second God is briefly mentioned, but by no means worked out in detail, the same thesis takes the form: "The Father of the universe has a Son, who also, being the first begotten Word of the God, is a God."[2] Two arguments are adduced to prove this thesis, the first based upon theophanies, the second upon passages in the Old Testament where God is represented as speaking to some other God.

The argument from theophanies is as follows.[3] Justin quotes to Trypho the passage where God appeared to Abraham under the oak of Mamre, and the great discussion occurred concerning the burning of Sodom and Gomorrah. According to the account in Genesis two ordinary angels accompanied One who must definitely be recognized as God, for He entered into the tent to announce the coming birth of a son to Sarah and promised to return later; when He did return He is explicitly called God by the Scriptures.

[1] Dial. 56. 4 (275 C).
[2] Ap. I 63 15 (96 C).
[3] Dial. 56 entire.

But this God cannot be the same as the God who rules over all He is a messenger God who finally secures permission from the God of heaven to rain fire and sulphur upon the cities of Sodom and Gomorrah. There must then be two Gods, One who remains in Heaven and One who appears in theophanies. Justin goes on to quote the appearance of God in the incidents of Jacob's dream of the spotted rams and goats, Jacob's wrestling, the changing of Jacob's name at Luz, Jacob's dream at Bethel,[1] and a little further on the appearance in the burning bush.[2] In another passage he says that Christ was the Angel with whom Moses communed· on the occasion when he had lost faith in the promise of food.[3] In all these passages Justin's emphasis is upon two points, first upon the independent personality of this Being who can be manifested to man, and second upon His divine nature. "He is called God, and He is and shall be God,"[4] Justin exclaims to his Jewish auditors who give their complete assent

It is in connection with the argument from theophanies that Justin makes his strongest assertions of the transcendence of God "He who has but the smallest intelligence will not venture to assert that the Maker and Father of all things, having left all supercelestial matters, was visible on a little portion of the earth,"[5] but Justin's attention here and throughout is primarily not upon the nature of God but upon the existence of the personal Second God

Philo, who inherited his prejudice against theophanies from Plato,[6] is clearly in the direct line of ancestry of Justin's protest, and a comparsion between Justin's and Philo's interpretations of theophanies is illuminating Though Philo, like Plato, argued against theophanies from the unchangeableness of God,[7] he inclined like Justin

[1] Dial 58
[2] Dial 60
[3] Dial 126 6 (356 C)
[4] Dial 58 9 (281 D).
[5] Dial 60 2 (283 B)
[6] Rep II 380 D ff See above p 127
[7] De Somnus I 231 ff (I 655, 656)

to base the argument more commonly upon the trans-cendence of God than upon His unchangeable perfection Philo had no thesis to prove from the appearances of God to man, and mentioned the incidents in his writings only as Scriptural inconsistencies with God's character which must be explained away Consequently he cared little for general consistency in his explanations of how these incidents really happened, so long as in each individual case he could rid the Scriptures of their primitive anthropomorphism An excellent illustration of Philo's object is the passage in which he goes into the matter of the appearances of God in some detail [1] He begins with the quotation, "I am the God who was seen by thee in the place of God "[2] Are there then, Philo asks, two Gods? By no means, for only the one God who is truly God may be called ὁ θεός, but there are numerous beings who are loosely called θεός without the article In this Scriptural statement, says Philo, the reference to the second God is to the Logos But a few lines below Philo says that God can appear as He is to incorporeal souls, but that He must, without actually changing, appear in the semblance of an angel when there is need of appearing to a corporeal man Again after a digression Philo adds that it is not surprising that God took the form of an Angel so far as appearance went (though without changing His nature), for man could not endure to see God as He truly is. But those who are unable to bear the sight of God look upon His image, His Angel Logos, as Himself Philo is obviously not concerned here as to whether he calls the medium of theophany "angels", "an angel", or the "Logos", far less is he appealing to any secondary deity His sole object in treating the passage at all is to free the Scriptures from an apparent anthropo-morphic aspersion upon God.[3] Such after Philo was the

[1] De Somniis I 227 ff (I 655, 656) Cf similarly De Somniis I 69 ff (I 631) and De Mut Nom 15 ff (I 581)

[2] Gen xxxi 13

[3] It is because Philo finds his doctrine of Logos, Logoi, and lower divine beings in general a frequent escape from embarrasing blind alleys that Friedlander has strikingly but on the whole in-

incentive which led the poet Ezekiel to identify God in
the burning bush with the Logos·

ὁ δ' ἐκ βάτου σοι θεῖος ἐκλάμπει λόγος.[1]

The Jews carried on the same thought in the Talmudic
use of the Memra to explain theophanies and all other
physical or anthropomorphic references to God in the Old
Testament. It was the Memra who was the cloud leading
the Children of Israel in the wilderness, as well as the
Deity which gave the Law on Sinai.[2] But here as in
Philo the device is not an end in itself, for not the
conception of the Logos or Memra, but the doctrine of
God, is the interest of the commentators.

It is thus apparent that Justin, in proving the existence
of a second personal God from theophanies, has used
material from Greek Judaism,[3] but has given it an
implication never found in any Judaism, and in deducing
therefrom a second divine Personality has come to conclusions which Jews have always felt to be unjustified.

Similar is the case of the second argument to prove
the existence of a Second God. This argument is based
upon Scriptural passages where God is represented as
speaking to another God or to other Gods, or where
mention is apparently made of two Gods. Justin considers
to whom the ποιήσωμεν of Genesis i. 25 could have been
addressed. Jewish teachers, he asserts, vary in their explanation of this passage. Some say God addressed Himself in soliloquy, others that He addressed the "elements,
to wit the earth and other similar substances of which we
believe man was formed," while others say that He spoke
to the angels who themselves proceeded to create man's
body.[4] But these suggestions are of no help, says Justin,

accurately generalized· "The Logos is only an emergency device
(Notbehelf) in order to be able to explain Creation." (Bibl. 222) p 38

[1] Euseb Pr. Ev. IX 29 (p. 441).

[2] Weber, Judische Theologie, pp 180—184.

[3] Cf. The Philonic nature of Justin's comment on the incident of the "three men" who appeared to Abraham, above
pp. 114 ff.

[4] Dial 62. 1 ff. (285 A ff) Who these Jewish teachers were
we cannot now ascertain. Justin's summary of their teachings
reproduces a Tannaitic tradition (but with one important modi-

for God addressed another person who was numerically distinct from Himself and a rational being To prove this statement Justin adduces the passage, "Behold Adam has become as one of us, to know good and evil" Clearly the person addressed must have been rational. Other passages which are found useful witnesses to the existence of a second rational personal God are: "The Lord made me from the beginning of His ways for His works,"[1] etc.; "The Lord says to my Lord;"[2] "Thy throne, oh God, is forever and ever . . . . . God, even thy God, hath annointed thee," etc.[3] Trypho is by this time quite willing to admit the existence of a Second God who is distinct from the Father of All in number, but who fully deserves the title of God[4]

So far as I know, Justin is here the first to attempt a term for personalities in the Godhead. He frequently uses ἕτερος ἀριθμῷ which is always, and on the whole wisely, translated "numerically distinct", but which meant to Justin "different in person."[5] This sharp personality of Justin's Logos is the element which distinguishes it from the Philonic Logos more than anything except its incarnation. Feder, who attempts to minimize the Philonic

fication): "With whom has He taken counsel? 1 With the Creation of Heaven and earth (that is the elements which Justin has mentioned) . . . . 2. With Himself . . . . 3 He took counsel with the Angels and said to them, Let us make, etc" (Mish Gen Rabba c. 8, p. 7 c, d, from Goldfahn [Bibl. 389] p 245) Goldfahn says that such passages are frequent, but that in no orthodox Jewish tradition were the Angels ever represented as creators of the human body Philo of course teaches a very similar doctrine (see above p 114, n 1 and below p 211), and the idea certainly came originally from Plato's Timaeus Justin may be actually denying a doctrine from some Jewish Gnostic Sect. See Philo, De Opif Mundi 72—75 (I. 16. 17). Justin is here apparently summarizing all Jewish comments upon the passage which he could find, and so has combined orthodox and unorthodox Jewish traditions

[1] Dial. 61. 3 (284 C), Prov viii 21 ff
[2] Dial 56 14 (277 B), Ps cx 1
[3] Ibid, Ps xlv. 6, 7
[4] Dial. 63 1 (286 B)
[5] Dial 56. 11 (276 D); 62 2 (285 C); 128 4 (358 C); 129. 1, 4 (358 D, 359 D)

influence upon Justin, draws up six points of contrast between the Justinian and Philonic Logos.[1] In four of his six points the distinction is purely in the matter of the personality of Justin's Logos. But nothing could be more inaccurate than to conclude that Justin was not influenced by Philonic tradition merely because his Logos or Second God is personal, while the Logos of Philo is not, or because Justin, when discussing theophanies and the Second God, usually prefers to call the Second God Christ rather than the Logos.[2] The Philonic arguments and materials, as will shortly appear more clearly, are present in Justin's writings in marked detail.

B THE ORIGIN OF THE LOGOS
1. MANNER OF ORIGIN

Justin has two main methods for explaining how the Logos came into being

The first explanation centers around the word *begotten,* or its synonyms, and may be best summed up by Justin's phrase πρωτότοκος τῷ ἀγεννήτῳ θεῷ.[3] God begat this begotten thing before all creation.[4] Justin did not intend to imply creation in the origin of the Logos, for though he represents Trypho as using the word ποιέω in that connection,[5] Justin himself did not use it, and while he does not contrast the term "begotten" and "made" as Christianity soon came to do, the contrast is clearly in his mind by his pointed avoidance of the latter term. So he quotes from Prov. viii. 21 ff. where Wisdom describes her origin in terms both of creation and begetting, but he quietly

---

[1] (Bibl 350) p. 143

[2] As he does even in the Ap I 62 3 (95 B), and of course almost throughout the Dialogue In Dial 113 4 (340 D) theophanies are even referred to "Jesus".

[3] Ap I 53 2 (88 A); cf also πρωτόγονος τοῦ θεοῦ Ap I 58. 3 (92 B), and πρωτότοκος τοῦ θεοῦ Ap I 46 2 (83 C) etc Justin does not distinguish between the two words πρωτόγονος and πρωτότοκος. Only the latter is found in the New Testament, while the former is the word preferred by Philo See Abbott (Bibl 454) p 571.

[4] Dial 129 4 (359 B).

[5] Dial 64 1 (287 C)

ignores the first term in expounding the passage to lay
stress on the conception of begetting [1]

But helpful as the terms γέννημα and πρωτότοκος are
in distinguishing the two Gods, and adequate as they
might have been for ordinary use, especially with Christians
converted from popular Palestinian Judaism or from the
heathenism of popular mythologies, both words are much
too anthropomorphic to suffice in explaining the origin
of the Second God to one at all acquainted with philosophy
Justin retains, and is personally fond of using, the simple
explanation of the Logos as "begotten", but he is aware
that he must explain such a conception in philosophic
language if he is to appeal to educated minds   The
difficulty with the analogy of begetting, aside from its
anthropomorphic connotations, lies in the fact that it implies
an abscission from and a diminution of the begetter, both
of which Justin is most careful to deny

The origin of the Logos was secondly typified by other
figures such as were in common and increasing vogue
in the philosophy of the day to represent *emanations*,
and which Hellenistic Judaism had long found useful
Justin found no single figure adequate for his purpose,
and could describe his conception only by combining
several figures.

By the figure of light from the sun [2] Justin expressed
his conviction that the Logos was still one with the
Father, because the process of His begetting or emanation
(a term which Justin does not use) was attended by
no abscission   The light has no independent existence
apart from the sun, but is only an effulgence from the
sun   When the sun sets, Justin points out, the light
disappears. So the Logos is not an existence independent
of the Father   According as the Father wills it, there
radiate from Him Powers which may go forth, as some
do, only to return and vanish in the great Source from
which they have gone out,[3] or which may be sustained in

[1] Dial 129. 3, 4 (359 A, B)

[2] Dial 128 3, 4 (358 B ff)

[3] By contemporary science, when a light went out it recalled its
beams, or fiery extensions, back into itself As a source of light God would
have this same power, but arbitrarily See Athenagor Supplic 10 3

a permanent outflowing if the Father so will. Such permanent outflowings are the angels of permanent existence. But though permanent they have no independent existences and represent no abscission from the Source. They are permanent beams from the Eternal Light. Δυνάμεις was a word for rays in Justin's vocabulary. In one passage he speaks of δυνάμεις from the sun in a way to suggest that the meaning of the word as actual light rays would be perfectly intelligible to his audience.[1] But since Justin thought of light as a fiery stream actually flowing from a fiery source,[2] his meaning might perhaps be more accurately illustrated for us today by a river.[3] God is an eternal and infinite source, from which, without diminution of the source, flow streams of water. These streams may be named, bridged, treated as independent reality, but they actually have no existence apart from the water which flows from the source. Cut from the source the water ceases to flow, and the river has vanished. So the permanent angels are permanent outflowings of the power of God. Of these the Logos is chief. He is the first effulgence, the first outflowing, and by far the most important, but His existence is in no sense independent of the Father. Thus does Justin protect himself from the charge of ditheism. There are two Gods, but only one source, only one ultimate existence.

But helpful as is this representation of the origin of the Logos, Justin does not feel that it is adequate, for any figure of outflowing from a source inevitably suggests a diminution of the source. Water that flows out from the source into the stream, no less than light which reaches the earth from the sun, has left the source, and by however small a proportion, the source must have been diminished. He therefore balances the figure of light from a source by the figure of fire from fire.[4] One may light a second torch from a burning first torch without having taken at all from the fire of the first torch.

[1] Dial. 121. 2 (350 A). See below p. 246.
[2] Cf. Hans Leisegang, Der Heilige Geist, I. i. (Leipzig 1919), p. 31.
[3] For this figure see Athanasius, De Sententia Dionysii, 18.
[4] Dial. 128. 4 (358 C, D); cf. 61. 2 (284 C).

God must not be conceived of as having flowed out
into the Logos in such a way that there is any diminution
of the source. There can be no cutting off or departure
from the οὐσία of God, as this figure by itself might
seem to suggest. Nor is God exhausted by his outflowings;
He remains eternally unchanged in spite of them. This
outflowing of the δυνάμεις from the Father must not be
considered in any sense as a process inevitable from the
nature of God. A power goes forth only when God wills
it to do so. Hence the Logos, angels, and all powers,
are the result of an action of God's will.[1]

Justin's thought of the emanation of the powers from
the Father, of which the Logos was the chief, is thus
to be found between the two figures. Light from a source
illustrates the radiating of divine powers without abscission
from the Father, or the extension of a single οὐσία into
a plurality of persons. Fire from fire illustrates a giving
forth from a source without any diminution of the source,
while at the same time sharpening the individuality of
the emanation.

Both the figures of fire from fire and of beams from
a light as illustrations of the dissemination of spiritual
power from God had been clearly expounded in Philo.
Of fire from fire Philo speaks in commenting upon, "I
will take up my spirit which is upon thee, and I will
pour it upon the seventy elders." Philo says, "But
think not that this taking away could be by means of
cutting off and sundering, but as would happen from
fire, which even though it kindled ten thousand torches
remains in the same condition, in no respect diminished."[3]
Of light from a source of light Philo says, "Being itself
archetypal source of light (αὐγή), the eye of God throws out

[1] On the freedom of God see above p. 135. Duncker
(Bibl 339) is probably right in concluding that Justin, in making
the Logos the expression of God's will, was protecting the character
of God as a Being who loved and cared for the world, but Justin
himself never draws such a conclusion.

[2] Numb. xi, 17.

[3] De Gigant 24, 25 (I 266). See above p. 46. Justin seems
here however still closer to the figures of the Tannaim than to those
of Philo. See below pp 189 ff

innumerable rays, not one of which is a sensible, but all are intelligible." [1]

Justin has one more important figure to explain the emanation of the Logos from the Father Justin makes the following statement which loses half its force in translation because of the double sense of the word Logos Λόγον γάρ τινα προβάλλοντες, λόγον γεννῶμεν, οὐ κατὰ ἀποτομήν. ὡς ἐλαττωθῆναι τὸν ἐν ἡμῖν λόγον. προβαλλόμενοι.[2] "In giving forth anything rational we beget speech, not giving it forth in such a way as to make an abscission so that the rational in us is diminished." Justin could use the same word "Logos" to express both the process of thought which lay behind an utterance, and the utterance itself, so that the passage may be paraphrased: in telling our thoughts to others, while something has gone out from us our thought life has not in the least been diminished within us. Justin does not use the scientific terms, but he has obviously in mind the distinction between λόγος ἐνδιάθετος and λόγος προφορικός which we have seen[3] were terms of contemporary Logic But it is particularly interesting to note Justin's use of the figure As thought can be transmitted from one man to another without the thought of the first man having in the least been diminished, Justin says, so the Logos has gone forth from the Father without the slightest division or diminution of the *Father*. That is, Justin stops just short of carrying the figure too far and representing a cosmic duality of the Logos, a cosmic λόγος ἐνδιάθετος and a cosmic λόγος προφορικός. If the figure must be pressed into the cosmic, it was God Himself who was typified by the human λόγος ἐνδιάθετος, while the Logos was typified only by the human λόγος προφορικός. The point is interesting for two reasons, first because Justin stops just short of a step which was very soon taken, when Theophilus explicitly taught a stage of existence of the Logos which could be described as the λόγος ἐνδιάθετος of God [4] But

[1] De Cherubim 97 (I 156) et passim On Light as a title for the Logos see below sect E 5
[2] Dial 61 2 (284 B, C)
[3] See p. 19
[4] Ad Autol II 22 (100 B) et passim

the second reason for interest here is the fact that Philo
also comes very close to ascribing the two human logoi to
God,[1] so close that Gfrorer says that it was only by in-
advertence that Philo did not complete his figure by an
explicit sentence.[2] Philo however does refrain from taking
the step, and Drummond has pointed out that Philo here
knew perfectly well what he was about, and that he refused
to take the step because the figure did not quite fit his
theories of the Logos. A theologian of a slightly more
developed stage than Justin, then, dared to make an assertion about the Logos which Justin, like Philo, did not yet
care to make, and one feels that only a very close
dependence upon a Philonic tradition could have brought
him so near to speaking of a cosmic λόγος ἐνδιάθετος and
yet kept him from doing so.[3]

In general the lightness with which Justin touches the
problem of the emanation of the Logos is well explained
by Irenaeus. The emanation theory was the only theory
which was at hand to explain philosophically the origin of
the Logos, but the doctrine was extremely dangerous to
use, for it was the chief weapon of the Gnostics. Irenaeus
criticizes people who ascribe all steps of human ratiocination
to God, for we have no right to be certain that God thinks
by the same processes as ourselves, and still less have we
the right to represent each step in the process of God's
thought as an emanation, itself father of the next emanation-
step Not only so, says Irenaeus, but the representation of
emanations at all is a contradiction, for it is impossible to
conceive of anything as proceeding out from the Infinite
and Omnipresent.[4] Justin is not, like Irenaeus, prepared to
give over the whole thought of emanations, but he clearly
uses the conception with the greatest caution, and is careful
to keep figures only as figures, and not to represent them as

[1] Vit. Mos II. (III) 127 (II. 154), see Drummond II. 171 ff.
[2] Philo und die judisch - alexandrinische Theosophie Stuttgart 1835. I. 177, 178.
[3] See below p. 165. n 1.
[4] Adv Haer. II 13 entire

assertions of actual events in the Godhead.[1] But however inexplicable was the begetting or procession of the Son from the Father, that some such thing must have happened was witnessed to Justin by the palpable fact that the Second God did exist.

2 TIME OF ORIGIN

Unfortunately Justin has avoided or not recognized the problem of the time at which the Logos was begotten from the Father, and has given us little from which to infer what his opinion might have been All of Justin's figures, whether of begetting or procession, suggest the previous existence of the Source from which the Logos came forth, and Justin has nowhere attempted to soften the temporal implications of his illustrations He knows nothing, at least says nothing, of the Logos as being eternal.

The begetting of the Logos probably took place as a preparatory step toward creation Certainly it did not take place after creation The Logos is the "Beginning before all created things"[2] and Justin probably thought that He was the beginning, immediately after which came the created things. This is the sense in which he understands the πρωτότοκος πάσης κτίσεως, for in one passage the Logos is described as πρωτότοκος πάσης κτίσεως καὶ ἀρχὴ πάλιν ἄλλου γένους[3] that is, the Logos was the first born of all creation, and now (by His incarnation and saving power) marks the starting point of a race for a second time, the spiritual race of Christians The parallelism will probably hold good For as the incarnate Logos marked the beginning of Christian people, so the Logos, though Himself not created, marked the beginning of created things, which seems to mean that the *begetting* of the Logos marked the beginning of created things The inference is very remote, but slightly suggests that the Logos was begotten not long before creation.

---

[1] Justin also, but much more slightly, reproaches those who identify the thought processes of God with goddesses Ap. I 64 4 (97 B)

[2] Dial 62 4 (285 D)

[3] Dial 138 2 (367 D) On the title ἀρχή see below, section E 4

Justin has given us but one bit of real evidence for the time of the procession or begetting of the Logos, but the meaning of that passage is much' disputed. ὁ δὲ υἱὸς ἐκείνου, ὁ μόνος λεγόμενος κυρίως υἱός, ὁ λόγος πρὸ τῶν ποιημάτων καὶ συνὼν καὶ γεννώμενος, ὅτε τὴν ἀρχὴν δι' αὐτοῦ πάντα ἔκτισε καὶ ἐκόσμησε, κτλ.[1] "But His Son, the only Son properly so called, the Logos who was with Him and was-begotten before the Creation, when He created and set in order all things through Him at the beginning," etc. The controversy which is still unsettled concerning the passage springs from the problem of the reference of the ὅτε. Semisch proposed to take the ὅτε only with γεννώμενος, and hence to distinguish two stages in the existence of the Logos-Christ.[2] At the first stage He was an impersonal attribute, the Logos of God, and as such was eternal. But at the beginning of creation this hitherto impersonal and unbegotten attribute was begotten, and for the first time became a personality. In other words Semisch tried to find in this passage a doctrine of a divine λόγος ἐνδιάθετος and λόγος προφορικός which we have seen Justin pointedly avoided in another passage Aside from the danger of basing so large an inference upon so slight a foundation, the objections are potent against even a possibility of Justin's having meant here to distinguish betwen συνὼν and γεννώμενος. Justin has expressly marked the two words as parallel by the double καί, so that it is quite forced to associate the ὅτε with the word γεννώμενος alone. The passage seems only to mean that when God created the world the Logos was already in existence and dwelling with Him, and was of assistance in the process of creation [3]

We must then agree with Holland that concerning the time of the emanation of the Logos Justin knows only that the Logos was already-existent and at hand to assist in creation, but that Justin has apparently made no attempt

---

[1] Ap. II 6 3 (44 D, E).
[2] (Bibl. 118) II. 278 ff. Otto, Veil, Pfattisch, et al. agree with Semisch, von Engelhardt, Donaldson, etc, disagree. Feder seems undecided
[3] On the creative activity of the Logos see below pp 161 ff

to speculate about events in the timeless eternity which lay behind creation.[1]

C. *THE NATURE OF THE LOGOS*

From Justin's arguments for the existence of a Second God, and from his descriptions of the begetting of the Only Begotten, it has appeared that Justin was attempting to explain a birth or begetting in the Godhead which produced a Second Person without any separation or division of the Godhead. But in general Justin found his Philonic figures of the unity of the οὐσία much less important than the dual divine Personalities, and consequently he makes the real basis of his argument for monotheism not the unity of οὐσία but the subordination of rank of the Second God. The Logos, in passage after passage is represented as subordinate to the Father. Probably the figure of Light beams from a source of light expressed his conceptions much more fully than he wanted explicitly to admit. Bosse has accurately pointed out that in the title ἕτερος θεός the term θεός is of much less importance than ἕτερος.[2] It is quite true that in places Justin checks himself from making the distinction between God and the Logos too sharp, as in the passage where he says that the Second God is "distinct from Him who made all things: I mean He is distinct in number but not in intellectual initiative."[3] But even here, where Justin has apparently asserted the equality of the Logos with the Father, a second glance will at once reveal the fact that to deny independence γνώμη is quite the reverse of asserting equality of rank. The sentence is ordinarily rendered as,

---

[1] (Bibl. 153) pp. 573, 574. But here Holland is quite wrong in representing Justin's interest as primarily cosmological rather than theistic. Cosmology was at that time, with the exception of mysticism, the only approach to theism, so that when Justin wished to describe reality in the pre-creation Logos he naturally would have used cosmological language to do so. But Justin's real interest was not in cosmology, but in the personal Father and His Son Jesus Christ.

[2] (Bibl. 345) p. 22.

[3] Dial. 56. 11 (276 E) ἕτερός ἐστι τοῦ τὰ πάντα ποιήσαντος θεοῦ, ἀριθμῷ λέγω ἀλλὰ οὐ γνώμῃ.

though γνώμη here were equivalent to θελήματι, will, but it means much more than that. It means that though the Second God is a distinct personality He yet has no impulsive power in His thinking, for there is only one such centre in the Godhead, the ὄντως θεός. The beam of light has an independent existence, in a sense that it can be treated as a thing in itself. It can be broken by a prism, reflected in a mirror, or checked by a screen without anything having happened to the source. It is intelligible to speak of a light *and* its beams, making a plurality of number. Nevertheless the beam remains nothing in itself apart from its source. So the Logos, while different in person or number from the Source, has no independence of intellectual initiative in Himself. He is never a cause, but only a means, the personal vehicle through whom God may express His will and intentions. "For I say that He (the Second God) has never done (or said) anything other than what He who made the world, above whom is no other God, has wished Him to do or say."[1] So Justin says again that Christ "is also God according to His (God's) will, His Son, and He is an Angel because He ministers to Gods purpose (ἐκ τοῦ ὑπηρετεῖν τῇ γνώμῃ αὐτοῦ)."[2] But the similarity between Christ and the angels is deeper than one of function. It has been seen that His origin was of the same nature as that of the angels, and at least in this point His character is like theirs For though the angels were granted freedom of choice[3] they are not self-directed. There are not two or more centers radiating δυνάμεις λογικάς but only One, and to that Center Christ, as the angels, must look for direction as well as origin. It is this similarity of nature between the Logos and the angels which prompted Justin, to the great discomfort of later Christian Apologists, to say that the objects of Christian worship were God, "and the Son who came forth from Him and taught us those things, and the host of other good angels who follow Him and are

[1] Dial. 56. 11 (276 D)

[2] Dial 127 4 (357 B), cf. Dial 60 3 (283 C).

[3] Ap II. 7. 5 (45 D). αὐτεξουσίαν; cf. Dial 88. 5 (316 A).

made like to Him," etc.[1] This passage Father Martindale has recently wished to explain as meaning "and the others, the ministering angels," by a familiar Greek idiom[2] But such an interpretation is dubious from the fact that Justin describes the origin of the Logos and of the angels as of the same nature. Justin's confusion of the Logos as a distinct and unique existence, and at the same time as similar ultimately to the angels is entirely Philonic. For Philo has passages where the Logos seems a unique existence, as when he identifies it with the κόσμος νοητός but in other passages he repeatedly calls the Logos an Angel[3] and one of the δυνάμεις of God, and gives it the angelic title ὑπηρέτης.[4]

But in spite of Justin's identification of the metaphysical nature of the Logos with the angels, no greater injustice can be done Justin's thought than to regard the Logos as adequately described in terms of His angelic character The Logos is the *Only* Begotten, the only one properly called Son of God, and it is impossible to suppose that Justin thought of the Logos as simply the chief of the Angels If He is an angel in nature, He is not one in rank, for He alone, except the Father, merits the titles κύριος and θεός.

The title θεός which Justin repeatedly insists is properly applied to the Logos is very hard to define, for Justin by no means meant to teach that there are two First Gods. To express the distinction between the First and Second Gods Justin took over a locution which Philo was the first to my knowledge to have defined, that is the distinction between ὁ θεός and θεός, which has already been quoted[5] Justin had no occasion to define this distinction

---

[1] Ap I 6 2 (56 C) τὸν παρ' αὐτοῦ υἱὸν ἐλθόντα καὶ διδάξαντα ἡμᾶς ταῦτα, καὶ τὸν τῶν ἄλλων ἑπομένων καὶ ἐξομοιουμένων ἀγαθῶν ἀγγέλων στρατόν.

[2] (Bibl 169) p 67 n 1

[3] e g De Somniis I 239 (I 656) τὸν ἄγγελον αὐτοῦ λόγον

[4] In Dial. 57. 3 (279 E) Justin has Trypho called the Logos ὑπηρέτης τοῦ ποιητοῦ τῶν ὅλων θεοῦ. Cf. Philo, De Nomin Mut 87 (I 591) ἄγγελος ὑπηρέτης τοῦ θεοῦ, λόγος, and Quod Deos immut 57 (I 281) suggested by Thirlby

[5] See above p 144

as Philo did, for apparently it was a perfectly familiar manner of speech. It was indeed familiar enough by the time when the Fourth Gospel was written to enable its use without definition in that Prologue which is only intelligible on the assumption that the writer was summarizing in familiar language a familiar conception. The Prologue says, ὁ λόγος ἦν πρὸς τὸν θεόν, καὶ θεὸς ἦν ὁ λόγος. But Justin departs from the Philonic use to make θεός not only a title distinguishing Him from the First God, but also a mark of the superiority of the Logos to the other angels. Philo says that many may loosely be called θεός, but Justin indicates the title as the distinction of the unique rank of the Logos,[1] though in the Apology he prefers the equally Philonic term θεῖος λόγος.[2] Justin says that the Logos is θεός because He is the Son of God,[3] but this means nothing. However when he says that the Logos is θεός because it is the will of the Father that He should be θεός[4] we have a statement of much greater significance. For this statement recalls the fact that Justin says the Logos is Son of God because God wills it. Indeed all of the glory and power which the Logos possesses is His, not by His own right but by the will of the Father. He is ὁ κύριος ἡμῶν κατὰ τὰ θέλημα τοῦ πέμψαντος αὐτὸν πατρὸς καὶ δεσπότου τῶν ὅλων[5] God gave His glory only to His Christ.[6] Christ Himself

[1] The title is thus used · Dial 48. 2 (267 C); 56. 8 (276 B), 125 3 (354 D); 126. 2 (355 C), 127 4 (357 B); 128 1, 4 (357 D, 358 C). It must however be borne in mind that Justin is by no means a nice writer, and does not check his terminology. Hence when he has just quoted an Old Testament theophany in which the God of the theophany is called ὁ θεός, Justin occasionally applies the article to the God of the theophany. Donaldson (Bibl. 143) pp. 227 ff. has entered into elaborate analyses of the passages where Justin does so, and has offered some ingenious explanations But the carelessness of Justin deserves no such ingenuity.

[2] Ap I 10 6 (58 D), 33 9 (75 D), 36 1 (76 D) The term θεῖος λόγος would be more easily intelligible to people not familiar with the Philonic tradition than the simple θεός. The Apology was probably designed for readers unacquainted with the Philonic tradition, the Dialogue for readers who had such acquaintance.

[3] Dial. 125 3 (354 D); 128. 1 (357 D).

[4] Dial. 127. 4 (357 B)

[5] Dial. 140 4 (369 D)

[6] Dial. 65. 3 (289 E).

received from the Father the title of King, and Christ, and
Priest, and Angel, and such like other titles which He bears
or did bear.[1] The Logos is worshipped because God wills
it.[2] The Logos is then θεός, κύριος, Son, King, Christ, Priest,
Angel, glorious, and worshipful only because God wills this
to be the case. Otherwise, we must conclude, He would
be merely like any of the other angels. For the Logos was
an emanation of Power, a permanent δύναμις like all the
other permanent δυνάμεις, but by the will of God granted
powers, glory, and eminence so far superior to the others
that He alone is properly called Son, and Lord, and to Him
alone is the word θεός (or θεῖος) to be applied.

D. COSMIC SIGNIFICANCE OF THE LOGOS

Justin's conception of the cosmic significance of the
Logos must be reconstructed from fragmentary references.

We have seen that He called Christ the πρωτότοκος πάσης
κτίσεως καὶ ἀρχὴ πάλιν ἄλλου γένους.[3] If the new race was
considered by Justin in the Pauline mystical sense of existing in Christ, or of Christ in us, which we shall see good
reason for believing to have been Justin's view, it may be
that this parallelism of Justin's may be taken as implying
that as Christ is the mystic Person in whom all the new
race dwells, and who dwells in the new race, so all
creation is sustained and permeated by the First Born
of God.

A clearer hint of the cosmic significance of the Logos
is found in the discussion of the cosmic significance of the
Cross.[4] Justin finds in the Cross an omnipresent mystic
symbol. The sails of ships hung on crosses indicate the
power of the Cross on the sea; ploughs are crosses which
mould the dry land, tools are for the most part made in
the shape of a cross, and show that the Cross is all-powerful
in manufactured articles (which Justin seems to be following
Platonism in representing as a distinct sort and class of

[1] Dial 86 3 (313 C).
[2] Dial 93 2 (321 A).
[3] See above p. 147
[4] Ap. I 55 entire

existence); the human form is in the shape of a cross
formed by the projection of the arms from the body; the
face is especially marked with the cross by the projection
of the nose, while respiration through the nose indicates a
special and immediate linking of spirit and matter in man
The Cross is a symbol of human power and achievment,
for it is carried as a banner before all state processions,
while it is the form adopted by sculptors as that best
adapted to symbolize deity (for it has been seen that the
human form is cruciform). The Cross is thus an omnipresent symbol But what does it symbolize? Justin says
that the Cross is τὸ μέγιστον σύμβολον τῆς ἰσχύος καὶ ἀρχῆς αὐτοῦ,[1]
the most important symbol of His strength and rulership, so
that any cosmic significance of the Logos in the passage
depends upon the reference of the αὐτοῦ. Does it refer to
Christ, or merely to the Cross? The immediate context
helps not at all in deciding this matter, but since Justin has
been speaking of Christ in the preceding chapters, the
probability is strong that Christ was intended here. If that
is the case, the passage as a whole will mean that as the
Cross is found everywhere, in all classes and sorts of existence from the elements to the mind and power of man,
so is the cosmic Christ or Logos the guiding and sustaining
force of the universe.

A similar hint of cosmic importance of the Logos is
found in the strange passage where Justin finds the Cross
referred to in a statement of Plato in the Timaeus.[2] He
refers explicitly to the passage in the Timaeus where Plato
describes the disposal of the Animus Mundi in the world
by a splitting of the Animus Mundi and joining of the two
halves to form a Greek Chi. This Chi, says Justin, was
intended by Plato to represent the Cross Astonishing a bit
of Platonic interpretation as this is, it obviously implies some
sort of resemblance between the Logos-Christ and the
Animus Mundi of Plato, and at least makes clear that Justin
thought of the Logos as a cosmic Being.

Again Justin hints at a cosmic significance of the

[1] Ap. I. 55 2 (90 B).
[2] Ap. I. 60 1 (92 E); cf. Timaeus 36 b, c.

Logos by using the adjective βασιλικός in the expression, "The Logos, than whom, after God who begat Him, we know that there is no ruler more, kingly and more just" (βασιλικώτατον καὶ δικαιότατον, superlative used for comparative).[1] Here the ruler is a royal ruler, but His kingdom is still undefined. But in view of the implication of these terms in current speech it seems likely that the reference is here as in the other passages to a cosmic significance and function of some sort of the Logos.

Justin gives but one clue to what may have been his real thought of the cosmic significance of the Logos, namely the fact that he uses the expression λόγος σπερματικός. It has been seen[2] that in Stoic physiology λόγος σπερματικός represented a very fine gas which flowed, among other bodily senses and functions, into the damp seminal fluid, and which was the active element, the truly germinal property, of the entire sexual excretion. When this gaseous element from the male united with a similar gaseous flow in the female, germination took place. As a figure this term was applied to God to indicate that in the universal Matter there were two elements, the active and the passive. The active element was called the λόγος σπερματικός or the πνεῦμα indifferently, with the understanding in connection with both terms that they referred to a very fine gas which was the dynamic element in matter. It was this dynamic element which caused in Matter the flow in cycles of the Stoic universe and which made possible the coming into being of the various phenomena of the universe. The term was apparently a very familiar one, for it appears in many philosophical schools and is used by people who had little philosophical training.[3] In the dualistic philosophies such

[1] Ap. I. 12. 7 (59 E).

[2] See above Introd pp 16 ff.

[3] Origin in Joh. xx 2—5, 13, 37; c. Cels I 37, IV 48, Athenag Suppl 6. 4. For its more philosophic application in Christian theology see the Commentary upon Gregory of Nyssa in Karl Gronau. Poseidonios und die judisch-christliche Genesis-exegese, Leipzig - Berlin 1914, pp 113 ff. Cf. C. H. Kirchner· Die Philosophie des Plotin, Halle 1854, p 144; Zeller III. ii, 139 (140 n. 1).

as Platonism and Neo-Pythagoreanism, the term was used
to represent that spiritual (1 e. gaseous) effluence from
God whose entering into matter caused it at first to take
on form, and afterwards to have the power of growth and
generation. Philo speaks of the Logos as ἡ σπερματικὴ τῶν
ὄντων οὐσία, the germinal substance of all things.[1] The passage is a very difficult one, but from the general meaning
of the adjective σπερματικός we can see that Philo means
that the substance (οὐσία) of all things is a spiritual effluence from God, the Logos. It had two functions, the
creative and the ruling. That is, Philo is using a physio-
logical term legitimately to figure the relation between God
and the world. The Logos as spermatic had to do with
creation and providence, was at once a spiritual principle
of life (i e a πνεῦμα) and a regulating principle which could
rule the world. The Logos by this conception, while an
extension of the Being of God, is fundamentally a mediator.
The Spermatic Logos of physiology presupposed a person
out of which it could flow, and a substance or material
into which it could flow, by a projection into this substance the Spermatic Logos could function in producing
a new life and form similar to the source whence it
had come.

There is no reason to suppose that Justin did not so
understand the term when he used it, as a spiritual effluence from God, bringing the life and intelligence of God
into the world of matter. Unfortunately he has little to
say about the Logos as spermatic. But that he regarded
the title as a legitimate one for the Logos cannot be denied.
All men, says Justin, have a part of the Spermatic Logos
in themselves,[2] and Justin contrasts the part which is in

[1] Quaest in Ex II. 68, Harris, Fragments of Philo, p 67.
Freudenthal, Max, Die Erkenntnislehre Philos von Alexandria,
Berlin 1891, p 27, n 3, says that the word σπερματική means
"hier doch wohl nichts anderes als ‚schopferische Kraft‘" However not only has Freudenthal made a noun of an adjective, but
Philo in the next sentence represents δύναμις ποιητική as one of
two offshoots from the σπερματικὴ οὐσία, so that σπερματικὴ οὐσία
must itself mean more than Freudenthal allows

[2] Ap II 13 3 ff (51 C ff)

men with the Spermatic Logos in totality.[1] The Logos as an entirety is the σπέρμα τὸ παρὰ τοῦ θεοῦ.[2] On the whole there are grounds for supposing that with Justin as with Philo the projection of this spiritual principle from God into Matter was the real creative act. So can Justin's statements that the world was made by God and no other be best reconciled with his insistence that the world was made διὰ τοῦ λόγου.[3] For as the outflowing Spirit of God the Spermatic Logos would be truly God, not separated nor distinct from God, and the activity of the Logos would be still the creative work of God Himself. If the Spermatic Logos be thus understood, the cryptic passage becomes clear in which Justin says that God is averting the final catastrophe of the world διὰ τὸ σπέρμα τῶν Χριστιανῶν, ὃ γινώσκει ἐν τῇ φύσει ὅτι αἴτιόν ἐστιν.[4] For here the seed of the Christians, the Spermatic Logos, is correctly referred to as the Universal Cause in nature. Such again is the significance of Justin's comparison between the creation of the animal world and the incarnation.[5] Christ became incarnate, says Justin, by the power and will of the Creator of the universe, just as Eve came into existence from one of Adam's ribs, and in the same way as all living things were *begotten* in the beginning by a logos of God. The comparison is profoundly illuminating. We know that Justin thought that the Logos from God entered

[1] Ap. II. 8. 3 ff (46 C ff).

[2] Ap. I 32. 8 (74 B)

[3] For the presence of a μέρος τοῦ σπερματικοῦ λόγου in man see below Chapter VII p 214 f

[4] Ap. II 7. 1 (45 B) Veil (in loco) thinks that this statement of Justin reproduces the thought of Aristides Apol. 16 1, 6· "Ut homines qui deum cognoverunt supplicationes ei offerunt quae aptae sunt ei ad dandum et sibi ad recipiendum, et ita aetatem suam consummant. Et cum benificia dei in se agnoscant, ecce, propter eos pulchra quae in mundo sunt, profluunt .. Et mihi haud dubium est quin Christianorum propter precationem mundus consistat." But Justin's language suggests a much deeper thought than the passage of Aristides See below p 282

[5] Dial 84 2 (310 C) δυνάμει καὶ βουλῇ τοῦ τῶν ὅλων ποιητοῦ γενόμενον . . . . . ὡς καὶ πλευρᾶς μιᾶς τοῦ Ἀδὰμ ἡ Εὔα γέγονε, καὶ ὥσπερ τἆλλα πάντα ζῶα λόγῳ θεοῦ τὴν ἀρχὴν ἐγεννήθη.

11*

into the womb of Mary and became the God-man Christ [1]
If Justin's comparison is to have meaning then he must
imply that the creation of the animal world was a begetting
in which the Spermatic Logos was projected into something.
So Eve came into existence by the projection of such
Spermatic Principle into the rib of Adam The result of the
one action was the God-man Christ. The result of the
other was the creation or begetting of Eve, or of the
animal world.

In this passage we see that Justin's λόγῳ θεοῦ is an
instrumental dative, and not a dative of agent. The same
instrumental dative, or the instrumental preposition διά is
used in speaking of the activity of the Logos in the creation
of the physical universe The preposition ὑπό is never
used in that connection. So Justin says, "And God said,
Let there be light; and it was so. So that by means of
a logos of God (λόγῳ θεοῦ) the whole world was born
from a substrate about which also Moses had previously
spoken." [2] Here not only is the λόγῳ θεοῦ mentioned exactly
as in the case where the action of the Logos of God in
producing the animal world was compared to the action of
the δύναμις θεοῦ in Mary, but the action of this same
principle is extended to the physical universe, and the
recipient of the Logos is specified as chaotic matter. The
projection of the Logos of God into this matter resulted
in the *birth* of the physical universe. Again Justin says,
"God, having taken thought (ἐννοηθέντα) by speech (by a
logos, διὰ λόγον) made the world " [3] Here the manner of
the procession of the Spermatic Logos into matter is
made clear. God thought and then uttered His thoughts
The utterance of the thought (as recorded in the Genesis
story) was that projection of the Spermatic Logos of God
into matter which produced the world. Such an interpretation of the words of Justin is justified by a comparison
of Justin with Philo [4] The expression comes from Genesis

[1] See below pp 235 ff.

[2] Ap. I. 59. 4, 5 (92 D). For the significance of the reference to matter here see below pp. 207 ff

[3] Ap I. 65. 5 (97 B).

[4] Quod deos sit immut 33, 34 (I. 277); 49 (I 280)

vi. 6, on the basis of which same verse Philo distinguishes the ἔννοια and διανόησις of God. The first is the thought, the second the projection of the thought of God It was this projection of the divine ἔννοια, of the Logos, the divine διανόησις which formed, according to Philo, the phenomenal world.[1]

In all these passages it must be noticed that the Logos is entirely impersonal, as fitted the impersonal philosophic Spermatic Logos which Justin was using. But as all the Christian doctrine of the Logos is complicated by the insistence upon personality in the case of a fundamentally impersonal conception, so is Justin's Spermatic Logos complicated by a single passage where Justin speaks of the Spermatic Principle of creation as a Person, or rather asserts the identity of this principle with the personal Logos-Christ. After speaking of this divine Personality Justin says, "At the beginning He (God) created and set in order all things through Him (δι' αὐτοῦ)."[2] But we can now see in the light of Justin's other declarations that this statement is only an attempt to add glory to the pre-incarnate Christ by identifying Him with the Spermatic Principle of creation. If an impersonal λόγου is understood for the αὐτοῦ the sentence becomes identical in meaning with those we have just explained. That is, when Justin thinks of creation and its process he speaks of the emission of the Seminal Logos from God entirely impersonally.

---

[1] We seem to be here very close again to the λόγος ἐνδιάθετος and the λόγος προφορικός which has just been denied to both Philo and Justin. But if such a distinction may be read into both writers in these passages, in the case of both the distinction would be meaningless. In fact the passage in Philo represents an awkward escape from the Old Testament passage rather than a fundamental part of his thinking. With Philo, God was utterly too abstract to have thoughts, which He could express. There emanates from God the Logos Principle of intelligence, but even the κόσμος νοητός is the Logos which has emanated. The Forms are not the thoughts of God, for God is properly above Form and hence above thoughts. There is thus no room for significance in Philo for a λόγος ἐνδιάθετος. Since Justin is obviously here only echoing Philonic phraseology, it is unjustified on the basis of this one passage to ascribe the twofold Logos conception to him

[2] Ap. II. 6. 3 (44 E).

When he thinks of the Christ he asserts the identity of the personal Logos-Christ with this Spermatic Principle. But the personality of this Spermatic Logos had nothing to do with creation. It never acted as an inferior creating deity, a δημιουργός. God is, by this figure, represented as coming into the closest of all relationships with Matter, that of sexual intercourse. Of course Justin is not crass enough to represent this in anthropomorphic myth, and rather describes the emission of the Seminal Principle in the figure of "speech". But there was no personal Deity or Mediator between God and Matter functioning *as a personality*. The creating Personality was One, the Supreme God.[1]

The Apology and Dialogue are thus at one on the doctrine of creation. There is room in the Apology for all the insistence of the Dialogue upon the fact that one of the chief characteristics of the Highest God was His activity as the personal Creator of the world, and that there was no higher God than the Creator.[2] Completely misunderstanding Justin's doctrine of creation, von Engelhardt has imputed to Justin precisely the belief which Justin was most anxious to refute. For he says that in Justin God is so completely separated from the world that He could create the world only through a Being who was at once divine and not divine.[3] But in the Dialogue Justin proves the existence of the lower Deity in answer to a request from Trypho that he substantiate the Christian doctrine of the existence of a God other than the One who made all things.[4] In precisely the same spirit Justin turned against

[1] One other passage, Dial 114 3 (341 D), has been made to bear upon this question by a change of text The passage is not adduced as evidence, for the reason that determining texts by reference to an author's doctrines, and then determining the doctrines by the changed texts has never seemed a profitable sort of scholarship But if the change suggested by Otto (see note in loco) is accepted, there is no discrepancy between the passage and the doctrine of creation here described

[2] Dial 11 1 (227 E), 56. 4, 11 (275 C, 276 D): 60. 5 (284 A)

[3] (Bibl 313) p 481

[4] Dial 50 1 (269 D); 56. 3 (275 B, C)

Marcion with the assertion that he would not have believed the Lord Himself (Christ) if He had announced any other God than the Fashioner and Sustainer of all things.[1] Directed against Marcion, Justin's remark shows at once the incentive of his insistence upon God as the personal agent of creation. It was one of the chief doctrines of Gnosticism that God was so remote from the material world that creation could only have been the work of a sub-deity, and Justin's insistence upon the fact that God created the world is part of his anti - Gnostic Apologetic. Still by the identification of the pre-incarnate Christ with the Spermatic Logos of creation, Justin plainly regards the Logos as being the chief medium of creation. To use Philo's adjective, the Logos, while not ὁ δημιουργός, was ποιητικός.

Philo also said, as we have seen, that the Spermatic Logos implied a second δύναμις in the Logos, the βασιλική as well as the ποιητική. It is probably in harmony with this conception that Justin's use of the adjective βασιλικός, which before seemed undefined, is to be referred, and with this also the identification of the Logos with the Animus Mundi of the Timaeus and the cosmic omnipresence and power of the symbol of the Cross. The seminal principle, once projected, not only formed the new child but remained as the ἡγεμονικόν of its constitution, according to Stoic physiology. So the Seminal Logos of God, the σπέρμα τοῦ θεοῦ, remained as the cohesive and ruling force in the universe. Such a conception could be expressed in personal terms with less misrepresentation than in the case of the creative activity of the Spermatic Logos, and the transition was easy from a personalized cohesive force in the universe to the world ruling Christ of eschatological speculation. But still it must be remembered that as a ruler of such an origin, the Logos was still a subordinate, and when necessary, an impersonal, effluence from the Father, so that Justin had no thought of removing the Father beyond the possibility of providential care over the world

[1] Fragment I. (ed. Otto) from Irenaeus Adv Haer IV. 6

E TITLES APPLIED TO THE LOGOS

There is no more illuminating aspect of Justin's discussion of the Logos for revealing the true nature of the material with which he was building, than the matter of the titles by which Justin says the Logos is mentioned in Scripture The following is only a selection. Several titles, θεός, κύριος, ἄγγελος, δύναμις, etc., have already been explained.

1. The statement is four times made of the Logos that "The East is His name (ἀνατολὴ ὄνομα αὐτῷ)," [1] with reference to Zach. vi. 12. The application of this verse to the Logos had already been made by Philo, who said that ἀνατολή here could not refer to a man of body and soul, "but is most properly applied to that incorporeal One, who differs in no respect from the divine image of God." [2] Philo could only have been thinking of the Logos when he wrote this.

2. Another title for the Logos is Stone or Rock (λίθος καὶ πέτρα), which Justin derives from several Old Testament passages.[3] Philo in commenting upon the rock from which water flowed in the wilderness says that this rock is "the Wisdom of God (which term Philo frequently equates with the Logos) which as the highest and first rock He cut off from His own Powers, from which He gave drink to God-loving souls."[4] Philo is obviously writing with the "stone cut out without hands" in mind, and this Philonic exegesis is accurately preserved in Justin, who in commenting upon the same verse as a description of the Logos says that it was so cut out, "to signify that it is not the work of a man, but of the will of the Father and God of all things, who caused Him to go forth

[1] Dial. 100. 4 (327 C); 106. 4 (334 B); 121 2 (350 A ; 126 1 (355 C).

[2] De Confus Ling. 62 (I. 414).

[3] Dial 34. 2 (251 D); 36. 1 (254 C), 70. 1 (296 B), 76. 1 (301 B); 90 5 (318 B); 100 4 (327 B); 113 6 (341 A); 114. 2, 4 (341 D); 126. 1 (355 B)

[4] Leg Al. II 86 (I. 82) St. Paul is a parallel dependent upon Philonic exegesis for identifying Christ with a rock See I Cor. x. 4.

(προβάλλοντος αὐτόν)."[1] Justin's phraseology constitutes an accurate description of a δύναμις of God.

3 The Logos is the Ἀρχή. In one passage Justin insists that the Second God was begotten as the Ἀρχή before all created things, not ἐν ἀρχῇ, but Christ was Himself Ἀρχή.[2] In the same way the term is twice used by Philo in lists of titles of the Logos.[3] I have not been able to find whence Philo derived the word as a title of the Logos, but the probability is that he like Justin based it upon Proverbs viii. 22.[4]

4. Justin is the first to use the word ἡμέρα as a title for the Logos according to our records, though the word had a varied history in later Christian controversy[5] Justin does not explain the meaning or origin of the title, though later writers (Clement of Alexandria, Eusebius, Augustine) derived it from "This is the Day which the Lord hath made."[6] In commenting upon the use of the word in Justin, Trollop made a guess that "possibly ἡμέρα may be synonymous with φῶς",[7] a guess that has never received any attention But an important clue to the meaning of the term, and the passage from which it was originally derived, is found in a passage in Philo, where "Day", though not used as a Logos title, is yet very pointedly associated with the Logos[8] Philo is

[1] Dial. 76 1 (301 B)

[2] Dial 62 4 (285 D)

[3] De Confus Ling 146 (I 427), Leg. Al I 43 (I 52)

[4] Although Philo, in the only passage where he quotes Prov viii 22, while using it as a description of Creation, has according to our text πρωτίστην where the Septuagint reads ἀρχήν. Feder (Bibl 350) p 127 n 9, has attempted to explain the title ἀρχή in Justin from the proposition of Aristotle, πάντα γὰρ τὰ αἴτια ἀρχαί (Met Δ I 1013 a. 17). Upon this Feder bases the statement that in Greek philosophy ἀρχή signifies "die erste, nicht weiter ableitbare Ursache der Dinge" Feder has obviously converted an unconvertible proposition

[5] Dial. 100 4 (327 B) See Rendel Harris, "A New Title for Jesus Christ", The Expositor, 8th Series, Vol XIV, London 1917, pp. 145—151

[6] Ps cxviii 24

[7] See Trollop, ed Dial p 209 n 30

[8] De Opif. Mundi 35 (I 7) See foregoing context

commenting upon the division of light from darkness to form day, though it is of the making of the κόσμος νοητός rather than of the physical world that he is speaking. The light he clearly equates with the Logos,[1] but he becomes very obscure in accounting for darkness which must be represented in the κόσμος νοητός because it is found in the physical world, but which is still most anomalous as part of a conception (the κόσμος νοητός) which he has just wholly identified with light. Philo tries to find a solution by including both in the κόσμος νοητός, but partitioning them off from each other by the two barriers, evening and morning Such an expedient, however, threatens seriously the unity of the κόσμος νοητός, one of its chief characteristics. He hastens to add then that though evening and morning partition light from darknesss, they do not divide the unity of the Intelligible World, but constitute unity when taken together The totality of light and darkness, morning and evening, are thus represented by the single word ἡμέρα, which consequently must be treated as a unity As such the word "Day" can not be modified by the adjective "first", but is properly called in Scripture "one". "The evening and the morning are *one* day," and this locution, Philo explains, is necessitated by the nature of the κόσμος νοητός. The totality ἡμέρα must then be treated exactly like the κόσμος νοητός, for it symbolizes the κόσμος νοητός, symbolizes it so closely that no adjective can be applied to the first which is not suitable to the second That is, ἡμέρα is an appropriate title for the Intelligible World. But as such it would be a title for the Logos, for Philo frequently equates the Logos and the Intelligible World It seems most probable then that the title ἡμέρα for the Logos came to Justin as part of his tradition from Hellenistic Judaism

5. In view of the preceding, and of the description already given of the origin of the Logos as light from a source, little further comment need be made upon the fact that Justin calls Christ ὁ μόνος ἄμωμος καὶ δίκαιος φῶς.[2]

---

[1] De Opif. Mundi 31 (I. 7) τὸ δὲ ἀόρατον καὶ νοητὸν φῶς ἐκεῖνο θείου λόγου.

[2] Dial. 17 3 (235 B).

Though the Logos is identified with light in the Fourth Gospel, the identification is clearly not original there, but looks back to the Alexandrian speculation.[1]

6. The σοφία of God as a term for the Logos was one of the earliest titles used in Hellenistic Jewish expositions. Justin uses it several times[2] basing it, like his Jewish predecessors, upon Proverbs viii. 22.[3]

7. Justin says that the Logos is called "ἀνήρ and ἄνθρωπος because He appears in the likeness of such form as the Father wills,"[4] or because He appeared to Abraham ἐν ἰδέᾳ ἀνδρός, to Jacob ἐν ἰδέᾳ ἀνθρώπου.[5] These sound very much like a title which Philo ascribes to the Logos, ὁ κατ' εἰκόνα ἄνθρωπος.[6] Justin also says that He is called ἀνήρ by Ezekiel,[7] but he gives no passage, nor does Philo throw any light upon such a derivation.

8. Two titles must next be considered together. Justin calls the Logos or Christ "Israel" and "Jacob", and is evidently fond of using the two titles together.[8] He expounds the names as signifying only a parallelism between Jacob, who was surnamed Israel and who gave his name to the Israelites, and Christ from whom the Christians have received their name. Philo uses "Israel" as a title of the Logos, and explains it to mean "Him who sees God".[9] So the "House of Israel" signifies the human soul in which dwells the νοῦς which is capable of seeing God, that is,, the Universal Intelligence in the individual soul.[10] "Jacob" is not used as a Logos title by Philo but the fact that Jacob is still commonly called Jacob after his name has been changed to Israel typifies to Philo the fact that the Logos, who made the change, cannot

---

[1] Wisdom is called ἀπαύγασμα φωτὸς ἀιδίου in Wisd vii 26
[2] Dial 62. 4 (285 D), etc.
[3] Cf. De Ebrietate 30, 31 (I. 361, 362).
[4] Dial 128. 2 (358 A).
[5] Dial 58. 10 (281 E)
[6] De Confus. Ling. 146 (I 427)
[7] Dial. 126. 1 (355 B).
[8] Dial. 123. 8, 9 (353 A, B); 126 1 (355 B
[9] De Confus Ling 146 (I. 427); De Mut. Nom. 81 (I. 590)
[10] De Somniis II. 172, 173 (I. 681).

make anything permanent and unchanging.[1] Jacob is contrasted with Abraham whose name was changed once for all by God. If these interpretations of the names Jacob and Israel ever reached Justin he has abandoned them for a Christian explanation. But it is not all unlikely that the two titles were originally suggested to him by Greek-Jewish tradition.

9. A still more definitely Christian title is $\pi\alpha\theta\eta\tau\acute{o}\varsigma$, which Justin says is applied to the Logos by Isaiah.[2] The word seems to be a Christian inference from Is liii. There was probably no trace of the term in Jewish Logos titles, for twice Trypho singles it out as particularly inappropriate for the Second God.[3]

10. Justin's favorite title $\pi\rho\omega\tau\acute{o}\tau\sigma\kappa\sigma\varsigma$ is a verbal variant of Philo's $\pi\rho\epsilon\sigma\beta\acute{o}\tau\alpha\tau\sigma\varsigma$ $\theta\epsilon\sigma\tilde{o}$ $\upsilon\acute{\iota}\acute{o}\varsigma$, $\pi\rho\omega\tau\acute{o}\gamma\sigma\nu\sigma\varsigma$, etc.[4] The word which Justin uses may have come immediately from St. Paul, but it seems more likely that both found it in Hellenistic Jewish tradition, for only so would St. Paul's use of the term have had significant meaning to his readers.

11. It will be sufficient to mention two more titles of the Logos which Justin likes to use together, "Priest" and "King".[5] Justin derives the title "Priest" from the verse in the Psalms made familiar in the Epistle to the Hebrews, "Thou art a priest forever after the order of Melchizedek."[6] Philo does not use this verse from the Psalms, but finds in Melchizedek a figure both of the Kingly and Priestly character of the Logos.[7]

There can no longer be any doubt that in his titles for the Logos Justin has received much from a Philonic tradition. But even the impulse to speak of the Logos by many names has come through the same tradition. Philo,

---

[1] De Mut. Nom. 87 (I. 591)
[2] Dial. 126 1 (355 B) et al.
[3] Dial. 36 1 (254 C), 39 7 (258 D).
[4] De Agr. Noe. 51 (I 308); De Confus. Ling. 63 (I. 414), 146 (I. 427); De Somniis I. 215 (I. 653); Leg. Al. III 175 (I 121).
[5] e. g. Dial. 118 2 (346 B)
[6] Ps. cx. 4.
[7] Leg. Al. III. 79 ff. (I 102, 103).

like Justin, is not only always interested in finding new
names which he can apply to the Logos, but is fond
of drawing up lists of such names He even uses as one
title of the Logos πολυώνυμος, "many-named".[1] Drummond
has shown that this title itself came from the Stoics
and that the multiplication of names for the Logos was
one of the Stoic methods of expounding its nature.[2]
Philo adopted this method from the Stoics, but worked out
Old Testament names to take the place of the Stoic names
from Greek mythology. But that Justin took over his
inspiration for explaining the nature of the Logos by
titles not directly from the Stoics but from Greek-Jewish
tradition is amply demonstrated by the overwhelmingly
Greek-Jewish character of his names and derivations.

F. CONCLUSION

In describing the Logos Justin has had to reckon with
at least three different traditions. First and foremost there
was the Christianity of Synoptic tradition, which was to
Justin the authoritative source of Christian teaching, but
with which was now associated the fundamental conviction
that Jesus of Nazareth was the Son of God, a divine Personality. Second there was a large Greek-Jewish tradition
which Christians were regarding with great favour, and in
terms of which they had now for some time been attempting to explain the divine character of Jesus. Third there
was the Gnostic tradition already strongly working in Christianity. The first of these demanded above all reverence for
God and the *Person* of Jesus Christ, and to this Justin
was always true. His Logos was always a divine *Personality*. The Greek-Jewish tradition had for its central
point the One God, and explained the divinity of the Second
God in terms which obliterated its personality. Philo conceived first and foremost of the God who was Himself
Absolute but who radiated Powers by which the world was

[1] De Confus Ling. 146 (I. 427); Leg. Al. I. 43 (I. 52)
[2] Drummond, Philo I 88, II. 206, 270 πολυώνυμος was used
in the first line of the Hymn of Cleanthes as preserved in Stob
Ecl. I. 30

created and sustained. It was ultimately a matter of no importance to Philo whether he summarized this radiation of Powers under the singular "Logos", or spoke of them as "Logoi", "Powers", or "Angels", for it was in any case the impersonal radiation of power from the Father which he had in mind. The Logos of Philo was thus truly undivided from the Father. But in order to get the separate Personality for the Logos which the Christian tradition demanded, Justin was compelled to make far more of a division between God and the Logos than Philo had done. As a follower of Greek Judaism Justin denied that there could have been any division of the Second God from the First. As a Christian he asserted the separate Personality of the Son, and was thereby forced to describe a subordinationism of the Logos to the Father which was of quite a different character from Philo's description of subordination. But the Gnostic leaven in Christianity, whose working Justin was trying to check, prevented Him from conceiving of any sort of cosmology wherein the Logos could act consistently with His truly subordinate character. Granted the Logos as an emanation distinct in nature and activity from the Father, the entire Gnostic point of view was at once admitted.

In trying to solve the problem presented by these three factors which were together shaping the Logos doctrine, Justin appears not to have been aware of the possibilities of his figures representing the plurality of personality in the single οὐσία which the Church later adopted as the official explanation. He would probably have welcomed the suggestion as a priceless boon had it been made to him, but in its absence he was forced to develop a doctrine of the Logos which expressed the Logos Personality in a subordinationism which possessed little cosmic significance or value.

The Logos of Justin has indicated its sources with gratifying clarity. Thus far we have seen no reason whatever to think that Justin was working Platonic or Stoic doctrines over directly into Christianity. Specific Stoic elements, such as had not already been used in Hellenistic Judaism as witnessed by Philo, have thus far not appeared at all, or have been mentioned by Justin only to be rejected with scorn. When Justin attempts a comment upon a Platonic document his suggestion ludicrously illustrates how little he understood of its real significance. But in point after point we have found the closest similarity between Justin's and Philo's speculations. Much of Philo's deeper thought, conspicuously the Intelligible World, has either not reached Justin or has been beyond his power of adaptation to the Personal Son of God For Justin was primarily not a speculative thinker but a Christian who wanted to find for Apologetic use an explanation of his experience through Christ in terms of what he thought was sound science. Throughout his writings it was not the science but the experience through Christ to which he gave first heed. As a result he describes in Greek-Jewish terminology a Logos doctrine which was as strange to Greek Judaism as to the Synoptic tradition. But as a Logos doctrine it is still recognizably the Logos of Philo which Justin has in mind, though popularized, diluted, intensely personalized, and re-presented as incarnate in the historical Jesus Christ.

In all this there is little reason to see in Justin a lonely pioneer. Begun with St. Paul, explicit in the Fourth Gospel, the pagan Christian community had been brought up from the beginning with the idea that the divine Christ of their experience was to be identified with the Logos of Hellenistic Judaism, and there is no reason to doubt that their leaders had long and commonly been working the mine of Greek Judaism to explain Christianity in philosophic language. Only on such grounds is it conceivable that Justin's Logos should have been unhesitatingly received by his fellow Christians, who had early been made sensitive to the approach of heresy by Gnosticism and reactionary Judaism, and should have gone unchallenged until the Sixteenth Century.

CHAPTER VI

THE HOLY SPIRIT AND THE LOWER POWERS

It has been seen that unique in rank as Justin conceived the Logos to be, the origin of the Logos was
ultimately described in terms which were also used to account for the origin of an unnumbered host of other superhuman beings. When one tries to reconstruct what Justin
probably believed about these beings, difficulties multiply.
For the material in Justin on the subject is not only very
scanty, but is on many points contradictory, so that probably
the more vague the subject is left the better Justin's actual
notions are represented He, like most people of his time,
was almost animistic in his belief that the universe was
swarming with superhuman, invisible powers, some weak,
others strong. So much Justin knew, but he was certain
of very little more about them The fact of their existence
was daily if not hourly in his mind, but their nature, functions, mode of action, and interrelation he had not attempted
systematically to explain

A. THE HOLY SPIRIT

There is no doctrine of Justin more baffling than his
doctrine of the Holy Spirit, and no doctrine which has
been more differently understood Orthodox writers have
tended to find the doctrine of the Christian Trinity in Justin's writings,[1] while others have denied any personality
whatever to the Spirit, and insisted that ultimately "Logos"
and "Spirit" were two names in Justin's mind for the same
conception.[2] Von Engelhardt represents a middle school

[1] e g Stahlin (Bibl. 318) p. 10
[2] See e g Paul (Bibl 344) 1890 pp. 571—576; Clemen
Bibl 324); Duncker (Bibl 339) pp 37—39

which sees in Justin's Spirit a distinct Personality but which denies real divinity either to the Logos or the Spirit.[1]

Justin mentions the Holy Spirit mainly in connection with prophetic inspiration When he wishes to explain the baptismal formula he states of the Holy Spirit that He was the inspirer of the Prophets[2] Consequently Justin's doctrine of the Spirit is best approached from the point of view of his theory of inspiration.

Justin is quite a child of his time in his theory of prophetic madness Peoples of all nations understood in the same way the ecstasy of inspiration, and had the profoundest respect for oracular utterance It was because this respect for inspired utterance was so universal that Justin could use the Hebrew Scriptures for Apologetic arguments with people who were utterly outside the pale of any Hebraistic influence. "That the Prophets are inspired by no other than the Divine Logos, even you, as I fancy, will grant," Justin fearlessly says to the heathen[3] For inspiration meant practically the same thing in the mystery religions,[4] in oracular utterances,[5] to Plato, to the ancient schools of the Prophets,[6] to Philo[7] It is because Justin and the early Christian community had nothing to add to the doctrine that they theorized little about it The Christians were busy expounding the peculiar doctrines of their Faith, and had no occasion to speculate about conceptions common to Christianity and the heathen world An inspired man was thus to all people of the time one whose faculties had come to be completely under the control of a spirit or god. He was "out of himself", had lost all initiative, had

[1] (Bibl 313) pp. 141 ff.

[2] Ap I 61 13 (94 E)

[3] Ap I 33 9 (75 D)

[4] Cf Toussaint, L'Hellénisme et l'Apôtre Paul Paris 1921 p 60

[5] Represented accurately by the Sibyll Oracul Ed Geffcken [II] II 4, 5 p 26.

οὐδὲ γὰρ οἶδα
ὅττι λέγω, κέλεται δὲ θεὸς τὰ ἕκαστ' ἀγορεύειν.
From (Bibl 118) II 19. n 1.

[6] Cf I Sam. x 10

[7] Quis rer div Haer 259 ff (I 510)

sometimes even lost conciousness, and had become a passive medium through which the god or the divine spirit spoke or acted

Such a theory of inspiration was Justin's. In one passage, where Justin quotes a description of a prophetic vision from the Old Testament, Justin explains that the prophet was in an ecstasy in which his physical senses, particularly those of sight and hearing, were completely quiescent.[1] He nowhere else uses the word ecstasy, or implies so complete a submergence of the normal personal activity of the Prophet, and it is not right, as has frequently been protested, to conclude from this one passage that Justin regarded ecstasy as the normal prophetic state.[2] But though he nowhere else speaks of prophecy as coming out from ecstasy, the words of the prophet are always regarded as divine utterances, and not the words of the prophet himself. Justin says, "When you hear the utterances of the Prophets spoken as it were by a person, you must not suppose that they are spoken by the inspired men themselves, but by the Divine Logos who moves them."[3] The Psalms were "dictated" to David by the Holy Spirit.[4]

In Justin's day such a theory had only to be stated to be credible Only one point concerning the theory of the inspiration of the Prophets did he think required elucidation Other oracles spoke out in a recognizable way. If a myth told the story of a visit to an oracle, the words of the oracle alone were regarded as definitely inspired. But Justin wished to find inspiration not only in formal prophetic utterance but in the entire Old Testament, much of which was in the form of simple narrative. Statements made

[1] Dial. 115 3 (343 A)   The complete incompatibility of physical sight with such spiritual sight as could be capable of perceiving an appearance of the Lord is discussed by Philo in the De Mut Nom 3 ff. (I 578 ff.)

[2] (Bibl. 394) p 44   In n. 3 Heinisch refers to others who have made a similar protest   Semisch is carried into an overstatement of Justin's theory of inspiration by the fact that he treats the Cohort ad Graec as genuine. This work actually goes much further than Justin to describe the prophetic trance

[3] Ap. I 36 1 (76 D).

[4] Dial 34. 1 (251 B).

about the past,[1] as well as the future statements made
in all connections, even by the Israelitish mob,[2] were used
indifferently by the Christians to furnish a prophetic background for their Faith. Such a prophetic authority needed
a defence to which Justin devotes considerable attention
in the Apology The explanation given is that multifarious
as the form of the utterance may be, it is always the same
Spirit (or Logos) inspiring the utterance.[3] For the Spirit
may assume various roles, act various parts, and hence speak
in various characters Justin's phrase for this playing of
parts is ἀπὸ προσώπου. The Spirit speaks ἀπὸ προσώπου τοῦ
πατρός,[4] τοῦ Χριστοῦ,[5] τέκνων Ἀβραάμ,[6] τῶν ἀποστόλων,[7] but
the Spirit must be recognized as the speaker in every case,
regardless of the form of utterance.

It is interesting as contributory evidence for the ultimate source of Justin's metaphysical ideas to find that this,
the only point which seems at all valuable in his treatment
of the theory of prophetic inspiration, had already been
expounded in the same words by Philo. Philo also wished
to regard as inspired many statements in the Pentateuch
which were not in prophetic form. He justified his doing
so by saying that prophetic inspiration may take several
forms, but that whether the prophetic utterances were
spoken ἐκ προσώπου τοῦ θεοῦ or ἐκ προσώπου Μωϋσεως, their
character as inspired words is unchanged.[8]

There is however one original attempt at explanation
of a difficulty about inspiration, and, like most of Justin's
own contributions it obscures more than it clarifies. Justin
wishes to justify his use of scriptural statemements in the
past tense as prophetic utterances foretelling what Christ was
to be and do. Such a use of Scripture is perfectly legitimate,
he says, for when the Prophetic Spirit was absolutely
certain that an event would take place, He prophesied

[1] Ap. I. 42. 1 ff (80 B).
[2] Ap. I. 47. 1 (84 A).
[3] Ap I 36 entire.
[4] Ap. I. 37. 1 (77 A).
[5] Ap. I. 38. 1 (77 C).
[6] Dial. 25. 1 (242 B)
[7] Dial. 42. 2 (260 D).
[8] De Vita Moses III 188 (II. 163)

it as though it had already happened.[1] It does not
seem to occur to Justin that by such an explanation he
has discredited every other form of prophecy in the defence
of what he recognizes to be only one among many forms
He would certainly have repudiated the implications of his
own statement that the Holy Spirit was only guessing
when the prophetic utterances were put in the future tense

Indeed Justin seems to have had very few clear ideas
about the person and nature of the Prophetic Spirit He
believed in general that inspiration was a filling of the
prophet by the Spirit Prophets were οἱ ἐμπνεύσμενοι.[2] But
sometimes the Spirit which inspired was called the Holy
Spirit,[3] sometimes the Prophetic Spirit,[4] sometimes the
Logos,[5] and sometimes God.[6] Of these terms, "Holy
Spirit" and "Prophetic Spirit" are used in the majority of
instances, and are terms almost constantly to be encountered
throughout Justin's writings But did he think of a Personal
Spirit, or was this only a convenient and intelligible term
for one aspect or activity of the Logos? The question
cannot be answered with certainty In one passage Justin
says that inspiration of the Prophets must be referred to
none other than to the Divine Logos.[7] Again the utterances of the Prophets have been spoken by the Divine
Logos who has moved or changed them.[8] But when he
mentions the threefold baptismal formula and explains the
nature of each of the three Persons referred to, it is the
Holy Spirit who is described as the One who foretold all
things about Jesus through the Prophets.[9] To choose
arbitrarily between these contradictory statements is only to
do violence to the one rejected. Von Engelhardt has with

[1] Ap. I 42 2 (80 B).
[2] Ap I 36. 2 (76 D).
[3] E g Dial 25 1 (242 B)
[4] E. g. Ap I. 31 1 (72 B) This expression was Jewish,
and is twice to be found in the Targums. See Weber, Judische
Theologie pp 190 ff
[5] Ap I 36 1 (76 D). See Ap. I 33 9 (75 D); Ap II
10 7 (49 A)
[6] Dial 84 1 (310 B)
[7] Ap I 33 9 (75 D)
[8] Ap I 36. 1 (76 D)
[9] Ap I 61 13 (94 E)

little explanation declared that Justin referred prophetic inspiration ultimately to the Logos, and considered the Holy Spirit to be only the personal agent whom the Logos used for that purpose.[1] Von Engelhardt adduces no evidence for the suggestion because there is none to adduce. One must frankly admit that Justin leaves unsettled the matter of the agent of inspiration. For though Justin thus confuses the Logos and Holy Spirit, it must be recognized, with Semisch,[2] that the confusion is one of function, and that confusion of function is possible without confusion of personality

But against the personality of the Holy Spirit reproaches have been adduced other than Justin's confusion of prophetic agency. Justin in one passage states explicitly· τὸ πνεῦμα καὶ τὴν δύναμιν τὴν παρὰ τοῦ θεοῦ οὐδὲν ἄλλο νοῆσαι θέμις ἢ τὸν λόγον, ὃς καὶ πρωτότοκος τῷ θεῷ ἐστί.[3] Since the time of Lange, at least, this passage has seemed to many to be decisive proof that to Justin the πνεῦμα and the λόγος were two names for the same person[4] But the passage, as Semisch argues,[5] is not decisive for a general conclusion about the nature of the Spirit because the statement in its context is not intended to be general. Justin has been speaking of the δύναμις καὶ πνεῦμα which Luke records overpowered Mary with His glory[6] as the result of which she became pregnant. Justin's own theory of the incarnation, as will be seen later,[7] was that the

[1] (Bibl. 313) p. 160.

[2] (Bibl 118) II. 311.

[3] Ap. I. 33. 6 (75 C).

[4] Ausführliche Geschichte der Dogmen I. (1796) p. 107

[5] (Bibl. 118) II. 309; Donaldson (Bibl 143) p 267 as usual repeats Semisch.

[6] Κατασκιάζειν, as Hatch has pointed out, means in late Greek not "to overshadow", but to overpower by a dazzling brilliancy. Read in that sense the passage in Luke has a meaning which translations have ordinarily obscured The detailed discussion of Leisegang on the meaning of this word would have been much improved had he read Hatch. See Leisegang, Pneuma Hagion. Leipzig 1922. pp. 25—31.

[7] See below p. 235 Justin in thus thinking of the Logos, rather than the Spirit, as the agent of incarnation is clearly following the same tradition as that recorded in the Protevang.

Logos came down and entered into the womb of Mary, acting as His own agent of incarnation. Accordingly Justin insists that the Spirit and Power mentioned in the traditional account of the Incarnation was the Logos Since the Logos was of course a Spirit and a Power of God, such an identification was perfectly legitimate, and in no way effects the fact that Justin might have believed in another Spirit which was properly *the* Spirit

It is a more serious reflection upon Justin's belief in the personality of the Holy Spirit that in the Dialogue there are only two divine Personalities described, the Father and the Son. Had we only the Dialogue from which to reconstruct Justin's conception, it would be impossible to account for the repeatedly mentioned Holy Spirit who inspires prophecy. But it must be born in mind that the Dialogue does mention the Holy Spirit frequently, and confuses Him with the Logos as inspirer of the Prophets less than the Apologies But the Dialogue does not purport to be, even so slightly as the First Apology, a statement of Christian doctrine It is an essay upon a definite theme, and much stress cannot be laid upon omissions of extraneous matter. A probable reference to the Holy Spirit is found in the Dialogue, where if the reference actually be to the Spirit the thought is quite impersonal.[1] Justin distinguishes between the way in which Christ now dwells among the Christians and the way in which He is to be with them after the Second Coming He is now with men δυνάμει, but will then be with them ἐναργῶς. The language is of course

---

of James, xi. 2, καὶ ἰδοὺ ἄγγελος κυρίου ἔστη ἐνώπιον αὐτῆς λέγων· μὴ φοβοῦ, Μαρίαμ, εὗρες γὰρ χάριν ἐνώπιον τοῦ πάντων δεσπότου καὶ συλλήψῃ ἐκ λόγου αὐτοῦ. But the passage is not witness to the fact that Justin used this Gospel. He may have had the Gospel, but if he did he by no means regarded it as having the same authority as the Synoptic tradition. It seems still more likely that the conception that the agent of incarnation was the Logos was part of Justin's oral tradition which he in this passage is trying to reconcile with the written Gospel record representing Mary as having conceived of the Holy Ghost. See, contra, Heinisch (Bibl. 394) p. 140 n. 2 and Zahn (Bibl. 181) I ii 539 Anm. 1.

[1] Dial. 54. 1 (273 D).

Aristotelian, and probably the famous δυνάμει—ἐναργῶς antithesis of the philosopher was proverbial in Justin's day. But did Justin intend a pun upon δυνάμει, and imply that the Holy Spirit, now present with the Church, is the presence of Christ δυνάμει? It is highly probable that Justin intended such an inference, and if so he was thinking impersonally of the Spirit. But one cannot be certain of the meaning here of δυνάμει, because later in the Dialogue Justin speaks of Christ as appearing in the Old Testament theophanies δυνάμει.[1] The meaning of neither passage is clear, and each obscures the other.

Furthermore in two passages of the Dialogue the Holy Spirit is mentioned in a way that must be admitted to be impersonal. The locution "pouring the Spirit on all flesh" seems to Dr. Paul to be incompatible with a personal conception of the Spirit.[2] Dr Paul has evidently not noticed that the expression occurs in an Old Testament quotation,[3] and hence cannot be taken as evidence for Justin's views on so delicate a point But still it must be admitted that the conception of pouring the Spirit, and of baptism in the Spirit, are impersonal.[4] In the other passage Justin speaks of the transference to John the Baptist of the Spirit of God which was in Elijah.[5] There is no intelligible explanation of this passage in terms of a personal Spirit. Trypho asks Justin how such a thing could happen, and Justin's only explanation is a Scriptural precedent, the transference to Joshua of the spirit of Moses. But the precedent no whit explains the metaphysics of such a transition of Spirit, and there is no material for reconstructing what Justin may have thought. As a matter of fact Justin probably did not in the least understand it himself, but was simply passing on part of the Christian tradition about John the Baptist Nevertheless it is apparent that impersonal references to the

---

[1] Dial. 128. 1 (357 D). The meaning of δυνάμει, several times repeated in this chapter is very obscure. See p. 256.

[2] (Bibl. 344) 1890. pp 571—576, from Pfättisch (Bibl 385) p. 47.

[3] Joel ii 28.

[4] Dial. 29 1 (246 C).

[5] Dial. 49. 3 ff. (268 C ff.).

Spirit, whether in the form of Old Testament quotation or of Christian tradition, do not disturb Justin at all.

Did he then believe in a personal Spirit? Aside from the fact that Justin's mention of the Prophetic Spirit is usually personal, there is considerable evidence to show that he did believe in a personal Spirit Justin writes the following exposition of some passages in Plato "And as to his (Plato's) speaking of a third, he did this because he read, as we have said above, that which was spoken by Moses, that the Spirit of God moved upon the waters For he gives the second place to the Logos which is with God, who he said was placed crosswise in the universe, and the third place to the Spirit who was said to be borne upon the water, saying 'and the third around the third' "[1] Here Justin is clearly thinking of two Beings similar in nature although unequal in rank, the Logos and the Spirit Again he says that the devils imitated the Scriptural conception of the Spirit moving upon the waters by setting up statues to Cora at springs, and worshipping her there as the daughter of Zeus[2] Justin must then at least sometimes have understood the Spirit to be an offshoot of God, and personal, in order for his parallelism to hold Justin four times quotes the formula, "In the name of the Father and of the Son and of the Holy Spirit,"[3] on one of which occasions he explains the significance of each term and gives a personal activity to the Spirit as well as to the other two, saying that the Spirit through the Prophets foretold all things about Jesus He says that the Christians regard Jesus Christ as in the second place after God, and the Prophetic Spirit in the third place[4] Again he says that the Christians worship the Holy Spirit, but lists the Spirit not only after the Father and the Logos, but also after the angels[5] Still Justin's mention of the Spirit here implies a distinct Person.

[1] Ap I 60 6, 7 (93 B ff), cf Plato Tim 36 b, c, and Plato (?) Epist II p 312 e
[2] Ap I 64 1 ff (97 A)
[3] Ap I 61. 3, 13 (94 A, E), 65 2 (97 D), 67 2 (98 C)
[4] Ap I 13 3 (60 E)
[5] Ap I. 6 2 (56 C)

Justin prefers then to speak of the Spirit in personal language as a Being distinct from both the Father and the Son He confuses the functions of the Spirit with those of the Logos, and he has no objection to speaking of the Spirit impersonally, but he would apparently ordinarily think of the Spirit as a distinct person Still it must be admitted that the Spirit was never so vividly personal to Justin as was the Logos-Christ Herein Justin is at one with the overwhelming mass of Christians of all time. By the Incarnation the person of the Logos was given a sharpness of detail which the Spirit has never achieved. It spite of the dogma of the Trinity, the Holy Spirit is still commonly spoken of, and thought of even in most orthodox minds, as "It" The same mystical experience may still correctly be described indifferently as God in us, Christ in us, or the Spirit in us But the Spirit is not on that account thought of as personally identical with either Christ or the Father The term Spirit has still its own distinctive connotation, though the connotations may or may not be personal at any given time. So Justin regarded the Holy Spirit as a Person, the third in divine rank, but allowed himself to speak impersonally of the Spirit when he found the impersonal language more convenient

As to the origin or generation of the Holy Spirit Justin gives little information Justin had but one theory for the generation of Divine Beings, that of emanation from the One Divine Source. In the Dialogue, much as he wished to make the Son different from the other celestial beings, we have seen that Justin had to represent the Logos as produced in the same way as the other δυνάμεις τοῦ θεοῦ. Of a distinction between created and uncreated celestial persons about which Semisch labours Justin knew nothing. The Logos, like the lowest angel, was ultimately a δύναμις of God There is no reason for trying to imagine for Justin a different sort of emanation of the Holy Spirit The Rays from the Divine Light varied in importance The Spirit was no ordinary δύναμις, but a δύναμις of God Justin must have considered Him Indeed so completely did Justin regard Him as a power of God that we have seen in one case, where Justin is listing the divine objects of Christian worship, that he puts the entire group of angelic personalities before the Holy Spirit,[1] though in point of rank Justin ordinarily thought of the Spirit as before the other powers. The Dialogue leads us to suspect that the Spirit was not divine in the sense in which the Son was divine. But as to what sort of divinity Justin would ascribe to a Divine Person whom the Christians worshipped, who yet was not included either as ὁ θεός or as θεός in the Dialogue, he gives us no information.

Doctrine of the Trinity Justin had none. Justin believed in One God the Father, and neither the Logos nor the Holy Spirit nor any other power could be ranked with the Father. The Logos was divine, but in the second place; the Holy Spirit was worthy of worship, but in the third place Such words are entirely incompatible with a doctrine of the Trinity

The functions of the Spirit have already in part been described. Pre-eminently the Spirit was the inspirer of the Prophets In one passage Justin shows how, since the coming of Christ, a great change had taken place in the operation of the Holy Spirit Before the Incarnation the Spirit had operated upon the Prophets apparently directly from God. But when the Spirit settled upon Christ at the baptism, it rested from its former mode of activity and thenceforth became the Spirit of Christ, to be given out to men only by Christ.[2] But Justin's explanation of the incident of the descent of the Spirit upon Christ must be used with caution. The explanation comes out as a *tour de force* to avoid a difficulty, suggested by Trypho, that Christ could not have been of divine nature, else He would have had no need of having the Spirit rest upon Him [3] As divine, it was urged, Christ would already have possessed all that the Spirit had to give The incident of

[1] Ap. I. 6. 2 (56 C).

[2] Dial. 87. 3 ff. (314 C ff)

[3] Trypho does not suggest that Is. xi 2 has reference to the baptism of Jesus But the discussion in Chapters 87 and 88 show clearly that this verse had been connected with the incident of the baptism to substantiate the adoptionist position.

Christ's baptism must have been a most perplexing one
to Christians who had accepted the Logos theory, for it
was and is the chief evidence of adoptionists. Justin's
explanation of the incident very dubiously represents his
actual opinion of the activity of the Spirit with the Prophets.
It would have been more in harmony with his usual confusion of Logos and Spirit in the Prophets to say, with von
Engelhardt,[1] that Justin regarded the Spirit as always having
been the Spirit of the Logos, while from this exposition we
should be led to infer that the two were united for the
first time at the baptism of Christ But in speaking of
Christ's baptism, if Justin has been unfair to the pre-
Christian activity of the Prophetic Spirit, his explanation
of the event precisely represents his theory of the activity
of the Spirit in his own day The Spirit was found
by Christians in their worship of Christ. Christian baptism
is baptism in the Spirit.[2] The gifts of the Spirit, wisdom,
knowledge, understanding and counsel, might and piety,
fear, (sc. of the Lord) and others which had formerly
been bestowed on the Prophets are now given through
Christ by grace to those who believe in Him according
as each man is worthy.[3] It is easily possible to find
Christians possessing these gifts which before the coming
of Christ had been given only to the Prophets.[4] Christian
illumination, the guide to truth which made Christianity
the supreme philosophy, came from the Holy Spirit.[5]

The Holy Spirit was to Justin, then, the guide of piety,
the gifts of the Spirit were the goal of spiritual endeavour.
It is likely that had we a sermon of Justin addressed to
Christians we should hear more of the Spirit, but the
controversial documents which we possess have no occasion
to enter minutely into the heart of Christian worship and
aspiration. Semisch closes his discussion of the theory
of the Holy Spirit in Justin's writings by saying that the

[1] See above p. 181 n 1
[2] Dial 29. 1 (246 C).
[3] Dial. 87. 4 (314 D).
[4] Dial. 88. 1 (315 B).
[5] Dial. 4 1 (221 C).

Holy Spirit was too idiomatically Christian to be intelligible
to outsiders, and that Justin on that account allows a
temporary confusion with the Logos.[1] But was the Holy
Spirit to the heathen a "strange name and conception"?[2]
One wonders how much the Christian Spirit differed from
the δαίμων of Socrates.[2] But even granted (which I do
not by any means grant) that it was strangeness which
made Justin hesitate to expound the Holy Spirit to the
heathen, surely the Holy Spirit was not strange to the
Jews. The Holy Spirit as the inspirer of Prophecy and
the guide of piety is certainly one of the Christian heritages
from Judaism. John the Baptist preached no riddles, and
his statement that his Successor would baptise in the
Holy Spirit was the statement of a Jew to Jews. The
Holy Spirit became Christian when the gifts of the Spirit
became also the gifts of Christ, when the indwelling Spirit
was in a sense the indwelling Christ also. But not the
doctrine of the Spirit but the doctrine of Christ was the
novelty which was at once attacked from without and
studied within Christianity. Little explanation is made of
the Spirit during the first two Centuries of Christian
writing because the Spirit of whom Christians spoke, except
that He came from and through Christ, was too well known
both in Hellenism and Judaism to need an introduction, was
too traditional to need defence.

[1] (Bibl 118) II. 331

[2] A valuable collection of material on the Holy Spirit is
Hans Leisegang's new work: Der Heilige Geist, das Wesen und
Werden der mystisch-intuitiven Erkenntnis in der Philosophie und
Religion der Griechen. I Teil: Die vorchristlichen Anschauungen
und Lehren vom Pneuma und der mystisch-intuitiven Erkenntnis
Leipzig und Berlin 1919. II Teil: Pneuma Hagion: Der Ursprung
und Geistbegriff der synoptischen Evangelien aus der griechischen
Mystik. Leipzig 1922. Leisegang has brilliantly demonstrated how
universal was the notion of the Divine Spirit, but he is
carried away with the Greek element, and does not give sufficient weight to the Hebrew doctrine. To assume as he does
(e. g. II Teil, pp 45 ff.) that the Philonic doctrine of the
Spirit is in every particular Greek is to beg a very large
question.

B. THE LOWER POWERS.

Of the other powers in addition to the Holy Spirit
it has already been said that though Justin had an ever-
present sense of their existence, he had little explanation of
their origin or nature. His only account of the origin
of the angelic host has been already mentioned, but should
be here examined in detail "The Father, when He chooses,
say they, makes His power to spring forth (προπηδᾶν ποιεῖ)
and when He chooses, He recalls it to Himself. In this
way, they teach, He made (ποιεῖν) the angels. But it has
been taught that there are certain angels which always
exist, and are not reabsorbed into that out of which
they have sprung." [1] There seems still to be some misunderstanding as to Justin's intention in this passage.
Heinisch appears to think that Justin is controverting the
doctrine of the origin of the angels here described.[2] But
Justin is doing no such thing. He has just stated his
great thesis that God who appeared to Moses in the
burning bush was the Second God, Christ, and now he
proceeds to deal with a counter argument which had been
raised by Jews to this thesis. Some people, he says, deny
such an interpretation and assert that the appearance here
was actually that of an angel. But, they insist, the appearance of an angel does not involve a second divine
Personality, as the Christians claim, for the angels are a
company of powers who are continually proceeding from
the Father, and as continually being reabsorbed in the
original Source. The appearance of one of these then as
a representative of God by no means involves the existence
of a Second God. This is all very true, Justin admits, but he
insists that there are certain angels who, though generated
in the same way, are permanently sustained, and do not
lose their personality by reabsorption into the Source.
Now the particular Power, or Angel who appeared on
the occasion in question was of such a kind, but of unique
dignity. And so Justin goes on as we have already seen,
to describe the generation of the Christ. Justin has not

[1] Dial. 128 3, 4 (358 B, C).
[2] (Bibl. 394) pp. 139, 140.

controverted a syllable of the doctrine of angels proposed
by his hypothetical opponent. But he has claimed that
the opponent has only half stated the doctrine, and that
the part concealed is the part applicable to Christ. The
doctrine of the emanation of these angels, whether of
temporary or permanent existence, seems to Justin to need
no proof, but to be sufficiently well known and widely
believed so that he could use the conception to explain
the origin of the Second God.

Justin's doctrine of the origin and nature of the
angels is much illuminated by comparison of the passage
under discussion with some of the sayings recorded from the
Tannaim. There is preserved a comment upon the description in the book of Daniel (vii. 9, 10): "His throne was
like the fiery flame, and his wheels as burning fire A
fiery stream issued and came forth from before him:
thousand thousands ministered unto him, and ten thousand
times ten thousand stood before him." The comment
is: "Every day are ministering angels created out of
the Stream of Fire singing songs of praise and perishing,
for it is written, 'New are they every morning, for great
is thy Grace'." The same passage continues: "An angel
is created out of my word from the mouth of God; for it
is written 'Through the word of God even the heavens
were created, and through the breath of his wrath all
his company'." [1]   Another parallel, which Goldfahn does
not suggest, is even closer to Justin's thought. The following conversation is recorded between two very early
Tannaim:

"*Hadrian*: You say no angel emanation sings praises
twice, but that God daily creates new angels, which sing
a song in His honour, and then depart; whither do they go?

"*Joshua* (b. Chananja): Thither whence they were
created.

"*Hadrian*: Whence were they created?

"*Joshua*. Out of the Stream of Fire.

"*Hadrian*: And how is it with this Stream?

[1] Chagiga 14 a.   Goldfahn (Bibl. 389) p. 114.

"*Joshua*: It is as this Jordan, which ceases not to flow day and night.

"*Hadrian* And whence comes this Stream of Fire?

"*Joshua·* From the sweat of the beasts at the Chariot of God, which flows from them under the weight of the Chariot of God."[1]

Weber insists that, in addition to the temporary angels, who have no independent existence, the Rabbinic theology taught also that there were permanent emanations from God, with permanent existences.[2]

Justin's angelology is clearly dependent upon this tradition which seems to have been strictly Palestinian, grown up upon the statement quoted from the Book of Daniel, if that statement does not itself show that at the time of its composition such a conception of the origin of angels was already extant. The closeness of Justin's thought to that of the Rabbinic passage is apparent when it is recalled that δυνάμεις in Justin's account of emanation is used in a double sense, that of·powers, superhuman personalities, and that of rays. Both meanings are found elsewhere in Justin. Since a ray of light was regarded as a stream of very fine fire flowing from the source, it is clear that Justin's description of the δυνάμεις radiating from the Father meant to him a fiery streaming from the central fiery Source, while the second meaning of the word implied to his mind, and to those of his readers, something of personal existence at the same time.[3] But as Justin, in representing the angels as permanent, even personal, rays from God is clearly Palestinian, he is just as clearly not Philonic. Philo was troubled by the angels, for while he believed in them as a good Jew, they had little place in his metaphysics. Accordingly he at one time seems to identify them with the powers which were impersonal emanations from God;[4] at another time with

---

[1] Gen rab 78; Echa. to 3 : 23, from Bacher, Die Aggada der Tannaiten I (2. Aufl.) p. 172.

[2] Weber, Judische Theologie. pp. 166 ff

[3] Cf. above p. 148.

[4] Cf. Ling. 168 ff. (I. 430 ff.). See Drummond, Philo II. 148 ff. Drummond has not made his point here of a distinction

the demons,[1] or with souls not yet born[2] His object
in thus classing the angels with some other familiar conception is to reduce their importance so that they could
by no means be made parallel to the gods of the heathen
and hence suggest polytheism. With the same purpose he
at times even denies them any existence at all, and says that
the angels of the Old Testament were visions of God
Himself who appeared as an angel in order to come within
the power of comprehension of mortals in the flesh.[3] With
such speculation Justin has nothing to do. He holds here
unmistakably to his Hebrew tradition.

Did Justin understand this entire emanation process
to be a sort of creation? It is notable at first that
Justin says here that by this process the angels were
"made", and that he uses the Greek word ποιεῖν which
later, at least, was used in Christian theology as a specific
term for creation. Did Justin so use the word? At first it
seems to appear that he did think of the angels as
"created", for ποιεῖν is applied to the angels on three
other occasions,[4] in two of which they are classed together
with men as "made",[5] and in all three passages are said
to have been made with free power of choice. But in
these passages it is asserted of the angels that they were
"made like men", not in the process of their origin, but in
virtue of the fact that both men and angels are endowed
with free power of choice. For the origin of the angelic host
we must then rely entirely upon the single passage first
quoted. But here though the angels are said to be "made",
the process by which they were made is entirely different
from that described elsewhere for the creation of men, but
precisely the same as that which produced the Son of
God. Indeed the statement most strongly suggestive of

of powers and angels. The identification is clear, but not necessarily
did Philo always think of the angels as powers, nor of the powers
as angels

[1] De Gigant. 6 ff. (I. 263 ff.).
[2] Ibid.
[3] De Somniis I 232 (I. 655) See above Chapter IV.
[4] Ap II. 7 5 (45 D), Dial 88 5 (316 A), 141. 1 (370 B)
[5] Ap. II. 7. 5 (45 D); Dial. 141. 1 (370 B).

creation in the passage is made in connection with the origin of the Second God rather than of the angels, though we understand that it should apply to them as well For Justin makes it distinctly plain that the emanation which generated the Son was put forth from God by an act of God's will. If this passage seems then to represent the angels as created, the same must with even greater confidence be said of the Son of God Actually Justin thought of neither the Son of God nor the angelic host as created By the same process each was begotten, generated from the Father

Justin thus conceived of two sorts of angels, the temporary and the permanent Were either or both of these groups made up of distinct personalities? On the whole, Justin probably thought of the permanent angels at least as personalities, but he has nothing to say of outstanding angelic persons such as later were understood in Christian teachings

The question of the angels' relation to Divinity, or their claim to divine character, has been made a pressing one by Justin's mention of the angelic host as one of the objects of Christian worship, listed even before the Holy Spirit [1] The passage bears all the ear-marks of genuiness, and is not to be dismissed by altering the text or by ingenuity of explanation. Does Justin regard this pleroma of personal emanation as itself divine? Justin continually insists in the Dialogue that there is only one God the Father, and that there are only two divine Personalities, which may perhaps be extended to include the Holy Spirit But that there is any pleroma of divinities is precisely the thought that he is controverting alike in the Apologies and the Dialogue The only illumination I have been able to find for the passage is the fact that Philo represents Moses as praying to the powers,[2] which may conceivably be a philosophic reflection of a popular angelolatry. If such was a popular practice in the Judaism of the Diaspora, it may be that Justin's statement

[1] Ap. I 6 2 (56 C).
[2] De Plant 46 (I. 336). Moses prays to τὸ αὐτεξούσιον τοῦ θεοῦ κράτος αὐτοῦ καὶ τὰς ἵλεως καὶ ἡμέρους δυνάμεις.

Goodenough, The Theology of Justin Martyr.   13

is a survival from such an antecedent. It is however inconceivable that the angels, whether in Judaism or Christianity, were worshipped as more than intermediaries, who would bear petitions directly to God. It is not at all impossible that the Christian doctrine of the mediation of Christ, and later of the Saints, has had such a forgotten ancestry. But we are here in the region of pure conjecture. Actually, Justin's statement that the Christians worshipped the angels hangs unsupported in the air.

As to the nature of the angels, it is highly probable that Justin followed his Palestinian Jewish tradition still further, and thought that the angels were made of fire. The angels were made of fire in the Epistle to the Hebrews,[1] while Weber shows that the Palestinian tradition of the angels was also that they were so constituted.[2] Nothing would be more natural than so to think of the angels in view of the description of their fiery origin. That Justin so believed, and that the origin of his belief was ultimately the Palestinian tradition is witnessed by his explanation of manna, the food of angels, as well as of the phenomenon of the angel's eating before the tent of Abraham. For Justin says that angels must receive nourishment of some sort because the Scripture says that the manna which the Children of Israel ate in the wilderness was the bread of angels (ἄρτον ἀγγέλων).[3] Here Justin follows the Septuagint rendering of the Hebrew "bread of the mighty", but the Septuagint itself was quite true to the Palestinian tradition in interpreting the "mighty" in this verse as the angels, for such was Akiba's understanding of the passage. So explicit, indeed, was Akiba's explanation that it sounded to his opponent Ismael as too crass, and provoked the rejoinder: "Go out and tell Akiba that he is wrong; for do the angels eat? Much more does the expression signify a nourishment which is entirely absorbed by the members."[4] In another passage

[1] Hebr. i. 7.

[2] Weber, Jüdische Theologie. pp 166 ff.

[3] Dial 57 2 (279 C). See Ps. lxxviii. 25.

[4] Bar. Joma 75 b, from Bacher, Die Agada der Tannaiten. I (2 Aufl) 245.

it is denied that manna is the *bread* of angels on the basis
of the passage, "Bread have I not eaten."[1] The Hebrew
tradition made the angels thus a consuming fire which
was nourished by some celestial substance that was consumed or devoured by the angels as fire consumes fuel, but
not as human beings consume bread. In the light of this
Hebrew belief Justin's remarks about the angels' eating
become at once intelligible. He thus explains the circum-
stance where the angels *(including the Logos)* ate before
the tent of Abraham: "The Scripture which says that they
ate bears the same meaning as when we would say about
fire that it has devoured (κατέφαγεν) all things; yet it is
by no means to be understood that they ate, masticating
with their teeth and jaws."[2] Here is clearly a reproduction
of the Palestinian Jewish thought. The angels are made
of a fiery substance which consumes nourishment; but they
do not eat food after the manner of men. One has only to
glance at Philo to feel how pre-eminently here we are in
the midst of a Palestinian rather than a Hellenistic Jewish
tradition. Manna was by Philo explained as "heavenly
wisdom, which God sends from above to those who have
a longing for virtue."[3] Semisch concludes from Justin's
comment upon the angels' eating that he considers the
angels as having a bodiliness between the corporeality of
man and the pure spirituality of God.[4] Aside from the
ambiguity of his language Semisch is on treacherous ground.
That Justin ever conceived of immaterial reality is most
doubtful. The material figures by which the procession
of emanations was represented always speak of a source
as material as the emanation, and insist upon the identity
in character of the fire which is lighted with the fire from
which the new flame has been kindled. The very word
πνεῦμα was of course a material expression, and it is certainly
beyond anything Justin says to conclude that in applying
the word to God Justin purified it entirely of its physical

[1] Goldfahn (Bibl 389) p 112 (No 13).
[2] Dial. 57. 2 (279 C
[3] De Mut Nom 259 (I 618).
[4] Semisch (Bibl 118) II. 342. "Diese Körperlichkeit als ein
Mitteldíng zwischen reiner Geistigkeit und menschlicher Leiblichkeit.'

13*

implications Since all the powers and demons, even the evil ones, were to Justin also πνεύματα, [1] it is impossible to speak of a "spirituality" which God has but which cannot be applied to the angels. Indeed the word spirituality (in modern use of most uncertain meaning) is well avoided in any such discussion.

Justin probably thought of the powers or angels ordinarily as in human form. In this the imagery of the Old Testament would have helped him. He even carries his attack against mythology so far as to say that the statues of the gods have the names and *forms* of the evil demons, not the form of God.[2] We are told little about the faculties of these beings. The whole spirit world, after the Father and the Logos, seems not to be omniscient. Spirits are easily deceived, though of course they know more of God's ways and plans than an uninspired human being. The demons imitated the prophecy about the coming Incarnation, but on many details missed the point of the prophecy.[3] The angels, called here "the rulers in heaven", seeing the returning Christ in his loneliness and humility did not recognize their Lord in such disguise.[4] In thus setting a limit upon the intelligence of the angels Justin is quite in accord with the teaching of Jesus that the day and hour of the Second Coming were not known to the angels of heaven, but only to God.[5]

But if the angels of heaven were not omniscient, Justin was confident that they had freedom of choice.[6] "God, wishing men and angels to follow His will, resolved to make them self-determining (αὐτεξουσίους) to do righteousness; possessing reason (μετὰ λόγου) that they may know by whom they were made, and through whom they, not existing formerly, do now exist; and with a law that they

[1] Dial. 7. 3 (225 B); 30 2 (247 B); 35 2 (253 A); 76. 6 302 A).

[2] Ap. I. 9. 1 (57 C, D). For the relation between demons and other powers see below p. 198

[3] Ap I. 54 4 (89 C)

[4] Dial 36 6 (255 B).

[5] Mat xxiv 36

[6] On the freedom of the angels see further p. 230

shall be judged by Him, if they do anything contrary to right reason (τὸν ὀρθὸν λόγον); and of ourselves we, men and angels, shall be convicted as having acted sinfully unless we repent "[1] It is remarkable that Justin seems to include angels among those needing repentance and salvation. Justin says nothing which will help the understanding of this statement. His insistence upon the free power of choice of angels was of course a part of his theodicy. If some of the angels were sinful, as some very clearly were, either God had made them sinful or they had made themselves so. To represent God as the cause of sin was of course impossible. Justin had to take the other alternative and represent the angels as free moral agents in order to be able to blame the bad angels for their own sinfulness. But Justin probably did no choosing in the matter, for he had merely to continue to follow the Palestinian Jewish angelology. It is recorded that Pappos at one time interpreted, "Man has become as one of us," as meaning, "Man has become as one of the angels." Akiba added to this the comment that to be as one of the angels meant to have free power of choice, to go either the way of life or the way of death.[2] Justin expressly rejected the interpretation of the passage, "Man has become as one of us," as referring to the angels, for he had need of this passage to prove the existence of a Second God,[3] but he retained the conception that man was like the angels in having free power of choice. Unfortunately Justin says no more about an atonement of the angels, and it is useless to try to build a theory of angelic atonement upon this passage. Justin thought usually, it appears, in terms of good and of bad angels. The first he worshipped, the second were all destined for damnation, and there is no other hint of a passing from the bad class to the good class, or of any further lapses among the angels than those which had long ago occurred. The power of choice of the angels then seems to have played a vital

---

[1] Dial. 141 1 (370 B, C), cf. 140 4 (370 A); 88 5 (316 A); Ap. II. 7. 5 (45 D).

[2] Bacher, Die Aggada der Tannaiten. I. (2. Aufl.) p. 318. By an oversight Bacher has omitted a reference for this quotation.

[3] Dial. 62. 3 (285 C); 129 2 (359 A)

part in Justin's system only in defending the righteousness of God who had permitted some of the good angels to fall.

The circumstances of this evil event are described by Justin as having taken place in connection with the angels' exercise of care over men in the world. The statement of Justin about this function of the angels presents in itself a perplexing problem. Normally the angels were regarded as the messengers of God, but in one passage Justin says: "God, when He made the whole world, and subjected things earthly to man .... committed the oversight ($\pi\rho\acute{o}\nu o\iota\alpha\nu$) of men and of all things under heaven to angels whom He appointed over them."[1] Did God then exercise providence only through the angel company, while He Himself in Platonic remoteness was unconcerned about the world of matter? The entire teaching of Justin is opposed to such a theory. To enlarge upon this passage upon the basis of the Timaeus, as does Pfättisch,[2] for example, is to misunderstand Justin entirely. It is inconceivable that he thought of the angels as anything more than the messengers and helpers of God. They were God's footmen, not his vice-regents. The idea of giving certain angels certain definite tasks is to be seen in Hebrew tradition as old as the cherubim who guarded the garden of Eden. But the cherubim in the garden of Eden were not considered as the gods of the garden of Eden, nor as rulers acting on their own initiative. No more did Justin regard the angels appointed to watch over various parts of the world as rulers in God's place.[3]

The occasion of the fall of the wicked angels was this their appointment as overseers of the world. Justin goes on from the above quotation to say, "But the angels, overstepping their appointment, were drawn to have intercourse

---

[1] Ap II 5. 2 (44 A)

[2] Pfättisch's peculiarly unsatisfactory work is typically fallacious in its treatment of angels. See (Bibl. 385) pp. 37 ff. Pfättisch overlooks the fact that it was part of the Christian tradition before Justin that the angels in a sense supervised the world, for such a statement is preserved in almost the same words from Papias Fragment 4, quoted below p. 200 n. 5.

[3] Cf Athenagoras, Suppl 24 3 ff ; Enoch xxi 6, Josephus Ant. I. 3

with women, and begat children who are called demons ".
So far as I know this statement of Justin is the first record
we have of the conception that the union of angels and
human women produced demons. The Hebrew reads that
the "children of God" were attracted by women, and in
uniting with them begat giants.[1] The phrase "children
of God" was translated in the Septuagint as "angels of
God", and accordingly it is stated in Philo,[2] Josephus,[3]
and the Book of Enoch,[4] that the union of angels and
human women produced giants. Justin is the first to substitute demons for giants, or at least to understand the
giants to be demons, though Athenagoras[5] and Tertullian[6] both followed Justin later. Justin may have been
speaking of this fall of the angels more in detail in a passage in the Dialogue which has apparently been mutilated[7]
Trypho is represented as indignant at something which
Justin has just said about the sin of the angels as having
been a revolt against God. But the statement of Justin
against which Trypho directs his protest is so obscure
upon the subject of the angels, makes indeed such slight
and passing mention of them, that the remark objected to
by Trypho must be lacking from our text. Had Justin
actually been describing his doctrine of the fall of the
angels at greater length, it is not surprising that the passage
was later mutilated, for Justin's explanation was afterwards
expressly rejected by Christian theologians. Indeed not
only were the demons not allowed to be identified with
the giants of this verse of Scripture, but the translation of
the Septuagint was itself challenged, the "children of God"
was restored in place of the "angels of God",[8] and the

[1] Gen vi 2
[2] De Gigant 6—27 (I 263 ff)
[3] Ant I 3.
[4] Enoch xxi 6.
[5] Suppl. 25. 1.
[6] Apol 22
[7] Dial. 79 1 (305 B)
[8] Philastrius, Haer 107, 'Quae de gigantibus assent quod
angeli miscuerint se cum feminis ante deluvium, et inde esse natos
gigantos suspicatur" Augustine also calls the doctrine a fable,
Civ. Dei XV. 23.

verse was explained as the union of the sons of Seth with the daughters of Cain.[1]

Veil has made a bad guess that Justin first evolved his theory of the fall of the angels by elaborating the argument of Aristides Apol. 8, where the misdeeds of the Greek gods with mortal women are cited against their divine character.[2] Justin is probably here still following Christian tradition from Palestinian Judaism. The Ebionites had the same explanation as Justin of the production of demons by intercourse of angels with human women,[3] and Semisch's analysis of their statement is quite convincing that both they and Justin had received the same Jewish tradition, rather than that Justin had his doctrine from the Ebionites.[4] Further the fragment of Papias already mentioned seems to have been taken from a statement of a similar, if not the same, tradition,[5] so that it is quite possible that Justin is here only the first whose record has reached us of a tradition which had long been incorporated from Judaism into Christianity.

But after the unfortunate lapse of the angels, and the begetting of their demonic children, both the fathers and sons were called interchangeably demons or evil angels.[6] Together they constituted an army of evil powers which

---

[1] Chrysost. in Gen. 6, Homil. 22. On the history of this doctrine see Baumgarten-Crusius, Compend. der Dogmengeschichte Leipzig 1846, II. 213 Anm. e. The note is probably by the editor Hase.

[2] (Bibl. 80) p. 120. chap. 4 n. 1.

[3] Clem. Homil. 6. 18 (I. 677)

[4] Semisch (Bibl. 118) II. 389—392

[5] Fragment 4, 'Ενίοις δὲ αὐτῶν, δηλαδὴ τῶν πάλαι θείων ἀγγέλων, καὶ τῆς περὶ τὴν γῆν διακοσμήσεως ἔδωκεν ἄρχειν, καὶ καλῶς ἄρχειν παρηγγύησε, καὶ ἑξῆς φησίν· Εἰς οὐδὲν δέον συνέβη τελευτῆσαι τὴν τάξιν αὐτῶν; from Gebhardt, Harnack, Zahn. Patrum Apostol. Op. I. ii (1878). p 94. Notice here that the rulership is given to the angels who were *formerly* divine, but that they in no respect fulfilled their τάξιν. Cf. Justin's remark. "the angels παραβάντες τήνδε τὴν τάξιν." Ap II. 5. 3 (44 B). If Justin is thus verbally reproducing Papias, it seems likely that the parallelism of ideas goes much further than this limited fragment reveals.

[6] Ap I. 5. 2 (55 E), Dial. 70. 4 (306 B).

was much more real to Justin than the host of good angels which he reverently names before the Holy Spirit.

The company of demons and fallen angels was led by an arch fiend Satan,[1] who fell in an uniquely sinful manner. It was he who deceived Adam and Eve, and as a result of this treachery he was cursed and fell with a great overthrow.[2] His name, said Justin, is a Hebrew compound meaning Apostate Serpent[3] Justin had a much more elaborate account of the fall and activity of this Serpent or Apostate than he cares to narrate, for on one occasion he but mentions the subject to drop it with the remark that with this matter it is aside from his present purpose to deal[4] From what height Satan fell we can only judge from the statement that he was εἷς τῶν ὀρχόντων,[5] an expression which is probably to be found more complete elsewhere as οἱ ἐν οὐρανῷ ἄρχοντες,[6] when it means the angelic host. The title may have reference to the rulership which God gave to particular angels[7] Satan then, from our meagre information, was apparently one of the many angels thus given duties in the universe, but was the first and chief apostate of the group.

The activity of the evil host is manifold. Their evil presence is everywhere felt. They are the princes in Tanis,[8] and Damascus,[9] they stand by the altar while the priest sacrifices,[10] they even appear before God Himself[11] Magicians of all sorts help them in their evil

[1] Dial 131 2 (360 C). Here the demons are called the army of Satan, understanding καί as explanatory Cf Ap. I 28 1 (71 A).

[2] Dial 124. 3 (353 D); 79. 4 (306 A).
[3] Dial 103. 5 (331 B), 125 4 (354 D).
[4] Dial 124 3 (353 D)
[5] Ibid.
[6] Dial 36 6 (255 B).
[7] See above p. 198.
[8] Dial 79 3 (305 D)
[9] Dial. 78 9 (304 D)
[10] Dial 79 4 (306 A)
[11] Ibid

work,[1] while wicked men are tools in their hands[2]
Their attack on mankind Justin divides into two kinds[3]
First they try to rivet men to this world and to things made
by hands, by which he probably means to the sins and
lusts of matter and mammon, which in Justin's day, not
only to Christians but to all serious people, was an adequate
description of the way to destruction. But some men
persist in trying to walk by a larger view of life. These are
attacked in the second way, for the demons try to lead
them into fallacy, and to undermine their philosophic
temper of reasoned self-control and superiority to the
material phases of life[4] In connection with this latter
activity Justin has conceived that the demons mask themselves as the gods of the Greeks, in order to mislead men
by their bad example.[5] Further the demons have, listened
carefully to the utterances of the Prophets and have tried to
caricature the events foretold in order that when they came
to pass the events themselves might seem to be as absurd
and blasphemous as the demonic imitations.[6] This has
particularly been evident in the case of the Virgin Birth,[7]
and of the birth of Christ in a cave, which is parodied in
Mithraism.[8] But bold and clever as the demons have
been, they have failed to grasp the prophecies of the Cross,
and hence have never caricatured that supreme event[9]
Since the coming of Christ they have been as busy as before
if not busier[10] Their attack upon the truth has been

[1] Ap. I. 26 2 (69 D); Dial. 69. 1 (294 D); 78. 9 (304 D).
In this last passage the magi who came to the new born Christ
were magicians from Damascus, and witnessed that Christ at His
birth had broken the power of the demon ruling there. A similar
idea was long prevalent in the Church See Semisch (Bibl 118)
II 383 Anm. 9 for references.
[2] Ap I 5 3 (56 A)
[3] Ap. I. 58 3 (92 B)
[4] Ap I. 28 4 (71 C).
[5] See above p 108.
[6] Ap. I. 53, 54, 64.
[7] Ap I. 33 3 (74 E)
[8] Dial 78 6 (304 A), 70. 1 (296 B).
[9] Ap. I 55. 1 (90 B
[10] See fragment II (ed. Otto), from Irenaeus Cont Haer V
26 2

continued in the form of the institution of heresies by which
they hope to pervert the knowledge of the true way as
revealed in Christ,[1] and by parodies of the Christian
cultus, especially of baptism in the heathen temple puri-
fications,[2] and of the Eucharist in the mysteries of Mi-
thras [3] They have now entered into a large extension of
an activity which had been only occasionally undertaken
before the coming of Christ, namely the attack upon good
men externally by persecution through men who are subject
to demonic direction [4] So great is the activity and power
of this host for doing what are apparently wonderful miracles that Justin feels he has little advantage in stressing the
miraculous power of Jesus as witness of His divine
character The countercharge has been made, says Justin,
that a wonder worker is a person in league with demons,
and that hence, since Jesus was a wonder worker, He must
have been in league with demons.[5] Justin accepts the
reasoning as generally valid outside of Christianity, though
he believes that Christian miracles are worked by inspiration
of the Spirit, but he is aware that he has little material
with which he can demonstrate a distinction between
Christian and non-Christian miracles

Justin believes in demonic possession as did the
authors of the Synoptics, and apparently Jesus Himself [6]
But he makes a statement, surprising at first glance, that
possession by demons is possession by souls of the dead [7]
However, the introduction of "souls" as a further complication of Justin's demonology was quite to be expected in
view of his strong tradition of angelology and demonology
from Hebraism Josephus says that the so-called demons are
the souls of evil men [8] Philo has this tradition in mind in

[1] Dial 82 3 (308 D). Ap I 56 1 (91 A), 58 1 (92 A)
[2] Ap I 62 1 (94 E)
[3] Ap I 66 4 (98 C)
[4] Ap I 5 3 (56 A), Dial 131 2 (360 C,
[5] Ap I 30 1 (72 A)
[6] Ap I 18 4 (65 A); Ap II 6 (45 B)
[7] Ap I 18 4 (65 A); cf also W Baldensperger, Urchristliche Apologie: Die ältesten Auferstehungskontroversen Strassburg
1909 p 13
[8] Bel Jud VII vi 3

the passage where he says that souls, demons, and angels
are to be distinguished only in name, for they are all three
actually the same.[1] The confusion of terms was clarified
by Tatian soon after Justin's time, for Tatian denied that
the demons who attacked men were human souls.[2]

But malignant and terrible as is the activity of the
demonic host, it is not altogether beyond control. Before
the coming of Christ the demons were controlled when
exorcised in the name of the God of Abraham, Isaac, and
Jacob,[3] and now their power has been broken by the
coming of Christ, as was symbolized by the coming of the
magi to the infant Christ.[4] Christ is now Lord over the
demons, and they are always subject to exorcism in His
name.[5] The ritual of exorcism evidently culminated in a
recital of the creed, especially that part relative to the life
and death of Jesus Christ.[6] When this form of exorcism
was used the power of demons, who had defied all previous
exorcisms, was at once broken.[7] Thus fortified the Christians might hope to succeed in the struggle against the
unending activity of these evil spirits. At the end, the
triumph of the Cross, which was a triumph over the
demons,[8] would be finally demonstrated, and they would
be completely subdued,[9] and damned.[10] It is the foreknowledge of this event which makes Satan desperate, and
has prompted him since Christ's death to a complete

[1] De Gigant. 16 (I 264).
[2] Tatian, Orat. 16. 1
[3] Dial. 85. 3 (311 C)
[4] Dial 78 9 (304 D)
[5] Dial. 85 1, 2 (311 B), 76. 6 (302 A); 111. 2 (338 B);
30 3 (247 C); Ap II. 6. 6 (45 A)
[6] Ap. II. 6. 6 (45 A); Dial. 85 2 (311 B). Otto, n. 7 in loco,
gives references to similar passages in other Christian writers. Was
this not the original use of the Creed, introduced into Christian
worship to purify the place of meeting as well as the worshippers
of all demons?
[7] Dial 85 3 (311 C)
[8] Dial. 94 2 (322 A), cf 41 1 (260 A); 49 8 (269 C) On
this point see Behm's excellent notes (Bibl. 321) p 480
[9] Ap. I. 45. 1 (82 D).
[10] Dial. 76 3—6 (310 C ff).

abandonment of all restraint in his evil activity against men [1]

In Justin's demonology we are as close as in any of his doctrines, with the dubious exception of his ethics or eschatology, to the mode of thought and the ideas of the Synoptic Gospels.[2] Justin is thus close to the Synoptic conceptions, not because he was expounding the Synoptic statements about demons, but because in his tradition about demons from Palestinian Judaism he had the same background on the subject as the Synoptic writers. To think that Justin's demonology is a system worked out by himself on the basis of borrowings from Platonism[3] or Ebionism,[4] is to speak from a partial knowledge of the real nature of his demonology as Hebrew parallels enlighten it. Justin felt no need of softening the animism of his belief in demons, as Philo had done, because to Justin the existence of demons was a self-obvious fact, and his was not the sort of mind which made itself useless trouble He and the Christians about him were abundantly satisfied with the simple explanations of demons which Hebrew tradition furnished, and with the assertion that the demons as described in this tradition were to be controlled by the power of the name of Christ. The chief attention of the Christianity of Justin's day was centered upon winning in the never ending fight against the actual incursions and seductions of the demonic host.

[1] Fragment II. (Otto) from Irenaeus Cont Haer. V. 26. 2.

[2] See Conybeare (Bibl 328) pp 597—599

[3] For old writers see references in Semisch (Bibl. 118) II. 387 Anm. 1. The mistake has recently been renewed by Pfättisch (Bibl. 385).

[4] E g Credner (Bibl 416) I. 98

CHAPTER VII

THE CREATED WORLD

A. MATTER

Justin's theory of the germinative activity of the Logos as a spermatic principle introduced by God into the material substrate has already been discussed.[1] It remains here to examine what Justin has to say of the material substrate. The evidence is most unsatisfactory, for, aside from insuring the divine origin of the world and the good character of the Creator,[2] Justin has little interest in the process by which the universe came into existence. He has, as we have seen, connected the creative Word of God of the Genesis account with the Spermatic Logos of the Greek and Greek-Jewish traditions. But when he had done this, his mild speculative curiosity about the Creation ceased, and he was content to take the remainder of the Genesis narrative quite literally. His utter lack of scientific interest is nowhere better illustrated than in the fact that though a doctrine of matter was necessary to complete his doctrine of the Spermatic Logos, and though the origin and nature of matter were among the most important points of philosophic and religious discussion of the day, Justin seems to have no interest in the

[1] See above pp 161 ff.
[2] Justin, in correction of the Gnostic idea that the δημιουργός was a bad rather than a good deity, adds to a statement of Jesus as follows, "No one is good but God, *the one who made all things.*" Ap. I. 16. 6, 7 (63 D, E); cf. notes by Veil and Blunt (following Veil) in loco That this additional phrase was not in Justin's text is witnessed by his quotation of the same saying of Jesus in another connection See Dial. 93. 2 (321 A).

subject whatever The few statements in which he mentions matter have been very differently interpreted. It is universally admitted that Justin thought of God as having created the world out of unformed matter Indeed Justin says this much explicitly.[1] But whence came this matter? Did it constitute an eternal existential antithesis to God, or was it itself a creation of God in an unformed state, and then made into the phenomenal world? Or is there some third explanation?

The answer to these questions, if answer may be given at all, depends upon the interpretation of a single passage in the First Apology Justin has been developing his thesis that the philosophers of Greece derive their doctrines from the writings of Moses and the Prophets,[2] and proceeds to give the following illustration

"And that you may also learn that it was from our teachers that Plato borrowed his statement that God, having altered matter which was shapeless, made the world, hear the utterances exactly as made by Moses, who, as has been shown, was the first prophet, and was older than the Greek writers Through him the Prophetic Spirit indicated how and out of what ingredients God in the beginning fashioned the world, as follows: 'In the beginning God created heaven and earth And the earth was invisible and unfurnished, and darkness was upon the deep, and the Spirit of God moved upon the waters. And God said, Let there be light And it was so' So that both Plato and his followers and we ourselves have learned, and you may learn, that the whole world came into being by means of a logos from God out of the existing substance about which also Moses had already spoken."[3]

A persistent interpretation of this passage represents Justin as here criticizing a doctrine of Plato Plato, says Justin by this interpretation, is right in asserting that God made the world by shaping it out of an unformed

[1] Ap I 10 2 (58 B)

[2] See above p 105

[3] Ap I 59 entire. λόγῳ θεοῦ ἐκ τῶν ὑποκειμένων καὶ προ-δηλωθέντων διὰ Μωυσέως γεγενῆσθαι τὸν πάντα κόσμον. For the significance of the λόγῳ θεοῦ here see above p 164

material substrate, but is quite wrong in thinking that this material substrate was eternally existing. For according to the account of Moses, God created heaven and earth, and then began the process of shaping the world from the matter that had thus been described as having been created in an unformed state.[1]

Before criticizing this interpretation it must be noticed that the passage hangs quite unsupported. Several other passages have been adduced to support the above theory, but none of them give any information at all as to the origin of matter. In one passage Justin says that in the beginning God created all things good from unformed matter.[2] In another he speaks of God as having turned or changed darkness and matter, and as thus having made the world.[3] Semisch even tried to use as evidence the statement that a world like ours could not be eternal in itself, but must have been made by a Creator.[4] The irrelevancy of the last passage to the question of the origin of matter needs no comment; the two former passages at least mention matter, but do not give the slightest hint as to whether it was eternal or created, unless the τρέψας of the second quotation be misunderstood. For τρέψας means turning or changing, and cannot of course be understood as creating.

The interpretation of the first quoted passage then is not assisted by any other statement of Justin, except perhaps his declaration, "When we say that all things have been arranged and brought into being (κεκοσμῆσθαι καὶ γεγενῆσθαι) by God we seem to be expressing a doctrine

---

[1] This interpretation, stated clearly by Otto (see n 6 p 159 in loco), is most elaborately developed by Semisch (Bibl. 118) II 336 ff His arguments have been reproduced more or less completely by Weizsäcker (Bibl. 311) p. 84, von Engelhardt (Bibl 313) pp 139 ff., La Grange (Bibl 167) pp 149 ff, Windisch (Bibl. 333) p 8 (who says that this denial of the eternity of matter is the starting point of Justin's theodicy), and Blunt (Bibl 43) n 10 in loco, to mention only a few

[2] Ap. I 10 2 (58 B)

[3] Ap. I. 67 7 (99 A) τὸ σκότος καὶ τὴν ὕλην τρέψας κόσμον ἐποίησε.

[4] Dial. 5. 2 (223 A).

of Plato."[1] This last statement of Justin's accentuates an aspect of the main passage under discussion which has usually been disregarded,[2] namely that Justin mentions pre-creation matter at all only to assert that the Mosaic and Platonic doctrines are identical For Justin says no syllable in the passage which can be taken as indicating a contrast at any point between the doctrines of creation of the two He declares that Moses and Plato both alike taught that when God created the world He altered matter and gave it form whereas before it was formless. But if Justin is not criticizing Plato, did he still believe that the words, "In the beginning God created heaven and earth,' where a description of the creation of unformed matter, as theologians later interpreted them?[3] The only ground for attributing such a doctrine to Justin is the presence of the plurals ἐκ τῶν ὑποκειμένων καὶ προδηλωθέντων διὰ Μωυσέως, with which he refers to the material substrate. Here προδηλωθέντων is a modifier of ὑποκειμένων agreeing with it in number while the καὶ is intensive, to be translated "also" Justin is here only saying then that τὰ ὑποκείμενα from which God made the world have been mentioned by Moses But it will be at once recognized that τὰ ὑποκείμενα is a Stoic word for ultimate matter, and that the Stoics used the singular and plural interchangeably to indicate the single material substrate which they regarded as underlying and constituting all things[4] Τὰ ὑποκείμενα, in referring to matter, does not then imply a plural but rather a singular reference, and is here much more naturally to be understood with ἡ γῆ which was ἀόρατος καὶ ἀκατασκεύαστος, than with the two words "heaven and earth" The invisible and unfurnished earth, then, is the unformed

---

[1] Ap I 20 4 (66 D) Such a doubling of terms to describe creation is frequent in Justin. Semisch (Bibl 118) II 337 wishes to represent this use of doublets as a contrast between the creation matter and the shaping of the world out of matter Cf Ap II 6. 3 (44 E), Dial 11 1 (228 A) But without other evidence that Justin held such a view, it cannot be considered that he believed in the doctrine from this mannerism of speech

[2] Except by Pfattisch (Bibl 385) pp 96 ff.

[3] Cf Theophilus, ad Aut II 10

[4] See Zeller III 1 pp 93 ff Engl. Tr · Stoics p 101 n 3.

material substrate which Justin asserts was common to
Plato and Moses. How Justin understood the first sentence,
that God in the beginning created heaven and earth, he
does not indicate, and in the absence of evidence it is
natural to assume that he understood it correctly as the
topic sentence of the description of creation which follows.
There seems to be no valid reason for reading into the
passage a doctrine that matter was itself a creation of God.

But if it cannot be said that Justin taught the creation
of matter, it is equally erroneous to go to the other extreme
and insist that Justin believed in the eternity of matter
in the full Platonic sense of an existential antithesis to
God.[1] To do so is to misrepresent Justin's unphilosophic
mind, for he had no interest in matter further than to
assert that out of it, in an unformed state, God made the
world. The origin and nature of matter, one of the most
burning questions of contemporary philosophic speculation,
did not arouse his curiosity. A parallel to this indifference
to the nature of matter can only be found in Palestinian
Judaism. While the Platonic and Stoic schools, with which
Justin is often represented as being more in accord than
with Christianity, made the origin and nature of matter
the basis of most ethical and many metaphysical doctrines,
and while Hellenistic Judaism had taken over a late Platonic
and Pythagorean view of life as a dualism between God
and matter, Palestinian Judaism like Justin regarded matter
as a fact rather than as a problem. Palestinian opinion
is not consistent as to the origin of matter. One tradition
says that when God created the world He found shapeless
matter ready at hand to be used.[2] Another tradition says
that this matter was itself created[3] But the question

---

[1] This extreme conclusion mars Pfattisch's otherwise excellent
analysis of this passage. See (Bibl 385) pp. 96 ff. The best
comment on the passage is by Möller (Bibl 307) pp. 146—149

[2] Rab. Josh b Chananja thought it sufficient explanation of
creation to say that God created the world out of the six elements
which are stated figuratively in Gen 1 2 (Bacher I. 171) Weber,
Jüdische Theologie. pp 200 ff, says that the creation of the world
out of a previously existing matter was the persistent Talmudic tradition.

[3] Gamalied II answered R. Josh b Chananja that these six
elements were also created Bacher I 81.

had never caused much comment or controversy because it had no importance in Jewish eyes. By neither of these two traditions for the origin of matter were the origin of evil and the origin of matter considered as having any connection with each other This is exactly Justin's position. It was the identity of-evil with matter which gave to philosophic schools and Hellenistic Judaism their keen interest in the origin of matter. Justin lacked this incentive, and was not sufficiently philosophical to have interested himself in the problem on other grounds.

The purpose of creation, Justin explains, was the benefit of the human race.[1] All earthly things were directly made subject to man, while the heavenly elements and seasons, and the laws which govern them, though not of course subject to man's control, were still ordained for man's profit.[2] Of a real explanation of the purpose of creation Justin has no trace. Why God should have wished to create a human race to be thus favoured by the rest of creation Justin does not explain. The later orthodox Christian doctrine that the purpose of creation was a display of the goodness, and the revelation of the glory of God, came into Christianity also from the Hellenistic-Judaistic tradition,[3] and Justin himself seems to believe that God was motivated to create the world by His goodness.[4]

B. MAN

• In general Justin could say with Philo that man was created from the material elements [5] The body at least

[1] Ap II. 4. 2 (43 C, D).
[2] Ap. II. 5 2 (44 A); cf. Dial. 41. 1 (260 A).
[3] Cf Philo De Cherub. 127 (I 162).
[4] Ap. I. 10 2 (58 B)

[5] Dial. 62. 2 (285 C) τὰ στοιχεῖα, τοῦτ' ἔστι τὴν γῆν καὶ τὰ ἄλλα ὁμοίως, ἐξ ὧν νοοῦμεν τὸν ἄνθρωπον γεγονέναι. Cf. Philo, Opif. Mundi 146 (I. 35). The body συγκέκραται ἐκ τῶν αὐτῶν. γῆς καὶ ὕδατος καὶ ἀέρος καὶ πυρός, ἑκάστου τῶν στοιχείων εἰσενεγκόντος τὸ ἐπιβάλλον μέρος πρὸς ἐκπλήρωσιν αὐταρκεστάτης ὕλης, ἣν ἔδει λαβεῖν τὸν δημιουργόν, ἵνα τεχνιτεύσῃ τὴν ὁρατὴν ταύτην εἰκόνα.

was shaped by God Himself,[1] and Justin would have nothing to do with those Jewish teachers who said that the body of man was a creation of angels.[2]

Justin's psychology has already been partially discussed in connection with his analysis of Platonism under the guidance of the Old Man. It was then found that Justin regarded man as endowed with a soul which included apparently all his non-bodily constitution except the reason, and which was probably to be considered as possessing a sort of mentality, and as being the seat of personality The soul however was not especially exalted, though higher than the body, because human souls and animal souls were of the same nature. To this soul was granted a ζωτικὸν πνεῦμα which never became an integral part of the soul, but which imparted life and true reason to it. It was the business of man to guide his soul by this reason, and thus to make his soul worthy of retaining the πνεῦμα. The important assumption in this description, that the πνεῦμα imparted reason as well as life to the soul, was made formerly on the basis of analogy with the doctrines of contemporary Platonism which Justin clearly had in mind in writing the introduction to the Dialogue. A study of the remarks of Justin about human psychology in the rest of his writings confirms the impression that Justin believed man was thus equipped both with a personal soul and in addition with a divine element which at once gave life to the soul and imparted the highest reason.

From the few passages outside the introduction to the Dialogue where the soul is mentioned, we may conclude that Justin thought of it as a very human thing. It is no more to be conceived that God has a soul than that He has fingers and feet [3] Justin must have had material connotations with the word soul because he insisted that souls, after the death of the body, are still ἐν αἰσθήσει, have power of sensation,[4] and he probably regarded the

---

[1] Dial. 29. 3 (246 E). Here God is represented as having *personally* formed even the foreskin.

[2] Dial 62. 3 (285 D). See above p. 145.

[3] Dial. 114. 3 (342 A)

[4] Ap. I. 18. 3 (65 A).

soul as the seat of sensation in the body. Certainly the soul is the seat of desire[1] and hope.[2] But the soul has higher powers than sensation, emotion, and desire. It is in a sense intelligent. For Justin speaks of a "soul" which is confined by ignorance as being hard to change,[3] so that he must have thought of both ignorant souls and souls which had some sort of knowledge. That is, the soul had to do with conceptions as well as with sensations and emotions. Similarly he exclaims that it should be far from a self-controlled soul to have certain erroneous conceptions about the gods.[4] In both of these last references the soul evidently is intelligent to some extent, and in both, ψυχή might as well be translated "person" as "soul." Indeed the soul was the determining center of personality. Not the body, and, as we shall see, not the spirit or higher mind, but the soul is the focus of personal existence. It is the merging of personalities to make one great personality, the Church, which Justin describes as "being in one soul."[5] The survival of the soul after death involves the survival of the personality.[6] The great need of man is to make this soul pure,[7] for when the soul is pure the person is himself pure.

Justin does not account for the origin of the soul. He probably did not think it existed before its appearance in a body, or at least he did not describe the soul of one man as the re-incarnation of another. In the introduction to the Dialogue Justin examines this Platonic belief and completely rejects it; the soul is something begotten (here in the sense of created),[8] and hence cannot be the eternal subject of metempsychosis. But Justin says that though souls are begotten, they are not begotten in connection with

[1] Dial. 8. 1 (225 B)
[2] Dial. 44. 4 (263 B).
[3] Ap. I. 12. 11 (60 B).
[4] Ap. I. 21. 5 (67 C).
[5] Dial. 63. 5 (287 B).
[6] Dial. 105. 4 (333 A).
[7] Dial. 14. 2 (231 D).
[8] Dial. 4, 5.

the body.[1] That is, Justin also expressly rejects the
Aristotelian belief that the soul was σώματός τι,[2] a property
or attribute of the body, in the sense that no soul can
exist where there is no body. Apparently in Justin's
opinion each soul is begotten to be joined to a particular
body but in its begetting it is an independent existence.
The reason for Justin's rejection of the Aristotelian doctrine
is obvious. Aristotle concluded from his explanation of
the soul that the soul could not survive the death of
the body. Justin, wishing to teach a doctrine of the immortality of the soul, was accordingly careful to keep the
soul's origin and nature independent of that of the body.

But Justin speaks repeatedly of a part of man which is
much more intimately connected with the Divine Logos
than he admits in the case of the soul. In every man
there is a divine particle, his reason, which at least before
Christ's coming was man's best guide in life, Justin
believes.[3] Only as one directs his soul life by the
leadings of reason can he become pure. An individual man
can live μετὰ λόγου or ἄνευ λόγου as he pleases,[4] but the
consequences are for himself to bear. What distinguished
the ancient philosophers was the fact that they were
exceptional men who had lived μετὰ λόγου, and their reward
is not lost by the fact that they were killed by man
living ἄνευ λόγου.[5]

Justin has two terms for this higher divine principle
in man. He called it a part of the Logos,[6] or of the
Spermatic Logos,[7] or the πνεῦμα in man.[8] The apparent
discrepancy of these terms has already in part been explained in the discussion of the Spermatic Logos.[9] What-

[1] Dial 5. 2 (223 B) ὅλως κατ᾽ ἰδίαν καὶ μὴ μετὰ τῶν ἰδίων
σωμάτων . . . . . αὐτὰς (ψυχὰς) γεγονέναι.
[2] De Anima 417 a. 14 ff
[3] Ap II. 10. 8 (49 A) ὁ ἐν παντὶ ὤν might mean "all pervading", but probably means "present in every man".
[4] Ap. I 46 3, 4 (83 C, D).
[5] Ibid.
[6] Ap. II 10. 8 (49 A)
[7] Ap. II. 13. 3 (51 C)
[8] Dial 6 2 (224 C)
[9] See above pp. 16, 161.

ever else may have been the activity of the Spermatic Logos, it is present in a unique form in man. For while it probably is the ζωτικὸν πνεῦμα in all other forms of life, in man it is a σπέρμα in the specially technical sense of being the principle of resemblance between man and the Ancestor of whose Spermatic Logos he is constituted. That is, its presence is a higher intelligence like to the mind of God. But the presence of the Spermatic Logos is a presence of the Logos Himself in man. It has been customary, since Duncker's exposition, to think of a contrast between the σπέρμα παρὰ τοῦ θεοῦ, that is the personal Logos, and the Spermatic Logos in man, on the understanding that the Logos fragment in man is an emanation from the Logos, in the same way as the Logos Himself is an emanation from God, and hence that as the part of the Logos in man is inferior to the entire Logos, so the entire Logos is inferior to God.[1] But Justin betrays no sense of such a contrast. The Logos, he thought, was a spermatic effluence from God which appears in fragments in individual human beings Justin confuses the subject by asserting the incarnation, and hence the personality, of this seminal spiritual effluence from God as a totality. But the fact that he has left strict philosophy to personalize sharply the totality of the Logos does not imply that he has changed also the significance of the "part" of the total Logos or νοῦς. We have already seen that to say that the human mind is a τοῦ βασιλικοῦ νοῦ μέρος[2] does not imply a mutilation or partition of the βασιλικὸς νοῦς. The βασιλικὸς νοῦς. or the Logos, can be present in partial representation in the human constitution without itself being divided. So as the Logos according to Justin is God's Spermatic Logos, or the Sperma of God, it can be present in man without a second emanation or series of emanations from itself, and at the same time without being divided. The higher mind of man is thus itself the Spermatic Logos of God. The inferiority of the human mind to the Logos is the inferiority of a part to the whole, not of a derivative to its source.

[1] Duncker (Bibl 339) pp 25 ff
[2] Dial 4. 2 (221 E).

A single statement of Justin throws light upon two phases of this divine presence in man. Justin has been describing the fact that Socrates lived his life in harmony with what of the Logos he could apprehend. It was accordingly Christ that Socrates was unwittingly following, for Christ "was and is the Logos in every man, and it was He who foretold all things through the Prophets . . . . . For He (Christ) is a power of the ineffable Father, and not the mere instrument of the human reason"[1] Here again it is asserted that it is the universal Logos Himself, and not a seed from the universal Logos, which is present in *all* men, and that through this spiritual presence may come the inspiration to prophecy. The implication is clear. At ordinary times the higher mind plays a co-ordinate part in the human constitution, though it always should be the guide of all the lower parts But occasionally this spiritual divine element is greatly expanded. With the expansion comes supernormal perception of the truth, immediate apprehension of divine thought, and, either then or later, expression of the truth thus revealed. Such inspiration, we have seen, is usually though not always attributed to the Spirit But here 'the confusion of Spirit and Logos is complete, and makes abundantly clear the fact that to Justin the Spermatic Logos, in man as well as universally, is a spiritual flow rather than a "kernel".

This sort of inspiration we have seen to have been the great source of metaphysical knowledge in Justin's opinion. But there was an inferior method of getting at such knowledge. For, small an amount of this divine seminal Spirit as each man has, if he disciplines himself properly he may make some progress by it toward understanding the truth and pleasing God. For the operation of this particle in man is one of immediate perception of the truth. It is the principle which produces the likeness between man and God In true Stoic fashion Justin taught that the presence of the Spermatic Logos implies μετουσία καὶ μίμησις, participation and resemblance.[2] By

[1] Ap. II. 10. 8 (49 A)
[2] Ap II 13 6 (51 D).

the presence of the sperma we have participation in the divine Source of the Logos, that is in God Himself, and are granted similar characteristics. The similar characteristics can only refer to rational potentiality, for so only in that day could any likeness between man and God have been considered possible. The sperma provides man with "natural conceptions" (φυσικὸς ἔννοιας),[1] just as the presence of the higher mind accounted to Aristotle for the innate knowledge of the axioms upon which all knowledge in his opinion was founded. Especially, Justin is convinced, is this true in the moral realm. All men know certain general principles of right and wrong, he argues,[2] because all man have this particle of the Divine Mind within them. The Father has always taught men through the Logos to do the same things as Himself.[3] This has been the way of living the Christian life before the coming of Christ. As one suppressed his lower nature, and lived according to the direction and light of this divine guide he was a follower of Christ, in a partial sense (ἀπὸ μέρους) knew Christ[4] For this reason the Christians claim as part of their system whatever has been well and rightly said at any time and under any conditions, for no one can speak the truth except in proportion to his share in the Spermatic Logos[5]

The presence of this particle implies an active not a passive apprehension. What truth the philosophers and historians have been able to discover and relate they have *found* and *reasoned* out by the instrumentality of this fragment of the Logos.[6] As Puech has well observed, Justin's language implies not mystic contemplation so much as active rational inquiry. The highest part of man is not a capacity but a force and power This agrees with Justin's calling the highest part of man a spirit of life, and is in

[1] Dial. 93. 1 (320 D)
[2] Ap. II 8 1 (46 B ff.).
[3] Ap. II 9 2 (48 A)
[4] Ap. II. 10. 8 (49 A).
[5] Ap. II. 13. 3 (51 C) ἀπὸ μέρους τοῦ σπερματικοῦ θείου λόγου.
[6] Ap II. 10. 2, 3 (48 C). Cf. Puech (Bibl. 334) p 67 n 1. and the translation of Veil which is here excellent

harmony with the best thought of the Greek world about
the highest intelligence in man Justin conceived that the
true object of knowledge was Deity. Christ, Justin says,
was the incarnation of the entire Rational Principle, while
Socrates had only a part of the Rational Principle [1] But
the activities of the part of the Rational Principle in Socrates led him to a partial knowledge of the Logos-Christ,
that is of the Rational Principle as a whole. Socrates'
knowledge was ἀπὸ μέρους, and did not embrace τὰ πάντα
τοῦ λόγου. In other words the Logos was functioning in Socrates with partial success to discover by rational investigation the entire Logos. The Rational Principle as a whole,
the Logos-Christ, in turn functions by rational investigation
to discover the Father and to reveal Him to all men. Accordingly, as all rationality is an effluence from the Father,
its activity may be described as ever back toward the
Father. The same conception Justin expressed in the introduction to the Dialogue as follows: after asserting that
a part of the βασιλικὸς νοῦς is in us, he says that as the
βασιλικὸς νοῦς sees God, so it is also possible for us by
means of our minds to comprehénd divine things [2]

It is quite evident from the nature of the particle of
the Logos in a man that it is not the seat of his personality.
The individual has a share in the divine effluence, and
receives certain intellectual abilities thereby, but the center
of personality of this indwelling part of the Logos is not
in the individual man but in the Universal Logos. Feder
has tried to minimize the connection between the Logos-
Christ and the sperma in every man, but without conviction [3] The totality of the Logos is the personal Christ,
the sperma in man is a μέρος of this personal Logos. Such
a conception is of course utterly foreign to the true signification of the terminology. To distinguish the personality
of the Spermatic Logos from the personality of the Source
was a contradiction of terms. But such contradiction of
terms had for at least decades been the Christian explanation of the divine personality of Christ, and Justin

---

[1] Ap II. 10 1, ·7, 8 (48 B—49 A). Cf below p. 240
[2] Dial 4. 2 (221 E).
[3] (Bibl. 350) p. 137

is here only passing on the tradition which he had received

The activity of the Logos or Spirit in man is particularly the object of demonic attack. Once the demons can
suppress its influence, darken its light,[1] the soul is
helplessly in their power. The soul is at once the battlefield
and prize of victory between two warring factions, the
demons and the Logos in man. Ordinarily the demons are
victorious, but occasionally the battle has gone the other
way. The victory of the Logos means a victory over the
baser elements of the soul, a raising of the moral tone of
the soul, and hence its purification and preparation for
salvation after death. Victory of the demons means the
exaggeration of the lower elements of desire in the soul,
which the demons use as their allies in the struggle,[2] and
consequently the total unfitness of the soul for future life
with God.

In a real sense the soul can turn the tide of this
struggle. Justin everywhere is positive in his assertion that
the results of the struggle are fairly to be imputed to the
blame of each individual. The Stoic determinism he in-
dignantly rejects. Unless man is himself responsible for
his ethical conduct, the entire ethical scheme of the universe
collapses, and with it the very existence of God Himself.[3]
The presence of the higher reason in the soul removes all
excuse. Men were made λογικοί καὶ θεωρητικοί,[4] and there
is in the soul of every man the ability to ally himself with
this part.

The will is thus a function of the ψυχή, of the personality. The higher intellect would of course exercise no
compulsion upon the soul. It can lead and persuade,[5] but
cannot do so against the will of the soul.[6]

Whether Justin ever actually thought of a trichotomy
or not is difficult to say. Philosophers who taught

[1] Ap. I. 10. 4—6 (58 B ff.)
[2] ibid.
[3] Ap. II. 7. 3 ff. (45 D ff.).
[4] Ap. I. 28. 3 (71 C).
[5] Ap. I. 10. 4 (58 D)
[6] For Justin's argument in favor of human freedom see below p. 226

practically the same doctrine varied in calling this rational
principle only the higher part of the soul, or a separate
and co-ordinate part of the human constitution   Justin is
not greatly interested in the question because from the
ethical point of view the decision is quite indifferent. In
either case the lower instincts of man are to be made
subject to the higher intelligence which is alone divine and
immortal of its own right and nature On the whole however
Dialogue 6 seems slightly to turn the balance in favour of
a presumption that Justin believed in a threefold division
of human nature. There, it has been seen, Justin concludes
that the soul of itself is not immortal, nor even alive. It
only lives in virtue of there having been put into it a living
Spirit, which we have concluded was to be identified
with the μέρος τοῦ σπερματικοῦ λόγου. Also careless as Justin
usually is in terminology, he never outside the introduction
to the Dialogue confuses the word ψυχή with this higher
intelligence. The indications seem to point to the fact that
he believed in a human trichotomy [1]

Whence had Justin this doctrine of the higher nature
of man, the μέρος τοῦ σπερματικοῦ λόγου? It has been seen
that though Justin is using the terminology figuratively, he
is surprisingly careful in his use of terms about the Spermatic Logos to keep the figure accurate, except in attributing
personality to the Spermatic Logos. That the σπέρμα in man
involved both μετουσία and μίμησις could not be improved
upon as a description of the Stoic doctrine The use of
this terminology is indeed usually represented as Justin's
personal elaboration of Christianity in the hope of making
Christianity attractive to Stoics.[2] But is Justin personally
borrowing direct from Stoicism? "The supposition is an
unnatural one," said Neander; "forming our estimate of
Justin especially from his own writings, we could hardly

[1] If Justin believed in trichotomy, which seems very likely,
the soul was part of the creation of man from the dust τὸ πλάσμα.
ὃ ἔπλασεν ὁ θεὸς τὸν Ἀδάμ, οἶκος ἐγένετο τοῦ ἐμφυσήματος τοῦ
παρὰ τοῦ θεοῦ. Dial 40 1 (259 A). Cf below pp 240 ff.

[2] E. g Duncker (Bibl 339) pp. 25 ff , Feder (Bibl. 350) p 137,
and Puech (Bibl. 334) pp. 71 ff., alike represent Justin as importing
Stoic terminology, but unable to adapt himself to it accurately
because of his Platonic bias

give him credit for possessing versatility of mind enough
to range so freely in a circle of ideas which had merely
been borrowed from abroad to answer a present purpose "
The judgment of Neander can only be justified by the
discovery, outside Justin, of a link which his psychology
might have had to connect it with that of the Stoics Such
a link is to be found in Philo

It has been already seen that Philo applied the adjective Spermatic to the Universal Logos with apparently the
same meaning as the word bears in Justin Philo had, while
much more elaborate, a conception very similar to that of
Justin about the presence of the Logos in the soul of man
as the organ of the soul for metaphysical knowledge When
man was made, Philo says, the thing that God formed from
the earth was the mind which was to be infused into the
body but had not yet been so infused (The body was made
by the lower powers and not directly by God) This mind
would have been a very earthly thing had God not breathed
into it δύναμιν ἀληθινῆς ζωῆς. By this act the earthly mind
became a soul intelligent and truly living [1] That is, Philo,
while retaining a dichotomy, had the same distinction as
Justin between the earthly mind and that Divine Spirit in
man whose presence furnished true intelligence and life at
the same time. Thus far Philo and Justin, with the exception of the dichotomous division, are perfectly agreed [2]
The same argument is to be found in the matter of the
metaphysical nature of this divine Life-Intelligence Power
which was breathed into the earthly mind of man That
which was inbreathed was itself the only true νοῦς in man.

[1] Philo Leg Al I 32 (I 50), somewhat abridged An elaborate analysis of this passage will be found in Hans Leisegang's
Der Heilige Geist, I 1 (Leipzig und Berlin 1919) pp 85 ff Leisegang s otherwise highly valuable treatment of Philo's doctrine of
th πνεῦμα is marred by his regarding the πνεῦμα too much as an
independent conception, while he does not pay sufficient heed to
the intricate complication between the πνεῦμα and λόγος of Philo
[2] The origin of Justin's trichotomy is ordinarily assigned to
I. Thess v 23. See Semisch (Bibl 118) II 363, Heinisch (Bibl 394)
p. 167 But caution must always be exercised in saying that any
statement of Justin comes from a definite literary source Trichotomy is also found in Josephus, and was probably widely believed
See Josephus, Ant I 1 2

The soul already possessed νοῦς, a ἡγεμονικῶν of the soul
But with the inbreathing of God there came into this νοῦς
such a spirit of intelligence as transformed it from being
unworthy to being a mighty instrument which could even
in a similar way inspire the rest of the body Philo continues his discussion by contrasting that which was breathed
into the ideal type man, and that into the human man
The ideal type man, says Philo, received the actual Spirit
of God, but the man made from matter can have not the
full Spirit but only a faint vaporous exhalation from the
Spirit like the fragrance of spices [1] The closeness of this
idea to the spermatic logos of the Stoics will be at once
recognized For the physical spermatic logos of the Stoics
was a vaporous presence in the damp, a part of a flow
of inexpressibly fine vapour which might go out from any
sense organ to constitute that sense, but which flowing into
the damp of the seminal fluid was called the spermatic
logos The cosmic spermatic logos of Philo was the gener-
ative substance of all things, generating an effluence which
is the spirit in the human man, but which is only properly
present in the Heavenly Man, the Platonic type man [2] The
similarity to Justin's thought is made more striking when
it is recalled that the Heavenly Man of Philo, which he
here says alone can receive the Logos entirely, was one of
the first Hellenistic Jewish conceptions applied to Christ
by St. Paul.[3] Similarly Philo says that the souls of more
perfect men are nourished by the entire Logos, but that
we must be content to be nourished by a part of it
(μέρει αὐτοῦ) [4] Here is the thought of a contrast of a part
of the Logos with the whole, and (from the context) the
notion of relatively large apportionments of the Logos ac-

[1] Leg Al I 42 (I 51). It will be noticed that the double
emanation of Logos from God, and of human πνεῦμα from the
Logos denied above to Justin is admitted by Philo. Justin had
no need of such a doctrine when he had rejected Philo's intermediary type man from creation For the type man is only partially to be compared to the Logos-Christ of Justin

[2] On Philo's Spermatic Logos see Karl Herzog, Grundlagen
und Grundlinien des philonischen Systems, Leipzig 1911, pp 36—40

[3] E g I Cor. xv. 45

[4] Leg Al III 176 (I. 122).

cording to the virtue of the individual Again Philo speaks of God as sowing seeds in men which cause them to bring forth the fruits of virtue "God, opening the wombs, sows good actions into them When the womb has received virtue from God it does not bring forth to God, . . . but to me, Jacob, for it was for my sake, probably, that God sowed seed in virtue, and not for His own "[1] Likewise Philo says that that which "openeth the womb of the mind, so as to enable it to comprehend the things appreciable only by the intellect, or of the speech so as to enable it to exercise the energies of voice, or of the external senses, so as to qualify them to receive the impressions which are made upon them by their appropriate objects, or of the body to fit it for its appropriate stationary conditions or motions, is the invisible σπερματικὸς καὶ τεχνικὸς θεῖος λόγος "[2] Here is a perfect jumble of Stoic figures. The Logos is itself the σπέρμα which empowers every human function, including the activity of the mind The important point for our purpose is Philo's obvious familiarity with the Stoic doctrine of the spermatic logos, the use of the technical language figuratively in connection with the Universal Logos, and the conception that the presence of this Spermatic Logos in man was an incomplete presence of the universal λόγος-πνεῦμα, which empowered the lower mind to grasp metaphysical truth (τὰς νοητάς). So Philo says that every man in virtue of his intelligence is inhabited by the Divine Logos [3]

It is clearly quite unnecessary to go beyond the supposition, which we have already seen much reason for making, of a strong Philonic tradition in Justin's Christianity, in order to account for Justin's doctrine of the Spermatic Logos, and with it for his psychology [4] It is

[1] Leg. Al. III 181 (I. 123)

[2] Quis rer div. Haer. 119 (I. 489)

[3] De Opif Mundi 146 (I 35) πᾶς ἄνθρωπος κατὰ μὲν τὴν διάνοιαν ᾠκείωται λόγῳ θείῳ, τῆς μακαρίας φύσεως ἐκμαγεῖον ἢ ἀπόσπασμα ἢ ἀπαύγασμα γεγονώς. A statement of Philo's views on this point will be found in modern philosophical terminology in Karl Herzog, op, cit., pp 85 ff

[4] Friedländer has unsuccessfully tried to connect Justin's fragment of the Logos in the heathen with the early Jewish saying

probably an early form of the same tradition in Christianity which was expressed in the words, "In him was life,
and the life was the light of men, . . That was the light
which lighteth every man which cometh into the world."[1]
The entire conception is only difficult for us because of our
instinctive connotation of kernel or grain with the word
seed. Once it is understood that Justin's generation thought
of the seminal, germinal force in a seed as being a spiritual
gaseous presence, it is easy to see how Justin's few remarks
about the Spermatic Logos might not be going beyond a
very popular comprehension of his subject.

At death the body was cut off from the soul, while the
soul, still retaining the spirit, continued to live Justin finds
proof of the survival of the soul after the death of the body
in necromancy, divinations upon children of abortive birth,
spiritualistic evoking of the departed, the power of magicians through their familiar spirit, mad men and de-
moniacs (who were possessed by souls of wicked dead man),
and the oracles, as well as in the literary testimony of
Empedocles, Pythagoras, Plato, Socrates, the pit of Homer,[2] and the descent of Odysseus.[3] But the few remarks
which Justin makes in passing concerning the state of existence of souls after death are so contradictory as to make
certainty about his beliefs impossible. For example he says
that after death the souls of all men are ἐν αἰσθήσει,[4]
but in another passage that the souls of the blessed live
ἐν ἀπαθείᾳ καὶ ἀφθαρσίᾳ καὶ ἀλυπίᾳ καὶ ἀθανασίᾳ.[5] The two
passages may be reconciled perhaps on the basis of a contrast between the life of the wicked and good souls after
death, but the first statement is clearly intended as applying
to all souls. All dead men go to Hades, we may infer from
the statement of Justin that God did not allow Christ to
remain in Hades like an ordinary man.[6] But Hades itself

that the Hebrews had the entire word of God, while the Gentiles
had only half. Cf (Bibl 222) p 88, 143 Anm 1

[1] John 1 4, 9
[2] Odys xi 25
[3] Ap I 18 2—5 (65 A B).
[4] Ap I 18 3 (65 A)
[5] Dial 45 4 (264 B).
[6] Dial 99 3 (326 C)

seems to have been divided. For Justin says (in the person
of the Old Man) that at death the souls of the good in a
better place, the souls of the wicked in a worse place,
await the coming judgment.[1] But they are there not cut
off from human and demonic annoyance The souls of the
wicked apparently join the demonic host at once upon
death It is they whose presence in human beings causes
demonic possession.[2] But even though in a better place
in Hades, the souls of virtuous men are also in great danger
of demonic captivation. For in one passage Christ is represented as praying that His soul, after His death, may not
fall under the power of necromancers or evil angels of any
kind, and Justin gives the slavery of the ghost or soul of
Samuel to the Witch of Endor as an example of the danger
even the best of men encounter after death.[3] Christians
may be spared this ignominy by praying like Christ for
special deliverance; but since Samuel, one of the Old Testament saints who are to be saved, suffered such an indignity,
his condition may be taken as typical of the state possible
for all souls awaiting the resurrection. Justin denies as a
terrible heresy the belief that at death souls return at once
to God. To be Christians men must believe in a resurrection
from the dead which all souls await.[4] But Justin is
insistent that all souls survive death; the good souls live
eternally, the bad souls so long as God wishes them to
exist and be punished.[5] Justin did not explain this statement, but it is intelligible in terms of the psychology Justin
elsewhere elucidates. When the wicked soul is sufficiently
punished the πνεῦμα is withdrawn, and thereupon the soul
at once ceases to exist. But Justin also says, and more

[1] Dial 5 3 (223 B) Feder thinks that this means
that the division of souls for heaven and hell takes place
at death But he is certainly wrong. Justin's language does
not in the least suggest heaven. See (Bibl 350) p 247
n 5.

[2] Ap I. 18 3 (65 A)

[3] Dial. 105 3 ff (333 A, B), cf. Ap. I. 18. 3 (65 A).

[4] Dial. 80. 4 (307 A).

[5] Dial. 5. 3 (223 B): cf 88. 5 (316 A) where Justin says that
punishment is alloted to each sinner according to the discretion
of God

usually thought, that the punishment of hell is eternal.[1]
Justin's views about the Resurrection and Judgment will be
discussed under his Eschatology.

C. SIN

It has been stated that Justin believed in man's moral
freedom, as well as in moral freedom for the angels. He
would have nothing to do with predestination, and
stops in his argument repeatedly to explain away any
such implication which might appear in Scriptural passages he is quoting. There is, Justin believed, a sort of
physical necessity which is about us. We are begotten
without our knowledge or consent and brought up into bad
habits by wicked training. As such we may be called the
children of necessity. But we all have an opportunity to
become children of choice if we accept the new birth of
baptism.[2] 'In other words, we are brought up in a world
where the environment prompts a normal choice of sin
But every man is born intelligent and capable of making
the choice for good for himself, and hence he alone is
responsible if he refuses to choose properly.[3] Justin adduces
Scriptural proof of human liberty, and even asserts
that the famous Platonic dictum, "The blame is his who
chooses, but God is blameless," was taken by Plato directly
from Moses.[4] In almost the same words Justin says in the
Dialogue that neither men nor angels have ever been made
wicked by God's fault, but each man by his own fault is
whatever he shall appear to be.[5] God's foreknowledge
of future events which makes prophecy possible does not
imply predetermination.[6] Similarly in God's providential
care and rulership in the world Justin says that there has

[1] Ap. I 8. 4 (57 B); 18. 2 (65 A); Ap. II. 1 2 (41 C); Dial
130 2 (359 D), cf. below p. 287.
[2] Ap. I. 61. 10 (94 C).
[3] Ap. I. 28 3 (71 C). See above pp. 219
[4] Ap I. 44 1—8 (81 B—E); cf. Plato, Republic, X 617 e
[5] Dial. 140, 4 (370 A). οὐκ αἰτίᾳ τοῦ θεοῦ οἱ προγινωσκόμενοι
καὶ γενησόμενοι ἄδικοι, εἴτε ἄγγελοι εἴτε ἄνθρωποι, γίνονται φαῦλοι
ἀλλὰ τῇ ἑαυτῶν ἕκαστος αἰτίᾳ τοιοῦτοί εἰσιν, ὁποῖος ἕκαστος
φανήσεται.
[6] Dial. 141 2 (370 C).

never been any real encroachment of the moral freedom of man. God would warn Mary and Joseph of the coming massacre of the innocents and bid them fly to Egypt, but He would not prevent Herod's committing the crime by killing him. This would be using compulsion on human beings, and compulsion God does not see fit to exercise.[1] He says that those who are prepared aforetime and repent and are baptised, will be saved,[2] but here repentance can be taken as defining the nature of the preparation for baptism which Justin had in mind, so that the statement in no way implies determinism Similarly Justin speaks of Christians as being called through Christ to the salvation prepared beforehand by the Father,[3] but the echo of Pauline phraseology cannot be pressed against Justin's frequent and sweeping statements of the freedom of moral choice which all men possess. For Justin states the issue fairly. Without free choice for all men there is no reason for thinking of the universe as moral in any sense, and the meaning of God as ruler of the world, if not His personal existence itself, is completely lost [4]

But with man equipped with knowledge of what is right and wrong, and with complete freedom to choose, why does the vast majority of humanity choose the wrong ? Justin answers this question by appealing not to a racial taint of sin from the first man, but to the activity of the demons The sin of Adam is typical of our sin; the sins of our ancestors result in an evil atmosphere into which we must he born, a constant evil influence in which we must grow up,[5] but there is no inherited guilt, and no racial depravity aside from the totality of individual offences. "Behold ye die like men and fall like one of the princes," means according to Justin that we all die like Adam and Eve (that is like men) and fall like the Serpent, who as one of the princes fell with a great fall because he deceived Eve Each man might have become free from suffering

---

[1] Dial. 102. 2 — 4 (328 D, 329 A)
[2] Dial 138 3 (368 A).
[3] Dial 131. 2 (360 C), cf Romans ix. 23
[4] Ap II. 7. 9 (46 B)
[5] Ap. I 61 10 (94 C).

and death like God if he had kept God's commandments,
but instead of doing so each man wrought his own death
for himself. As every man, then, has power like Adam and
Eve to become a god, and a son of the Highest, so shall
each man by himself be judged and condemned.[1] Justin
speaks of an analogy between Mary and Eve. The activity
of the Serpent began with Eve. Eve conceived from the
logos of the Serpent and brought forth disobedience and
death. Mary conceived from the Logos of God, and
brought forth a Son by whom God destroys the serpent
and the angels and men who are like him, but saves from
death those who repented their wickedness and believe
upon Him.[2] The analogy is not worked out in detail. As
it stands the passage might be harmonized with a doctrine
that subsequent generations after Eve were in bondage to
disobedience and death because of her act, but it can as
well be interpreted as referring to a succession of sinners
who followed Eve's example. Such we gather from other
passages was Justin's belief. The human race has fallen
under the power of death and the guile of the Serpent
from the time of Adam (not from the offence of Adam),
and each member of the race has committed personal
transgression. Men and angels alike are free to make their
own decision on the important question.[3] That is, the
activity of the Serpent began with Adam and has continued
ever since that time.

For our sins are not due to an inherited guilt, but to
the fact that, hampered by the bad environment and influences in which we form our habits, and by the fact that
the demons from Satan down are busy in unceasing activity
to try to mislead us, the little divine element in us is
hopelessly overpowered, and we of our own wish consent
to follow the demons into disobedience. The only inherited
tendency to sin in man seems to have been τὴν ἐν ἑκάστῳ κακὴν
πρὸς πάντα καὶ ποικίλην φύσει ἐπιθυμίαν, "the naturally wicked

[1] Dial. 124. 3 (353 D ff.).
[2] Dial. 100. 5, 6 (327 C).
[3] Dial. 88. 4, 5 (316 A). On translating ἀπὸ τοῦ 'Αδάμ,
"from the time of Adam", cf. Dial. 92. 2 (319 C) ἀπὸ 'Αβραὰμ
μέχρι Μωϋσέως . . . . . ἀπὸ Μωυσέως and Mattes' (Bibl. 306) exhaustive
analysis of the passages

lust in every man which draws variously to all manner (of vice) "[1] But this ἐπιθυμία in man Justin must have regarded as one of the parts of the soul from creation, and cannot be taken as an inheritance of guilt from Adam.

Weber's description of the doctrine of universal depravity in the Talmudic literature precisely corresponds to Justin's belief. The Jews, according to Weber traditionally held that the fall of Adam brought death upon the race, put men under the influence of Satan, and made God more remote But free will remained so that there is no idea of Sin as a universal necessity. There is no inherited sinfulness which has any actuality apart from the commission of acts of sin [2] Philo retained the doctrine of free will as a popular explanation of the origin of human sin, but said that in reality the human mind could produce nothing on its own initiative, and that ultimately all action was of God It is only to the uninitiated that one can speak of free choice.[3] Drummond admits himself at a loss to reconcile the various statements of Philo about free will,[4] but the explanation is not difficult Philo accepts the Jewish doctrine of free will as well enough for practical purposes, and often speaks as though the popular doctrine were correct But those initiated, that is those who can rise from the simple Jewish traditions to a philosophic point of view, may see a deeper truth underlying free will We cannot agree then with the statements of von Engelhardt[5] and Windisch[6] that because Justin's doctrine of free will is not to be traced to any Old Testament or New Testament

[1] Ap. I 10 6 (58 D) ποικίλη seems to have been a familiar Cynic description of the evil nature of lust and pleasure The word is thus used also in Philo, Leg Al II 74, 75 (I 79), and Justin probably had it from his Hellenistic Judaistic tradition See Heinemann's note 2 in loco to his translation of the Leg Al (Breslau 1919, p 75, n 2)

[2] Weber, Judische Theologie, 224, 239 ff

[3] Drummond has collected the Philonic testimonies to the doctrine of free will, I 346—350, though he has not quite correctly interpreted them

[4] Drummond, Philo, II 347 note

[5] (Bibl 313) p 160

[6] (Bibl 333) p 14

statements, it must therefore have been taken direct from Greek philosophy. For whether Justin's tradition came directly from Palestinian Judaism, or indirectly through Hellenistic Judaism, his doctrine of free will as the explanation of human sin is exactly the doctrine common to popular adherents of both sects of Judaism

Windisch has further misrepresented Justin in arguing that a choice between good and evil, a knowledge of good and evil, such as Justin teaches, implies an objective good and an objective evil from which man may choose.[1] Justin would not have accepted these implications of his statements. He did not believe in an objective evil. Indeed, positive evil would in Justin's mind have been a contradiction in terms. Knowledge of good and evil is knowledge of the good, and knowledge that it is evil to depart from the good. Practically the heaped up sins of generations appear to represent an objective, positive evil which man may choose in preference to the good. But this evil is not an ontological antithesis to the good. Why the demons should have chosen to rebel against God Justin does not explain But once they rebelled and made themselves into an army of renegades determined to defeat the purposes of God in man, their evil influence was the positive evil with which man was called upon to do battle God is accordingly free from all responsibility in the origin of sin. He has made only the good The necessity of attributing freedom of choice to the angels becomes apparent, for only by their having been free of choice could they have changed themselves, without any shadow of responsibility on God's part, from angels to demons, from the helpers to the cosmic enemies of God Granted the existence of the evil demons, which was to Justin's mind as patent a fact as sunshine, they must either be the followers of an evil principle in ontological opposition to God (as the Manichaeans taught); or have been the evil creation of the good God, which is unthinkable; or have made themselves evil. Justin accepts

[1] (Bibl 333) p. 14 "Die Wahlfreiheit hatte zwei Objekte zu ihrem Gebrauch: Gut und Böse. Das Böse ist das eine Glied eines kontrár-gegensatzlichen Begriffspaares." Windisch has here the reasoning of von Engelhardt (loc cit) in mind

this last proposition, not because he had any adequate explanation of the fall of the angels, but because if the angels had made themselves evil he could defend the character of God without necessitating ontological dualism between good and evil. Man is a sinner because he allows the demons to lead him into rebellion against the Law of God which every man has within him as part of his divine equipment for life.[1] He is in need of salvation, for his rebellion has made him like the demons, and worthy to share their condemnation. But it is a race sinfulness made up of the sins of individual men, rather than a race corruption inherited from a fallen first parent, which, Justin thinks, Christ came into the world to counteract.

It must then be noticed that Justin has no trace of a horror of sin as sin. His conversion was not in the least prompted by a "conviction of sin", and the sin-sickness of the seventh chapter of Romans has no echo in his writings. Sin is an act of rebellion against God, not a state of corruption. Sin must result in damnation, and without a doctrine of future rewards and punishments morality has no meaning. So, as we shall see, Justin looks for a salvation which will remove the penalty of sin and ensure escape from hell. But in his regarding human sin from the point of view of the activity of the demons, if he departs from the Pauline conception it is not to become more philosophical, but more primitively Christian in the sense of being more in accord with the notions of popular Judaism. The point has been clearly demonstrated by Dr Conybeare [2] In the Synoptics, and even in the Fourth Gospel,[3] the origin of sin is the fault of demons who enter into a man and prompt him to sin, while the conception of redemption in the Synoptics, especially, is exclusively expressed in terms of exorcism. Similarly the struggle with demons is the outstanding characteristic of Justin's scheme of salvation

[1] Dial 141. 1 (370 B).
[2] (Bibl 328) see especially p 582
[3] Cf the instance of Judas in John xiii 2

CHAPTER VIII

CHRIST

Justin Martyr lived in an age which was marked at once by the decadence and yet the transitional character of its thinking. The magnificent attempt of the classic philosophers to read the mystery of life by the sheer power of their own rational efforts had patently failed. Philosophers were arguing against philosophers, while each compounded his own theory of the universe by an eclectic harmonizing from the same few great sources of philosophic lore. The spectacle was regarded as a confession of failure by those outside the professional philosophic ring, and was secretly so interpreted by the philosophers themselves. For all schools of thinking and all classes of men admitted that the human constitution, in its normal condition, has no faculty which is sufficient in itself to guide men to the truth, or to bring them to that salvation which, under various explanations, all classes of men were seeking. The philosophers still looked upon the human mind as a divine thing, and glorified the rational processes of man as the manifest presence of Deity in the soul. But all schools put their main hope of being truly reasonable not so much in their own efforts and practice in reasoning as in the expansion of this reasoning faculty by a larger and ever larger indwelling of the divine νοῦς or λόγος. They found their peace of mind in dwelling not upon the powers of man as man, but upon the privileges of man as a part of God. The solution of their difficulties they found in a mystical union of self with the Universal Mind if they were of the Platonic tradition, or in a mystical sense of conformity to the decrees of Fate or the Universal Law if they were of the Stoic tradition.

The unphilosophic world similarly was seeking salvation from itself. The salvation it sought was only a popularization of the salvation for which the philosophers strove By magic and mystery, rites and initiation, the man of the street sought likewise a sense of union with the divine, and an assurance that death would not mark the end of his existence But however they explained it, both philosophical and unphilosophical men looked to a revelation, to an act of God, for their salvation They could not save themselves, only as the God would come and dwell in them and enlighten them, could they hope to know adequately or follow the Way In Plato's time it had been sufficient to declare that all men knew the right and wrong, and that each man chose for himself, while God was blameless. But that was not sufficient theodicy in Justin's day. The God whom the people of his generation demanded was one who did something for men besides leaving them to make their own choice He must be a God who would help when men cried for assistance against the cruel odds all must face who wish to live according to their higher light. The Jews in the Dispersion who had the Law but could not keep it had long been in this position, and had long been as one of the many cults who were seeking in all possible ways for the God who could diplace their weakness with His strength

In this quest Christianity was not the first cult to shout Eureka, but it shouted it with a sustained conviction which eventually made it victor over all its rivals. It shouted it, most importantly, from crosses and in the arena, before judges and in the faces of executioners. The ancient world was amazed at such conviction, perceived that these despised people had the supernormal spiritual inspiration and enlargement of power which all were seeking, and, in spite of the predjudices which shut Christianity off from respectability, became Christian

And so while Justin's age was one of decadence, it was also one of transition In the philosophic world the breakdown of intellectual courage produced Neo-Platonism In the popular world it resulted in the wide-spread acceptance of Christianity. The bitter enemity between the two which at first characterized their relations gave away inevitably before a recognition of their similarity of purpose, and led to their ultimate amalgamation. Christians shouted their Eureka not only because in the Person of Jesus Christ they found their ideal, but because from that Person they believed that they were receiving the spiritual illumination, power, and peace which their souls were craving.

Justin's Christianity was precisely of this sort. Reason had been to him of no avail, the innate apprehensions of ethical truth had not been sufficient. He turned to a revelation, begun in the Prophets, culminating in Jesus Christ, which showed him the way. Christianity said, and Justin believed, that the Universal Reason, the beneficent Spirit, which men were everywhere seeking, had at last been made available to men by having become incarnate in the person of Jesus Christ. In Mary's womb the Mediator and. Messenger of God, the Cosmic Reason, had become a human Being.

The divine human Person in whom Justin found his salvation was in his eyes also the Jewish Messiah Extended as are Justin's demonstrations of how Christ fulfilled Old Testament prophecy, they do not lead one to believe that Justin associated a proportionate importance with the conception of Jesus' Messianic character. As an apologetic argument, to prove the antiquity of the Christian faith and the essential unity between revelation such as was given to the Jews and revelation in Christ, the Messianic character of Jesus was of the greatest significance. It gave probability and background for the Christian worship But as to the significance of the Messianic character of Jesus for Gentiles, Justin has little to say. The contrast between Christianity and Judaism was in Justin's mind complete. It is the Son of God, the incarnate Logos, the Personality revealing the will and dispensing the mercy of God which attracts Justin's personal worship.

Justin practically ignores the problem of the purpose of the Incarnation as such He has only one passage in which he comes near to speculating upon it. The conception of the Son of God by the Virgin Mary Justin contrasts with the conception of disobedience and death by the virgin Eve after her intercourse (συλλαβοῦσα) with the logos of the Serpent.[1] But the passage appears to be only a literary figure suggested by the two virgins, both impregnated by a logos, rather than a complete antithesis between the fruits of the two We have seen that no true doctrine of original sin is here implied,[2] nor is there any indication of a Pauline conviction of a racial significance in the Incarnation

Justin's story of the Incarnation follows the narrative of Luke very closely, but with one important variation Justin knew nothing of the mediation of the Holy Spirit in the impregnating of Mary His tradition was the same as that which has come down to us. He says that the δύναμις of God, coming upon the Virgin, overwhelmed her and caused her while yet a virgin to conceive. Here is no mention of the Holy Spirit, but Justin introduces the Holy Spirit into the annunciation at a place where our text has no such reading, "Behold thou shalt conceive of the Holy Spirit, and shalt bear a Son " Whether Justin had a different reading, or whether he is not recalling from memory all the details in the right order, is a matter of no importance for us here, because in either case it is clear that both Holy Spirit and the δύναμις θεοῦ were included in Justin's tradition, and that the two were, as in Luke, identical But in spite of his tradition Justin did not understand the significance of the words, at least as they were later interpreted, and said that this δύναμις θεοῦ, or πνεῦμα ἅγιον was none other than the Logos.[3] Justin of course thought of the Logos as a δύναμις θεοῦ.[4] as well as a Holy Spirit [5] We

[1] Dial 100. 5 (327 C)

[2] See above p. 228

[3] Ap I. 33 6 (75 C). τὸ πνεῦμα οὖν καὶ τὴν δύναμιν τὴν παρὰ τοῦ θεοῦ οὐδὲν ἄλλο νοῆσαι θέμις ἢ τὸν λόγον, ὃς καὶ πρωτότοκος τῷ θεῷ ἐστί, ὡς Μωϋσῆς ὁ προδεδηλωμένος προφήτης ἐμήνυσε. See above p. 181.

[4] Cf. Ap I 23 2 (68 C), 32 10 (74 B), 60.5 (93 B), Ap II 10 8 (49 A); Dial 105 1 (332 C)

[5] See Semisch (Bibl. 118) II. 310. This is the only passage where the Logos is called a Spirit, but we have seen how the Logos, from the figure of the Spermatic Logos, was probably conceived of by Justin as a spiritual effluence from God See above pp 161 ff

have seen no grounds for concluding that Justin identified the Holy Spirit and the Logos personally, but that it is very possible that he had no clear notion of either their metaphysical or functional distinction. He at least had not sufficiently clear a notion of the Holy Spirit to suppose that He could introduce the Logos into the womb of Mary. Such a function on the part of the Holy Spirit would have implied a parental relation and hence a superiority of the Spirit over the Logos. Justin did not wish to be obliged to reconcile such a contradiction with his usual doctrine that the Spirit was subordinate to the Logos, so he cut the knot by representing the Spirit and δύναμις θεοῦ of this passage as only other names for the Logos.

But this explanation of the traditional account of the Incarnation was not the only one Justin suggests. For in two passages, one in the First Apology and the other in the Dialogue, Justin suggests that the δύναμις was a δύναμις τοῦ λόγου. The statement in the Apology is that "through the agency of the δύναμις of the Logos He was born of a Virgin as man in accordance with the will of God who is Father and Ruler of all things,"[1] which is explained in the statement in the Dialogue that "Christ has come according to the δύναμις of the omnipotent Father which was given to Him."[2] The δύναμις of the Logos mentioned as the agent of incarnation in the Apology was thus something given to the Logos. It has been suggested that Justin meant by this δύναμις a personal Power, the Holy Spirit,[3] but it is much more likely that Justin meant here only that God endowed the Logos with power to become incarnate. A glance at Justin's manner of speaking makes this clear. In one passage Justin says that Christ, as a δύναμις of God, had done by His own δύναμις what Plato had declared to be most difficult for men; Christ had found the Father of all and declared Him to men, ... for He is a

---

[1] Ap. I 46. 5 (83 D, E). διὰ δυνάμεως τοῦ λόγου κατὰ τὴν τοῦ πατρὸς πάντων καὶ δεσπότου θεοῦ βουλὴν διὰ παρθένου ἄνθρωπος ἀπεκυήθη.

[2] Dial. 139. 4 (369 A). ὁ Χριστὸς κατὰ τὴν τοῦ παντοκράτορος πατρὸς δύναμιν δοθεῖσαν αὐτῷ παρεγένετο.

[3] By Trollope, Dial. in loco.

power of the ineffable Father.[1] Justin means that the Logos, as a δύναμις of God, had God as His natural object of knowledge, but that this knowledge did not come to the Logos in passivity by a mystical impartation, but by the exercise of His own faculties or powers. That is, the δύναμις of the Logos means here a faculty or ability of the Logos, not a personal Power. In this same sense Christ is said by Justin to have possessed a mystic power of God, by which He could overcome the demons[2] Here again the power is definitely an ability given Christ by God. . Justin's object in thus speaking of a power of the Logos is easily explained, for it is only a part of Justin's device for impressing upon his readers the subordination of the Son to the Father. The ability or faculty by which the Logos could vanquish the demons, or even could Himself know God, was nothing of Christ's own, but had been imparted to Christ by the Father to whom Christ "referred all things."[3] The power thus given was still the Father's, for Christ made no boast of ever having done anything of His own will and strength,[4] but it was not a personal Power, but only power which Christ had from the Father. It will thus be apparent that in declaring that Christ became incarnate διὰ δυνάμεως θεοῦ or τοῦ λόγου, Justin means in each case that God empowered the Logos to enter into the womb of Mary. There is not the least implication of a mediating personality in the Incarnation. The Logos, of His own God-given power, entered into the womb of Mary.[5]

---

[1] Ap. II. 10. 6—8 (48 E, 49 A).

[2] Dial. 49. 8 (269 C); 30. 3 (248 D).

[3] Dial. 98. 1 ff. (324 D ff.).

[4] Dial 101. 1 (328 A).

[5] The traditional character of the conception that Christ was completely subject to the Father, and received commandments and ability to execute the commandments from the Father, is demonstrated by the similarity between an element of Justin's theory of the Resurrection of Christ and a statement in the Fourth Gospel Justin says that on the third day after the Crucifixion Christ rose from the dead, ὁ ἀπὸ τοῦ πατρὸς αὐτοῦ λαβὼν ἔχει, Dial. 100. 1 (326 D). The Fourth Gospel says: ἐξουσίαν ἔχω θεῖναι αὐτήν (sc. τὴν ψυχήν μου), καὶ ἐξουσίαν ἔχω πάλιν λαβεῖν αὐτήν. ταύτην τὴν ἐντολὴν ἔλαβον παρὰ τοῦ πατρός μου. John x. 18, cf Mat. xi. 27

Justin has no explanation of the way in which the
Logos acted upon Mary.[1] He is content with the Lukan
figure by which the Logos ἐπισκίασεν Mary, overwhelmed
or overpowered her by His divine brilliance. Such a
dazzling approach of Deity, we learn from the Gnostic
tradition, was in itself normally attended by divine impregnation according to the thought of the time,[2] and Justin adds
no refinement to this explanation. A virgin birth was the
process of incarnation chosen because this process did not
involve the sin of intercourse.[3]

The Incarnation was however in a sense a process of
creation. The Incarnation was an operation of the power
and will of the Creator of all things, in the same way as
Eve was made from one of Adam's ribs, and as all -living
beings were created in the beginning by means of a logos
of God.[4] It is in this sense that the fragment of Justin
in Irenaeus must be understood, "unigenitus filius venit ad
nos suum plasma in semet ipso recapitulans."[5] But the
assertion of so remarkable a phenomenon needed evidence
and defence. Justin considered that he had sufficiently
proved his case when he first removed its antecedent improbability by comparing the Christian story with the
myths of divine-human intercourse and children in the
Greek legends. He insists that the Virgin Birth of Christ is
no more incredible than the stories of the birth of Per-
seus,[6] Dionysus,[7] or Hercules,[8] though these myths are
only crass demonic imitations of the truth, because they
represent the deity as having intercourse with human wo-

[1] As Eusebius did later for example when he compared the
impregnation of Mary with Prophetic inspiration. See Leisegang,
Pneuma Hagion   Leipzig 1922. p. 41.

[2] Cf. Iren Adv. Staer. I. iv 5.

[3] Dial. 23. 2 (241 B); cf. Semisch's note on the passage,
(Bibl. 118) II 406 n. 2   The mss reading has been much disputed here. Cf. Otto, n. 8, in loco See also Ap. I. 21 1 (66 E);
33 4 (75 A)

[4] Dial. 84. 2 (310 B). Cf. above pp. 163, 228.

[5] Iren. c Haer. IV. 6. 2

[6] Ap. I. 22. 5 (68 B); Dial. 70 5 (297 B).

[7] Dial. 69 2 (294 D)

[8] Dial 69 3 (295 A).

men.[1] Having removed the antecedent improbability, Justin seeks to establish an antecedent probability by proving that the Virgin Birth was long ago foretold by the Prophets. He adduces Is. vii. 14, "Behold a Virgin shall conceive", and against all the opposition of Trypho maintains his contention that the words refer to the birth of Christ.[2] The "Stone cut without hands" indicated the divine nature of His birth;[3] Christ's blood was made by God not man, as typified by the blood of the grape[4] Actual contribution of evidence to the Virgin Birth Justin does not make. In only one point does he improve upon the accounts of Luke and Matthew. He traces the Davidic line of Christ not through Joseph but Mary.[5] Indeed Justin's own belief in the Virgin birth has not the ring of conviction which he manifests on other points. He accepts the doctrine, but does not care to rest his whole case upon it. In both the First Apology[6] and the Dialogue[7] he admits that the Virgin Birth is not an essential part of the Christian Faith, and says that the divine nature of Christ can be proved quite independently of the story of His birth

By the divine impregnation of the Virgin Mary, then, a God-Man came into being. Justin insists upon the fact that the Person thus born was both divine and human. Christ, a crucified man, was the first born of the unbegotten God, who shall Himself be appointed judge of all men;[8] He was given the second place after God[9] Most of the statements about the relation of the Logos to the

[1] Ap. I. 21 2 (67 C); 25. 2 (69 B); Dial. 67. 2 (291 B)
[2] Ap. I 33 1 (74 E); Dial 67 1 (291 A); 71 3 (297 C), 84 1 (310 A)
[3] Dan. ii. 34. Dial. 76 1 (301 B) et passim.
[4] Gen. xlix. 11. Dial 76. 2 (301 B) et passim.
[5] Dial 43 1 (261 C), 45 4 (264 A), 100 2, 3 (326 D, 327 A); 120 2 (348 B)
[6] Ap. I, 22. 1 (67 E)
[7] Dial 48. 2, 3 (267 B—D)
[8] Ap. I 53. 2 (88 A).
[9] Ap I. 13. 4 (61 A). The apparent adoptionism of this phraseology must not be understood of the incarnate Christ It has been shown that Justin regarded the Logos emanation as singled out by God for peculiar dignity among the other emanations See above p 158

Father already discussed are made by Justin to describe
the Christ. They apply as fully to the incarnate Christ as
to the pre-incarnate Logos.[1] Indeed it is Justin's great
argument that whereas in man there is only a part of the
Spermatic Logos, Christ is the Entire Logos. Justin states
his doctrine as follows: "It thus appears that our doctrines
are more exalted than all human lore, for Reason in its
entirety (that is Christ who appeared for our sake) became
both body, and reason, and soul. For whatever the philosophers or lawgivers have ever uttered or discovered well,
they have worked it out by discovery and dialectic by
virtue of a part of the Logos (sc. with which they were
endowed). But since they did not understand all about
the Logos (who is Christ) they likewise contradicted themselves frequently . . . Christ was the Logos who was and
is in every man; as such He was partly known by Socrates,
and He foretold future events, speaking both through the
Prophets and in His own person when He became of like
passions (sc. as ourselves) and taught these doctrines."[2]
The significance of the latter part of this passage for anthropology has already been discussed. Here it is only necessary to notice two points First the incarnate Christ is
here completely identified with the entire Logos. Second
the entire Logos, Justin says, became body, logos, and soul
There is no idea in Justin's mind that the Logos simply
assumed a body, or that He took on humanity. In the
incarnation the Logos became a man in all three respects,
body, soul, and logos or spirit. We have seen grounds,
entirely aside from this statement, for thinking that Justin
regarded man as composed of three parts, body, soul, and
the third part which Justin called indifferently a fragment
of the Logos or the Living Spirit. Here, in this statement
about the incarnation, Justin shows at once that to him
"body, soul, and logos or spirit,"[3] was a formula inter-

[1] Cf. e. g Dial. 100. 4 (327 B); 125. 3 (354 C); 93 2 (321 A)
[2] Ap. II. 10 In the last sentence the clauses have been
slightly rearranged.
[3] The fact that Justin mentions these three in an order to
which we are not accustomed, body, logos, and soul, cannot cause
any real difficulty as to their meaning

changeable for the total constitution of man, and at the same time that he believed that the Logos of God became entirely a man Christ was, as body, soul, and spirit, the Logos become man. He was not man in body, or in body and soul, and divine in a higher part of His nature, He was not human in body and soul, but possessing the entire Logos in place of the usual fragment of the Logos; He was man entirely inasmuch as He was a being made up of body, soul, and spirit, but He was the Logos entirely inasmuch as this body, soul, and spirit was what the Logos Himself in His entirety had become

Justin's use of the tripartite formula for the human constitution of Christ has often suggested comparison with Apollinaris' teachings. There is however a great difference between them Apollinaris was working on the problem of the relation of human and divine natures, and in the end denied any reality to the human nature Apollinaris' real difficulty was the standing of the flesh of Christ. If it was human, there could be no salvation through it. Apollinaris answered in brief that as flesh of God, the flesh of Christ was not ὁμοούσιος ἡμῖν [1] Apollinaris' error was that he sacrificed the humanity of Christ to secure a consistent divinity The "soul" which he in later life admitted to be a part of a human constitution would, in the case of Christ, like the flesh of Christ, be θεός, as a ψυχὴ θεοῦ. [2] That is, Apollinaris is thinking in terms of the ἐνσάρκωσις τοῦ λόγου, while Justin is thinking in terms of the Logos as having become a man Justin resembled Apollinaris in teaching a trichotomous division of the human constitution, but was utterly unlike him in his approach to a doctrine of Incarnation, and in

---

[1] Fragm 161 (ed Lietzmann p. 254). Apollinaris says that this is too downright a statement of his position, but that there is little to be said against it He preferred to consider the flesh of Christ as ὁμοίωμα rather than ὁμοουσία. When Apollinaris would say that ὁ κύριος Ἰησοῦς Χριστὸς . . . . . καὶ μετὰ τῆς σαρκὸς ὁμοούσιος τῷ μόνῳ θεῷ (Fragm 153, ed Lietzmann p 248), he had indeed little ground for objecting to the doctrine that the flesh of Christ was not ὁμοούσιος ἡμῖν.

[2] Paraphrasing Fragm. 153 (ed Lietzmann p 248)

his application of trichotomy to Christology. So Justin says that "Jesus Christ is the Son and Messenger of God, who formerly, being the Logos, appeared at one time in the form of fire, and in another in the likeness of bodies; now, by the will of God He has become man for the sake of the human race."[1] That is, Jesus Christ is at once the Logos of God who used to appear in theophanies, and that same Logos become a man.

. The Christ was truly a man. He became ἄνθρωπος ἐν ἀνθρώποις[2] not ἄνθρωπος ἐξ ἀνθρώπων.[3] His blood was not from the human race but from the power of God. Humanity had no more to do with the making of the blood of Christ than with making the blood of the grape.[4] He is no human product, no ἀνθρώπινον ἔργον.[5] These statements together with Justin's declaration that Christ was not of human seed, are all made to prove that He was born of a Virgin. But they go much further than they need to go for such a purpose, since they deny to Christ all relationships with the human race, and their implication is not softened by admitting any contribution which the Virgin made to the formation of the God-Man. The process of man-becoming took place in the womb of the Virgin, but His blood was not made from Mary's blood, His flesh was not her flesh. The Virgin was an instrument in the process. Christ was made flesh διὰ τῆς ἀπὸ γένους αὐτῶν παρθένου, and as such He claimed to be descended from Adam, whence He received the title "Son of Man."[6] But Justin insists that the title "Son of Man" should more properly take the form "*Like* the Son of Man", which indicates truly that he was a man, but not with human connections.[7] Christ was a new creation, like the first creation of old, made directly by God.[8] Thus the Logos

[1] Ap. I. 63. 10 (96 A). Reading a comma after πρότερον. Cf. Donaldson (Bibl. 143) p. 233.
[2] Ap. I. 23 3 (68 C)
[3] Dial 76. 2 (301 B); 54 2 (274 A).
[4] Dial 54 2 (274 A).
[5] Dial. 76. 1 (301 B).
[6] Dial. 100. 3 (327 A).
[7] Dial. 76. 1 (301 A).
[8] Dial. 84. 2 (310 B) see above p. 238.

did not assume humanity, but became a human being. He was a man like men, but He had no real blood relationships with the human race

But the humanity of Christ, though unique and not received from other men, was truly humanity.[1] Justin repeats with emphasis the fact that the coming of Christ, at least in the first advent, was παθητὸς καὶ ἄδοξος καὶ ἄτιμος καὶ σταυρούμενος.[2] He had become a man truly capable of suffering.[3] Justin is found of using the adjective ὁμοιοπαθής to show Christ's complete similarity with other men in His humanity.[4] He truly had flesh and blood.[5] He grew from true infancy [6] to manhood by normal steps; He ate normal food [7] Justin explicitly contradicts a docetic view of the sufferings of Christ when he says that in the Garden of Gethsemane Christ trembled in His heart and bones, His sweat fell down like drops of blood, His heart melted in His belly like wax. All this happened, Justin explains, that we might recognize that the Father for our sake wished His Son truly to experience such suffering, and that we might not say that as Son of God He did not feel what was happening to Him and being inflicted upon Him [8]

But though He was thus human in His bodily life and growth, Christ had at all times His full powers as the Logos of God. As the Logos laid aside no part of His divine nature, as was explained above, so He was still able of His own God-given power to find God just as before the Incarnation, and was still able to speak the entire truth which men with only a fragment of the Logos had been able to find but imperfectly. Christ spake inspired truth not as the Prophets, who were moved

[1] Dial. 98 1 (325 A). ἀληθῶς γέγονεν ἄνθρωπος ἀντιληπτικῶς παθῶν.
[2] Dial. 110 2 (336 D), cf Dial 14 8 (232 D), 32. 2 (249 C), 36. 6 (255 B) et al.
[3] Dial 99. 2 (326 B).
[4] Ap. II. 10 8 (49 A); Dial 48 3 (267 C).
[5] Ap. I 66. 2 (98 A)
[6] Dial 84 2 (310 B)
[7] Dial. 88. 2 (315 C).
[8] Dial. 103. 8 (331 C, D)

by a power outside themselves, but by the exercise of
His own God-given faculties in finding the truth and
declaring it.[1] Even as a child just born the demons
recognized His supremacy by the coming of the magi.
These had formerly been under bondage to the demons,
but the coming of Christ gave the magi power to revolt
from their bondage, and the visit to Christ was in thankful
recognition of their new Master.[2] Even at His birth,
concludes Justin, Christ was in possession of His power.[3]
It is with this view of Christ as the entire Logos become
a true man while yet remaining the Logos that Justin
comments upon the incidents recorded from the life of
Christ.[4]

Justin tells the story of the birth of Christ by harmonizing the accounts of Matthew and Luke,[5] only adding
his strange interpretation of the mission of the magi,
and the detail that Christ was born in a cave [6] After His
normal growth to manhood [7] He occupied Himself as a
carpenter in making ploughs and yokes[8] until at about
the age of thirty [9] He was publicly proclaimed to be
the Son of God by the circumstances of His baptism by
John At that time a fire was kindled in the Jordan, the
Spirit descended upon Him in the form of a dove, and
a voice said, "Thou art my Son, this day have I begotten
thee " Justin's protest against the natural implications
of this incident, namely that Jesus came to baptism an
ordinary man and was here chosen to be the Son of

[1] Ap. II 10. 6, 7 (48 E).

[2] Dial. 78 entire.

[3] Dial 88 2 (315 C).

[4] Feder (Bibl. 350) devotes pp 247—263 to the subject "Das
Leben Jesu nach Justin."

[5] See note 2.

[6] Dial. 78. 5 (304 A); cf. Protev Jac xviii. 1, Is. xxxiii. 16.
Donaldson (Bibl. 143) p. 237 says that Justin got this information
from the passage of Isaiah mentioned, but this is impossible Justin
was uniting traditional fact with prophecy, not declaring all prophetic catchwords to have been facts

[7] See note 3.

[8] Dial. 88. 8 (316); cf. Ev Thomae xiii 1.

[9] See note 3.

God, annointed as such by the Spirit, and declared to be
such by the Heavenly Voice, has already been examined
in connection with Justin's doctrine of the Spirit. The
change of text in the saying of the Heavenly Voice had
not yet been made, or at least the change had not
reached Justin, and he was bound to make some sort of
explanation of the incident. The Spirit had therefore,
Justin says, worked among the Jewish Prophets, but when
it descended upon Christ in baptism it ceased from such
activity, rested in Christ, and was thenceforth dispensed
not to Jews but to followers of Christ. But Justin does not
press this point, is content to let the baptism and its
meaning go if he can avoid the obvious implication of the
narrative. So the Voice is interpreted as a mere proof of
Christ's divinity to men,[1] and an invitation to salvation
by knowing Christ.[2] Whatever the passage may mean,
Justin is saying, it must not mean that Christ at this
time received His powers. For with these divine powers
Christ was born.

The temptation which followed the baptism was only
a typical incident from the entire career of the Logos.
His name was from the beginning Israel, which signifies
a man overcoming a power, Justin explains, and the temptation in which Christ overcame the power which is called
Satan was only one of Christ's many victories over Satan.[3]
The significance of the passage for the work of Christ
will be discussed later.

Justin firmly believed in the power of Christ to work
miracles. It was prophecied that Christ should have such
powers,[4] and Justin, in a world where miracle workers
were everywhere known, had no reason to question this
power in his Lord. But because miracles were so common,
they were not adequate evidence for His divine Sonship.[5]

[1] Dial 88. 6 (316 B); cf. Dial. 8. 4 (226 B)
[2] Dial 88. 8 (316 D) This is the generally accepted explanation of an obscure passage.
[3] Dial 125. 3, 4 (354 C—355 A) Understanding the τότε of
section 4 (355 A) as indicating a temporary departure
[4] Ap. I. 48. 1 (84 C), Dial. 69. 4 ff. (295 C ff)
[5] Ap. I. 30.

and Justin gives the miracles actually very little attention. He asserts that the miracles of Simon Magus and Menander were the work of magical power, that is of demonic intervention,[1] and implies that the Christian miraculous power is of the Spirit.[2] But the nature of Christ's miraclous power he does not discuss.

The teaching of Christ, which he quotes exclusively from Synoptic tradition (with the exception of a few passages not in our canonical records),[3] Justin regards as a power in its own right. "The word of His truth and wisdom is more inflaming and more illuminating than the rays (δυνάμεων) of the sun, even piercing into the depths of the heart and mind."[4] Here Justin is thinking temporarily of the radiation of power from Christ as though Christ were Himself a source. But that such was not Justin's real explanation is shown in the assertion that Christ's preaching (His logos) was a δύναμις θεοῦ.[5] Justin does not leave the impression that the Logos was ever a source of radiation of Powers. God Himself was the one source, and the Logos was always to be regarded as a mediatorial subordinate, not as a coordinate source of life. Christ found God and declared His message to men by the exercise of His God-given faculties, but the message which was uttered, the spiritual force which went from Him to men, was not originally a δύναμις Χριστοῦ, but a δύναμις θεοῦ. The conception of the Christian message as a Word of Power is familiarly Pauline, and will be discussed further under Justin's doctrine of salvation. Justin regarded the unique character of Christ's teaching as in itself sufficient demonstration of the Christian claim for His Messianic character and divine Sonship.[6]

[1] Ap. I 26. 2 (69 D ff.); 56. 1 (91 B).

[2] Dial. 87. 5, 6 (315 A, B)

[3] A collection of such passages is to be found in Otto, Dial., ed 3, p. 590, 591.

[4] Dial. 121. 2 (350 A) See above p. 149.

[5] Ap. I. 14. 5 (62 D), cf. Dial. 102. 5 (329 C).

[6] Cf. von Engelhardt (Bibl 313) pp. 178, 179. In addition to evidence there quoted see Dial 76 3 (301 C).

Justin's comment upon the events of the week preceding the Crucifixion have little interest for his theological position except in the matter of his interpretation of the incident of the Garden which has already been discussed, and of the Last Supper which will be examined in connection with his doctrine of the Eucharist.[1]

Christ was arrested on the day of the Passover and after His trial by Pilate was crucified on the same day.[2] That the Crucifixion of Christ was the supreme incident in the drama of the humanized Logos is attested again and again in Justin's reverent allusions to the Cross. He finds references to the Cross in all parts of the Old Testament.[3] He sees the Cross in every aspect of nature.[4] He reads it into Plato's Timaeus.[5] The Cross is the supreme symbol of Christ's strength and rulership.[6] It is the horn of a unicorn which shakes the peoples of all nations from idolatry, that is from demon worship, and turns them to the worship of God.[7] The place in Justin's scheme of salvation which the Cross held will be discussed later. Justin adds to the Synoptic account of the Crucifixion only a few minor details of the mockery of the bystanders.[8] The soldiers at the Crucifixion cried out, "Judge us."[9] After the Crucifixion the disciples fled and denied Jesus,[10] an action which they repented after Christ's Resurrection.[11]

At death Christ descended into Hades. Justin says of this that the following passage has been taken out from the text of Jeremiah by the Jews; "The Lord God remembered His dead people of Israel who lay in the grave; and He

[1] See pp. 271 ff.
[2] Dial. 111. 3 (338 C) For the date implied by this statement see Otto n. 10 in loco.
[3] E. g Dial 73. 1 (298 C); 86 entire: 97 entire; Ap I 35. 7 (76 B).
[4] Ap. I. 55 entire.
[5] Ap. I. 60. 5 (93 B).
[6] Ap. I. 55. 1 (90 B); cf. above p. 159.
[7] Dial. 91. 3 (319 D)
[8] Dial. 101. 3 (328 B) On the text cf Otto notes 13 and 14 in loco.
[9] Ap. I 35. 6 (76 B)
[10] Ap. I. 50. 12 (86 A).
[11] Dial 106 1 (333 C)

descended to preach to them His own salvation."[1] Justin does not apply this directly to Christ, but apparently the verse was so familiar in that application that it needed no comment. In another passage Justin points out the ignorance of the people who supposed that they could put Christ to death, and that Christ would then remain in Hades like an ordinary mortal.[2] Here the emphasis is upon the word "remain" But Christ did not "remain" in Hades, for He received from His Father the ability to rise from the dead on the third day after the Crucifixion,[3] or was raised from the dead by the Father.[4]

In His earthly carer, Christ was completely sinless.[5] But Justin says that notwithstanding His sinlessness, Christ was in need of salvation from God like any other man.[6] Not in virtue of the divine Sonship, not by His own strength or wisdom, could Christ be saved. Without God even He was lost. But the meaning of this salvation is indicated in a statement that Christ was saved in being raised again after His death.[7] That is, though Christ was sinless, once He had died He was like every other man in being completely in the power of death Only an act of God could bring Him back from Hades into real life again. It is true that He had a sort of life in Hades, but true life, such as earth, and better still, such as heaven knows, would have been forever denied Him had not an action of God taken Him away from the land of the dead. The risen Christ

---

[1] Dial. 72. 4 (298 C). Not found in our texts, and supposed to be a Christian interpolation It is twice quoted by Irenaeus, once as from Isaiah and once from Jeremiah. C Haer. III. 20. 4, IV. 22 1. The tradition of such a Scriptural passage is very old, however, for it clearly is assumed as familiar in I Pet. iii. 19, and iv. 6 Cf Gosp. of Nicodemus. Donaldson (Bibl. 143) p. 239 goes too far in his reaction against Semisch (Bibl. 118) II 413 in not admitting the presumption which Justin's word's make in favor of his belief in Christ's descent into Hades.

[2] Dial 99. 3 (326 C).

[3] Dial. 100. 1 (326 C)

[4] Ap. I 45 1 (82 D); Dial 95. 2 (323 A), 106. 1 (333 B).

[5] Dial. 17. 1 (234 D); 102. 7 (330 A); 103. 2 (330 C); 110 6 (337 D).

[6] Dial 102. 7 (330 A), cf. Dial. 101. 1 (328 A).

[7] Dial. 73. 2 (298 C)

returned to heaven with all the marks of His earthly career upon Him, so much so that He was at first not recognized by the Heavenly Host.[1] Now in heaven He is being detained by God until proper preparation has been made for His second coming [2] While Christ awaits He is sitting upon the right hand of God [3]

[1] Dial. 36. 5 (255 B)
[2] Ap I. 45. 1 (82 D), cf. Hebr. x. 19
[3] Dial. 32. 3 (249 E)

CHAPTER IX

REDEMPTION AND THE CHRISTIAN LIFE

It has been seen that according to Justin's view the human race is made up, practically without exception, of sinners. In spite of the fact that God has given to all men a divine guide to righteousness, and a free will by which they may, if they choose, live according to the eternal principles of right, men, under the influence of the demons and a sinful environment, actually choose the wrong. As a result we are all in urgent need of salvation, else, having chosen to follow the demons rather than the Logos, we shall be condemned by Him at the last judgment to suffer with the demons in eternal fire. Justin in no passage betrays a horror of sin as such, but he has a most vivid conviction of the imminent and frightful character of damnation.

Thus with him the preparation for salvation is begun on earth in the forgiveness of sins, but salvation is actually received only when at the judgment the Christian is taken from the ranks of doomed humanity to be included in the number of the blessed. The Christians are brands snatched from the burning. They have lost their old filthy garments, but do not get new pure ones until the establishment of the eternal kingdom.[1] Justin says that as Noah was saved by water, faith, and wood, so shall those who have been prepared by baptism, faith, and the power of the Cross escape the coming Judgment of God.[2] This last statement is perhaps the best way in which Justin's views may be expressed. The operation of grace which cleanses the soul from sin is a preparation for that salvation which is not received until the judgment day. Purity of life is a prerequisite for

[1] Dial. 116. 2, 3 (344 A, B)
[2] Dial. 138. 3 (368 A).

salvation, not a result of it, for Justin says that harlots and
sinners of all nations, who have received the remission of
sins and who no longer commit sins, are to be saved [1]
Salvation is synonymous with entering into the kingdom of
heaven [2] It is the same thought which Justin expresses
in representing this ultimate salvation as a delivery from
death   The kingdom into which good Christians are to
enter when they are finally saved is one of eternal and
unfailing life   So in this sense we have seen that Christ
Himself, once dead, was like every dead person in need of
salvation if He were to become alive again [3] Hence the
work of Christ is expressed in terms of crushing death
"By the Son, God brings freedom from death to those who
repent of their sins and believe upon Him." [4] Death became
despised in the first advent, and in the second appearance
of Christ it will "cease completely from those who trust
Him and live well pleasing to Him, for death will not exist
any more after this when the one class shall be sent to be
punished unceasingly, but the others shall live together in
freedom from suffering, and decay, and grief, and death." [5]

Only one passage has with any probability been adduced [6] to show that Justin conceives of salvation as a
present deliverance from sin rather than as a future deliverance from death and hell   The passage is Justin's
analogy between the Cross of Christ and the saving power
of the brazen serpent   Those who believe on Christ receive
"salvation from the fangs of the serpent which were wicked
deeds, idolatries, and other unrighteous acts," for Christ on
the Cross has "broken the power of the Serpent which oc-
casioned the transgression of Adam" [7] The significance

[1] Dial 111 4 (338 D)   The context immediately before this
statement shows that the σώζονται here means "they are to be
saved"

[2] Ap. I 16 8, 9 (64 A)   The kingdom in Justin is of course
always eschatological

[3] See above p 248

[4] Dial 100. 6 (327 D)

[5] Dial 45. 4 (264 A, B)

[6] As, e. g., by Donaldson (Bibl 143) p 242, and Stahlin
(Bibl 318) p 38

[7] Dial. 94 2, 3 (322 A, B)

of the passage for the power of the Cross will be considered
later. That Justin considered forgiveness of sins as a part
of the preparation for salvation is obvious from the statements already quoted, but it is quite exceptional to his usual
manner of speech to call that forgiveness itself "salvation"
as he does here. He ordinarily thinks of forgiveness only
as a preparation for salvation, and his loose confusion of
the end with the means in this instance cannot overbalance
the great frequency with which he speaks of salvation
as something eschatological.[1] In this respect Justin is in
accord with St. Paul, who regarded salvation as only made
actual in the future though as a present expectation it was
in a sense already in the believer's possession [2]

The work of Christ for salvation is primarily directed
against the demons. Here is the cause of all sin God made
man of such a nature that he would normally have chosen
the right, and lived by the guidance of the Logos fragment
within him. But even if one does choose so to live, he
cannot long unassisted continue to act in a way pleasing
to God The demons are so powerful in their seductiveness
that they must be destroyed, or man must be equipped with
power greater than he normally has, if he is not sooner or
later to become their victim. Against this demonic activity
Justin seems to think that God opposes the Logos. A war
in heaven is not described by Justin, nor is there any
eternal struggle between good and evil But it seems a
particular activity of the Logos to oppose the demons,
as the Logos is the particular object of demonic attack
through humanity. Before the Incarnation the demons had
been consistently victors in all but a few isolated individual
cases, but that was because the full demonic power was
being exercised against fragments of the Logos seriatim.
The tide of battle is now turned because Christ, as the
entire Logos, represents a concentration of all the small
logos elements into a single force against which the demons
are powerless At the second coming the word will be

[1] Cf. e. g. the frequent future references in Dial. 47.
[2] Cf. Handbuch zum N. T. III, An die Römer, erklärt von
Prof. Hans Lietzmann, 2. Aufl., Tubingen 1919, p. 29, note on
Romans i 16.

finally spoken which will end their activity forever Meanwhile each man may have the benefit of the entire Logos to whose united strength he can appeal, and in the power of whose totality he need have no fear of the outcome

The operation of this collected power of the Logos in man is first that of a revelation. To Justin it is inconceivable that anyone can be convinced of the Christian doctrine of the future, that eternal happiness or eternal agony hang upon our conduct in this life, without such an overmastering determination to choose the good that even death by torture will by every man be unhesitatingly preferred to the certain penalties that await sin after death Philosophy has inklings of this doctrine, but the revelations of the Spermatic Logos in every man, while perfectly true, do not bring the unmovable conviction that can defy the activities of the demons The demons darken the light of the higher mind They deceive and lead astray the race,[1] they are robbers[2] who steal its counsels. They make slaves and servants of men[3] But the apprehension of truth which before was weak has now been made abundantly strong in the illumination given by the teaching and person of Jesus Christ The long succession of revelation, all pointing toward the culmination in Christ, and fulfilled in Him to the smallest detail, has given to the teachings of Christ an authority which attends the utterance of no other man. And when Christ came, His teaching was, as Justin reads it, of the future coming, of the dread Day of the Lord, and of eternal rewards and punishments, while He spoke many maxims and guides for us as to how we should prepare ourselves for the great division of humanity.

Thus far Justin justifies the statements of von Engelhardt and Windisch that he rationalized the doctrine of salvation. According to their view, Justin teaches that Christ gave light and information. He destroyed the demonic influence, increased the true knowledge of man, and so made it possible for men to purify themselves by choosing the higher life In Christ man is awakened, by

[1] Ap I. 54. 1 (89 A)
[2] Fragment in Tatian, Oratio ad Graec. 18 2, 3
[3] Ap. I. 14. 1 (61 B)

a revelation of the complete Logos and of the plan of creation and of the future, to a recognition of his moral powers and inherent kinship with God as a partaker in the Spermatic Logos. There is no change in the relationship of God to man in a forgiveness of sin. Only is there change on the part of those men who choose to claim their kinship with God and to use the latent power that is in them This true liberty is consummated after death in a συνουσία with God. The reason why there can be no such change on the part of God as Christian theology represents, they explain, is that Justin's God is impersonal, while the God of Christianity proper is personal [1]

We have already seen that Justin's God is most certainly personal. As to the doctrine of salvation itself even what Justin says of Christ as teacher makes room for a mystic working of the personal God upon man which goes much further than von Engelhardt would admit.

For the great difficulty with von Engelhardt's criticism is that he has vastly overestimated certain aspects of Justin's theology So he has not noticed that even in the representation of salvation as knowledge, Justin gives active power to the knowledge. The Gospel story and the Christian doctrine are in Justin's thought themselves an active force, a δύναμις from God Christ received from God a special message (λόγος), and was not to be killed until after He had delivered it to men.[2] This logos was active, a power flowing from Christ like the gushing of a mighty spring, so that when He kept silent it was as if such a rush of water had suddenly been cut off. The dynamic quality of the word of Christ was illustrated by the easy way in which it had vanquished all the teachers of Judaism.[3] The power of the words of Christ is no whit diminished by time. Justin speaks in the present tense, saying, "The word of His truth and wisdom (that is, Christ's true and wise preaching) is more inflaming and illuminating than the rays of the sun, even piercing into the depths of the

[1] See (Bibl. 313) pp. 195 ff., (Bibl. 333) pp 14—19. Cf. Harnack, Dogmengeschichte I (1909) p. 543.

[2] Dial. 102. 5 (329 C).

[3] Ibid.

heart and mind "[1] The Christian revelation is thus not a coldly convincing lecture on metaphysical or ethical theory. It is a burning force which sets the heart afire. In this Justin's doctrine is clearly Pauline: βραχεῖς δὲ καὶ σύντομοι παρ' αὐτοῦ λόγοι γεγόνασιν· οὐ γὰρ σοφιστὴς ὑπῆρχεν, ἀλλὰ δύναμις θεοῦ ὁ λόγος αὐτοῦ ἦν [2] says Justin, clearly making use of the Pauline contrast. καὶ ὁ λόγος μου καὶ τὸ κήρυγμα μου οὐκ ἐν πειθοῖς σοφίας λόγοις, ἀλλ' ἐν ἀποδείξει πνεύματος καὶ δυνάμεως, ἵνα ἡ πίστις ὑμῶν μὴ ᾖ ἐν σοφίᾳ ἀνθρώπων, ἀλλ' ἐν δυνάμει θεοῦ. [3] The word which the Apostles went forth to preach was likewise possessed of strength [4] Justin illustrates in his autobiographical remarks the working of this illuminating power When the Old Man left him, he says, he found suddenly burning within him a fire of love for the Prophets and Christ [5] The significance of the knowledge of the doctrine then is not simply a marshalling of facts before the mind of man so that he will be able to make the choice of life more fully advised of its consequences, but an impartation of illumination and power We may now fight the demons not with a part of the Logos but with its entirety. In the possession of the Christian message we are possessed of the entire Logos, and in that vast increase of power we are invincible Justin gives no details for the working of the entire Logos in human psychology But the entire Logos, he believes, is made subjective in every Christian by the acceptance of the preaching of Christ and the Apostles The δύναμις θεοῦ has been sent to us through Jesus Christ, and when the devil would tempt Christians this δύναμις rebukes him and he departs from us. For the Christians are vehemently inflamed διὰ τοῦ λόγου τῆς κλήσεως αὐτοῦ,

[1] Dial 121 2 (350 A), cf above pp 149, 246. The δύναμις is there shown to be originally from the Father

[2] Ap. I. 14 5 (62 D).

[3] I Cor 11. 4, 5 Cf Rom 1 16 . . . . τὸ εὐαγγέλιον δύναμις γὰρ θεοῦ ἐστιν εἰς σωτηρίαν παντὶ τῷ πιστεύοντι.

[4] Ap. I. 45 5 (83 A). τὸ οὖν εἰρημένον· 'Ράβδον δυνάμεως ἐξαποστελεῖ σοι ἐξ 'Ιερουσαλήμ, προαγγελτικὸν τοῦ λόγου τοῦ ἰσχυροῦ, ὃν ἀπὸ 'Ιερουσαλὴμ οἱ ἀπόστολοι αὐτοῦ ἐξελθόντες πανταχοῦ ἐκήρυξαν.

[5] Dial. 8. 1 (225 B)

"through the doctrine, or preaching, of His calling."[1] Christians live no longer κατὰ σπερματικοῦ λόγου μέρος, ἀλλὰ κατὰ τὴν τοῦ παντὸς λόγου (ὅ ἐστι Χριστοῦ) γνῶσιν καὶ θεωρίαν.[2] No one can say that to Justin's contemporaries γνῶσιν καὶ θεωρίαν could mean objective knowledge. It is a mystic apprehension which makes the entire Logos a factor of the inner life of the Christian. He no longer lives according to a part of the Logos; the part is swallowed up in the whole. And just as salvation comes from a mystical γνῶσις καὶ θεωρία, so it does not come from σοφία. Christ, says Justin, was like us. He could not be saved by His ancestry, His wealth, His strength (that is, any powers or faculties of His own), or His knowledge (σοφία).[3] Only an act of God, a power of God, can save a man. And that power is given to man through a mystic impartation of ἐπιστήμην τὴν ἄποπτον καὶ γνῶσιν τὴν ἀνέλεγκτον,[4] which is the δύναμις θεοῦ διὰ Χριστοῦ.

In this sense it is that Christ is here among men δυνάμει since His first coming.[5] The force of this conception is weakened in Justin by the fact that in one passage he puns upon δυνάμει. The Christians, he says, are called His robe since He always dwells among them δυνάμει, and in the second coming will dwell ἐναργῶς [6] The last phrase is an after-thought. It is true that Justin believed in a contrast as sharp as the Aristotelian contrast of δυνάμει and ἐναργῶς between the state of affairs now and those which are to obtain after the second coming But he believed also in a stronger and more real indwelling of Christ in Christians even in this interval between His two comings than the Aristotelian δυνάμει expressed For Justin comments in the First Apology upon the same figure as follows; the men who believe upon Christ are His robe, that is, those in whom the Logos in its entirety,

[1] Dial. 116 3 (344 A—C).
[2] Ap. II. 8 3 (46 C).
[3] Dial. 102 6, 7 (329 D ff)
[4] Ap. II. 13 3 (51 C).
[5] Dial. 138. 1 (367 C). For the implications of this passage for the doctrine of the Spirit, see above p. 182.
[6] Dial. 54. 1 (273 D)

the σπέρμα παρὰ τοῦ 'θεοῦ, dwells [1] ⟋The Power of God, the
Gospel dwells in man, and is itself the presence of the
entire Logos

It is very likely that Justin regarded this entire Logos
as coming into a man normally in what he calls the
φωτισμός. Christians are spoken of as τοὺς διὰ Ἰησοῦ φωτισ-
μένους. [2] Justin uses the word as a synonym for baptism,
and calls a baptized man one who has been illuminated,
as to say, one who had been baptized [3] But he explains the
term. "And this washing (baptism) is called illumination
since those learning these things (sc. the doctrine of
salvation) are illuminated in their understanding." [4] Baptism
is called in the Dialogue "the laver of repentance καὶ τῆς
γνώσεως τοῦ θεοῦ." [5] Clearly then φωτισμός, as a name for
baptism, has a real significance. ⟋The term was taken,
as Otto says, from the Mysteries. But it is not a mere
name of a rite it describes what Justin thought to be
the spiritual experience of one who is baptized [6]

⟍ It must be noticed that in this scheme of salvation
there has been no mention of the Cross, and that there
is no admission of a real significance for the Incarnation.
It is in the incarnate Logos that men come to know the
entire Logos, but the special value of the fact that the
Logos became a man is not included in this theory of the
work of Christ. But nevertheless Justin has a great deal to
say of the Cross So closely did he identify the Cross with
the Work of Christ that when he wished to prove the
Logos to be cosmic force in nature he sums up the
whole by proving the presence of the Cross in all the
elements and in all forms of life. For "the Cross is the
most important symbol of His might and rulership " [7]
So it is by the power of the mystery of the Cross as
typified by the horn of the unicorn that some in all

---

[1] Ap. I 32. 8 (74 B); cf. above pp 214 ff
[2] Dial 122. 1 (350 C) Cf Hebr. x 32
[3] Ap I 65. 1 (97 C), 61 13 (94 E).
[4] Ap I 61 12 (94 D).
[5] Dial 14. 1 (231 C).
[6] For Justin's theory of baptism see below pp 265 ff
[7] Ap. I. 55 2 ff (90 B ff.), cf Dial. 86 entire

nations, having been "horned, that is pricked,[1] have turned from empty idols and demons to the worship of God."[2] Justin may have here in mind the preaching of the Gospel which had a similar effect upon the hearts and lives of men. But if it is the Christian message which Justin has in mind, he states unmistakably that the supreme part of that Christian message is the Cross. Even more unmistakably does Justin make the Passion of Christ the act of Redemption when he says that Christ "served, even to the slavery of the Cross, for the various and many-formed races of mankind, acquiring them by the blood and mystery of the Cross."[3]

/ Justin may have connected the Cross with the breaking of the power of the demons because of the conspicuous part which the Cross played in exorcisms. The formula of exorcism which Justin has preserved lays great stress upon the Crucifixion.[4] The demons, he says, are "subject to His name and to the dispensation of the passion which He experienced"[5] Through the mystery (of the Cross) the power of the Serpent was destroyed.[6] /But just how Justin conceived that the Cross achieved this victory he does not explain. Indeed he speaks repeatedly of the demons as having been conquered "by the crucified Christ," but not "by the Crucifixion of Christ." The matter is made more complicated by the fact that at the temptation,[7] in exorcising demons,[8] even at His birth,[9] Christ had already complete power over the demons, was "Lord of the demons."[10] The Incarnation, whose purpose is never made very clear, is at least twice alluded to as

---

[1] Κατανυγέντες, cf. Acts ii. 37 κατενύγησαν τῇ καρδίᾳ.

[2] Dial 91. 3 (318 D).

[3] Dial. 134. 5 (364 C).

[4] Dial 85. 2 (311 B); cf. Dial. 30. 3 (247 C).

[5] Dial. 30. 3 (247 D). τὰ δαιμόνια ὑποτάσσεσθαι τῷ ὀνόματι αὐτοῦ καὶ τῇ τοῦ γενομένου πάθους αὐτοῦ οἰκονομίᾳ.

[6] Dial. 94. 2 (322 A).

[7] Dial 125. 4 (354 D)

[8] Dial. 49. 8 (269 C)

[9] Dial. 78. 9 (304 D ff.).

[10] Dial 85. 1 (311 A, B); cf. 100. 6 (327 D).

finding its object in the destruction of the demons.[1]
The concealed power of God was in Christ the crucified,
before whom the demons and all the principalities and
powers will be revealed, and the devils condemned.[2] We
must then agree with von Engelhardt that the Cross
receives little real significance in Justin's writings as
marking the triumph of Christ over the demons.[3]

Justin deals more directly with the problem of the
significance of the Crucifixion, when he says that Christ
took upon Himself a curse for the sake of men when
He was crucified. Justin's argument on this point is
apologetic, but his meaning is tolerably clear so far as he
goes. He begins by challenging Trypho as to why God
would command Moses to break His own Law against the
erection of images by telling Moses to set up the brazen
serpent.[4] Justin himself answers that the reason is that
men are healed from the bites of the serpents by the
Cross. Christ, as one who hung upon a tree, was accursed
in the eyes of the Law. This was all foreshadowed in
the action of Moses in breaking the Law to make an
accursed image of a serpent, that the people might be
saved from the bites of the serpents. But why and in
what sense did Christ become accursed? All men, Justin
explains, have become accursed in the eyes of the Law
because all men whether Jews or Gentiles have failed
in some particular in the observance of the Law, and
thereby have brought upon themselves a curse. By dying
upon the Cross Christ became, in accordance with the
Law, an accursed person, but the curse which was upon
Him He took upon Himself, and it was, we infer, a
collection of all the curses upon the entire human family.
This collected curse Christ took upon Himself at the
wish of the Father, for the Father knew that the curse
would not abide upon Christ since He, the Father, intended
to raise Christ up after His death. The Son was thus
never in a full sense accursed. Blameless and unaccursed

[1] Dial. 45 4 (264 A), 125. 3, 4 (354 C, D): cf. 100. 6 (327 A).
[2] Dial. 49. 8 (269 C).
[3] (Bibl. 313) p. 270.
[4] See Dial. 94 and 95 for the argument.

in His own right, He took upon Himself our curses, and, Justin implies, dying with them upon Him, they died with Him. Thus Christ, though He fulfilled the saying that every man is accursed who hangs upon the tree, as the Jews insist, was never personally accursed. Justin therefore exhorts the Jews to recognize the real significance of this verse which they are using against Christ and the Christian faith, and to claim the privilege which the curse upon Christ opens to all men, that of becoming free from the curses which are upon themselves.

The disappointing part of the section is that two very important steps in the argument are omitted. That the curse which was upon Christ as a crucified man was identical with the collected curses of all men, and that these curses died with Christ, while Christ was raised up without them, Justin does not explicitly say. But the argument as a whole seems to imply both these steps with sufficient obviousness.

Justin may have had other explanations of the significance of the Cross, but this is the only explanation which he has allowed us to reconstruct.[1] Certain he is, however, that in the Cross of Christ and in the blood of Christ, the guilt of our sins may be removed. For Justin repeats many times that through the passion and the Cross men now have and have always had their only hope for salvation.[2] Christ's death was a sacrifice for our sins.[3] It is by the blood of Christ that our souls are washed pure of the old stains of sin[4] But if Justin has only traces of theories to explain the action of the Cross upon

---

[1] E. g. Justin says in Ap. I. 63. 16 (96 D) that "Christ endured both to be set at naught and to suffer, that by dying and rising again He might conquer death." But how far Justin carried this Pauline thought we cannot tell.

[2] Dial. 13. 1 (229 D), 17. 1 (234 D, E); 41. 1 (260 A). 43. 3 (261 D); 89. 3 (317 B); 94. 2 (322 A); 137. 1 (366 D), Ap. II. 13. 4 (51 D).

[3] Dial. 40 entire; 89. 3 (317 B); 111. 3 (338 C).

[4] Ap I. 32. 7 (74 A); Dial. 13. 1 (299 D), 24. 1 (241 D); 44. 4 (263 C); 54. 1 (273 D), 111. 3 (338 C).

the hearts of men, rather than a consistent doctrine which meant very much to him as a theory, and if he views the atonement rather from the practical than the theoretic point of view, the fact is not to be explained by calling him a "philosopher" Windisch has rightly interpreted Ap. I. 53 as indicating something of a hopeless feeling on the part of Justin to explain the Crucifixion on any theoretical grounds [1] The proof of an otherwise incredible fact, Justin there says, is the prophetic evidence for a Crucifixion, while we may only answer the question, "Why did God choose that way," by saying, "It was His will" But it was not, as Windisch implies, Justin's philosophic viewpoint which made him thus unable to explain the Crucifixion "A philosopher like Justin" had adequate explanation for little or nothing, whether in Christianity or in philosophy Nor is the absence of an adequate theory of the Crucifixion to be taken as an indication that the Cross meant little to Justin

From the point of view of Christ, then, the salvation of men was accomplished by a power which, coming from God through the crucified Christ, enlightened them and empowered them to overcome the demons and to choose to live according to the eternal moral verities Christ incarnate was the antithesis of Eve's offspring by the Serpent. As she produced disobedience and death, so did Mary produce the Son of God who destroys both death and the devil.[2] This achievment was accomplished supremely on the Cross and in the Resurrection. His death meant an atonement for the sins of all who care to claim it.

From the point of view of the Christian believer, salvation is to be hoped for after the following preliminary steps [3] First one must recognize the truth of the Gospel message; second one must repent of the sins which he has committed, third he must be baptized; fourth he must live a pure life thereafter until death Those who die after such a life may hope to be saved from death and destruction in

[1] (Bibl 333) p 29.
[2] Dial. 100 4, 5 (327 C); 45 4 (264 A).
[3] Dial 44 4 (263 C), 95 3 (323 B); 138. 3 (368 A).

the last day, that is to receive remission of sins rather than
punishment for their sin.[1]

/ On the importance of believing the Gospel Justin is
most explicit Along with those who have lived wickedly
will go to hell those who do not believe that those things
which God has taught us by Christ will come to pass.[2]
Von Engelhardt has rightly pointed out that in Justin faith
is not spoken of in the Luthero-Pauline sense of the term [3]
Von Engelhardt concludes from this fact that Justin is
primarily a heathen who did not understand Christianity
Feder and Martindale conclude from the same fact that
Justin was a true Catholic because he had the traditionalist
viewpoint as contrasted with the later individualistic interpretation of Christianity [4] /In his exposition of Christianity Justin's aim is not to expand or elaborate, but to
reproduce the doctrines of Christianity as he had received
them   Heretics, even those who made so slight a departure from the faith as to reject the intermediary period
when the souls of the just await the Resurrection, and who
believed that the just went to heaven at once upon death,
had no toleration from Justin [5]/It is true that he makes
room for the salvation of such men as Socrates and
Abraham, but in both cases it was because of their faith which
believed in the truth of the utterances of God Socrates
believed in the truth of the utterances of the fragment of
the Logos within himself, and lived according to the knowledge of right and wrong which his own higher mind gave
him, while ordinary men refuse to believe in the utterances
of the Logos within them, and hence surrender themselves
to the leadership and instruction of the demons Abraham
believed that what God said to him was true, and acted

[1] Dial 95 3 (323 B)
[2] Ap. I 19 8 (66 B)
[3] (Bibl 313) p 188   See below p. 264 n 2
[4] Martindale writes that to Justin "denial or distortion of the
taught traditional faith is anti-Christianity . . . The whole structure and scheme of Justin's Christianity is Catholic throughout:
the individualist and fideist theories of later ages do not so much
as dawn "
[5] Dial 80 4 (307 A)

accordingly.[1] God has spoken to us now through Christ.
/The first essential for salvation for us is, like Socrates and
Abraham, to take God at His word, and live according to His
instructions Echoes of a more mystical faith Justin has
But faith whatever else it may include must begin with
the intellectual acceptation of a revealed body of truth
There is no compulsion toward this acceptation. /We may
reject God's saving power if we will, for to refuse to believe
the truth of God's revelation is completely to resist the
grace of God Justin believed with St. Paul that the Gospel
is foolishness to one who will not accept it, but the power
of God unto salvation to anyone who believes it [2]/There is
no contradiction between the facts that we may refuse to
believe the Gospel, and that the Gospel is yet an active
power from God through Christ Once we accept the doctrine it will inflame us But Justin always preserves the
liberty of man to choose in the first place to accept or
reject the divine operation.[3]

Acceptance of the doctrines of Christianity must be
followed or accompanied by repentance.[4] /Christ died, it
would appear, not for all men, but only for those who are
willing to repent [5] Repentance is a condition of mercy,[6] a
prerequisite for baptism [7] "For the goodness and loving-
kindness of God, and His boundless riches, hold righteous
and sinless the man who, as Ezekiel tells us, repents of
sins "[8] Hence Justin's exhortations to repentance are urgent
in both the First Apology and the Dialogue [9] It is true
that he does not always include repentance among the

[1] Dial. 11 5 (229 A); 23 4 (241 B) To Justin, believing
God and acting according to His instructions were inseparable
See below pp 267 ff
[2] Rom 1 16 See above pp 254 ff
[3] Ap. I. 43 entire
[4] Dial. 26 1 (243 C)
[5] Dial 40 4 (259 D).
[6] Ap. I. 28. 2 (71 B); Dial 26 1 (243 C), 141 2, 3
(370 C ff)
[7] Ap I 61 10 (94 D).
[8] Dial 47. 5 (266 D ff); cf Ap I 61 6 (94 A)
[9] Ap. I. 40. 7 (79 A); Dial 95 3 (323 B); 108 3 (335 D).
118 1 (345 D), 138 3 (368 A)

essentials for becoming a Christian [1] But he certainly considers repentance at least as the normal way to secure the remission of sins However repentance is not in itself an act of purification. Von Engelhardt says that in the Apologies repentance is only a turning from the bad to the good, probably with sorrow for the past; man is saved by that act because he is thereafter no longer a sinner but a righteous man, and hence can not well be condemned by God as a sinner. God's only part in the change is to call men to repentance. Justin, says von Engelhardt, rejects the formula ὁ δίκαιος ἐκ πίστεως ζήσεται, and even ἡ πίστις σου σέσωκέ σε, for ἐκ μετανοίας σωθήσεσθαι. [2] But a glance at the context of this formula shows at once that Justin does not use it as a general formula for salvation in the single passage where it appears. Justin has been trying to account for the delay of the second coming, and says that that great event is awaiting the fulfillment of the number of those who are to be saved There are still more to come in, says Justin; some shall be saved by repentance, and some are yet to be born That is, Justin means here no more than that there are still men who shall repent and be saved. Von Engelhardt gives repentance a disproportionate emphasis, for he makes repentance itself the act by which a man purifies himself from sin, while the forgiveness of sin by God is merely the declaration by God that the repentant man is

[1] E g. Dial 28. 4 (246 A). Here the γνῶσις τοῦ θεοῦ καὶ τοῦ Χριστοῦ αὐτοῦ and the observance of τὰ αἰώνια δίκαια are the sole requirements for becoming a friend of God

[2] (Bibl. 313) p. 191; cf. Ap, I. 28. 2 (71 B). Von Engelhardt here shows the great disadvantage of his method of expounding Justin's theology. He begins with the Apologies, which are of course more pagan in point of view and argument than the Dialogue, and draws extreme conclusions therefrom for the Greek character of Justin's thinking. Then he treats a few problems in the Dialogue, but never checks the two together to come to Justin's real thought between the two. It may be possible to come to so extreme a conclusion as von Engelhardt has done when one considers the Apologies alone, for they have comparatively little to say, for example, about repentance. But the error of his conclusion appears at once when the statements about repentance in the Dialogue are considered. This evidence von Engelhardt ignores.

no longer a sinner [1] But Dial 141 gives quite another account of the relation of the two / Justin is here explaining the necessity for repentance: "If they repent, all who wish for it can obtain the mercy of God, the Scripture foretells that they shall be blessed, saying, 'Blessed is the man to whom the Lord imputeth not sin'; that is, having repented of his sins, he may receive remission of them from God, and not as you deceive yourselves, and some others who resemble you in this, who say, that even though they be sinners, but know God, the Lord will not impute sin to them. We have as proof of this the one fall of David, which happened through his boasting, which was forgiven then when he so mourned and wept, as it is written But if even to such a man no remission was granted before repentance, and only when this great king, and annointed one, and prophet, mourned and conducted himself so, how can the impure and utterly abandoned, if they weep not, and mourn not, and repent not, entertain the hope that the Lord will not impute to them sin?" [2] /Here repentance is represented as an indispensable preparation, but only as a preparation, for that remission of sin which comes from God, and which we have seen is given to men through the blood of Christ Von Engelhardt is right in making repentance itself the free act of man The mercy of God is to be had by those who wish for it and repent. Always the human volition is left free to choose But the human volition is not empowered to cleanse away the guilt of past acts / We may always obtain remission of sins by repenting, but it is always God who acts through Christ to forgive

/The change of character consequent upon repentance is normally brought about in baptism Baptism is thus described [3] The candidate is first to be convinced of the truth of the Christian doctrine He next promises to live by Christian precepts, and enters upon a preparation of prayer and fasting which is shared by the congregation When this has been completed he is brought to the water where he receives the washing with water "in the name of

[1] (Bibl 313) p. 192.
[2] Dial 141 2, 3 (370 C, D)
[3] Ap. I. 61 2 ff (93 D ff.)

God the Father and Lord of the universe, and of our Saviour Jesus Christ, and of the Holy Spirit, thereby being regenerated in the same manner in which we were ourselves regenerated." The washing with water was prophesied by Ezekiel as a putting away of evil from the soul, and was possible only to men who had repented The candidate "washes himself" which may mean that he goes under the water unassisted while the formula of baptism is being repeated over him,[1] but which probably refers to the fact that this is a birth which cannot be possible without the complete concurrence of the will of the person baptised. In the fleshly birth our wills have no part, but the second birth is impossible without our assent /The middle voice does not, however, indicate that we *purify* ourselves in baptism We there receive, not achieve the remission of sins.[2] Baptism is the washing in behalf of remission of sins, and into a rebirth[3] But the new birth is not merely negative in character It is here that man receives the great enlightening from God which gives the power of the entire Logos in place of the defeated fragment which man naturally possesses[4]

Baptism is thus a regenerative rite. Veil is wrong in saying that it merely expresses outwardly an experience which has already happened within the soul[5] /Justin does not regard the ceremony as mechanical or magical,[6] but the new birth, while spiritual, actually does take place during the external rite, and, in a sense which Justin does not explain, by the instrumentality of the external rite The spiritual character of baptism, and the impotence of any ceremony, especially a ceremony of purification, apart from the attitude of mind of the participant, is further explained in the Dialogue. Justin says there that the old rites of Judaism were broken cisterns, for they were performed without a turning from evil doings "Baptize the soul from

[1] See Blunt (Bibl 43) p 92 n 9
[2] Ap I. 61 10 (94 D)
[3] Ap I. 66 1 (98 A)
[4] See above p. 257
[5] (Bibl 80) p 91, c 61 n. 2
[6] Semisch (Bibl 118) II 432 ff. is right in his argument on this point against Credner and Otto

wrath and from covetousness, from envy, and from hatred, and, lo! the body is pure "[1] But the spiritual circumcision which alone is of any value for purification, Christians receive in baptism,[2] which is a laver of repentance and of the knowledge of God[3]

/ But Justin did not regard baptism as an essential for salvation. The heroes of the Old Testament, as for example David, were purified by God at once upon repentance,[4] and repentance was alone necessary for salvation for those who might sin after they had become Christians.[5] Not even repentance is named as necessary for salvation in such cases as Socrates and Enoch, while any man, whether "Scythian or Persian, if he has the knowledge of God and of His Christ and keeps the everlasting righteous decrees, is circumcised with the good and useful circumcision, and is a friend of God, and God rejoices in his gifts and offerings '[6]/But nevertheless baptism is the normal way for becoming a Christian, and ordinarily the second birth or spiritual circumcision must thus be found. It is probably to the Christian sacraments and particularly to baptism, that Justin refers when he says that salvation is only to be received by faith and the observation of the mysteries[7]

\ Only adult baptism could have been known to Justin. The second birth in baptism was a matter of the free choice of the candidate, in contrast with the fleshly birth. This could only apply to adult baptism, or to baptism after an age when at least the form of consulting the inclination of the candidate could be carried out.

But salvation is not achieved by the new birth in baptism. Even admitting the strongest force of Justin's conceptions of the φωτισμός, man is only empowered in

[1] Dial 14 1, 2 (231 C, D).
[2] Dial 43 2 (261 C, D), cf Col ii 11, 12.
[3] Dial 14 1 (231 C).
[4] Dial 141 2, 3 (370 C, D), cf above p 265
[5] Dial 47 4 (266 D)
[6] Dial 28 4 (246 A)
[7] Dial 44 2 (263 A) The discussion in the preceding chapter and the statement at the end of this chapter make the reference of these "mysteries" tolerably definite

baptism with a divine force with which he can achieve
salvation For at the judgment nothing will be taken into
consideration but man's moral character as witnessed by
his actual deeds in life. / Christian baptism and repentance
have insured a fresh start for the new convert He may be
sure that his old sins will not be brought up against him at
the judgment. It has further given him a new power He
has now the entire Logos as a force in his own life by
which he may be guided, instead of the faltering fragment
with which he began life / But this means only that he is
empowered to earn salvation by his own conduct, not that
he is already accepted into kinship with God. One who
lives aright, like Socrates or Abraham, though he has never
heard of the Christian doctrine of salvation, has far better
hopes for the last day than a Christian who has not lived
a good life / Grace in Justin's mind did not take the place
of human effort. God by grace will so equip a man that
he can have a fair chance in the struggle against the influence of the demons, but man must still fight for he can
still fall Just as eternal punishment seemed to Justin as
immoral, meaningless, and hence not a true doctrine, unless
each person punished is himself responsible for his sin, so
eternal happiness and reward only become an acceptable
doctrine when the recipient is conceived of as having
earned the right to his blessing

In terms of Justin's psychology, the action of the
φωτισμός is apparently a replacement of the entire Logos
for the fragment, but of course man at the Judgment is to
be judged for his personal character, that is, for the condition not of his spirit but of his soul ┌ The proper aim of
man is to make his soul a fit habitation for the spirit His
chances for doing so are hopeless when he has only the
fragment, but are sure when he has the entire Logos. Still
he earns the final approbation of God, not for having
the entire Logos in his soul, but for having guided his soul
by the leadership of this entire Logos /This is still the
achievment of the individual man It is by a co-operation
of work and grace that salvation is achieved God gives
the power, and without this special grant of power man is
helpless; but man must use the power once it is given, or

he is one of the unworthy Christians whom Justin despises as worse than the heathen

In this Justin would not have agreed with the Luthero-Pauline conception of grace which could not be earned or affected by human efforts. His conception of divine morality was much more instinctively true than Luther's. /But in making the test for salvation ethical rather than mystical Justin is in accord with the spirit of the best at once of Judaism and of the Synoptic tradition To rule Justin out from the true Christian succession because his view of religion was ultimately ethical, and because he saw in the Cross of Christ a means whereby we may receive power from God to live lives worthy of His friendship, is inconceivably narrow The best Catholic tradition has never agreed with Luther's rejection of the Epistle of James, and insistence that the Christian was saved by his faith, to the exclusion of a wholesome emphasis upon his moral life Justin, as we have seen, follows St. Paul in a great many details. It is not at all impossible that his belief in the Gospel Message as a Power of God in the believer's heart represents St. Paul's conception of faith with greater accuracy than the Protestant definitions of the Sixteenth Century. In any case he is much more true than those Protestant theologians to the thought of his Master when he insists that the test of a tree, in God's sight as in man's, is the quality of its fruit, and that the fruit God wants is not so much mysticism as purity of soul expressed in ethical integrity

/Justin had a divine guide to conduct in the sayings of Jesus The true ethical ideal has been pronounced by Christ, he says, in the double commandment, love of God and of one's neighbor To love God with a whole heart excludes worship of any other God, and includes reverence to Christ because God wishes us to revere Him. To love our neighbour means both to pray and to work for that to befall the neighbour which we should particularly like to have befall ourselves A neighbour is any human being whatever,[1] and hence includes our enemies The

[1] Dial, 93. 2, 3 (321 A, B)

Christians die in persecution praying for their persecutors, and refuse to give the least retort to accusations.[1] They pray for the Jews and call them brothers, in spite of the hatred the Jews bear them.[2] The Christians have given up personal ambition for wealth and have all things in common.[3] They are so strict in their reverence for truth that they refuse to take an oath with mental reservations.[4] They are peaceful instead of warlike.[5] The Christians live in remarkable sexual purity. They never marry except for the begetting of children, and are perfectly continent out of matrimony.[6] Each man sits under his own vine, that is, Justin explains, with his own wife.[7] All sorts of demon worship and magic have been given up, and the Christians now serve the one God alone.[8] Justin quotes most of the moral maxims of the Sermon on the Mount, and demands that anyone who is not living according to these teachings be punished, for such can be a Christian only in name.[9] The Christian doctrine, he says, enjoins civil obedience, and he quotes the incident of Christ and the denarius, but says that rulers must beware how they conduct themselves, for as they have been given much by God, He will require much from them again.[10] Justin's ethics are clearly based upon the Synoptic tradition. In only one point does he present a contrast to New Testament ethics. He goes much further than St. Paul and prohibits absolutely the eating of meat offered to idols.[11] The fact has been frequently exaggerated to show that Justin was not of a Pauline school of Christianity. Justin's point of view seems not in the least to warrant such a generalization. Justin lived nearly a hundred years after St. Paul, and in the meantime Christian

[1] Dial. 18. 3 (236 A).
[2] Dial. 96. 3 (323 D); 108. 3 (325 D)
[3] Ap. I. 14. 2 (61 C).
[4] Ap. I. 39. 4, 5 (78 C)
[5] Ap. I. 39. 3 (78 B); Dial. 110. 3 (337 A).
[6] Ap. I. 29 entire; 14. 2 (61 C); 15. 1—8 (61 E ff.).
[7] Dial. 110. 3 (337 B)
[8] Ap. I. 14. 2 (61 C)
[9] Ap. I. 16. 14 (64 C).
[10] Ap. I. 17 entire.
[11] Dial. 35. 1 ff (253 A ff).

experience might well have found that St Paul's liberal counsel on the matter of meat offered to idols was impracticable. The eating of meat offered to idols by any Christians had probably become so scandalous to most Christians that it had seemed advisable to debar its use altogether. It is not the only instance where orthodox Christianity has been forced to set aside one of St. Paul's practical counsels. But Justin has very few such restrictions for Christians. In general it is by lives of peace, honesty, purity, and love to all men that he thinks God is to be pleased and the ultimate happiness won. / The eternal moral law of which all men have had inklings is to Justin practically complete in the Sermon on the Mount. He can imagine no higher ethical standard

As part of the Christian life Justin speaks in several passages of the Eucharist. But no element of Justin's teaching has been so much disputed. He has been demonstrated as teaching every known theory of the Eucharist, and in spite of the fact that the literature on the subject is very large, the disagreement among later expositors of his Eucharistic theory is as profound as that of fifty years ago.

Justin describes two celebrations of a sacred meal. The first is the closing rite of baptism and is the more important description of the two [1] At the conclusion of the baptismal ceremony the new member is brought to the place of meeting (evidently the baptisms were not performed at the meeting place, probably in an open stream), where are assembled all the brethren. The company is made up of those who have become Christians by the steps already described, that is of those who believe in the truth of the Christian doctrines, who have been washed for the remission of sins unto regeneration, and who are living according to Christ's instructions. Their object in meeting on this occasion is to unite in prayer for the newly baptized member and for themselves and all others, "that, having learned the truth, they may be accounted worthy to be in their works good citizens and keepers of the commandments, so that they may be saved with everlasting

[1] Ap I 65, 66 entire.

salvation." At the conclusion of these prayers they salute one another with a kiss. Then are brought to the president of the brethren bread and a cup of wine mixed with water. The president takes these and offers a special prayer of praise to the Father of the universe through the name of the Son and the Holy Spirit, and of "thanksgiving at considerable length for being counted worthy to receive these things at His hand. And when he has concluded the prayers and thanksgivings, all the people express their assent by saying Amen." Then "those who are called by us deacons give to each of those present to partake of the bread and wine mixed with water over which the thanksgiving was pronounced, and to those who are absent they carry away a portion."

The second description of the celebration of the Eucharist is of that which was done each Sunday at the weekly meeting of the Christians.[1] This service was opened by a reading from the Prophets or the Memoirs of the Apostles which varied in length with the time at the company's disposal, and which was followed by an address of instruction and exhortation by the president. The company then stood and prayed, and at the conclusion of the prayer the elements were brought in and distributed as before described, after the president had "offered prayers and thanksgiving according to his ability." This last phrase which has caused considerable difficulty seems on the whole best understood as indicating an extemporary prayer. The service was accompanied by a collection for the poor and needy.

Thus far the description has been sufficiently straight-forward and clear. On only two points of the account has there been any important difference of opinion. The standing of the president and deacons in Justin's narrative is undefined, and has consequently been open to conflicting interpretations /The president is a man who conducts the Eucharist, preaches to the congregation, and has charge of the community funds and of the relief of the distressed. But Justin has not given a phrase of indication that the

[1] Ap. I 67. 1—5 (98 C—E).

president was a specially ordained person rather than one
who held a temporary office of pre-eminence in the
congregation [1] Likewise the deacons might as well have
been the deacons of Congregationalism as of Catholicism
from Justin's description. Justin tells us practically nothing
about Church organization. He was evidently one in whose
thinking the theory of the Church meant comparatively
little. The Christians constitute the garments of Christ,
he says,[2] but their organization was not a part of the
scheme of salvation. It is unfair to infer from this silence
that the church organization was unsystematic, or that
church theory interested Justin's contemporaries as little
as it did him. But unless Justin keeps silent upon the
question of Church theory for apologetic reasons, his
instruction in theology could not have put so much stress
upon the subject as Christian instruction of later centuries.

The other point which Justin's description of the
celebration of the Eucharist has raised is the matter of
whether the elements of the Eucharist are described as
being bread and wine or bread and water. The discussion
upon this point was opened by an interesting dissertation
by Professor Harnack defending the thesis that Justin's
elements were bread and water [3] But Harnack's argument
depends upon some serious changes of text, and consequently has been judged on the whole as unconvincing.

It is, more particularly, upon the Eucharistic theory
of Justin that discussion is still unsettled. Justin's words
appear to the present writer to represent so primitive a
mode of thought about the Eucharist that the advanced
or detailed interpretations which have been given to his
statements seem for the most part more interesting from
the speculative than from the historical point of view.
The statement which has always constituted the center
of controversy is the following "For not as common bread

[1] Veil's note 5 to c 65 (p 97) is an excellent instance of a
discussion which has gone far beyond the actual data. A theory
of Church government can only so be read into Justin

[2] Dial 54. 1 (273 D)

[3] (Bibl. 362) Harnack's opponents are indicated in the Bibliography in loco

or common drink do we receive these things; but just as Jesus Christ our Saviour, having been made flesh by the word of God, had both flesh and blood for our salvation, so likewise have we been taught that that food for which thanks was given by the word of thanksgiving offered by him (the president?), and by which our blood and flesh are by transmutation nourished, is the flesh and blood of that Jesus who was made flesh. For the Apostles in the Memoirs composed by them and which are called Gospels, have thus delivered to us the things which had been commanded to them; that Jesus took bread, and when He had given thanks, said, 'This do in remembrance of me; this is my body'; and that having similarly taken the cup and given thanks He said, 'This is my blood', and gave it to them alone." [1] The passage is most interesting, but inconclusive. Of the various interpretations that of Semisch is the most attractive. He saw in Justin's remarks a contrast and comparison between the Incarnation and the introduction of the divine Logos into the elements of the Eucharist. He concluded that Justin conceived of a new incarnation of the Logos in the elements; that the elements became united, not with the divine flesh and blood by consubstantiation, but with the Logos Himself by a fresh incarnation, by which the bread and wine became His flesh and blood without changing nature or ceasing to be bread and wine. [2]

---

[1] Ap. I. 66. 2, 3 (98 A, B) οὐ γὰρ ὡς κοινὸν ἄρτον οὐδὲ κοινὸν πόμα ταῦτα λαμβάνομεν· ἀλλ᾽ ὃν τρόπον διὰ λόγου θεοῦ σαρκοποιηθεὶς Ἰησοῦς Χριστὸς ὁ σωτὴρ ἡμῶν καὶ σάρκα καὶ αἷμα ὑπὲρ σωτηρίας ἡμῶν ἔσχεν, οὕτως καὶ τὴν δι᾽ εὐχῆς λόγου τοῦ παρ᾽ αὐτοῦ εὐχαριστηθεῖσαν τροφήν, ἐξ ἧς αἷμα καὶ σάρκες κατὰ μεταβολὴν τρέφονται ἡμῶν, ἐκείνου τοῦ σαρκοποιηθέντος Ἰησοῦ καὶ σάρκα καὶ αἷμα ἐδιδάχθημεν εἶναι. οἱ γὰρ ἀπόστολοι ἐν τοῖς γενομένοις ὑπ᾽ αὐτῶν ἀπομνημονεύμασιν, ἃ καλεῖται εὐαγγέλια, οὕτως παρέδωκαν ἐντετάλθαι αὐτοῖς· τὸν Ἰησοῦν λαβόντα ἄρτον εὐχαριστήσαντα εἰπεῖν· τοῦτο ποιεῖτε εἰς τὴν ἀνάμνησίν μου, τοῦτ᾽ ἔστι τὸ σῶμά μου· καὶ τὸ ποτήριον ὁμοίως λαβόντα καὶ εὐχαριστήσαντα εἰπεῖν· τοῦτό ἐστι τὸ αἷμά μου. καὶ μόνοις αὐτοῖς μεταδοῦναι.

[2] Semisch (Bibl. 118) II. 437 ff. The same interpretation has recently been made by G. P. Wetter, Altchristliche Liturgien: I. Das christliche Mysterium. Göttingen 1921. p. 143.

/But on the whole it must be admitted that Justin has given here no theory of the Eucharist. He says only that the bread and wine which are blessed, and by which our bodies are nourished, are the flesh and blood of the Christ who has been incarnate, and as such that they are no ordinary food and drink. To go beyond this into an explanation of how the bread and wine becomes or may be called the flesh and blood of Christ is to go beyond our evidence.

Equally baffling are the references to the Eucharist in the Dialogue. In chapter 41. 1—3 (260 A, B) /Justin describes the Eucharist as a celebration prescribed by Jesus Christ in memory of the suffering which He endured on behalf of those who are purified in soul from all iniquity. The thanksgiving which the name of the sacrament implies is offered for two things, first for the fact that God has created the world and all things therein for the sake of man, second "for delivering us from the evil in which we were, and for overthrowing principalities and powers with a complete overthrow through Him who suffered according to His will." The bread and cup of the Eucharist are sacrifices offered to God, by which the name of God is glorified. We have here probably a very early form of the prayer of thanksgiving for our creation and preservation, and perhaps more phrases of the present Prayer of General Thanksgiving were then in use.[1] /But in spite of the fact that Justin here calls the Eucharist a sacrifice by which God is glorified, he still offers no explanation of the Eucharist, whether as to its nature or as to its operation upon the communicant. The sacrament seems indeed to be rather a celebration for benefits already received than a source of new blessings.

In another passage Justin states that the prophecy "Bread shall be given him, and his water shall be sure," refers "to the bread which our Christ gave us to do (ποιεῖν), in remembrance of His being made flesh for the sake of His believers, for whom also He suffered; and to the cup which He gave us to do (ποιεῖν) in remembrance

[1] Cf. Ap. I. 13. 2 (60 D).

ot His own blood with giving of thanks."[1] Here Justin
has clearly St Paul's account of the institution in mind,
and is giving the Apostle's words a sacrificial interpretation. But still he gives no basis for a theory of
the Eucharist

In another passage, Justin speaks of the Eucharist as
a sacrifice presented by Christians through all the world.[2]
He admits that prayers and thanksgivings offered by worthy
men at any time and anywhere are perfect and well
pleasing sacrifices to God, but insists that the Christian
Eucharist is the only prayer and thanksgiving which has
been worthy to be called truly a sacrifice The Christian
offering then is apparently unique only in the degree
of its worthiness as a prayer and thanksgiving and not
because of any peculiarity of its nature.

Justin's remarks on the Eucharist, taken together,
show that he regarded it as the supreme form of worship.
In partaking of the sacrament which had been instituted
by Christ Himself Christians partook of the body and
blood of Christ, in remembrance of His incarnation and
suffering.[3] The sacrament was a sacrifice to God, of so
exalted a character that it alone could be truly called a
sacrifice pleasing to God. But theory of the Eucharist
he probably did not have at all. He was content to take
the spiritual blessing of the Eucharist without questioning
just how the elements he was eating had become, or in
what sense they could be called, the body and blood of
Christ But he makes quite clear that by his time the
separation between the Agape and the Eucharist was
complete, and that the Eucharist was celebrated as a conclusion to the rites of baptism as well as at the weekly
assembly of the congregation.

It would be wrong to close an account of Justin's
thought of salvation and the Christian Life without
protesting against too rigid a use of our sources   Justin

[1] Dial. 70. 3, 4 (296 D ff)

[2] Dial. 117. 1—3 (344 C ff).

[3] I cannot agree with Veil's distinction between St. Paul's and
Justin's emphasis in the Eucharist. Justin's reference of the sacrament to the death of Christ is even more significant than that to
the Incarnation See Veil (Bibl 80) n 2 to c 66. pp 103—106.

has little to say of a Christian life of mysticism and communion with God. His emphasis upon the ethical side of Christianity is very strong But before concluding, as has often been done, that Justin is barren of a mystical interpretation of the believer's life, one must take into consideration the apologetic and exoteric character of all the three genuine writings. Justin, in addressing outsiders, would naturally be concerned with giving evidence and with preaching conversion, heaven and hell, and the ethical standards and achievments of Christianity. Herein the contrast with St Paul is complete. While all of St. Paul's remains are intimate letters to Christians, all of Justin's are apologies to unbelievers It is almost as though, granted the verbal accuracy of the reports of St. Paul's addresses in Acts, we were restricted to that book alone for our knowledge of his thought In that case St. Paul the mystic might have been guessed, but could not have been known So it is utterly unfair to Justin to think that his Christianity is adequately represented in the apologetic documents that have come down to us He was certainly no such mystic as St. Paul, but he was certainly a Christian mystic. It was a hunger for mystic experience which he represents as his incentive in philosophic inquiry, and though there is little likelihood that the account of his philosophic quest is accurate, it still is plain that he regarded the philosophic sects in the light of mysticism rather than of philosophy proper He talks about the entire Logos as being in the Christians, but to Christians he would undoubtedly have been speaking, like St. Paul, of the indwelling Christ. It was not an external guide so much as the Christ within him from which he got his ideas and direction. The proper understanding of the Scriptures was to be had not by study or skill in reasoning, but by drinking of the living fountain of God.[1] If this passage refers to baptism, it refers clearly to the φωτισμός which is one of the most mystical interpretations of baptism ever given Trypho, as a Jew without this illumination, cannot comprehend the Scriptures.[2] But

[1] Dial. 140 1 (369 B).
[2] Dial 38 2 (256 C); 55. 3 (274 D).

Justin, as a partaker in grace, has been granted understanding.[1] Likewise the indwelling Logos repels the attacks of the demons "Though the devil is ever at hand to resist us." he says, "and anxious to seduce all to himself, yet the Angel of God, that is the Power of God sent to us through Jesus Christ, rebukes him, and he departs from us."[2] Justin may not have been a profound mystic. But he is still less a man who approached Christianity from a rationalist's point of view, or who restricted the operation of God to an acknowledgment that man had left the path of sin by his own free choice. He did not conceive of his own Christian life as lived from baptism till death guided only by his own mind, and warding off evil with only his own strength. The Christian may live his life and bravely face death inwardly led and inspired by Christ, and blessed and empowered by the gifts of the Spirit. "We continually beseech God by Jesus Christ to preserve us from the demons which are hostile to the worship of God, and whom of old times we served, in order that, after our conversion to God, we may through Him be blameless. For we call Him Helper and Redeemer."[3]

[1] Dial. 58. 1 (280 A, B)
[2] Dial. 116. 1 (344 A)
[3] Dial. 30. 3 (248 C).

CHAPTER X

ESCHATOLOGY

The first coming of Christ did not fulfill the Jewish
expectation, and was regarded by Jesus Himself as but a
tentative step toward the solution of the world's problems.
The early Church looked upon the coming in humility as
the foundation of their hope, but their hope itself looked
forward unto a fuller manifestation of the power of their
Saviour. To early Christians the first coming was utterly
meaningless apart from the consummation in the Parousia,
and it is one of the marvels of history that Christianity did
not collapse when its eschatological hope had to be in-
definitely postponed. St Paul in his later life saw the
danger of his early emphasis upon the second coming, and
it was probably his magnificent courage in facing and
correcting the mistake of his early thinking which opened
the way for the ultimate change of thinking of orthodox
Christianity. But the change was gradual, and was at first
possible only to the most thoughtful of the Church. Simple
Christians held to the plain statements of Jesus and of the
early Apostles, as many simple Christians still do today, and
insisted that Christ was yet to come to found an earthly
kingdom, while they interpreted the events of their
generation as indicating the probability of a momentary
fulfillment of their hopes.

Justin takes his place in this long line of simple
Christians to whom the written and oral traditions of early
Christianity in their literal significance have meant more
than the attempts of thoughtful men to reconcile them
with the facts of life. A Christian by Justin's definition
is a man who "has been persuaded that the unjust and
intemperate shall be punished in eternal fire, but that the

virtuous, that is those who live like Christ, shall dwell in a state that is free from suffering."[1] This statement represents Justin's real belief. His eyes were ever fixed upon the future. But it is quite characteristic of the sort of Christian thinking which Justin represents that in spite of the overwhelming emphasis he lays upon the second coming of Christ and the last judgment he has not a definite and consistent conception of what is to happen.

Proofs of the second coming of Christ Justin found chiefly in the Old Testament. The Christians had always to face the difficulty in proving the Messianic character of Jesus that the Jews utterly scoffed at their description of a Jewish Messiah, and at their claim that a crucified man could pretend to fulfill the Jewish expectations. The Christian answer as found in Justin was to take all that the Jews said of their Messiah and apply it to the second coming, while many new passages were adduced as being also Messianic, with the claim that they had been fulfilled in the first advent of Christ.[2] "He shall drink of the brook in the way, therefore shall he lift up the head," describes the humility and then the grandeur of the two comings.[3] In the first advent Christ was to be pierced; in the second advent they will look upon Him whom they have pierced and bitterly mourn[4] The glories of the prophecy of the dying Jacob are to be fulfilled in the second coming.[5] "He shall be the desire of the nations" can only refer to a second advent of Jesus Christ who is now the anticipation of the pious of every race.[6] Moses and Joshua together saved the Israelitish hosts. For Moses stretched out his hands, and Joshua led the army to victory. Moses with his arms outstretched symbolizes the first coming and the Cross; but Joshua whose name is the same as Jesus, symbolizes the second coming when the power of the name will finally be

[1] Ap. II. 1. 2 (41 C); cf von Engelhardt (Bibl. 313) pp. 199 ff.
[2] Dial. 14. 8 (232 D).
[3] Dial. 33. 2 (251 B); cf Ps. cx. 7.
[4] Dial. 32. 2 (249 D); cf. Zech. xii. 10, 12
[5] Dial. 52. 1 ff. (271 C), cf. Gen. xlix. 8—12.
[6] Dial. 52, 4 (272 B); cf. Gen. xlix. 10

victorious over the demonic hosts .[1] The two goats offered
during the fast are likewise symbols of the two advents.[2]
In the second advent all the marvels of the prophecies of
Daniel are to be revealed.[3]

This second coming is not to take place without adequate preparation, though as to the nature of the preparation Justin gives two contradictory explanations. Christ,
Justin says in the Dialogue, is to sit at the right hand of
God until God has made Christ's enemies His footstool.[4]
In the Apology Justin says that God will keep Christ in
Heaven until He has subdued His enemies the devils, and
until the number of those foreknown by Him as good and
virtuous is complete.[5] We should infer from these passages that Justin looked for an increased checking of the
demonic activity by the power of the first coming, and
that when these evil personalities have at last been conquered, and the number of the righteous completed, Christ
will come in glory. But Justin explains also that the Man
of Apostasy foretold by Daniel shall have dominion for a
time, times, and a half a time, and shall speak daring
blasphemies against the Most High.[6] The second coming
is to be preceded by a rampant propagation of heresy
which will deceive even many of the faithful.[7] In contradiction to his first quoted scheme these latter passages
would lead us to conclude that Justin looked for an increasingly evil time, which is to be consummated in the
person of the Man of Apostasy speaking strange things
against the Most High and doing unlawful things against
the Christians.[8] When the time of tribulation shall have
thus reached its height, Justin looked for the second advent. The contradiction of ideas is typical of the confusion
in which Justin was content to leave his eschatology in

[1] Dial. 111. 1 ff. (338 A).
[2] Dial. 40. 4 (259 C); cf Levit. xvi. 5 ff
[3] Dial. 31, 32.
[4] Dial. 32 3 (250 A).
[5] Ap. I 45. 1 (82 D)
[6] Dial. 32. 3 (250 A)
[7] Dial. 35. 2 ff. (253 A ff.); cf 51 2 (271 A, B).
[8] Dial. 110. 2 (336 D); cf. II Thes. ii. 3, 4.

spite of the importance with which he regarded it. Besides the time of apostasy and the coming of the Man of Apostasy, the suppression of the demons, and the fulfilling of the number of the righteous, Justin looked for one more sign of the advent. Elijah is to return a second time to be the herald of Christ, the immediate precursor of the great event.[1] But Justin tells us no particulars about this second reappearance of Elijah.

Justin looked for the Parousia momentarily. He advises the Jews in the Dialogue to make their decision for Christ with the least possible delay, because Christ is to be revealed in a very short time, and once He has come all opportunity for repentance will be closed.[2] The times are now running on to their consumation.[3] Justin refers to the statement in Daniel that the Man of Apostasy is to rule for a time, times, and a half a time,[4] and says that many people take this "time" to mean a century, in which case the Man of Apostasy would rule at least for 350 years. Justin says that it was urged that on the basis of this interpretation there will be ample opportunity for repentance and becoming Christian after the nature of the Man of Apostasy is fully established and revealed. But though this interpretation of "time" is certainly the traditional one.[5] Justin rejects it The Man of Apostasy could not possibly be allowed so long a period of rulership, he says. Once the last signs begin to appear, events will move very rapidly, and to Justin's thinking the Man of Apostasy was even then at the door. Justin says that the destruction of the world has been thus long postponed only because of the "seed of the Christians, which God recognizes as a cause in nature." [6] Here Justin has complicated an Old Testament idea of the saving from destruction of a city which included a small remnant or seed of righteous people, by punning upon the word σπέρμα. Apparently the σπέρμα

[1] Dial. 49 2, 3 (268 B, C).
[2] Dial. 28 2 (245 C)
[3] Dial. 32 3 (250 A).
[4] Ibid
[5] Cf Goldfahn (Bibl. 389) p 58.
[6] Ap. II. 7 1 (45 B)

which is an αἴτιον ἐν τῇ φύσει refers to the Spermatic Logos conception,[1] but the connection between this conception and that of a nucleus of good people who avert destruction from a large group of wicked people is hard to see, while the passage is not particularly simplified by denying to it any Spermatic Logos sense. For in that case the significance of the Christians for the *physical* universe is still unexplained. As a matter of fact Justin represents the Christians as earnestly looking forward to the end of this order of existence, and the destruction of the world, so that as they are to have no part in the destruction, it is hard to understand why the consummation should be delayed for their sakes.[2]

The beginning of the coming is to be a sudden appearance of Christ together with His angels in the clouds of heaven[3] The resurrection will follow immediately. This is to be a reuniting of the soul with the actual body discarded at death[4] Justin faces frankly the difficulty of the restoration of a decayed or destroyed body, but says that it is no whit more remarkable that God can reunite the elements which constitute a body, than that He can make a body in the first place from a small drop of human seed. Wonders great as the resurrection of the flesh are familiar. It is only the strangeness of this particular wonder that makes it seem impossible. With God all things are possible. "We shall receive again our own bodies, though they be dead and cast into the earth."[5]

From the Dialogue we should infer that the resurrection at this time will be the resurrection of the saints, who will then join Christ in an earthly rule in Jeru-

[1] See above p 163

[2] Otto's explanation (in loco) that the Christians are the reason why the world was created is at once not accurate to Justin's thought (for he says that the world was created for the sake of men in general), and still does not help to explain why these Christians should be regarded by God as a cause for delay in carrying out His plans for their salvation

[3] Ap I 51 8, 9 (86 E), 52 3 (87 A ff) Dial 31 1 (247 D)
[4] Ap I 19 entire
[5] Ap I 18 6 (65 C)

salem Justin speaks of a "holy resurrection"[1] which is to
be followed by a distribution to the Christians of an eternal
possession. As Joshua led the Children of Israel into Palestine and distributed the land, so shall Christ gather the
faithul and "distribute the good land to each one, though
not in the same way." Christ will then shine as a light in
Jerusalem eternally.[2] Again Justin says, "Christ came calling men to a . . . . living together of all the saints in the
same land whose possession He has promised, as has been
shown already Whence men from all parts, whether slave
or free, who believe in Christ and know the truth in His
and the Prophets' words, know that they will be with Him
in that land, there to inherit the things that are eternal
and incorruptible."[3] "Jerusalem will be really rebuilt," and
the Christians "will be collected and made glad with Christ,
along with the Patriarchs and Prophets and the holy men
of the Jewish race, and with those who were Jewish
proselytes before Christ came."[4] Since Justin seems to
imply that this rule in Jerusalem is to be preceded by a
renewing of heaven and earth,[5] we might, without further
information, be led to suppose that the "holy resurrection"
means the general resurrection, and that the coming of
Christ means an immediate judgment, the renewing of
heaven and earth, and the establishment of a new eternal
kingdom with the new Jerusalem as its capital, and all
Christians of all ages as sharing in the eternal rule.

But Justin is not always consistent with this comparatively simple eschatology. For he introduces an idea of a
special age of one thousand years during which this reign
shall be exercised from Jerusalem, the period to be preceded
by a resurrection of the just, and closed by a resurrection
of all (that is all others, the wicked), and the final
judgment. "But I and whatever Christians are of the true

[1] Dial. 113 4 (340 C) ἁγίαν ἀνάστασιν. which should be
understood as the resurrection of the saints though the text be not,
with Thirlby, changed to ἁγίων.

[2] Ibid.

[3] Dial. 132. 4, 5 (369 A); cf Donaldson (Bibl. 143)
p. 259

[4] Dial. 80 1 (306 B).

[5] Dial 113 5 (340 D)

faith understand that there is to be a resurrection of the flesh and a thousand years in Jerusalem which will have been rebuilt, adorned, and enlarged, as the prophets Ezekiel and Isaiah and others declare."[1] "And further, there was a certain man with us whose name was John, one of the Apostles of Christ who prophesied by a revelation made to him that those who believed upon our Christ would spend (ποιήσειν) a thousand years in Jerusalem, and that thereafter the general and, in short, the eternal resurrection of all men at the same time, and the judgment, would take place."[2] The character of existence and rulership which is to be given to the faithful during this period Justin does not describe. Semisch has inappropriately applied Justin's citation of the return of Christ to Jerusalem to eat and drink with the Disciples after His resurrection to the millenial period.[3] Justin in that passage means the post-resurrection appearances of Jesus, because he cites the instance among other events, which, already having happened, had fulfilled prophecy. Justin believes however that it is in this period that the prophecies of Isaiah lxv. will be fulfilled, and he probably understood the words as referring to actually material conditions.[4] For it is only after the general Resurrection that he applies the saying of Jesus, "They shall neither marry nor be given in marriage, but shall be equal to the angels, children of God being (children) of the resurrection."[5]

There seems to be no way of reconciling the millenium with the clear implication of Justin's other remarks that the new Jerusalem will be an eternal inheritance.[6] On the

[1] Dial 80 5 (307 B)
[2] Dial 81 4 (308 A, B).
[3] Dial 51 2 (271 A)   Semisch (Bibl 118) II 471
[4] Dial 81 entire
[5] Dial 81 4 (308 B)   Justin's quotation τέκνα τοῦ θεοῦ τῆς ἀναστάσεως ὄντες is probably an abridgment of Luke xx 35, 36. Since these words, without altering the text, can be taken in the sense in which I have translated them, that is in the sense of Luke's text, the translation of Reith (which follows Otto), "the children of the God of the resurrection" seems to introduce unnecessarily a discrepancy of sense between Justin and the text of Luke.
[6] Donaldson's remarks (Bibl 143) pp 261 ff, are excellent

other hand it is impossible to use the contradiction to soften
the unorthodoxy of Justin's chiliasm [1] The fact that the
millenial hope and the earthly kingdom from Jerusalem are
not mentioned in the First Apology is no argument either
for a separate authorship of the Dialogue and First Apology,
or for the inconsequential nature of Justin's belief in the
Thousand Years [2] The doctrine of the collapse of all earthly
power, and the rule of the world by the despised Christians
under the despised Christ at Jerusalem must have been a
most untactful piece of propaganda and apologetic to be
used in the non-Christian world That Justin has seen fit
not to mention such a doctrine in the Apology does not in
the least reflect upon the possibility that he believed in it
with all his heart Like the contradictory descriptions of
the preparation for the second coming, the contradiction
between the eternal rule from Jerusalem and the millenial
rule must be allowed to stand.

The event which Justin put either immediately after
the second advent, or at the close of the Thousand Years,
is the focus of Justin's eschatological thinking, if not of his
entire Christianity. For that all men will rise from the
dead, with their own bodies, to be judged before the throne
of God according to their deeds is the chief incentive in
Justin's mind to a holy life. He even threatens the Emperor
with damnation. "We forewarn you that you shall not escape
the coming judgment of God, if you continue in your injustice " [3] "And if you also read these words in a hostile
spirit you can do no more, as I said before, than kill us:
which indeed does no harm to us, but to you and all who
unjustly hate us, and do not repent, brings eternal punishment by fire." [4] All men, living and dead, even back to

[1] As does Feder (Bibl. 350) pp. 236, 237.

[2] The mention of the future kingdom in Ap I 11 is nothing
more than an extremely awkward attempt to avoid the subject.
The chapter has no significance for Justin's beliefs except to show
that the kingdom was a matter which he did not then care to
discuss Indeed the reign of Christ from Jerusalem is entirely
consistent with every word in the chapter.

[3] Ap. I. 68 2 (99 C).

[4] Ap I 45 6 (83 A, B)

Adam, will be haled before this tribunal.[1] The judgment, as always in Christian tradition, is to be based upon works. "Each man will go to eternal punishment or eternal salvation according to the merits of his conduct."[2] "Our Lord Jesus Christ said, in whatsoever things I take you, in these things also will I judge you"[3] As Isaiah was sawed in two with a wooden saw, so will Christ divide the human race at the judgment, some for the everlasting kingdom, some for unquenchable fire[4] Both men and angels are to be judged at the same judgment, as both alike have been given free will.[5] Christ is to be the Judge, acting, as always, for the Father. God, Justin says, will conduct the judgment διὰ τοῦ κυρίου μου Ἰησοῦ Χριστοῦ.[6] The office of Judge has been given to Christ (sc. by God).[7] This will be the final glorification of Christ The demons will here be finally and completely subdued and sent to eternal fires[8] while Christ, unchallenged, will become the eternal King and Priest.[9]

The damned go at once to the fires of hell. "Hell is a place where those are to be punished who have lived wickedly and who do not believe that those things which God has taught us by Christ will come to pass."[10] But here, as has already been pointed out,[11] Justin once more is not consistent From most of his remarks we should suppose that all men and angels not worthy of salvation are to be condemned to an eternal fire, where in spite of the fire they will retain their immortality in order to suffer forever.[12] Justin says explicitly that the punishment

[1] Dial 118 1 (346 A); 132 1 (362 A)
[2] Ap I 12 1 (59 B).
[3] Dial 47. 5 (267 A).
[4] Dial 120 5 (349 B)
[5] Dial 141 1, 2 (370 B).
[6] Dial 58 1 (280 B).
[7] Dial 46. 1 (264 B).
[8] Ap I 28. 1 (71 B), 52 3 (87 B).
[9] Dial 36 1 (254 C)
[10] Ap. I 19 8 (66 B)
[11] See above p 225
[12] Ap. I 18 2 (65 A); 52 3 (87 B); Ap II. 1 2 (41 C), Dial 130 2 (359 D)

of the wicked is not to endure only a thousand years, as
Plato said, but eternally.[1] But Justin also says that in
the eternal fire each man will suffer "according to the
merit of his deed, and will render account according to
the powers he has received from God."[2] Each man is to
be punished as God sees fit,[3] or for whatever sins he has
committed.[4] The wicked are punished so long as God
wills them to exist and be punished.[5] Justin is here
again retaining distinct traditions. It is idle to speculate
as to which he regarded as the true one.

In the matter of the world conflagration, which can
only be supposed to happen after the judgment, Justin again
suggests that he is retaining contradictory traditions. In
one passage Justin speaks of a doctrine of the Christians
which is vastly superior to the similar Stoic teachings.
Both believe that the world is to be consumed in a final
conflagration. But, says Justin, the ultimate destruction
of all things is not correctly described in the Stoic doctrines
of a metabolism of all things into each other.[6] It is evident
that Justin's criticism of the Stoic doctrine is based not
upon its aimless cycles,[7] but upon the Stoic identification
of God with destructible phenomena. For the Stoics
represented the eternal changing and dissolving matter
as itself deity, and it is against this notion that Justin
roundly protests. The Christians believe, he says, that
the end of the world will come by the raining of fire upon

---

[1] Ap. I. 8. 4 (57 B).

[2] Ap. I. 17. 4 (64 D, E) πρὸς ἀναλογίαν ὧν ἔλαβε δυνάμεων
παρὰ θεοῦ. This phrase suggests a greater or less share of the
δύναμις παρὰ θεοῦ in each man, which might indicate that the
Spermatic Logos, the highest power in each man, varies in amount
in different individuals. But as the reference in the passage is
very uncertain the statement was not adduced as evidence in discussing Justin's anthropology. Still the probability seems to favor
such an interpretation.

[3] Dial. 88. 5 (316 B).

[4] Ap. II. 7. 5 (45 D).

[5] Dial. 5. 3 (223 B); cf above p. 225.

[6] Ap. II. 7 entire, cf. Ap I..20. 4 (66 D).

[7] Such is Veil's interpretation in loco

the earth as God rained water in the days of Noah, and
that in the destruction all wicked angels, demons, and men
will perish. Only those who are Christians, whether before
or after Christ, it is to be inferred, will escape. Over against
this very explicit passage stand the passages already discussed of an eternal rule, with Jerusalem, and apparently
the earthly Jerusalem, as its capital,[1] which led Donaldson
to the statement. "Heaven was the peculiar habitation of
God, they assigned some definite place to dead Christians,
and they all looked forward to a complete renovation
of the earth ... Justin was therefore consistent in looking
to earth as the final habitation of the blessed."[2] Donaldson
can only be justified by allowing him to identify the
destruction of the earth already described with a statement
in the Dialogue that the Father will renew both heaven
and earth ἀπὸ καὶ διὰ Χριστοῦ.[3] But Donaldson does not
himself so interpret this latter passage,[4] and it is hard
to see how the renewing of the earth can be taken as
synonymous with its complete destruction. We shall have
to be content with leaving another unreconciled contradiction in Justin's eschatology. It must be recognized
that it is only in the Apologies we hear of the final
conflagration,[5] and only in the Dialogue that mention
is made of the eternal rule from Jerusalem, as well as the
chiliastic form of that tradition. But we have found already
too many inconsistencies in Justin's eschatology to draw
any hasty conclusions as to a different authorship of the
two works on that account.

But the divergence between the two doctrines about the
end of the world makes the doctrine of the future state of
the blessed different in the Apology from that in the
Dialogue. Von Engelhardt rightly concludes that the
destruction of the world with all the wicked, as described

[1] See above p 284

[2] (Bibl 143) p. 259

[3] Dial 113 5 (340 D)

[4] Donaldson looks upon this renewing as a process begun in
the Incarnation and consummated after the Judgment. Loc cit.

[5] Though that the world will perish is clearly the implication
of the argument in Dial. 5 1, 2 (222 E ff.).

in the Apologies, makes it essential to look to heaven as the place of the reward of immortality for Christians,[1] while it is just as fairly concluded by Donaldson from the statements in the Dialogue that earth was the scene of the ultimate happiness of the blessed.[2] But Justin becomes in some measure consistent with himself when he remarks about the condition of the blessed. In the Apologies he speaks of the saved as being immortalized[3] All men after death retain their powers of sense perception,[4] but this is said particularly of the wicked to insure the fact that they will feel the full horrors of the fires of damnation. The process of "immortalizing" may indicate the fact that the souls of the blessed will in some way be transformed, so that Justin is justified in speaking of the saved as existing in a state beyond sensation (βιώσαντες ἐν ἀπαθείᾳ).[5] In this state they will live with God (συγγενήσεσθαι τῷ θεῷ),[6] an eternal and pure life where nothing evil can cause disturbance[7] In the Dialogue they are similarly described as ἐν ἀπαθείᾳ καὶ ἀφθαρσίᾳ καὶ ἀλυπίᾳ καὶ ἀθανασίᾳ.[8] But one cannot see in these phrases the hunger of a Greek for freedom from the flesh. The passages are mere rhetoric, made up of the catchwords of the day for describing the future state of blessedness· Justin had no Hellenistic horror of the flesh. He only means that the blessed shall live eternally without a shadow of pain or sorrow, and with no diminution of powers.

Accordingly in the second coming of Christ Justin looked for a consummation of all his hopes. Christ Himself is to be Judge of all and Ruler in the new Jerusalem With Him and with God are to be the Christians, that

[1] (Bibl. 313) p. 205.

[2] Loc cit

[3] Ap I 21. 6 (67 D) ἀπαθανατίζεσθαι, translated by Dods "deified", following Otto's note in loco. Otto does not himself so translate, however, and the use of the word in Tatian's Orat ad Graec. 10 3; 16. 2; 25. 2 is not so strong

[4] Ap I 18. 1 (64 E); 20. 4 (66 D).

[5] Ap II. 1 2 (41 C).

[6] Ibid

[7] Ap. I 8 2 (57 A).

[8] Dial 45 4 (264 B), cf. 117. 3 (345 B).

is all those who have ever lived rightly, whether Jews, heathen, or followers of the incarnate Christ. Then will the problems of life all find their solution, and the justice of God be made manifest to every man. One of the chief values of a study of Justin's eschatology is the testimony it bears to the completely uncritical character of his thinking In spite of the overwhelming importance which he lays upon the doctrine of the future, he holds consistently to hardly a single important detail. The preparation for the coming is to be an increase of good things, at the same time a terrible riot of evil. The advent is to mean the founding of an eternal kingdom on earth, though the kingdom is to last only a thousand years, and though the earth itself is to be destroyed in fire The wicked are punished in fire not for a thousand years, but eternally, though Justin says that each man is punished in proportion to his crimes, and exists in the fire only so long as God wishes him to exist and be punished. If Justin could be thus uncritical in his use of tradition in this his most important doctrine, it can only be explained on the grounds that his was an inferior mind, and that to him the Christian life was immeasurably more important than its explanations or theology. On only one point in eschatology does he appear to reject a tradition which has come to him; he denies the Hellenistic doctrine of death as a release of the soul from the body to return to God, and instead retains the Palestinian Jewish notion of a resurrection of the body.

CONCLUSION

Justin's full title, St. Justin, Philosopher and Martyr,
is in part deeply deserved, in part misapplied That Justin
was a Martyr there is no reason to doubt, and there is
still less reason to doubt that his spirit burned with that
conviction and courage in life which in death transformed
executions into martyrdoms. But he burned also with a
gentler and purer flame than those of conviction and
courage, for the hand that traced the writings we assign
to his name, the heart that yearned for the soul of Trypho,
are unmistakably the hand and heart of a Saint The
world would be richer did it still possess some of the
quiet talks Justin used to give Christians in the upper
room above Martinus at the Timiotinian Bath. But while
we honour the Martyr and revere the Saint the fact must
definitely be admitted that Justin was in no sense a
philosopher. He was not a philosopher in that he had
had a philosopher's training, for we have repeatedly seen
that his use of philosophical terminology betrays only a
superficial and popular understanding of philosophical conceptions He was still less a philosopher in the sense that
he approached his problems from a cosmic or metaphysical
point of view. His excursions into the cosmic are necessitous
and inadequate attempts to gain a plausibility in philosophical obscurity for conceptions which as he usually held
them were not only unphilosophical, but often irrational
and contradictory. Justin is not even a philosopher in
the sense that he is concerned about consistency or system
in the beliefs for which he is willing and eager to die.
A tendency to analysis and criticism, the first traces of a
philosophical instinct, are completely absent from his
writings His Roman Catholic commentators are entirely

correct in insisting that he is first and always a traditionalist, whose chief desire is to explain Christianity as he learned it.

The Christianity which Justin learned could have differed from his own theology in only the smallest details, else he, like Marcion, would have been rejected by his own generation. It is inconceivable, for example, that he had learned from other Christians only so much of the Logos Doctrine as was to be found in the Fourth Gospel, and that he wrought out for himself the developments we have already described. He does not reveal the sort of mind by which intellectual pioneering is done. It is possible, though by no means certain, that he introduced a few phrases; he may have been the first to apply the Spermatic Logos conception to Christian Theology. But if he added anything to Christianity at all, it was not by transplanting foreign conceptions into Christianity, but by going deeper than ordinary Christians into a body of thought which was recognized as a legitimate source for Christian metaphysics. For Justin found Christianity an escape from speculation, not a barbarous faith which needed recasting and restating to be intelligible to Greek thinkers. Revelation, as he understood it, satisfied all doubts, settled all problems. The Prophets and Christ, in their perfect harmony, constitute the True Philosophy. Such a point of view is utterly inexplicable if Justin was a Greek in his thinking who never really understood the Christianity to which he had been converted, and who was trying to reconcile a mere Faith with the rationality of the Schools. It is Justin's chief joy in Christianity that what he teaches is not his own, but is the revealed and accepted Faith.

It must then be admitted that the Christianity of Justin's day had already its powerful tradition of orthodoxy, and thus that this tradition included: a God who was first the personal Father, and then as much as possible of the Philonic Deity; a Christ who was the Logos of Hellenistic Judaism, though only half understood, sharply personalized, and declared in His entirety to have been incarnate in Jesus of Nazareth; a host of other spiritual emanations from the Father of whom the most important was the Holy Prophetic Spirit; a company of evil spirits of all sorts of the type believed in by ignorant people everywhere, but recognizably akin to the demons of the Synoptic Gospels, a doctrine of Man, of which the elements are recognizably Philonic, but which falls immeasurably short of Philo's conceptions, a belief in the universal need for salvation, but only a feeble account of the cause of such a need; a popular (Palestinian Jewish) conception of sin as disobedience, rather than as a state of corruption; an overmastering conviction that eternal salvation was given through Christ, but only contradictory fragments of explanations of such a belief; a conviction that salvation was conditioned by man's conduct in this life; and a momentary expectation of the return of Christ when many great, but not certainly known, events would take place which would culminate in the judgement and division of humanity for heaven or hell In brief, the Christianity which Justin has described, with its foundation of primitive Palestinian Judaistic Christian beliefs, was almost entirely dependent for theory upon a Hellenistic Judaistic tradition which had been running in through the doors opened by St. Paul, and by the authors of the Epistle to the Hebrews and of the Fourth Gospel.

BIBLIOGRAPHY

The following bibliography goes again over the entire field although the invaluable work of E C Richardson (Bibliographical Synopsis to the Ante-Nicene Fathers Buffalo 1887 — reprint N. Y 1917 — pp 21—26) might appear adequate for the older literature Richardson omits a few important titles which had appeared up to the time of his first publication, but is still more at fault in including far too many items where the reference to Justin proves to be utterly inconsequential His list is, further, unclassified, and alphabetical rather than chronological The best classified bibliography is that by Baumgarten, published in the bibliographical supplement to his revision of Ueberweg's Geschichte der Philosophie II Berlin 1915, suppl p 37—39. But Baumgarten's bibliography is not complete for modern literature and does not attempt to cover publications earlier than 1840 Von Engelhardt (313) p 2—70 has written a very careful survey of the interpretation of Justin to his own day (1878), and Feder (350) p 14—31 has carried it on to 1906 Both these, however, take account only of literature discussing Justin's theology A bibliography which attempts to be complete, and yet to omit superfluous titles, and which furnishes a chronological and classified guide to the literature on Justin is lacking at present. Accordingly the compiler submits the following list in the hope that it may prove of service. A number of titles of course proved inaccessible, and have had to be taken over from various sources without checking, but this has been done as little as possible

CONTENTS

A Editions	.	296
B. Translations	.	298
1. Latin, 2 Danish, 3 English, 4. French, 5 German, 6 Italian, 7. Russian		
C General Literature	.	299
D Justin's Writings General	. .	303
E. The Two Apologies	.	304
F The Dialogue	.	305
G. Chronology	.	306
H. Text criticism and Expository Notes	.	307

I   Justin's Apologetic   .   .   308
J   Justin's Theology General   .   309
K   Justin's Logos Doctrine and Christology   311
L   Justin's Testimony about Sacraments and Ritual   312
M   Justin's Christian Ethics   313
N.   Justin and Greek Philosophy   .   .   .   314
O   Justin and Judaism (Palestinian and Hellenistic)   .   314
P   Justin and the Holy Scriptures   .   .   315
Q   Justin and the Creeds   .   .   318
R   Justin's Testimony to Contemporary Heresies   .   319
S   Pseudo-Justinian Works   319

A   EDITIONS (For fragments see also Group D)

1. *Guillardae, Carolae* Λόγος παραινετικὸς πρὸς "Ελληνας Paris 1539. 4⁰.

2. *Stephanus, Robert.* Opera Paris 1551. fol.

3. (Liturgical fragments) in: Liturgiae ss patrum Paris 1560 fol. p 121

4 *Stephanus, Henr* Epist ad. Diogn et Oratio ad Graecos Greek and Latin. Paiis 1571 (other eds 1592, 1595)

5 *Brunellus, Hier* Cohortatio In Ss patr orat et epist sel. I. 1, Romae 1586. 8⁰

6. *Sylbergius, Frid.* Opera Graecus textus correctus et Latina J. Langi versio emendata. Heidelb 1593 fol (also Lutet 1615. fol.).

7. *Morellus, Frider.* Opera (Gr et Lat) Paris 1615 fol. (also 1636 fol.) also Colon 1686 fol

8. *Halloix, Petr* De resurrectione Gr et Lat In Justini vita Duaci 1622 fol (also in Ill eccl orient. ser Duaci 1636 fol 299—329.)

9 *Grabius, J E* Fragmenta in Spicileg ss patrum Oxon 1699. 8⁰ Vol. II, p 177 also Ox 1714 8⁰.

10. — Apol I etc Gr. et Lat Oxon 1700 8⁰

11. *Koch, C* Dialogue. Kil 1700 8⁰

12 *Hutchin, H* Apologia secunda, oratio cohortatoria. Oratio ad Graecos, et de monarchia liber Gr et Lat Oxon. 1703 8⁰.

13. *Lequien, Mich* De resurrectione Gr. et Lat In Joannis Damasc. opera II. 756 ff Paris 1712 fol.

14 *Jebb, Sam* Dialogue, with lat by Langius Lond 1719 8⁰

15 *Thirlbius, Styanus* Apologiae duae et dialogus   Gr et Lat cum notis et emend Lond 1722 (cf 474).

16. *Maranus, Prud.* Opera Gr et Lat Paris 1742 (Benedict.) reprint Venet. 1747 (see 54)

17 *Thalemannus* Apologiae Lips 1755 8⁰

18 *Gallandius* Apologiae duae et dial In Bibl veterum patrum. Ven 1765 fol I p 413 et 595.

19 *Tellerus, Gul Abr* De Resur cum observatione Helmst 1766 4⁰

20. *Ashton, Car.* Apolog Gk and Lat w notes. Cant. 1768. 8⁰,

21. *Oberthur, F* Opera Gr et Lat. Wiiceb 1777 8⁰ (also 1794. 8⁰,)

22. *Göz, Johann Adam.* 2nd Apol and de Monarch Gk and German with notes and appendix Nuremb u Altdorf 1796.

23. *Augustus.* De resurrectione Gr. et Lat In Christ Patrist vol. I Leipz 1812. 8⁰.

24. *Hornemann, Ch Fr.* Dialogue. Gr. et Lat In. Scripta genuina Graecae patr apostol Pt III Havn 1829. 4⁰.

25. *Braunius, J W. J.* Apologies Bonn 1830, also 1860 (see 34)

26. *Otto, Joan Car Theod.* eques de Opera. Gr et Lat with notes. 1st ed Jenae 1842, 2nd ed 1847—1850. 3rd ed 1876—1881 all 8⁰. (cf 261 262)

27. *Trollope, W.* Apol prima w introd and notes Cambr 1845. 8⁰.

28. — Dial w introd and notes Cambr 1849 8⁰.

29. *Hoffmann* Brief an Diognetus Gr. u deutsch mit Einleitung u Erlauterung Meiss 1851 4⁰

30. *Hollen, W A* Brief an Diognetus hrsg u bearb Berl 1853 8⁰.

31. *Migne* Opera Patrol Gr tom VI Par 1857 8⁰ (after Maranus)

32 *Gildersleeve, B L.* Apologies, w notes N Y 1877 12⁰.

33. *Gebhardt, Oscar de* Epist ad Diognetum. Gr et Lat. In Patrum Apost Opera, ed. Gebhardt, Harnack, Zahn 2nd ed Lips 1878 Fasc I, Pt II, p 154—164. 3rd ed min Lips 1900 p 78

34 *Gutberlet, Constantinus* Apologiae (3rd ed of 25) Lips 1883 8⁰ (cf 269)

35 *Kruger, D G* Die Apologien Justins 2. Aufl Freib i B u Leipz 1896 4 vollig neubearb. Aufl. Tubing. 1915

36. Λεβεντόπουλος, 'Αθανάς Ap I—II Athens 1900 8⁰.

37. *De' Cavalieri, Dr Pio Franchi* Gli atti di S. Giustino. In Studi e Testi 8. (Roma 1902)

38. *Rauschen, Gerardus.* Apologiae duae In Florilegium patristicum. Bonnae 1904. 8⁰ Fasc alter.

39. *Pautigny, Louis* Apologies Texte grec, trad franç, introd et index Textes et documents pour l'étude historique du christ vol I. Paris 1904 8⁰.

40. *Knossalla, Joseph* Der pseudo-just Λόγος παραιν πρός "Ελλην. In. Kirchengesch Abhandl hrsg v. Max Schralek. Bd II p 107. Breslau 1904. 8⁰.

41. *Funk, F X* Epist ad Diogn In Die apostolischen Vater 2. Ausg Tubing 1906 pp 131—143 8⁰

42. *Archambault, Georges* Dial avec Tryph Texte grec, trad franç, introd., notes et index Textes et documents pour l'étude historique du christian. vols 8, 11 Paris 1909 8⁰

43. *Blunt, A W F.* The Apologies of Justin Martyr Cambridge Patristic texts, ed A J Mason Cambr 1911. 8⁰

44. *Pfattisch, Joan. Maria.* Justinus' Apologien Münster i W. 1912 Tl. I: Text, Tl II· Kommentar.

45 *Goodspeed, Edgar J* Die altesten Apologeten Texte mit kurzen Einleitungen Gottingen 1914 (Contains Ap I and II, and Dial)

B. TRANSLATIONS

1 LATIN See also 4. 6, 7, 8, 9. 10, 12. 13. 14, 15, 16, 20, 21, 23, 24
                          26, 31, 33.

46. *Pico della Mirandola, Giovanni Francesco* Admonitio 1506. fol
     Frequently reprinted. — See Richardson

47. *Postellus, Guil.* In· Evers. fals. dogm. Par. 1538.

48. *Perionius, Joach* Ap. I. In· De probatis, sanctorum historiis,
     collectis per L. Surium I V. Paris 1554. Colon. Agripp. 1574. fol
     Venet 1581 fol. Also in Bibl. Patr. Colon. 1618 fol T II.

49. *Gilenius, Sigism.* Opera Just. Basil 1555. fol

50 *Sainetis, Cl. de.* De Missae ritu ex Justini . . . . Apologia. In:
     Liturgia ss. patrum. p. 73 Antv. 1560, 1562.

51. *Langius, Joan* Just opera omn 3 vol. in 1. Basil 1565. fol.
     Paris 1575 16⁰ (w. Hippolytus) also in Bibl. patr. Lugdun
     1677. fol

52. *Billius. Jac.* De resurrectione, in his Damasceni opera. Paris 1619.
     fol.

53. *Rous, Fr.* Various works. in his Mella patrum omnium. Lond.
     1650. 8⁰.

54 *Prileszky, J. B* (Maranus version, see 16). Cassov. 1765 4⁰

55 Apologiae duae, ad Graec. cohort, De Monarch. liber In. St
     Matris catholicae eccl. dogmatum et morum ex selectis veterum
     patrum operibus veritas demonstrata Florentiae 1791. 4⁰.

56. *Caillou* and *Guillon* Par. et Brux 1829 8⁰. Mediol. 1830. 8⁰.

2. DANISH

57. *Muus, C. H.* Kjoebenh. 1836. 8⁰

3. ENGLISH

58. *Reeves, William.* Apologies of Justin Martyr, Tertullian, and Minucius
     Felix etc Lond. 1709. 2 v. 8⁰. 1716. 2 v. 8⁰

59 *Humphreys, David.* Resur. In his· "Athenagoras". London 1714. 8⁰.

60. *Brown, Henry.* Dialogue trans. w. notes. Oxf. 1755 2 v. 1846. 8⁰.

61. *Moses, Th.* Exh. to Gent. Lond. 1751. 8⁰.

62. *Dalrymple, D.* Edinb. 1778. 12⁰.

63. *Chevallier, F.* A translation of the Apologies, with a transl. of
     the Epistles of Clement. Camb 1833. 8⁰. Lond. 1851. 8⁰.

64. Bapt. and Euch. passages in Ap I and the Martyrdom In
     Records of the Church, No. 13 Tracts for the times vol. 1. Lond
     1834. 8⁰. Lond. 1839. 8⁰.

65 *(Davie, G. J.)* Wks. now extant of S. Justin the Martyr translated
     w. notes and indices. In Library to the Fathers of the Holy
     Catholic Church. vol. 40 Oxf. 1861. 8⁰

66 *Dods, Marcus; Reith, George; Pratten, B. P.* The Writings of Just.
     M. and Athenagoras. in Ante-Nicene Christian Library. Vol. II.
     Edinb. 1867 Amer. ed. Buffalo 1885. Vol. I, pp 163—302.

4 FRENCH See also 39, 42

67. *Maumont, Jean de.* Les oeuvres de S Justin . . . mises du Grec en Français Paris 1554 fol., 1559 fol

68. *Dupin, Martin.* Cohortatio Paris 1580 8⁰

69. *Fondet Pierre* Apol II Paris 1670 12⁰. 1686. 12⁰.

70. *Genoude (?)* In Pères de l'égl. Par. 1837—1843 8⁰.

5 GERMAN See also 22, 29, 218

71 *Hedius, Caspar* Cohort. Strasb 1529 fol.

72 *Glussing, J Otto* Epp Diognet, et Zen In his: Briefe und Schriften d Ap Männer Hamb 1723 8⁰ p. 443 ff

73 *Denis, M* Ap I In his Denkmale aus allen Jahrh Vindob 1795 8⁰ I i p 21 ff, Vindob 1830, I i 16 ff.

74 *Goz Jo A* De Monarchia. Norimb 1796

75. *Kestner, Aug* Orat ad Gent In his De Agape Jena 1819 8⁰ pp 333—337

76 *Brun, N. de* Dialogue Basil 1822 8⁰.

77 *Deckers* Ap I In Kath Monatsschr III (1828)

78 *Waizmann, J S* in: Sammtl. Werke der K.V. Kempten 1830 8⁰.

79 *Richard, P A* in Reithmayer-Thalhofer-Bibl. Kempten 1870 16⁰

80 *Veil, H.* Justins des Phil u Mart Rechtfertigung des Christentums (Apologie I u II) Eingeleitet, verdeutscht und erlautert Strassburg 1894

81. *Rauschen, Gerhard* Die beiden Apologien Justins des Martyrers, ubersetzt Kempten 1913 Bibliothek der Kirchenvater 12 Band Fruhchristliche Apologeten u Martyrakten I Bd pp. 55—155

6 ITALIAN

82 *Galliccioli, Giov Bapt* Venez 1799 8⁰

7 RUSSIAN

83 *Metodij, Jer* (De Monarch) Mosc 1783 8⁰

84. *Smirnov, M* (Selections) Mosc. 1783. 8⁰.

85 *Clementjewski, J* Dialogue St Petersb 1797 8⁰. Ap. I in Chiistijanskoje Tschtenje 1825 Ap II 1840

86. *Preobrazenskij* Mosc 1862/3

C. GENERAL LITERATURE

Only the more important of the earlier saints' lives and patrologies are here mentioned Of later Church Histories and Patrologies only those are named which made a contribution to the study of Justin Encyclopedia articles and church histories are represented likewise by only a few titles of independent value See also the Introductions to 16, 26, and 80, and the Appendix to 22

87. *Trithemius, Joan* De scriptoribus ecclesiasticis No 11 Par 1512 4⁰

88. *Langius, J* Comm in Just M Basil 1565 fol.

89. *Surius, Sam* Vitae sanctorum, ex probatis authoribus et mss codicibus edit Colon 1569 etc 13 April p 151 ff.

90. *Halloix, Pierre, S. J* Vita et documenta S. Justini Phil. et Mart. etc. Duaci 1622. 8⁰ 1636 fol. Reprinted in *Bollandi Acta Ss.* April 13 Vol. X, p. 101—119 Antv. 1675.

91. *Scultetus, Abr* De vita, scriptis et doctrina Justini M. In Medullae theologicae patrum syntagma Frkf 1634. I. 1 1—45

92. *Kortholdt, Christian* In Justinum martyrem, Athenagoram, Theophilum Antiochenum, Tatianum Assyrium commentarius Franc. 1686

93. *Cave, W.* Scriptorum Ecclesiasticorum Literaria etc London 1688—1698 Vol I Transl Engl and revised by *Henry Cary.* Oxford 1840. I. 228—257

94. *Tentzel. W. E.* Exercitationes Selectac Lips 1692 4⁰ pp 165—199

95. *Dupin, L. E* Nouvelle bibliothèque des auteurs ecclésiastiques, etc. Paris 1698 I 104—133

96. *Gundlingius, M. N. Hier* In (Buddeus) Observ sel litter 1700 II 89—113, 170—199

97. *Tillemont* Mémoires pour servir à l'histoire ecclésiastique des six premiers siècles etc Paris 1701 fol II 344—404.

98. *Nourry.* Apparatus ad bibliothecam maximum veterum patrum Par. 1703 I 350—470

99. *Clericus, J* Unparteiische Lebensbeschreibung einiger Kirchenvater und Ketzer Halle 1721 S 1—21

100 *Ceillier, Remy* Histoire générale des auteurs sacrés et ecclésiastiques Paris 1730 II 1—73, 1858, I. 408—448

101. *Jortin, J.* Remarks on Ecclesiastical History II (1751) 155 ff. "Character and Writings of Justin Martyr"

102. *Gerkenius, C Ch.* Dissert. de Just. M ad rel. christ. conversione admodum memorabili Leipz. 1753 4⁰

103. *Prileszky, Joh.* Baptist Acta et scripta s Justini, phil et mart Cassoviae 1765

104. *Cotta, F* Dissert de memorabilibus Justini M historicis atque dogmaticis. Tubing 1766 4⁰

105. *Gratianus, P C.* Dissert de memorabilibus Justini Mart hist atque dogmat. Tubing 1766 4⁰

106. *Cotta, J F* Vers ein. ausfuhrl. Kirchenhist des N T. Tubing. 1768—1773 §§ 284—290

107. *Schröckh, Joh. Mat* Christliche Kirchengeschichte Leipz. 1772 III 17—51.

108 *Rossler* Bibliothek der Kirchenvater Leipz I. (1776), 101—181

109. *Schram, P O* Analysis operum ss patrum et scriptorum eccles Augusta Vindelicorum 1780 8⁰ I. 295—524.

110 *Lumper, Gottfried* Historia theologica critica de vita, scriptis atque doctrina ss. patrum etc Aug Vindel. 1783—1799 II (1784) 48—316, 461—481, X (1793) 514—541

111 *Barrington, D.* Tomb of Justin Martyr. In Archaeologia V (1784) 143 ff.

112. *Jortin, J.* Tracts philos crit et misc London 1790 8⁰. II 102 —116.

113 *Hess, J J* In Bibl der heil Geschichte Zurich 1791. 8⁰. I 1

114. *Brown, J A* In Christian Observer. London 1801. III 619 ff, 717 ff

115 In Methodist Magazine London 1809 XXXII 3 ff

116 *Lamson, A* In Christian Examiner Boston 1825. VII, p 141 ff, 303 ff

117. *Kaye, John* Some Account of the Writings and Opinions of Justin Martyr Cambr and Lond 1829 Several later editions

118. *Semisch, Karl Gottlob* Justin der Martyrer, eine kirchen- und dogmengeschichtliche Monographie 2 Tle Breslau 1840, 1842, 8⁰

119. — Justin Martyr, his life, writings and opinions transl. (from 118) by J. E. Ryland 2 vols. (Vols 41 and 42 of the Biblical Cabinet) Edinb 1843 8⁰.

120 — Art Just Mart in Real-Encyklop fur protest Theol u Kirche 1 Aufl Bd VII pp 179—186

121. *Otto, Joh Carl Theodor* Commentatio de Justini Martyris scriptis et doctrina Jenae 1841 8⁰.

122 *Brown, J. A* In Christian Review Bost. 1841 VI, p 302 ff

123 *Permaneder, Michaelis* Bibliotheca Patristica Landishuti 1811— 1843 Vol I, 414—415; II, 98—149, 309—313, 943

124 *Reithmayr, Fr X* Rev. of Semisch (118) In Archiv fur theologische Literatur. Regensb 1842 I. 321—335, 632—662

125 *Hefele, C F.* Rev. of Semisch (118), and J Otto (26 and 121) In. Theol. Quartalschrift. (1843), 143—157

126 Life and Writings of Justin Martyr In Eclectic Review London LXXXI (1844), 186 ff

127 *Coffin, William H* The Lives and Times of the Most Distinguished Christian Fathers to the Close of the Third Century Baltimore 1846, 183—196

128. *Hefele, C. J.* Art. Justin Martyr in *Wetzer* und *Welte*, Kirchen-Lexikon oder Encyklopadie der Kath Theol und ihrer Hilfswissenschaften (1847—1851 V, 935—917)

129 Life and Writings of Justin Martyr; in Christian Review Boston 1850 p 353 ff

130 Life and Writings of Justin Martyr, in Kitto's Journal of Sacred Literature. Lond 1850 V. 253—301.

131. *Hepp, F* Geschichte der christl Kirche in Lebensbeschreib Mainz 1851 p 76 ff

132 *Otto, Joh Karl Theodor* Art Justin Martyr in *Ersch* und *Gruber* Allgemeine Encyklopadie der Wissenschaften u Künste Leipzig II XXX (1853), SS 39—76

133 *Sevestre* Dict patrol 1854 III 965—999

134 *Maurice, F D* Lectures on the Ecclesiastical History of the First and Second Centuries Cambr 1854 8⁰. 170, 207—216.

135. *Munnich, Christoph*, ed. of Kirchenhistoria of the Magdeburg Centuratorien 1855

136. *Brown, J. A* in Evangelical Review Gettysburg Pa 1855. p 151 ff

137. *Means, J. C.* Art Justin Martyr in *Smith.* Dict Gr and Rom Biogr 1859, II, 682—686

138. *Tobler* in Theol. Jahrbucher 1860

139. *Freppel, M L'abbe (Chas E)* Les Apologistes Chrétiens au IIe siècle Saint Justin Paris 1860.

140. *Aube, B* in Nuov. Biog Gen (Hoefer) XXVII (1861), 292—303

141. *Pressensé, E. de.* Histoire de l'Egl Chrét. IIe siècle Paris 1861 —1869.

142 — The Early Years of Christianity etc Transl (141) by *Annie Harwood-Holenden* London 1879 See Vol II The Martyrs and Apologists

143. *Donaldson, James.* A Critical History of Christian Literature and Doctrine. London II (1866), 62—344

144. *Stadler, Joh Evang* Art S. Justinus in Heiligen-Lexikon Bd III SS. 559—567

145 *Bohringer, Friedrich* Die Kirche Christi und ihre Zeugen, oder die Kirchengeschichte in Biographien 2 Aufl 2 Ausg Stuttgart 1873. I, 97—270

146. *Calogeras, N.* 'Ιουστῖνος ὁ φιλόσοφος καὶ μαρτύς In 'Αθήναιον II (1873), 359—380

147. *Worman, J H* Art Justin Martyr in Mc Clintock and Strong s Cyclopaedia of Bibl Theol and Ecclesiast Literature. N. Y 1874—81 IV. 1104—1110.

148 Die Bekehrung Justins. In Allgemeine evang-luther Kirchenzeitung. Leipz 1878. 409—413, 433—438

149. *Jackson, George A* Apostolical Fathers and Apologists of the Second Century N Y. 1879. pp. 140—186

150. *Lindsay, T M.* Art Justin Martyr in Encycl. Brit (9th Ed) XIII. 790—791

151 *Pressensé, E de* Art Just M in Encycl de Sc relig VII (Paris 1880). 576—583.

152. *Keim, Th* Rom und das Christentum Berlin 1881. 424—439 u a (s Register)

153 *Holland, Henry Scott* Art Just Mart. in Dict. Christ Biog (1882) III. 560—587.

154. Allard, Paul Histoire des présécutions pendant les deux premiers siècles Paris 1885 pp 281—295, 314—327, 365—373

155 *Zahn, Theodor* Studien zu Justin In Zeitschrift fur Kirchengeschichte VIII (1886), 1—84 I Justin bei Methodius und Paulus bei Justinus pp 1—20 II Justin's Schrift uber die Auferstehung pp 20—37 III Dichtung und Wahrheit in Justin's Dialog mit dem Juden Trypho pp 37—66. IV Justinus und die Lehre der zwolf Apostel pp 66—84 Answered by *Funk* (361)

156 *Martin, Mrs. Charles* Life of St. Justin Martyr. Lond 1890. 8⁰

157. *Hirth, Paul Emile* Justin Martyr, esquisse historique . These .. Genève 1893. 8⁰

158. *Meyrick, Frederick* The Life and Times of Justin Martyr In Lectures on ecclesiastical history delivered in Norwich Cathedral

Lond Edinb 1896 8⁰ p 53 ff Reprint London 1909 with title "Church leaders in Primitive times." p. 53 ff

159. *Willm, Pierre* Justin Martyr et son apologétique Thèse. Montauban 1897. 8⁰.

160. *Bonnuetsch.* Art Justin der Mart In Realencyclop. fur prot Theol. und Kirche 3 Aufl IX (Leipz 1901). 641—650.

161. *Pfleiderer, Otto.* Das Urchristentum. 2 Aufl. Berl 1902 II. 624—645, 681—704

162 *Rivière, J* S Justin et les Apologistes du deuxieme siècle Paris 1907

163. *Lebreton, Jules.* Art Just Mart. in Catholic Encyclop VIII. 580 —586

164. *Krüger, G* Art Just Mart. in Encyclop Brit 11th Ed XV p. 602

165. *Béry, A* St Justin, sa vie et sa doctrine. Paris 1911.

166. *Goodspeed, Edgar J.* Index Apologeticus sive clavis Justini Martyris operum aliorumque apologetarum piistinorum Lips 1912 8⁰

167. *la Grange, Le P M -J* Saint Justin, Philosophe, Martyr 2me Edit. Paris 1914.

168. *Ueberweg, Friedrich* Grundriß der Geschichte der Philosophie 10. Aufl von Dr Matthias Baumgarten II (Berl. 1915). pp 57—62 u. a S. Register.

169. *Martindale, C C* Justin Martyr London 1921

D JUSTIN'S WRITINGS

General treatises on the problem of the authenticity of the various works ascribed to Justin. The following is to be supplemented by Groups E, F, and S and 155 II Only the more important histories of Christian Literature are noted

170. *Herbig, Chr E* Commentatio Critica de scriptis quae sub nomine Justini circumferuntur. Vratislaviae 1833 8⁰

171. *Arendt.* Kritische Untersuchungen uber die Schriften Justin's des Martyrers. In Theol Quartalschr XVI (1834). 256—295.

172. *Mosinger, Georgio* Fragment of Justin In Monumenta Syriaca II (Oeniponti 1878). See p 7 no III notes p 17.

173. *Harnack, A* Die Ueberlieferung der griechischen Apologeten des 2. Jahrhunderts in der alten Kirche und im Mittelalter Leipz. 1882, (Texte u Unters I 1) S 130 ff see (177)

174 Fragments from the early history of the Christian Church Part 3 St Justin Martyr London 1882 8⁰

175. *Pitra, J. B.* Sancti Justini quae Syriacae supersunt fragmenta In: Analecta Sacra. Paris 1883 IV. 11—16, 287—292

176. — On 8 fragments attributed to St Justinus In: Analecta Sacra. Typis Tusculanis 1884. II. 285—287

177. *Hilgenfeld, A* Die Ueberlieferung uber d griechischen Apologeten des Christentums im 2 Jahrhundert u ihr neuester Censor (adv 173). In Zeitschr fur wissenschaftl Theol XVI (1883). 1—45

178. *Dräseke, J.* Zu den unter Justinus Namen uberlieferten christologischen Bruchstucken In· Jahrbucher fur protestantische Theologie X (1894). 347—352

179 *Harris, J R* Fragments of Justin Martyr. In The American Journal of Philology (1886), pp 33—37.

180 *Diels, Hermann.* Ueber den angeblichen Justin περὶ ψυχῆς. In: Sitzungsberichte d. Berl Akad (1891), 151—153.

181. *Zahn, Theodor* Geschichte des neutest Kanons. Leipz. u. Erl. II. ii (1892). S. 777 ff

182. *Harnack, Adolph.* Geschichte der altchristlichen Literatur. Leipz 1893—1904 I. 99 ff , II. 274 ff , 508 ff

183 *Holl, K* Fragmente vornicanischei Kirchenvater aus den Sacra Parallela. In: Texte u Untersuch V ii (Leipzig 1899), S. 36 ff.

184 *Pohl* Schrieb Justinus Martyr eine Erklarung der Apokalypse? In Historisches Jahrbuch (1910), 3 Heft

185. *Christ, Wilh. von* Geschichte der griechischen Literatur 5 Aufl. bearb. von *Wilh. Schmid* u *Otto Stahlin* II ii (Munchen 1919), pp 1028—1035.

186 *Bardenhewer, Otto* Geschichte der altkirchlichen Literatur 2. Aufl. (Freib i. B 1913). I. 206—262.

187 *Lietzmann, Hans.* Art. Justinus der Mart In. *Pauly - Wissowa,* Real-Encyclopadie der klassischen Altertumswissenschaft, X (Stuttg 1919) cols 1332—1337

E THE TWO APOLOGIES See also Groups G and H

188 *Tamburini, Pietro* Analisi delle Apologie di S Giustino Martie, etc. Pavia 1792

189. *Lange, S G* Dissert histor -crit , in qua Justini Mart apologia prima sub examen vocatur. Jena 1795

190 *Eisenlohr* Comment de argumentis Apol saec 2 Tub 1797 Reprint in *Pott* et *Rupert* Sylloge comment Theol II 114—202

191. *Junius, F J. J. A.* Dissertatio de Justino mart Apologeta adv Ethnicos Lugd Bat 1836. 8°

192 *Ritter, J J* Animadv in primam S Justini Mart Apol Vratisl. 1836

193 *Boll, F. C.* Ueber das Verhaltnis der beiden Apologien Justins des Martyrers zu einander In Zeitschr fur d hist Theol (Leipz. 1842), 3. Heft, p 3—47.

194. *Hagen, J A.* Beitrage zur Erklarung der ersten Apologie des hl. Justinus In Zeitschr f Philos und kath. Theol. N F IX (1848). 35—67.

195. *Schaller, L* Les deux apologies de Justin Mart au point de vue dogmatique Strassburg 1851

196 *Paul, Ludwig.* Zur ersten Apologie des Just Mart In Jahrb. fui klass Phil (1880), 316—320

197 Remarques sur la Ire Apologie de S Just M In Bibl choisie, II. 328—352; III. 372—391

198 *Grundl, Beda* De interpolationibus ex St Just Phil et Mart. Apologia secunda expurgendis Diss inaug (Wurzburg) Augusta Vindel 1891 8° (cf 201)

199. *Cramer, J A* In welke verhouding stande beide Apologieen van Just. tot elkanden etc In Theol Studien LXIV (1891), 313—357 401—436 Also separately printed 1892.

200. *Eberhard, Anselm* Athenagoras, nebst einem Exkurs uber das Verhaltnis der beiden Apologien des hl Just zu einander Progr. Augsburg 1895 8⁰

201 *Emmerich, Ferdinand S* De Justini phil et mart. apologia altera Comment philol acad reg Monaster 1896. 8⁰ (adv 198)

202. *Wehofer, Thomas M* Die Apologie Just des Phil u Mart in literaturhistorischer Beziehung zum erstenmal untersucht Romische Quartalschrift, Supplementheft 6 Rom 1897 8⁰ (cf 203)

203. *Rauschen, C* Die formale Seite der Apologien Justins In Theologische Quartalschrift 1899, S 188—206 (adv 202)

204. *Cramer, J A* Die erste Apologie Justins ein Versuch, die Bittschrift Justins in ihrer ursprunglichen Form darzustellen. In Zeitschr. fur die neutestamentliche Wissenschaft, V (1904), 154—162, 178—190, VI (1905), 347—368 (cf 186, p 217, n 1)

205. *Geffcken, Johannes* Zwei griechische Apologeten Leipzig u Berlin 1907. pp 97—104.

206. *Schwartz, E.* ed Eusebius, Kirchengeschichte 1909 III, p CLIV

207. *Antoniades, Baseleios* Ἑρμηνευτικὰ εἰς ῥῆσιν Ἰουστίνου τοῦ φιλ. καὶ μάρτ. καὶ εἰς ἀπόσπασμα τοῦ Σοφοκλέους In. Τεσσαρακονταετηρὶς τῆς καθηγεσίας Κ. Σ. Κόντου. Ἀθήναις 1909 p. 234

208. *Cessi, C* in Rivista di filologia e d'istruz class XL (1912), pp 64 —86.

209. *Hubik, Karl* Die Apologien des hl Just d Phil u Mait Literarhistorische Untersuchungen Theologische Studien der Leo-Gesellschaft, Nr 19. Wien 1912 8⁰.

210. *Jehne, Walter* Die Apologie Justins des Philosophen und Martyrers Dissert Leipzig und Munster 1914. 8⁰

F. THE DIALOGUE See also 155 III, 270 II, 395.

211. *Koch, Christian Gottlob* Justini mart cum Tryphone Judeo Dialogus secundum regulas criticas examinatus 1700 (cf 212)

212. *zum Felde, Albrecht* Epistula de Dialogo Just Mart cum Tryphone Judeo Sleswici 1700 (adv 211)

213. *zum Felde, Albrecht* Demonst invictae, dialogum in Tryph esse verum Justini factum Hamb. 1707. 8⁰.

214. *Danzius, J. A* Oratio de Tryphone, habita a. 1708. In Parerga Gotting (Gotting 1739 8⁰) I iv 80—91

215 *Jebb, Samuel* Proposals for printing a new edition of Justin Martyr's Dialogue with Trypho the Jew. n d 8⁰.

216. *Wetstennii, Joannis Jacobi* Novum Testamentum graece. 1751 I p. 66 (cf 217.)

217. *Krone, H J.* Diatribe de authentica dialogi Justini Martyris cum Tryphone Judaeo Middelburgh 1778 (adv 216)

218. *Gussmann, Franz* Tryphon und Justin, oder vom Judentum (incl transl. into German) Wien 1785 8⁰.

219. *Lobey-Lange, Samuel* Ausfuhrliche Geschichte der Dogmen oder Glaubenslehren der christlichen Kirche. I (1796), 137 ff.

220. *Münscher, Wilhelm.* An Dialogus c. Tr. Justino Mart. recte adscribatur, disquisitio. Marb 1799 4⁰ Reedited in· Commentationes theologicae. I ii. 184—214. Leipz 1826.

221 *Scharffenberg. G. H* and *D.* Comment academ. de Justino, Tertulliano, et Cypriano adv. Judaeos disputantibus. Lund Goth 1820. (20 pp)

222. *Friedländer, Moritz* Justin's Dialog mit Tryph , being the third study, in his Patristische und talmudische Studien. Wien 1878.

223. *Harnack, Adolph.* In: Texte u Untersuch. I iii. (1853). (cf. 224)

224. *Corssen* Die Altercatio Simonis Judaei et Theophili Christiani auf ihre Quellen gepruft. Berl 1890. (somewhat adv. 223)

225. *Funk, Franz X* Apost. Konstit. Rottenb. 1891 p. 72 ff. (answered by Harnack [182], I 101).

226. *Krauss, S.* In Jewish Quarterly Review, V. (1993). pp 123—134.

227. *Zöckler, O.* Der Dialog im Dienste der Apologetik Gütersloh 1894.

228. *Hirzel, Rudolf* Der Dialog Ein literarhistorischer Versuch. 2 Bde. Leipzig 1895. II. 368 ff

229. *Helm, Rudolf* Lucian und Menipp Leipz 1906 p. 42 ff.

230. *Freimann, M* Die Wortfuhrer des Judentums in den altesten Kontroversen zwischen Juden u Christen Ti II (Tryphon). In Monatsschrift fur Geschichte u. Wissenschaft des Judentums. Breslau 1911. 565—585.

231. *Preuschen, Erwin.* Die Echtheit von Justin's Dial gegen Trypho. In: Zeitschr. f d Neutest Wissenschaft 1919/20, Heft 3/4, pp. 102 —126 (cf. 232, 270 II)

232 *Fonck, Leop. S. J.* Die Echtheit von Justin's Dialog gegen Trypho. In Biblica. Commentarii editi a Pontificio Instituto Biblico. Roma II. 1921 342—347 (adv. 231)

G CHRONOLOGY. See also 182, 186, 209

233 *Longuerue, Louis du Four de* Dissertationes de variis epochis . . . de vita St. Justini martyris etc. Leipzig 1750 4⁰.

234. *Hoven, J D* De act. Minucii F. et ordine apol. Justini M. Campis 1762. 4⁰.

235. *Semisch, Karl* Ueber das Todesjahr Justins des Märtyrers. In· Theol. Studien u Kritiken. 1835, Heft 4, S. 907 (cf. 236)

236. *Stieren, Adolph.* Ueber das Todesjahr Justins des Märtyrers. In: Zeitschr. f d historische Theologie, 1842, Heft 1, S. 21—37 (adv. 235).

237. *Clinton, H. Fynes.* Fasti Romani Oxf. (1845—1850) I. 131, 139, II. 409.

238. *Volkmar, G.* Die Zeit Just d. Mart In. Theol. Jahrbb. XIV, Tubing. 1855, S. 227—283, 412—468 (cf. 239).

239. *Otto, Joh Carl Theod* Zu Dr Volkmars Abhandlung uber die Zeit Justins des Märtyrers In: Theol Jahrbb XIV Tubing 1855 S 468—470 (adv 238)

240. *Hort, F J A.* On the date of Justin Martyr In· Journal of class and sacr Philol. III. Cant 1857. p. 155—193.

241. *Keim, Theodor.* Die Zeit der Apologie Justins des Martyrers an Kaiser Antonin den Frommen In: Protestantische Kirchenzeitung fur das evangelische Deutschland Berlin 1873 S 618—621

242 *Usener.* In Religionsgesch Untersuch I (1889), 100—102, 106—108 (Date of Apol)

243 *Kruger, Gustav* Die Abfassungszeit der Apologien J, In Jahrbb. f. protest Theol XVI (1890), S 579—593.

244. *Kenyon* The date of the Apology of J M In The Academy; XLIX (1896) p 98

245. — Greek Papyri in Brit Museum II (1898) p 171 ff

246 *Zahn, Theodor.* Apostel und Apostelschulen in der Provinz Asien. In Forschung. z Gesch d Neut Kanons VI (1900), S 8—14

247 *Schwartz, Ed* In Nachrichten d. k Gesellschaft der Wiss zu Gottingen Philos -hist Kl 1907 S 369.

H TEXT CRITICISM AND EXPOSITORY NOTES

248. *Bull, G* De celebri loco J in Dialogo cum Tryphone disseritur. In his Judicium eccl. cath. (Oxon 1694 8⁰.) 164—192 Also in his Works (Oxf. 1846) VI, 187—235

249. *Dodwell, Henry* An explication of a famous passage in the dialogue of S Justin M with Tr, concerning the immortality of human souls London 1878 8⁰

250. *Hickes, G. A* A passage in J's first (commonly called his second) Apology vindicated against . . Whiston In Grabe's Some instances of the defects and omissions in Mr Whiston's collection of testimonies London 1712 8⁰ p XXXIV—LI

251 Locus Just Mart emendatur In Bibl Litter, being a Collection of Inscriptions, Medals, Dissertations, etc, An 1722 (Lond 1724 4⁰) VIII 1—28

252. *Oudin, Casimir* Commentarius de scriptoribus ecclesiae antiquis, etc. Lipsiae 1722 I, 179—203

253 Observationes in J M Apol I et Dial cum Tryph ed Thirlby In Miscellaneae Obss (Amst 1732) I, 363—372

254 *Harwood, Edw.* Note on a passage in Justin (Dial 48) In Gentleman's Magazine London 1783 p 831 (cf 255, 256)

255. *Row, T.* Answer to E Harwood on a passage in Justin In Gentleman's Magazine London 1783 p 904 (adv 254, cf 256).

256. *B., A* Note on a disputed passage in Justin In Gentleman's Magazine London 1786 p. 570—571 (adv 251, 255)

257 *(Bryant, James.)* Observations on a controverted passage in Justin London 1793 4⁰

258. *Mohler, J. A.* Ueber Justins Apol I c. 6 gegen die Auslegung dieser Stelle von Neander. In Theologische Quartalschrift Tubing 1833 S 49—60 (cf 259)

259. *Neander, A* Rechtfertigung seiner Auslegung der Stelle J's Apolog I 6 In Theologische Studien und Kritiken Hamburg 1833 S 772—6 (adv 258)

260. *Hasselbach.* Ueber d. Stelle in J. d. M. Ap I, p 56 In: Theol. Studien u. Kritiken Hamb 1839 XII, 329—392

261 *(Lange, Lobey.)* Critique of Otto's 1st edition (26) In Rohrs Kritische Prediger-Bibliothek Neustadt a d O 1844 XXV, 969—998

262. *Hase.* Critique of Otto's 2nd edit. (26). In. Journal des Savants Paris 1852, p. 619—630, 1853, p. 182—188, 363—370.

263. *Zeller* Noch ein Wort über d Ausspruch Jesu bei Justin Apol. I. 61 über die Wiedergeburt In Theol. Jahrbb. XIV (Tub. 1855).

264. *Volkmar, Gustav.* Ueber die Lesart des Claromontanus zu Anfang der größeren Apol J 's In Theol. Jahrbb. XIV (Tub. 1855). S 569—572.

265. *Schick, Aug. H* Ist das εὐχὴ λόγου τοῦ παρ' αὐτοῦ bei Just. das Gebet des Herrn oder nicht? In: Zeitschr. für die gesamte Lutherische Theoolgie und Kirche 1857 76—107.

266. *Nolte,* Conjecturae et emend In. *Migne.* Patrolog. gr. VI (1857), 1705—1738, 1763—1802.

267. *Volz, W. L.* Krit. Bemerkungen z J. Apol. I 66 In Theologische Studien und Kritiken. Gotha 1874 XXVI, 180—215

268. *Zahn, Theodor.* Zur Auslegung und Textkritik einiger schwieriger patristischer Stellen (Just Ap I 3, 4, 10) In: Zeitschr f. histor Theologie. 1875 S. 68—71

269 *Kihn, Heinrich* Rev of (34) in Theol Quartalschr. LXVI (1884), 497—500.

270. *Kruger, Gustav* Zu Justin In· Zeitschr. f. d. Neutest. Wissensch VII (1906), 136—139. I Zur οἶνος-ὄνος-Frage in Ap. u. Dial. II. Justin der Verfasser des Dialogs mit Trypho? (cf. 231)

271. *Burkitt, F. C* The oldest mss. of S. Justin's Martyrdom. In Journal of theol. Studies XI (Lond. 1909), p 61.

272. *Goodspeed, E J.,* and *Spregling, M.* A lost mss. of Just In. Zeitschr. f d. Neutestam Wissenschaft. XI (1910), 243—246.

273. *Pfattisch, J. M.* Psalm 110 (109) bei Just. In: Biblische Zeitschr. 1910, 3. Heft.

274. *Colson, F H* Notes on Just M., Ap I [14 (61. D), 23 3 (68. C): 28 4 (71 C); 22 6 (73 E), 66 (98. A); '67 (98 D, 99 B)] In. Journal of theol. Studies. XXIII (Lond 1922), 161—171.

I. JUSTIN'S APOLOGETIC

This list may be supplemented by Baumgarten's Bibliograph. Suppl. to Ueberweg's Geschichte der Philosophie II (Berl. 1915) Suppl S 35, 36, as well as by Group E.

275. *Tzschirner, H. G.* Geschichte d Apologet. (1805) I.

276 *Wurm.* Apol. v. Just, Tatian, Athenag Theoph. und Hermias. In Studien d. evangel Geistl. Wurt. I. u. (1828). 1—34

277. *Seibert, C. G.* J., d. Vertheidiger des Christentums vor dem Thron der Caesaren. Elberf. 1859.

278. *Bucheler, Franz.* Aristides und Justinus, die Apologeten Rhein Mus. XXXV (1880), S. 279—286

279. *Zahn, Jos* Die apologetischen Grundgedanken in der Literatur der ersten drei Jahrh. systematisch dargestellt Würzburg 1890

280 *Schmitt, Gregor* Die Apologie der drei ersten Jahrhh in historisch-systematischer Darstellung Mainz 1890

281. *Wernle, Paul* Die drei Stufen der altchristlichen Apologetik in religionsgeschichtlicher Bedeutung 1901

282. *Harnack, Ad* Der Vorwurf des Atheismus in den ersten drei Jahrh. Leipzig 1905. (Texte u Unt XXVIII, 4)

283. *Zockler, Otto* Geschichte der Apologie d Christentums Gütersloh 1907 S 35—51

284. *Koch, Wilhelm* Die altkirchliche Apologetik des Christentums In Theol Quartalschrift XC (1908) 7—33

J JUSTIN'S THEOLOGY GENERAL

To the following must be added the treatment of Justin in all histories of doctrine Those of especial importance for their treatment of Justin's doctrine are: *Semler, S G Lange, Baumgarten-Crusius, Baur, Neander, R Ritschl, Nitsch, Harnack, Schwane, Loofs, Seeberg,* and *Tixeront.*

285 Ὄρφεως ἔπη θεολογικά, ἐκ τῶν τοῦ ἁγίου Ἰουστίνου . . . καὶ τοῦ Κλήμεντος Ἀλεξάνδρεως καὶ τῶν ἄλλων συνειλεγμένα Paris 1588

286. *Lausselius, Petr* Dispunctio calumniarum quae St Justino Martyri inuruntur ab Is Casaubono Paris 1615 fol

287. *Biddle, John* The testimonies of Irenaeus, Justin M , Tertullian etc concerning that one God and the persons of the Holy Trinity, together with observations on the same London 1648 8⁰

288 *Cyprian, E La* Dissert de Clem Rom . . . . et Justini M. doctrina evang Coburg 1701 4⁰

289 *Chishull.* Some testimonies of Just concerning the immortality of the soul London 1708 8⁰

290 *Reuchlin, Fr Jac* Justini M extant doctrinae momentorum portionem primam (secundam, tertiam) August 1742—8 sm 4⁰

291. *Teller, Guil. Abr* Specimen doctrinae Justini de resurrectione carnis In. Fides dogmatis de resurrectione carnis per quatuor priora secula Halle et Helmst 1766. pp 81—85

292. *Leibes, Fr* Dissert S Just de praecipuis rel dogmat sententiam. Wirceb 1777 8⁰

293 *Oberthur* Dissert exponens Justini de praecipuis religionis dogmatis sententiam Wirceb 1777

294. Darstellung d ältesten Christentums aus d Schr Just usw In Beytrage zur Beförderung des ältesten Christenthums u d neuesten Philos Ulm 1791.

295 Worship of Angels London 1795 4⁰

296. *Credner, C. A* J.'s Vorstellungen von der Inspiration In Beitrage zur Einleitung in die Bibel-Schriften. Halle 1832 Thl I, S. 108 ff

297. *Georgii* Lehre v heil Geiste bei Just In Stirm's Studien d ev. Geistlichkeit Württemb X (1838), II 100 ff

298 *Gass, Wilhelm* Die unter J's d. M Schriften befindlichen Fragen an die Rechtgläubigen In Zeitschr f die hist Theol N F. VI. ı̇v (1812), S 35—154.

299. *Duncker L* Apologetarum secundi saeculi de essentialibus naturae humanae partibus placita. Part I (Just M) Götting 1844 4⁰. Part II 1850 (Zwei Universitatsprogramme)

300 *Schwegler, A.* Das nachapostolische Zeitalter in den Hauptmomenten seiner Entwickelung. Tubing 1846 I, 216—233, 359—363

301 *Ballou, H* Justin or the orthodox faith A D 150—165 In Universalist Quarterly Review. Boston 1846 III, 272 ff

302. *Kayser, August* De J M doctrina dissertatio histor Argentorati 1850 8⁰

303 *Otto, Joh Karl Theod* Zur Characteristik des heil Justin In Sitzungsberichte der Kaiserl Akademie der Wissenschaften Wien 1852

304 *Bungener* In Conférence sur le Christianisme aux 3 prem siècles Genève 1857

305. Anthropologie Justins des M In Der Katholik, N F I (1859), 423—443, 574—591.

306. *Mattes* Zur Lehre J's von der Eibsunde In Tubing. Theol. Quartalschrift III (1859), 367—407.

307 *Moller, W* Geschichte der Kosmologie in der griechischen Kirche 1860 S 112—188

308. *Aube, Barthelemy* Essai de critique religieuse de l'apologétique chrétienne au IIme siècle St Just phil et mart Paris 1861 8⁰ (later reprints).

309. *Chastel.* St J son sentiment sur la valeur de la raison humaine In Le Correspondent XXXI (1863), 189—206

310. *Ruggieri, E* Vita e dottrina di S Giustino, filosofo, martire Roma 1863 Cf Civiltà cattol E VI, 335—339

311 *Weiszacker. C* Die Theologie des Martyrers Justin In: Jahrbb f deutsche Theologie XII (1867), 60—119

312. *Dembowski, Hermann* Die Quellen der christlichen Apologeten Leipzig 1878

313. *Engelhardt, Moritz von* Das Christenthum Justins des Martyreis Erlangen 1878 8⁰ (cf 314, 315 316 317, 318, 319, 321)

314 *Harnack, A* Review of (313) In Theol Literaturzeitung III (1878), 632—637

315 *Drummond, J* Engelhardt (313) on J M In Theological Review, XVI (Lond 1879), 365—379

316. *Hilgenfeld, Adolf* Die neuorthodoxe Darstellung Justins durch M v Engelhardt (313) In Zeitschr fur wissenschaftl Theologie XXII (1879), Heft ı̇v, S 493

317. *Funk F X.* Review of 313 In Theol. Quartalschr. LXII (1880), 480—487

318. *Stahlin, Adolf* Justin d M und sein neuester Beurtheiler. Leipzig 1880 8⁰ (adv 313)

319. *Hilgenfeld, Adolf* Review of (318). In Zeitschr fur wissensch Theologie. XXIV (1881), 251—256 (adv both 313, 318)

320. *Dieckhoff, Aug Wilh* Justin, Augustin, Bernhard, und Luther. Entwicklungsgang christlicher Wahrheitserfassung. Leipzig 1882.

321. *Behm, Heinr. M Th.* Bemerkungen zum Christenthum Justins In Zeitschr. f. kirchl. Wissensch u. kirchl. Lehre. 1882. S. 478—491, 627—636 (adv. 313)

322. *Sprinzl, J.* Theologie Justins. In Linzer Theologisch-praktische Quartalschr. XXXVII (1884), 16—21, 283—292, 533—540, 778—787, XXXVIII (1885), 17—25, 266—272.

323 *Engelhardt, Moritz von* Art. Justin Martyr. In Realencyklopädie für prot. Theol. und Kirche 2. Aufl. VII, 318—327.

324. *Clemen, Carl Christian.* Die religionsphilosophische Bedeutung des stoisch-christlichen Eudamonismus in Justin's Apologie. Inaug.-Diss Leipzig 1890. 8⁰ (cf. 327)

325. *Purves, George T.* The testimony of J M. to early Christianity. Lectures delivered on the L P Stone Foundation at Princeton Theol. Seminary. London 1890 8⁰.

326. *Cramer, J. A.* Was leert Justin aangaaende het personlik bestaan van den heiligen Geest. In: Theol. Studien (1893), 17—35, 138 ff.

327. *Flemming, Ernst Wilhelm.* Zur Beurtheilung d. Christentums Justins d. M Inaug.-Diss Leipzig 1893. 8⁰. (adv. 324)

328. *Conybeare, F. C* The Demonology of the New Testament. In Jewish Quarterly Review VIII (1895—1896), 597—599.

329. *Craemer, O.* Die Grundzüge des christl. Gemeinglaubens um das Jahr 150, nach den Apologien Justins d. M In: Zeitschr. fur wissensch Theologie II (1896), 217—251

330 *Boucard, G.* Un philosophe chrétien au second siècle, St. Justin et sa première apologie. In L'Université catholique, N S. XXXI (1899), 77—102 Also sep. print Lyon 1899

331. *Liese, W.* Justinus Martyr in seiner Stellung zum Glauben und zur Philosophie. In: Zeitschr. fur kathol. Theologie, XXVI (1902), 560—570.

332. *Laguier, L* Le Millénarisme de St J. In Revue du Clergé Français XXXIX (1904), 182—193.

333. *Windisch, Hans Ludwig.* Die Theodizee des christlichen Apologeten Justin. Inaug.-Diss. Leipzig 1906 8⁰.

334 *Puech, Aimé* Apologistes grecs du 2me siècle de notre ere Paris 1912.

335. *Andres.* Die Engellehre der griech Apologeten. Paderborn 1914

K. JUSTIN'S LOGOS DOCTRINE AND CHRISTOLOGY
See also Groups J, N, and O, and 449.

336 *Seiler, Georg Friedr.* Christologia Justini M Erlangen 1775

337. *Burton* Divinity of Christ (1829), 32—61

338. *Dorner, J. A* Entwicklungsgeschichte der Lehre von der Person Christi. 1. Aufl 1839. 2 Aufl. 1845. Engl. Transl Edinb 1864. I, 264—279, 458—461.

339. *Duncker, Ludwig* Zur Geschichte der christlichen Logoslehre in den ersten Jahrhunderten: Die Logoslehre Just.'s d M Götting. 1848. 8⁰. (Abdruck aus den Gottinger Studien 1847.)

340 *Steeg.* Exposé de la doctrine de Justin M. sur la personne et l'oeuvre de Jésus Christ. Strassburg 1859.

341. *Waubert de Puiseau, D H* De Christologie van Just. M. In: Academisch Proefschrift. Leiden 1864. 8⁰

342. *Gass, W.* Das patristische Wort οἰκονομία. In Zeitschrift fur wissenschaftl. Theol. XVII (Leipzig 1874), 465—504

343. *Draeseke, J.* Zu den unter des Justinus Namen uberlieferten christologischen Bruchstücken. In: Jahrbb f. prot. Theol. X (1884), 347—352

344 *Paul, L.* Ueber die Logoslehre bei Just. M In Jahrbb f. prot. Theol XII (1886), 661—690, XVI (1890) 550—578, XVII (1891). 124—148

345. *Bosse, Friedrich.* Der praexistente Christus des J. M., eine Episode aus der Geschichte des christologischen Dogmas. (Inaug -Diss) Greifswald 1891. 8⁰.

346. *Aal, A.* Der Logos Bd II. Geschichte der Logosidee in der christlichen Literatur. Leipzig 1899 S 242 ff.

347. *Cramer, J. A.* Die Logosstellen in J.'s Apologien kritisch untersucht. In Zeitschr. f. die neutest Wissensch II (1901), 300—338.

348 — De logosleer in te pleitreden van Justinus In· Theologisch Tijdschrift (Leiden 1902), p. 144 ff

349. *Leblanc, J.* Le logos de S. Justin In. Annales de Philos. chrét. CXLVIII (1904), 191—197

350. *Feder, Alfred Leonhard, S J* Justins des M. Lehre von Jesus Christus dem Messias und dem menschgewordenen Sohne Gottes. Eine dogmengeschichtliche Monographie. Freib. i. Br 1906 8⁰.

351. *Pfättisch, J. M.* Christus und Sokrates bei Justin. In: Theol. Quartalschrift XC (1908), 503—523.

352 *Harris, Rendel* A new title for Jesus Christ In The Expositor. 8th Series XIV (Lond 1919), 145—151

L. JUSTIN'S TESTIMONY ABOUT SACRAMENTS AND RITUAL
See also 155. IV and 270. I.

353. *Burger, E. G.* Antiquitas liturgiae ev.-luth ex Justino M. demonstrata. Vitemb. 1755.

354. *Kestner* Die Agape. 1819

355. *Döllinger, Joh. Jos.* Die Lehre von der Eucharistie in d drei ersten Jahrhh. Mainz 1826 (cf 358)

356 Justin Martyr's testimony on Baptism. In Christian Review VI (Boston 1841), 302.

357. *Engelhardt, Joh. Georg Vit* Einige Bemerkungen uber die Geschichte der Lehre vom Abendmahle in den ersten drei Jahrhh. In: Zeitschr. f. d histor. Theologie (Leipzig 1842), 1. Heft, 3—20

358. *Höfling, Joh Wilh Fried.* Die Lehre der ältesten Kirche vom Opfer Erlangen 1851. S 43—70 (adv 355)

359. *Engelhardt, Wilhelm* Die Abendmahlslehre des Just Mart In Zeitschr. f luth Theol. XXXI (1870), 230—252 (consubs)

360 *Dreher, Th* Die Zeugnisse des Ignatius, Justinus, und Irenaus uber die Eucharistie als Sakrament. (Progr) Sigmaringen 1871 4⁰

361. *Funk, F X* Zur Apostellehre und apostolischen Kirchenordnung In Theol Quartalschr LXIX (1887), 355—359 (adv 155, iv)

362. *Harnack, A* Brot und Wasser, die eucharistischen Elemente bei Justin. In Texte u Untersuch VII ii. (1891), 115—144 (cf 363. 364, 367, 368)

363. *Zahn, Th* Brot und Wein im Abendmahl der alten Kirche In Neue kirchliche Zeitschr III (1892), 261—292 (adv 362, cf 365)

364. *Jülicher, A* Zur Geschichte der Abendmahlsfeier in der ältesten Kirche In Theol Abhandlungen, C V Weizsacker gewidmet Freib i B (1892), S. 215—250 (adv. 362).

365. *Harnack, A.* (answer to 363) In Theolog Literaturzeitung (1892), S 373—378

366 *Wilpert, Joseph* Die Eucharistie-Feier zur Zeit des hl Just M In. Fractio Panis Die älteste Darstellung des eucharistischen Opfers in der "Capella graeca". Freib i B. (1895), S 142—165

367 *Grafe, E.* Die neuesten Forschungen uber die urchristliche Abendmahlsfeier In Zeitschrift f Theologie u Kirche, V (1895), S. 101—138 (adv 362).

368. *Funk, F. X* Die Abendmahlselemente bei Justin In Theol Quartalschrift LXXIV (1892), S. 643—659 Improved and enlarged in his. Kirchengeschichtl. Abhandlungen u Untersuch I (1897), S 278—292 (adv. 362)

369 *Schewmler, A* Die Elemente der Eucharistie in den ersten Jahrhh Mainz (1903). S 26—43

370. *Feder, A.* Justin d M und die altchristliche Bussdisziplin In Zeitschr f kath Theol XXIX (1905), S 758—761

371. *Casel, Odo* Die Eucharistielehre des hl Just M. In. Der Katholik. XCIV. i (1904), 153—176, 243—263 331—355 414—436

M. JUSTIN S CHRISTIAN ETHICS

372. *Schmidt, J. A.* De Justini M theologia morali (Progr.) Helmstadtii 1698 4⁰.

373 *Staudlin.* Moral Justin's d M In his Geschichte der Sittenlehre Jesu II (Gotting. 1802), 93—121

374 *Charpentier, J P* Etudes sur les Pères de l'Eglise II (1853), 26—35

375. *Wolney, J* Das christliche Leben nach dem hl Just. d. M (Progr) Wien 1897. 8⁰.

N. JUSTIN AND GREEK PHILOSOPHY
See also 312, 313, 324, 330, and Groups J. and K

376. *Hahn, Immanuel E.* De platonismo theologiae veterum ecclesiae doctorum nominatim Just. Mart. et Clem Alex. corruptore. Wittebergae 1733.

377 *Rau, Joach. Just.* De philosophia Justini M et Athenagorae: resp. J. C. Kallio. Jenae 1733. 4⁰.

378. *Souverain* Versuch über den Platonismus der Kirchenväter, übersetzt und herausg. von Loffler. 2 Aufl Zullich 1792.

379 *Hugonin.* Des motifs qui ont déterminé St. Justin à abandonner le platonisme pour embrasser le christianisme In· Annales de Philosophie Chrétienne. XLII (1851), 459 ff

380. *Thumer.* Ueber den Platonismus in den Schriften des Justinus Martyr (Progr.) Glauchau 1880 4⁰

381. *de Faye, E.* De l'influence du Timée de Platon sur la théol. de Just. In Bibliothèque de l'Ecole des hautes études Sciences Religieuses VII (Paris 1896), 169—187

382 *Lebreton, J.* Théories du Logos au début de l'ère chrétienne In Etudes CVI (1906), 54 ff., 310 ff.

383. *Grabmann, M.* Die Geschichte d scholastischen Methode. I (Freib. 1909) 70 ff

384 *Pfattisch, P. Joan Mar.* Platons Einfluß auf die Theologie Justins In· Der Katholik I (1909), 401—419.

385. — Der Einfluss Platos auf die Theologie Justins des Märt Paderborn 1910.

O JUSTIN AND JUDAISM (PALESTINIAN AND HELLENISTIC)
See also 346, 451

386 *Rehling, Joh* Dissertatio crit de Samaritanismo et Hebraismo Justini M Wittenbergae 1729.

387. *Eichhorn, Joh Gottfr* Ueber die Quellen, aus denen die verschiedenen Erzahlungen von der Entstehung der alexandrinischen Uebersetzung geflossen sind In Repertorium für biblische und morgenlandische Literatur I (Leipzig 1777), 266—280.

388. *Stroth, Fr. A* Beitrage zur Kritik uber die 70 Dolmetscher aus Justin d M und anderen Kirchenvatern. In Repertorium fur biblische und morgenlandische Literatur II (Leipzig 1778), 66—123, III, 213—257.

389. *Goldfahn, H* Die Kirchenvater und die Agada; Abt I. Justin Martyr und die Agada. Vratisl. 1873 Offprint from H Graetz's Monatsschr. f Gesch u Wissensch. d Judenthums. XXII, 1873 (References in this dissertation are to pages in the Periodical.)

390. *Siegfried, Carl* Philo von Alexandria als Ausleger des Alten Testaments. Jena 1875 S 337 ff

391. *Grube, K L* Die hermeneutischen Grundsatze Just d Martyrers In Der Katholik I (Mainz 1880), 1—42

392 — Die typologische Schrifterklärung Justins d Mart In Der Katholik II (Mainz 1880), 139—159.

393 *Elter* De Just Monarchia et Aristobulo Judaeo. (Progr) Bonn 1893, 1894.

394 *Heinisch, Paul* Der Einfluß Philos auf die älteste christliche Exegese Barnabas, Justin, und Clemens von Alexandria Munster i W 1908.

395. *Harnack, A.* Judentum und Judenchristentum in Justins Dialog mit Trypho. In Texte u Untersuch III, ix, 1 Leipzig 1913 8⁰

396 *Bousset, D W* Judisch-christlicher Schulbetrieb in Alexandria und Rom Literarische Untersuchungen zu Philo und Clemens von Alex , Justin und Irenaeus Gotting 1915

P. JUSTIN AND THE HOLY SCRIPTURES.

Notice of Justin's testimony to the books of the New Testament is taken in every New Testament Introduction and history of the Canon Of such only a few of the more important are included here
See also 155, 184, 391, 392, 394

397. *Stroth, Friedr Andr* Fragmente des Evangeliums nach den Hebraern aus Just d Mart In Repertorium fur bibl u morgenl Literat I (Leipzig 1771), 1—59

398 *Paulus, H E G* Ob d Ev Justins d Ev nach d Hebraern sey? In his Exeget -kritische Abhandlgn Tub 1784

399. *Blessing, J L* De Justini M N. T citandi methodo In his Animadv ad Voltam de relig chr orig asserta Argent 1786 p 84 ff

400. *Weber, C F* Ueber d Evangelium Justins. In his Beytrage zur Geschichte d N T Canons 1791 8⁰ p 105 ff

401. *Corrodi* Versuch e Beleucht d jud u chr Bibel-Kanons 1792 Bd II

402 *Rosenmuller, J G* Historia et interpretationes librorum sacrorum in ecclesia christiana Heidburghusae I (1795), p 148—193.

403. *Eckermann* In Theolog Beitrage. V (1796) ii 168—170 (cf. 404).

404 *Heischkeil, D C* Ob J keine Spur zeigt daß er evang Schriften ein ausschließendes Ansehn beigelegt habe. In. *Augusti's* Neue theol Blatter I (Gotha 1798) II, 49—50 (adv 403)

405. *Emmerich, F C F.* De evangel secund Ebr Aegypt atque Just. Mart Argent 1807. 4⁰

406 *Mynster, J P* Ueber den Gebrauch unserer Evv in den Schriften Justins d. Mart In: *Mynster's* kleinen theol. Schriften. Kopenh. 1825 pp 1—48 transl from Danish, first publ in *Videns* Nabelige Forhandlunge I (1811), 126 ff

407. *Schutz, D F.* De Ev Just M. In his. Dissertationes de Evangeliis, quae ante Ev canon in usu Christ fuisse dicuntur Regiom 1812 II, 3—17

108. *Gratz, P. A.* Kritische Untersuchungen uber Justin's apostolische Denkwurdigkeiten Stuttg 1814.

109. *Olshausen* Ueber die von Justin gebrauchten Evangelien In his· Die Aechtheit der vier canon Evang (1823) p 331 ff

110. *Winer, G. Bd* Justinum Mart evangeliis canonicis usum fuisse. In. Commentationes theologicae (ed. *E F C Rosenmuller* etc) I (1825) i. 221—252

111. *Credner, K. A* De librorum N T. inspiratione etc I (Jena 1828), 53—60

112. *Rodhe, C. V.* Justini M. de Theopneustia libror sacr judicium Lundae 1830 8⁰.

113. *Lardner, N.* The credibility of the Gospel history In his· Works (1831). II, 125—140

114 *Mynster, J. P.* Justin und seine Evang. In. *Credner's* Beitrage zur Einleitung in die bibl. Schriften. I (Halle 1831), 92—267.

115. *Zastrau, David Friedrich* De Justini M. biblicis studiis commentatio hist.-critica, cuius posteriorem partem de Novi Test. studiis . . . . Vratislaviae 1832. 8⁰.

116. *Credner, Karl August* In his: Beitrage zur Einleitung in die biblischen Schriften Halle 1832—1838. I, 92—267; II, 17—98, 101—133, 157—311

117 *Otto, J. C T* Noch einige Beziehungen auf die Johanneischen Schriften bei Justin d. M und dem Verfasser des Briefes an Diognet. In. Zeitschr. f d. historische Theologie. Leipzig 1841. ii, 77—81.

118. — Beziehungen auf Paulinische Briefe bei Justin d M und dem Verfasser d. Briefes an Diognet. In. Zeitschr. f d historische Theologie. Leipzig 1842. ii. 41—57.

119 *Bindemann, E* Ueber die von Just. d M gebrauchten Evangelien. In. Theol. Stud u. Krit. II (1842), 355—482.

120. *Otto, J. C. T* Nachtragliches uber den Gebrauch neutestamentlicher Schriften bei Just d M und dem Verfasser d Br an Diognet. In: Zeitschr f. d. historische Theologie Leipzig 1843 i, 34—45.

121. *Semisch, Karl Gottlieb.* Die apostolischen Denkwürdigkeiten des Märtyrers Justinus Hamburg 1848 8⁰. (cf 425.)

122. *Hilgenfeld, Adolf* Die alttestamentlichen Citate Justin's in ihrer Bedeutung für die Untersuchung uber seine Evangelien In Theol Jahrbb. IX (Tübing. 1850). 385—439, 567—578

123. — Kritische Untersuchungen uber die Evv Justin's, der Clement. Hom., und Marcions Halle 1850

124. *Bonifas, Sam. E.* Des Evangiles employés par Just Mart. Thèse 1850.

125. *Grimm, Wilibald* Review of 421. In: Theol. Stud. und Krit. XXIV (1851), 669—702.

126. *Ritschl, Albert.* Ueber den gegenwärtigen Stand der Kritik der synoptischen Evangelien. In Theologische Jahrbucher (Tubing. 1851), 480—538; on Justin see pp. 483—493

427. *Volkmar, Gustav* Das Evangelium Marcion's Text u. Kritik, mit Rucksicht auf d. Evangelien d Mart Justin usw. Leipzig 1852

428. — Ueber Justin und sein Verhältniss zu unsern Evangelien Zurich 1853.

429. *Delitzsch, Franz.* Neue Untersuchungen uber Entstehung und Anlage der kanonischen Evangelien. Leipzig 1853. I, 31—40.

430 *Ewald, Heinrich* Ursprung und Wesen der Evangelien In· Jahrbucher der bibl Wissenschaft VI (Gotting 1853 1854); on Just. see pp. 59—64

431. *Zeller, Eduard* Die Apostelgeschichte nach ihrem Inhalt und Ursprung kritisch untersucht. Stuttgart 1854 SS 26—50

432. *Scherer, Eduard.* De la Formation du Canon du Nouveau Testament In Revue de Théologie et de Philosophie chretienne, publiée sous la direction de S Colani Strasbourg 1855 pp 193—217

433 *Baur, Ferd Christ.* Zur johanneischen Frage (1) Ueber Justin d M gegen Luthardt In Theol Jahrbucher XVI (Tubing 1857), 209—242 (adv. 446, earlier ed)

434. *Credner, Karl Aug.* Geschichte des neutestament. Kanons Berlin 1860 SS 3—22

435 *Volkmar, Gustav* Berichtigung zur ausseren Bezeugung des Johannes-Evangeliums In Zeitschr. f. wissensch Theol. (Jena 1860), 293—300

436. *Hilgenfeld, Adolf* Der Kanon und die Kritik des Neuen Testaments Halle 1863, SS. 24—28 etc., see Index

437. *Tischendorf, Const* Wann wurden unsere Evangelien verfasst? Leipzig 1866. SS 25—40.

438 *Willink, H D Tjeenk* Justinus Mart in zijne verhouding tot Paulus Zwolle 1868. 8⁰

439. *Lipsius, Richard Adalbert.* Die Pilatus-Akten kritisch untersucht Kiel 1871 (cf 440)

440. *Hilgenfeld, Adolf* Review of 439 In Zeitschr f wissensch. Theol (1871), 607—610

441. *Overbeck, Fr* Ueber das Verhältnis Justins d M zur Apostelgeschichte In Zeitschr f. wissensch Theol XV (1872), 305—349

442. *Hilgenfeld, Adolf* Die Apostelgeschichte und der M Just. In Zeitschrift f. wissensch Theol. XV (1872), 495—509

443. *Delitzsch, Franz.* De inspiratione scripturae sacrae quid statuerint patres apostolici et apologetae secundi saeculi. Lipsiae 1872.

444 *(Cassels, W)* Supernatural Religion London 1875 See enlarged edition London 1879 I, 282—428 (cf 445, 449)

445. *Lightfoot, J B.* Essays on the work entitled Supernatural Religion See Index (adv. 444)

446. *Luthardt.* St John the author of the Fourth Gospel. (1875), 52—66 (cf. 433)

447. *Drummond, James* On the alleged quotation from the Fourth Gospel, relating to the new birth, in Just M (Ap i 61) In· Theological Review XII (London 1875), 471—488

448. *Thoma, A* Justins literarisches Verhaltnis zu Paulus und zum Johannisevangelium In Zeitschr f wissensch Theol XVIII (1875), 383—412, 490—565.

449. *Sanday, W* The Gospels in the Second Century 1876 pp. 88—137 (adv. 444)

450 *Drummond, James.* Justin Martyr and the Fourth Gospel. In: Theological Review XIV (London 1877), 155—187, 323—333

451 *Abbott, E A* Art. "Gospels" In Encyclop. Brit (9th ed.) X, 816—818, 821—822

452. *Charteris.* Canonicity Edinb. and London 1880 pp. LIII—LXIII, 59—64, 114—127, 143—145, 156—158, 176—179, etc passim

453. *Westcott, Brooke Foss* A general survey of the History of the Canon of the New Testament Camb and Lond 5 edit 1881 pp 96—179

454. *Abbott, Edwin* Justin M and the Fourth Gospel. In Modern Review. (1882), 559—588, 716—756

455. *Paul, Ludwig* Die Abfassungszeit der synoptischen Evangelien Ein Nachweis aus Justinus Mart Leipz 1887 8º

456. *Zahn, Theodor* Geschichte des neutestamentlichen Kanons I. ii (Erlang und Leipz. 1889—1890), S 463—585

457. *Bousset, Wilhelm.* Die Evangeliencitate Justins d Mart. Inaug -Diss Gotting. 1890 8º

458. — Die Evangeliencitate Justins d Mart in ihrem Wert fur die Evangelienkritik von neuem untersucht Gotting 1891 8º

459. *Loisy, A* Hist. du canon du N T Paris 1891 pp 48—58

460. *Harnack, A.* Bruchstucke des Evangeliums und der Apokalypsen des Petrus. In Texte u Untersuch IX (1893), SS 38 ff

461. *Baldus, Al.* Das Verhaltnis Justins des Martyrers zu unseren synoptischen Evangelien Munster 1895

462. *Lippelt, Friedr G E.* Quae fuerint Justini M ἀπομνημονεύματα quaque ratione cum forma Evangeliorum Syro-Latina cohaeserint. Inaug -Diss Halle 1901 8º.

Q JUSTIN AND THE CREEDS
See best 350, pp. 264—288

463. *Heumann, Ch. A.* Symbola critica ad Justinum In Miscellan Lipsiens Nov (Lips 1744 8º.) III, 222 ff

464. *Harnack, A.* Vetustissimum Ecclesiae Romanae symbolum In Patrum Apostolicorum Opera, ed. Gebhardt, Harnack, Zahn 2 ed Lipsiae 1878. Fasc I, Pt ii, pp 115—112 (Justin pp. 128—132.)

465 *Bornemann, W* Das Taufsymbol Just d Mart In Zeitschr fur Kirchengeschichte III (1879), 1—27.

466. *Kunze, J.* Glaubensregel, hl Schrift und Taufbekenntnis. Leipz 1899. S 419

467 *Kattenbusch, Ferdinand* Verbreitung und Bedeutung des Taufsymbols i e Das apostolische Symbol Bd II Leipzig 1900. pp 279—298, 348 ff et passim Cf. Index.

R. JUSTIN'S TESTIMONY TO CONTEMPORARY HERESIES

468. *Lipsius, R A* Zur Quellenkritik des Epiphanius Wien 1865. pp. 57 ff et passim

469. — Die Zeit des Marcion und des Heiakleon In Zeitschr. f wissenschaftliche Theol. (Halle 1867), 75—83

470. *Harnack, Adolf* Zur Quellenkritik der Geschichte des Gnosticismus Leipzig 1873. Also in Zeitschr f historische Theologie II (1874), 143—226 (cf. 471)

471. *Lipsius, R. A* Die Quellen der altesten Ketzergeschichte. Leipzig pp. 5—36 Justins Angabe uber sein Syntagma wider alle Ketzereien und die Ketzerliste Hegesippos (adv 470)

472 *Hilgenfeld, Ad* Die Ketzergeschichte des Urchristenthums Leipz 1884. 8⁰ 162—341 et passim

S PSEUDO-JUSTINIAN WORKS

See also Group D and 155, ii

The following may be supplemented from the Bibliographical Appendix by Baumgarten to Ueberweg's Geschichte der Philosophie II (Berl. 1915), supp p 38, 39

473. *Postellus, Gul* Eversio falsorum Aristotelis dogmatum authore D Just. M Par 1552. 12⁰.

474. *Row, T* Difficulty in Justin M in the Oratio ad Graecos explained. Critique on Thirlby's Just. (15) In Gentleman's Magazine London 1783. p 551

475. *Mohler, J. A.* Ueber den Brief an Diognetus In: Gesammelte Schriften und Aufsatze. Regensburg 1839 I, 19—31

476. *Otto, Joh C Th.* De epistola ad Diognetum S Justini phil. et Mart. nomen . . . commentatio Jenae 1845 8⁰

477. *Hilgenfeld, A.* Der Brief an Diognetus In Zeitschr f wissensch Theol XVI (Leipz 1873) 270—280

478. *Keim, Th* Die Entstehungszeit des Briefes an Diognet In. Protestantische Kirchenzeitung f. d evangelische Deutschland Berlin 1873 285—289, 309—314

479. *Volter, Daniel* Ueber Zeit und Verfasser der pseudojust. Cohortatio ad Graecos In Zeitschr. f wissensch Theol XXVI (Jena 1883), 180—215.

480. *Draseke, J* Abfassungszeit d pseudojust. ἔκθεσις. In Zeitschr f wissensch Theol XXVI (Jena 1883), 481—496

481 — Die doppelte Fassung der pseudojust Ἔκθεσις πίστεως ἥτοι περὶ τριάδος In Zeitschr fur Kirchengesch VI (Gotha 1884), 1—45.

482 — Apollinarios von Laodicea Verfasser d. echten Bestandteile d. pseudojust. Schrift ἔκθεσις. In Zeitschr f Kirchengesch VI (Gotha 1884), 503—549.

483 — Der Verfasser des falschlich Justinus beigelegten Λόγος παραινετικὸς πρὸς Ἕλληνας. In. Zeitschr f. Kirchengesch VII (1885), 257—302

484. *Harnack, Adolf* Die pseudojustinische Rede an die Griechen (der syrische Text ist Uebersetzung einer freien Bearbeitung). In Sitzungsberichte d. Berliner Akademie 1896, p. 627 ff.

485. — Diodor von Tarsus. Vier pseudojustinische Schriften als Eigentum Diodors nachgewiesen. 1901

486 *Widmann, Wilhelm* Die Echtheit der Mahnrede Justins d. M. an die Heiden. In Forschungen zur christlichen Literatur und Dogmengeschichte. Mainz 1902 Bd III, Heft 1

487 *Gaul, Willy* Die Abfassungsverhältnisse der pseudo-justinischen Cohortatio ad Graecos Inaug.-Diss. Giessen. Potsdam 1902 8°

488. *Batiffol, B.* L'auteur véritable de l'ép ad Zenam et Seranum (The Novatian Bish Sisinnius in Constant. c. 400.) In Rev. bibl. Internat. V, 114 ff.

Frommannsche Buchdruckerei (Hermann Pohle) in Jena — 5114